Also by Sheila Rowbotham:
in Allen Lane and Penguin Books
Women, Resistance and Revolution

in Penguin Books
Woman's Consciousness, Man's World

Edited by Jean McCrindle and Sheila Rowbotham

Dutiful Daughters

Women Talk about Their Lives

Allen Lane

Allen Lane
Penguin Books Ltd
17 Grosvenor Gardens, London SW1W OBD

First published 1977

Copyright © Jean McCrindle and Sheila Rowbotham, 1977

ISBN 0 7139 1050 X

Printed in Great Britain by offset lithography by
Billing & Sons Ltd, Guildford, London and Worcester

To all the women we interviewed for the book,
with love and gratitude.

Contents

Acknowledgements

Our thanks to Peter Davidson, Asta Fink, Emma Hay, Jonathan Rée, Marsha Rowe and David Widgery for reading and encouragement; to Cathy Newman-Young and Ann Scarlett, who typed the transcripts; and to Lois Hobbs for interviewing Fiona MacFarlane.

Thanks also to neighbours, friends and family who looked after Claire.

Introduction

We chose this group of women from amongst our friends, our friends' mothers and contacts we have made through the women's movement. They are not supposed to be typical or representative, but simply individual women talking about their lives – how they see themselves, what they remember, what significance they give to personal and public events. They are nearly all from working-class or lower-middle-class backgrounds and they range in age from over seventy to the early thirties. The preponderance of Scottish women is due to the fact that one of us lived and worked there for a number of years.

A series of oral testimonies does not make a history. History is worked over more consciously; different sources open up various ways of looking at what happened. These interviews are fragments, as an individual life is a fragment and as an individual caught for a moment presents a fragment of a fragment. The personal oral account can be a source not for knowing that something was so, but for wondering about questions that are not often considered. So this should be seen not as a book with historical or sociological conclusions but as a stimulus to further investigation.

Many of the older women mention the shock, ignorance and guilt they experienced at the onset of puberty. Unable to talk freely with anyone because of the silence that surrounded women's sexuality, many of them hid the blood of menstruation rather than mention it to their mothers. Fiona McFarlane only realizes that periods are normal when she notices that advertisements for sanitary towels are too common for her experience to be exceptional; Barbara Marsh, from the West Indies, learns about periods from teenage magazines;

Maggie Fuller, too frightened to tell her mother that she is bleeding, eventually gets her aunt to explain, but is told to keep away from men when her periods are on and spends her adolescence running down the street, fearful of some unknown threat connected with her body. There was a similar embarrassment amongst the older women about developing breasts and pubic hair. Although the schools have done much to dispel ignorance for the younger generation, the self-disgust which many women feel about their bodies, and their sense of being strangers to themselves, are reinforced endlessly by advertising, with its emphasis on deodorants, body odours, hidden smells, unsightly blemishes.

Given what most of these women have had to endure in discovering their bodies and their sexual natures, it is not surprising that even for the younger women, who benefited from the more relaxed sexual code of the sixties and seventies, real sexual pleasure has not come easily. Christine Buchan and Irene McIntosh, both still in their thirties, only discovered how to have orgasms, and indeed what that actually meant, several years after they had been having regular sex with their husbands and boyfriends. The older women did not expect and certainly did not get enjoyment from their sex lives. Maggie Fuller's bewildered description of her failure to feel anything at all, except once when she conceived her second child, and Annie Williams's realization that at seventy she has never had an orgasm – 'I didn't know anything about being sexually satisfied, to me it was just a bloody nuisance' – have to be put alongside a younger working-class woman's statement: 'I was so repressed. None of my family talked about sex, I didn't even know what a period was.' There has been an increase in openness which undoubtedly helps women, but we should be wary of assuming that 'progress' is freeing us from all fears and inhibitions.

Contraception, of course, has been a major advance for all women, as has more access to abortion, but it still apparently requires an effort of the imagination for most men to realize the difficulties women face in having to worry about what type of contraception to use and the responsibility this continually throws on them. Annie Williams, desperate not to conceive again, went to one of the first Marie Stopes

Clinics before the Second World War, but her husband discovered she was using a cap and ripped it out of her as if his masculinity was threatened by its presence. Even after the War, when family planning was becoming gradually more available, Catherina Barnes could still be humiliated by a poised middle-class woman doctor: 'This woman hasn't a clue,' she says to a nurse while fitting Catherina with a cap. Another time Catherina has to trek from chemist to chemist in an agonizing search for the right size of diaphragm. We need to know far more about the early history of the birth-control movement and the extent to which information was being disseminated in the years prior to the 1960s, but these interviews show how much courage and determination it sometimes took to face the shame and silence about sex in order to try for a relationship in which pregnancy was not a constant threat.

There is plenty of evidence in these interviews that the fear of getting pregnant again, with no recourse to abortion except illegally, affected the attitudes of the older women to sex and their husbands. Annie Williams determines to go through with an abortion, an illegal one, but her husband refuses to discuss it with her or help her in any way; the trauma of the decision is left to her. Men are often staggeringly unsympathetic about the implications of such a decision, even now that abortion has been legalized. The relief a woman feels after an abortion can be enormous, but if there is any residual feeling in her that her pregnancy was part of a loving relationship, however impractical her ambiguity, she can nevertheless also feel deep emotional loss.

All of the women in this book have been married and all of them have children. Marriage is seen by most of them, young and old, as a convenient way of living with men and children. The bitterness and anger that some of them express are not directed primarily against men, but against a social structure which makes women relate to the world solely in terms of their relationships to men and children. It is clearly a structure which damages men and children, because it polarizes the feminine, interior, emotional, and the masculine, external, rational, to the detriment of both sexes. Annie Williams says about her husband: 'The only time I ever started to feel jealous

was when I had the children and Douglas was getting on so beautifully and I was crushed down and then I was jealous of everything he
did.' But on the whole men are seen by these women as having
muddled through the exhausting years of bringing up children, with
the sleepless nights and endless nappies, with a confused sympathy for
their wives. The sexual division of labour excludes men from equal
participation in the socializing of small children; we would like to see
as vast a literature on the effects of 'paternal deprivation' in the early
years of children's lives as there is on 'maternal deprivation'.

It is in fact the advent of children into their marriages which
causes by far the greatest tensions in these women's lives and forces
them into states of nervous irritation and sometimes near breakdown.
Linda Peffer sums up the total chaos that her first baby caused:
'Motherhood is the best-kept secret in the world. You never see a
TV programme where the woman's house is all in a mess.' That there
should be a search for more communal forms of living in which
fathers, mothers and adult friends can share in the upbringing of
children is surely a demand which as women we are increasingly
going to make.

All the interviews contain intense memories of childhood relationships in the family. 'I hate my mother; I respect her now but I don't
love her, she had too many kids and she was so work-worn, the poor
beggar.' Maggie Fuller is here expressing a bitterness about her
mother which is shared by most of the older women. We were
surprised by this hostility until we realized that teaching a daughter
her role as a future housewife can all too easily develop a sadistic
quality when the mother herself is tired, over-worked and oppressed
by her own existence.

In retrospect the women were able to feel more understanding of
their mothers, having realized from their own lives how hard it is
with small children, not much money and unceasing housework.
But they also made an explicit decision to behave differently towards
their daughters. Janet Daly, with all the poverty and hard work she
has had to endure, says: 'I used to say, how I was treated I'd never
treat mine.' Jean Mormont is delighted that her children can discuss
anything with her and Barbara Marsh is determined to tell her children

about periods and sex so that they will not have to find out through teenage magazines as she did. Obviously the change in attitudes towards children being expressed by these women raises complex problems. The desire for greater closeness and openness between parents and children has to be put alongside the widespread complaint, often aired through the media, that relationships between the generations are breaking down, especially in the area of sexual morality and behaviour.

Another preoccupation of these women is housing. They talk about housing not just in terms of material deprivation but also as an everyday fencing-around of what is possible in human relationships. Jean Mormont and Catherina Barnes, caught up in the severe housing crisis after the War, both had to live with relatives or in other people's houses, in cramped conditions which involved them in a network of relationships which were not chosen. Because women are at home with small children the housing situation affects them much more than their husbands. The way architects and planners, mostly male, have shut women and children up in individualized boxes on huge council estates with minimum facilities for communal sharing demonstrates how little women's needs have been taken into account in this as in many other areas. The involvement of thousands of working-class women in the post-war tenants' movement, the history of which has not yet been written, is evidence of their protest against this lack of concern.

The oral account can provide evidence not only in what is said but also in what is not said. The gaps and silences are as significant as the words. Accounts of school, for instance, are extremely sketchy, especially amongst the older women. Education appears as a remote process in which teachers behaved in mysterious ways. Even in the more recent experience of a young working-class girl like Linda Peffer, the class gulf between teachers and children could make her feel as if her identity were being taken away. Christine Buchan recalls having to learn two languages, one for school and one for home.

The younger women who passed upwards socially through education have been luckier. Irene McIntosh, from a working-class background, and Pat Garland, from a lower-middle-class background, belong to the generation which could move into higher education as a result of the 1944 Education Act and the increase in college and university places. These women welcome the opportunities which have come with education – opportunities for meeting different people and doing different things with their lives which their parents had not had. Work has had more meaning for them, has been an important aspect of their independent identity, and they have found ways of combining family life with satisfying work. But Barbara Marsh and Linda Peffer, as young working-class women without much education, are in a more traditional predicament. They are right at the bottom of the labour market, seen as unskilled casual workers, and having to cope as best they can with the demands of hard manual labour and bringing up young children.

The unevenness of the impact of education on women is clear. The conflict in values experienced by men who have been uprooted from their class has been artistically documented in novels and plays since the 1950s, but there is much less written about the feelings of women who have left both their class and the ways in which their mothers had been women, for the competitive world of academic and occupational advancement. There is also the predicament of working-class mothers who have watched their children vanish into an unknown world. They see this as an improvement but also as a denial of commonly accepted behaviour. Norah Kirk describes with a certain sadness how university changed her eldest son.

The women in these interviews vary in the significance they give to their working lives. Several of the women – Barbara Marsh, Maggie Fuller, Jean Mormont, Norah Kirk – have had a wide range of jobs, often taken up to supplement the family income when needed. But, where education or political involvement has been an influence, work means much more. Annie Davison, brought up in a Glasgow socialist family, describes her attempts to bargain for a decent wage as a young girl and Catherina Barnes, married to an active Communist, becomes a shop steward in her union. Linda Peffer, affected by some socialists she meets, tries to organize a union in the canteen in which she works. Her difficulties, and her feeling that the official trade-union structure remains alien to the work situation of women, are echoed in Jean Mormont's description of her attempts to recruit night cleaners into a union and to force a change in their appalling work conditions. Her story exposes not only the inadequacy of existing factory inspection but also the impotence of trade-union officials when faced with new demands. Employed women are often doing double shifts of work: one for an employer, one in the house; the one paid, the other not. Although more women are joining trade unions, they are often less active in them than male workers. If the reality of women's domestic labour were recognized and concerted efforts made to organize around their situation as a whole, many women would undoubtedly involve themselves more fully. The implications of this would also affect men. It might mean changing the times and places of branch meetings; it might mean male trade unionists agreeing to baby-sit or stay at home; it might mean making the language and rules more accessible and less alienating; it might mean challenging the present hierarchy of skill and power and the division between work and home. Finally, it might mean altering radically expectations of what work should be like, in what conditions it should be done, and who should be doing it.

Although most of the women had some connections with trade unions or political groups, the event which affected them most profoundly was political only in the most general sense – the Second World War. It took Jean Mormont into the ATS, where she could live a freer life than at home, meet a much wider range of people and observe different ways of relating between people – she mentions first noticing lesbians while in the forces. For Catherina Barnes the War meant Nazi occupation as well as the occasion for meeting her future husband. Norah Kirk and Peggy Wood, in completely different class situations, both knew what it was like to be separated for years from the men they loved. The war was exciting, or boring or painful, but it directly changed these women's lives and placed them in roles which they would certainly not have experienced otherwise. There is still a lot of research to be done on the different attitudes of men and women to their war-time experiences and to the return after the war to the familiar pattern of men at work and women at home.

Other political events of the period are mentioned rarely, except by one or two of the younger women who came into direct contact with political groups and ideas. But the idea of socialism as an alternative culture of the working class is vividly described by Annie Davison, who was brought up in the Glasgow Labour Movement between the wars. The pleasure with which she describes attending the Socialist Sunday School, spending weekends with the Clarion hikers, learning Workers' Esperanto, singing in the Socialist Choristers' Choir, cycling, camping, acting and propagandizing is in sharp contrast with the usual image of the post-war Labour Movement – dingy Party rooms, meetings in the back of the pub, marches in the rain, the language of 1917 and the emphasis on the factory-gate meeting. None of the political groups on the Left have taken women and children seriously except as tokens or tea-ladies, and the weakness of socialism must be intimately linked with this neglect. The imposed sterotype of the male worker does not fit the actual conditions of women's lives. A socialism which learned from the feminist movement would be concerned to work out ways in which people might become involved in changing their own lives, at home as well as at work.

Finally, a word about how we conducted, transcribed and edited the interviews. All the women were diffident at the beginning, finding it hard to believe that their lives could be interesting to anyone but themselves and their families. Once they began talking, however, we discovered in the women we were interviewing the same fascination we had found when women described their lives and shared their formerly private complaints in small groups in the Women's Movement. We were not looking for specific reminiscences, nor did we have questionnaires, so the flow of the talk could be determined entirely by the woman herself. There were hesitations, repetitions, silences, sentences which trailed off and thoughts left unfinished or contradictory, and as far as possible we have tried to make the transcripts readable without sacrificing that open quality. In addition some of the women wanted to cut out parts or change their names to protect relatives and friends, but we have kept the tapes for future reference.

We wanted to show through the interviews that if the experience of most women is regarded as unworthy of recording it is not because it is in itself uninteresting, meaningless or trivial, but because of the criteria which are normally brought to bear when the decision to record is taken. The Women's Movement has shown that shared individual experience is an important part of the social discovery of a common condition. In meeting together in a women's group we are connected by a conscious choice, by an explicit decision to break with the more familiar outlets for our dissatisfaction and to discover together what is social and shared in our experience. Once we can perceive what is common to women, change and transformation become possible and the cycle of guilt and personal recrimination can be broken.

Ideally we would have liked to have interviewed a group of men from similar class and regional backgrounds, asking them not only about their work but also about their relationships, their families, their feelings. We need to know more about men's lives and the consequences for them of the division of labour between the sexes, because women must be seen both autonomously and in relation to men if we are to assert a changing experience for both men and women. The autobiographies of this group of 'dutiful daughters' are a contribution to the cultural challenge by women of men's hold over the way in which the world is seen, felt, known and understood. This means challenging not only how women see themselves but also how men perceive themselves and their social relationships. We hope these histories strike a chord of recognition in those women, and men, who read them.

1.   Janet Daly

Janet Daly was over seventy years of age when we talked to her, which, together with her natural reticence, explains the poignant and disjointed nature of the interview. She had a strong Fife accent which we have tried to recapture by using Scottish spelling. She died of a heart attack while we were putting the book together, but her children were anxious that we should include her in the book.

Her own background was Scottish Presbyterian mining but she married into a large Irish Catholic immigrant family, also miners, her husband Jimmy Daly being an active member of the Communist Party in Fife and a trade-union agitator during the inter-war years. He was blacklisted by the coal owners for his politics, hence Janet Daly's constant moving around. Their eldest son, Lawrence, followed his father into the pits and left-wing politics and is now General Secretary of the National Union of Mineworkers. Willie Gallacher, whom she mentions in the interview, was Communist MP for West Fife for many years.

Childhood

'I was hard brought up.'

It was a hard life. It was a stepfather I had. I was hard brought up. Poor. He wasna good to me. There was a child of the second marriage. I was just put aside. We lived in a village called Kingseat. My stepfather was a miner. I had three brothers of my own and this half-brother. My mother took in washing, an' oot in the fields, ken, it was a hard life she had. I didna get on well wi' her, just the environment and tha', that you were brought up in.

My mother came from Tillicoultry. But so far as I ken, my mother had a hard life. She was one of fourteen that was left and this brother and his wife brought them up. And they'd a hard life. And she sort of passed it out on me. My stepfather was a good worker. His folks had been publicans, quite well off. But he was in the pits, aye.

You'd eat, it was sort of potatoes and chopped turnip, like, and we had meat as often as what you usually eat; no, we didn't go without meat. But I can always remember when I started to go out to work, there was this young brother of mine, my mother used to go to the bing for coal; she had to go to the bing, and I've seen her wi' near a hundredweight on her back, carrying it up the fields. She collected it wi' a pick. And she'd have a note, stuck up on the table, you know, for me coming home frae the factory. And she'd say my half egg was in the oven and whenever you've finished come doon to the dole – that's what they called it. And I had to carry the coal up on my back. We lived in a room and kitchen, a miners' row. The beds in the kitchen and in the room, my mother and father in the kitchen and all the children in the room; there were two beds. Just never thought nothing aboot it then, different noo. You wouldna dae that.

I'll tell ye, the cemetery, Dunfermline Cemetery, every Sunday, that's where we went and sat on the seat, that's what they did, the two o' them, and took me and my half-brother. No, really. And we used to look forward to it. No, there was no reason. It was funny wasn't it? It seemed that they loved to go there, just on a Sunday. They just sort of drifted away, my three brothers, my own three brothers you see . . . I think my stepfather had a lot to do with that.

I used to always hope for a sister, I used to think maybe they would think different, ye ken; this is just how I used to feel, that I wished I had a sister. I was the only girl in the family. I was treated differently, aye, no my ain three brothers, they were near marrying age, you know, older, but there were eight years between my youngest brother and me and then when the half-brother came along that made the difference, my stepfather had no time for me. And then my mother, she really, she gave in to him a lot just to keep peace and, of course, I got it. I just canna tell you, hen, I mean they were sort o' cruel. I never really had a girl's life like all the other girls' lives. I'd come home and I went to the washtub and things like that . . . It was terrible, aye, unless this young half-brother o' mine, you know there were a dance-hall next door and there'd be a dance on, a late dance, this was when I was in my teens, and he was eight years younger than me but if he said that he didna want to go an' sit in this dance, I didna get. Aye, an' I used to plead wi' him an' I would say, I'll gie you so much if he would want to go and then he would roar out and say 'I'm no wanting to go', and because Jim [the brother] wasna wanting to go, well I didna get. Well it was a case o' that until I was married.

I went to school in a small village called Hill o' Beath from five to fourteen. It was just a small village, there weren't many o' us. It was nice, you see. Your people were poor and it was a case o' when you were fourteen you had to go out and work.

Work

'You were put wi' an older woman . . . and they told you to get on wi' it.'

My mother had that job for me weeks afore I left the school. This supervisor, she was a supervisor in this factory, and she passed by the door to go to work, so my mother spoke to her, for to get me this job. I had this job weeks before I left. I left on the Friday and started on the Monday [laughs]. It was machines, like, hem-stitch, and plain stitch; it was a clothing factory, next to Dunfermline baths. It was all girls and all women supervisors. No men at all, you had to go up, way into the lab room which was where the men bundled all the stuff and put them in a lorry and took them doon to the bottom factory. We were in what you'd call the finishing-off department and then you'd have the factories wi' the big machines. You were put on wi' an older woman, for a few days, to learn the job and they told you get on wi' it . . . [laughs]. I loved it. I worked from seven in the morning to half past five at night. That was, well, that was your travelling hours within that. It would be eight in the morning. We went to the bothie for lunch and got a cup o' tea and take your own sandwiches. I loved working in the factory, well, it was away from the house. It was away frae hame.

I was a member of the Union. We paid three pence. Everybody was in the Union. This, what was his name, Davie Adamson I think you called him, on a Friday when you got your pay you just went round to him and paid your dues.

Well, I went to a factory in Dunfermline. And I was there till I was married. I got eleven and threepence a fortnight. There was the tramcars at that time, they took one and sixpence a week for that off at your works for the ticket to go back and forwards to your work. And I got a shilling pocket-money. I gave – I had to – the money to my mither. I got a shilling pocket-money, and then when I started to go wi' Jim I didna get nothing. She says, 'You dinna need money when you're going wi' a feller'. My mither bought the clothes. I can mind starting in the factory, and I hadna a coat, and she says, 'You'll get a coat when you work for it'. And I had boots, like tackity boots, and this mauve velvet dress, and that's how I went to the factory in Dunfermline, tae. And the first day I went I was with this Mary Tulloch, that was my pal, and we went up the tramcars, well the noise of the tackity boots on the stairs, I said, 'I'm no goin up again,' I says, 'everybody'll be looking.' Until eventually I worked for this coat; aye I still had to wear the boots. And I can mind the first pair of shoes that I got. There'd been a fire in Kingseat Store, and some of the boots were damaged, you ken, and mine's were like that, they were all drawn doon like this, and the sides of my feet were all sair [sore] and I said to a neighbour I liked them that way [laughs] . . . the leather was hard from the singeing.

Courtship and Marriage

'I used to think he'll no come back . . .'

I was twenty-one when I married, aye. She didn't stop me but she tried. And many a thumping I got. But I went back. I used to get the cane on my fingers and then on my knees. Aye, it was a hard life. It made me mair determined, to go wi' him. I mean there were a sort of friendship atween the four o' us. There were this Mary Tulloch and a boy and Jim and, I mean, if she had let us alane I don't suppose I'd have ever bothered. But she always kept at me. It was his religion. And the best of it is, he isn't religious. But what got her was because we were gettin' married in the Chapel. My oldest brother was worst, really, 'cause he was a beadle o' the Church and things like that. My three brothers and their wives were church-goers. They were against me marryin'. Jim didna mind. He just used to come o'er and whistle at the door, he never came in. Then the next thing, she'd let him in. She'd say, 'Oh well, let him in.' But if she take the roo at him, he was oot [laughs]. I used to think he'll no come back after that. The things she used to say.

It was one Sunday night, this Mary Tulloch, we went along a walk between Cowdenbeath and Kingseat and I met him there, and he says 'We're having a big dance on Friday', and he asked if I'd go, and I said 'Aye', but oh, I was terrified to tell me mither and I thought well I'll tell her the night; and I looked at her face and I said, oh, I better not tell her; I was terrified, and I ken I had to tell her, oh dear, so I did and then she says, 'Oh well, and now he'll come here for you. If he canna come to the hoose for you you're no going.' To have a look a' him. So he did. And then when she wasna in a very great mood, ken, she'd say, 'Well, you'd better go outside and meet the Irishman.' And I'll tell ye, he was better to her than her own sons. There were no pensions, many a ten shillings he used to gie her, well that was a lot then, he was really awfully good, and at the other end she thought the world o' him. Ach, it was a hard life . . .

I could remember that morning I was married. Of course, Mary Daly (that was Jim's sister), we went doon to hear Willie Gallacher doon at Burnt Island at the Miners' Gala – this was my honeymoon, ken. An' here I was dyin' to get to the ladies' room, well I hadna a ha'penny, an' I wouldna say to him, ye ken, to Jim, an' oh I was in agony that day until one time his sister says, 'Do you want to go to the lavatory?' I said, 'Oh Mary, I've been dying. Oh it was an awfu' job, ye ken. I got married, in the Chapel, I was christened a Catholic when I married, just before. I was brought up as a Protestant. My stepfather was dead before I was married, but my mither was dead against it. I used to get thumped, I used to get battered, and then she'd stop him comin' to the hoose, she'd say, 'Go outside if you want to, go away wi' an Irishman.'

We lived in his mother's room, in Hill o' Beath. In a miners' row. But she only lived a fortnight. She had dropsy. And the brother and the father just lived on wi' me. What a difference to my own home. There was somebody that loved you, I should say. Somebody that cared. Just at night, it was just like another world to ye, wasn't it? I stopped work because I was going to look after my husband's father and brother.

Married Life

'It was just like another world . . .'

I had my first seven children in nine year and a half [laughs]. I had nine, and a year before he died I had a loss, that was ten pregnancies I had. I was forty-six when Jimmy died. I had that loss in the January and he died in June. Ye didna seem to mind the children, you get used to it. I had three girls, and six boys. I lost two, one at ten months and one a year and ten months. One died of meningitis, through teething, cuttin' her teeth. There were nae midwives then, there was just an old woman that did this, all her life, and she'd had a big family too. She took ten shillings and that was for doing your washin', your nappies, takin' all the nappies away. She'd do that for five days until you were up on your feet and ready to go . . . [laughs].

We were five years in Hill o' Beath, and then we went to the Lothians. To a place called Penicuik. All the rest were born there . . . Lawrence went to a school in Edinburgh. There was much improvement. I mean, Jim never, it was just like this, he never took it if there was . . . his wages, I got them . . . there was never any question of keeping it off me or the family, never, he was good like that. And if he thought I was going to be short, well, he was there to see that, well, I had it. And it made that much difference. It seemed like heaven to what I was used to.

I worked just in the wartime. At the ammunitions. Jimmy had an accident at the time, and he was off work you see. Oh, he was very much against it . . . I've seen sometimes I would say, 'I think I'll go to the potato-gathering,' and he'd say, 'I ken who'll be wearing the troosers, it'll be you no me . . . I'll no go to the pit if you go . . .' And when I started in that factory, where the ammunition – oh, he didna like it, it was the idea of me working. He says, 'You've got plenty to dae, in here,' ye ken. Many a time I used to say, 'I think I'll go get a job,' and he'd say, 'Well you put the troosers on and I'll be at hame.' Maybe he thought that it made him feel inferior. He didna believe in women working . . . it was quite common that women didn't work then. With seven children, you were working half the night too. In the pit – I mean let's put it this way, if a woman's really tired she can sit down, and rest, but if a man's in the pit he canna dae that. But I was constant on my feet, I could never sit down.

It was his Saturday night. He went out wi' his brother. I mean, it was only two or three hours they was out, you couldna afford it. And you accepted that. He was that busy, ye ken; when he wasna reading he was writing, when he wasna writing he was oot, at the meetings, ye ken. And I accepted it; well, I knew before I married him what like he was, so there was no use in starting after he was married. I wouldna have convinced him anyway. He tried to convince me but I wasna having any. No really, I wasna interested. When I was young I never heard my parents talking aboot politics. It was either that you were Labour, I've heard them saying that when there was an election on. He was like Lawrence, aye at meetin's and tha'. Just after that accident Jim had, he stayed in a bit after that. That was five year afore he took this cancer. But before that, he was aye oot. You just accepted it. Well you'd that much for tae take up yer mind with other daein's that you just forgot that he was there . . .

Taking it all, I preferred married life to being single. Wi' the hard times and a'. Being put oot o' the hoose. I was expecting then, Rosie at the time, I already had two children; there was this day he [Jim] went to the pit and the men were all crowded at front coming up for to get their pay, and this man had a family and he was gettin' his wages arrested, see, for something. And of course, Jimmy went and stood in front of them all and said that they should tell the clerk that if that man didna get his pay, then there were none of us needed it . . . and when he went doon the pit the next day they tellt him he was needed at the pit-head, to tell him that he was oot. It was what they called the Fife Coal Company then; and the hoose, oh, Jimmy wanted me – I was expecting – to barricade the doors, that would keep them away . . . and I was in a state of . . . so, however we had to get oot. And, we'd naewhere to go, it was a Fife Coal Company hoose. Aye, we paid four shillings and threepence a week. I can mind this time, it was during the strike, I was expecting at the time, they made it up that they'd all march to the Poor Hoose in Dunfermline. Well it's a good trek to Dunfermline from Hill o' Beath, to the Poor Hoose where they would take your bairns. We'd all our bairns wi' us in prams, marching and singing. But they wouldna take us all in. Well then we held an open-air meeting, Jim was on the soap box . . . we had sandwiches and that. We ken fine they wouldna let us in.

We were lucky if we got four pound a week, that was a lot though. I mean, if you went with ten shillings you could get a lot of messages for that. We thought we were rich. And they tellt the men that anybody that took us in, in their room, they'd be put oot also, see. So we went to this boy, he was unemployed and he was living in Cowdenbeath, and he was in the Communist Party and he gave us a room there. Well Jim couldna get a job naewhere, ken, everybody kent that he was . . . We lived on the parish; we went and got a line for seventeen and sixpence to go to Lipton's, you didna get the money, but there were nae cigarettes and nae tobacco to be bought on it [laughs], you couldna get no clothes nor anything like that. Of course they wouldna give it to Jimmy anyway, he was a trouble-maker, he stuck up for his rights.

Well, he just couldna get a job and he decided that he would go to the Lothians, to Penicuik. He went there first, and here, he got a job in . . . Roslin. And that morning that he went to Roslin the pit-head manager says to him, 'The manager wants to see you before you go doon the pit.' Jim says, 'Oh,' so he waited and he says, 'You come from Fife, don't you?' Jim says 'Aye'. 'Well,' he says, 'we want no Reds here.' It was his name, travelled that quick and fast. So he said 'OK', because he kent he had me and the bairns. So he went doon the pit, ye ken. Then, something arose there, and we come back to Fife.

Fifteen times I've left, moved. We went from Hill o' Beath tae Cowdenbeath, from Cowdenbeath tae Kelty, from Kelty to that other place and from there to the Lothians, and we come to Glencraig, wi' bairns and all that, we just carted them all . . . we had very little furniture, just the sideboard and you just got that up and you were all ready to go. He was always shifting aboot, it was his activities, ye ken. That's what it was, the whole idea was just because he was political, he minded and carried it out. Although I believe he was quite right. He was standing up for the workers. But then the time came when he was gettin' put oot, they weren't allowed for to help him. They were going to be put oot too, you see. We had plenty of friends, but then they were afraid of their jobs.

I believe it affected their school [the children]. The like of Lawrence . . . We sometimes fell oot aboot it, but I kent I had to go. We ended up in Ballingry. He died twenty-five year ago [1949].

Children

'I used often say how I was treated I would never treat mine.'

I just let them think for themselves. Like they were all brought up Catholics; well, I said, 'When you leave the school, if you're sixteen and you think your way of being brought up is right . . . but if you want to change it to Protestant you're free to go.' And they are all Protestants, bar James – he married an Irish girl. Oh, very staunch they are. I'm just as happy. I don't really mind . . . But I never kept it up, I never could . . . I've seen the priest coming doon and the arguments he used to have wi' Jim. They'd be at it. The priest says, 'I bet you don't have the courage to come to the Chapel,' and Jim says, 'Just you wait till Sunday,' and he went . . . [laughs].

Well there was really nothing else to do but mining. One of the girls went into service and one in a factory. Rose went into service, with people who had money. Being a proper skivvy, doing all this dirty scurvy work. It was in Edinburgh; she lived in. She was four-teen, and they made her do all the dirty work. I went down to one once, as Rose got a letter out. When it came to it she wasna allowed a piece and marmalade or jam . . . This day that I did call in, she had lifted letters from the door and took them up the main stair to the woman, and she made her go straight back and go on the servants' door, what you've seen in pictures and that, but you wouldna credit it. So I wrote this letter, and Jimmy was working on the back shift, and I went over to Edinburgh, St Margaret's the house was called or something. And I brought her hame. He was an officer in the army, and his wife hadn't been well at the time. He was awfully nice, and he says, 'My wife really needs somebody to help, won't you come upstairs to the bedroom and talk to her, and thrash it out?' because I really resented that Rose was made a nothing. But if you'd heard the haughtiness of her. She was lying there all done up with her gowns and whatnot. We had an argument and I just really tellt her, I said that we were miners, miners' family, but I never brought them to skivvy after anybody. I says, 'We may be poor but she's not doing that. And she's no used to getting nothing for tea.' This one time Rosie had taken some marmalade and another lassie had spouted on her, so she cried Rosie up to the bedroom and said 'How dare you?' Rosie was terrified. So I brought her right hame wi' me. I knew she could get a job in Dunfermline.

I gi'ed them what I could gi'e 'em. And I used often say how I was treated I would never treat mine. Never. Aye, I gi'ed them well, to the best o' my ability.

2. Annie Williams

Annie Williams is in her seventies, married but living on her own in a small flat overlooking the sea. She and her husband decided to live separately after nearly fifty years of married life because, as she says, 'We'd been unhappy for a long time and I'd had enough.' He still visits her regularly and they both feel their relationship is much nicer than it was.

She has six children, all of them grown up, but one of them died in circumstances so upsetting that she could not bring herself to talk about it. Her youngest child, Ben, who was still suffering from a severe nervous breakdown when we talked to her, has now completely recovered. She hasn't worked outside the home since she was married, but worked as a nurse and a home help before her marriage.

Childhood

'I was ashamed to be on earth at all.'

Well, I suppose you would be interested really in how I had my stammer. It's a bit embarrassing, but I might as well tell you. I had a sort of half-brother, I should think he would be about twelve or thirteen, I couldn't have been more than three and a half. And he used to come into my bedroom at night and take me out of bed and fondle me. I never said a word, I was frightened to death, but it wasn't unpleasant, because he didn't hurt me or anything. Well then after that, I don't know whether one gets sexually aroused at that age, but we used to play like kids, take off our clothes and play hospitals and doctors. One day my mother came down and she caught us and she gave me a jolly good hiding. Well I didn't mind the hiding because she didn't hurt me, but the humiliation of it, and the guilt that I felt. Well then after that I started school and somebody said to me one day that the Inspector was coming, and I really think that could have been shock, and started me off, with this stammer. Well, this is my own idea of how it happened, I can't be sure but I am convinced it must be, because there isn't anything else. Even if I had asked my mother, how did this start, she probably wouldn't have known, you see, because in those days they didn't know anything.

Well, em, after this incident I didn't like my mother at all – I mean I used to help her, I used to do things for her, but I couldn't bear her to touch me. I loved my father, but I didn't see anything of him. He was what was called a cattle dealer, he came from a wealthy farming family. Then when he was about eighteen or so his people sent him to London, with his sister, to be an apprentice to the butchering. Well then when he came back from there he opened a shop of his own, and then he met my mother.

She was a little older than he was, and had been married before, and had had two sons. One was sent off to America directly he was born. Because my mother was a widow she had no means of support, so she had to go back to her own trade as a milliner. She was a widow for about six years, and she had this one son, Jim, who was brought up with her first husband's sister. They didn't have any children of their own and they had a butcher's shop, where my mother lived, and there she met my father. Well then they got married, and I was the first born. Now I think, I don't know about this, but I think my father would have liked to have had a boy. But ooh, he made such a fuss of me, and you know, when they had a child, about a year and three months after me, it was a boy, and my father would compare us and put us into races and say, 'She's the one that's going to win, she's the one that's going to win!' I think I really was a bit spoilt, I have heard, after that.

Then ages afterwards they had another one, a girl. Then they had this one that's in hospital, Frank. And then they had one other one, when my father was in the army – because in 1914 on the fourth of August he had to go, because he was in the Boer War and I suppose he was on the Reserve, or whatever it was. Then she had another baby, I think while he was in the army, and he died, so there was four of us. I didn't like my mother at all, not like my father. But I was particularly clever as a child, always coming top of the list, and I once won a scholarship with the highest marks in the whole of the valley, and I went to County School, and I had to travel by train to school about twelve miles away.

It was a very posh school. There were some kids that used to come up in big Rolls-Royces. But of course I was just a poor little scholarship girl, but never mind, I was all right. Anyway we – what's next now? Oh yes, even though I had a stammer I was particularly good at music, and before I went to the County School we used to have a little bit of a show every year towards Christmas time. I'm a great imitator, you know – I used to go to the pantomime, you know – did it all, my mother helped me with the costumes, it was Cinderella. And do you know what part I took? One of the ugly sisters. I never thought I was at all handsome or what it was. I remember crying to my mother one day because there was a young girl down the road, who, when I look back on her, she wasn't handsome at all – I don't suppose she was half so good-looking as I was. But she seemed to be sort of glamorous, you see. And I used to cry to my mother and say, 'All the girls are pretty except me.' My mother was awfully hurt about this, and she would say, 'I can't understand.' She was nice to me, but you see, because of this incident I never forgave her.

You see my mother made a profit on me, because when I went to this County School I had everything paid for – all my books, piano lessons, my fees – and then the Ministry of Pensions, because my father was in the War, made a big grant for her to buy my clothes and my sports equipment. She made all my clothes, practically, made all my gymslips and my blouses and everything. So she was able really to make a profit on it, you see.

But this little stammer I had worried them both to death. Before my father died they sent me to specialists, and ooh, I've had to talk with pebbles in my mouth, I've had to breathe, take deep breaths, and I had to sing. I learned to sing, and I went to learn elocution, and I could say poetry right through without a stammer at all, and as soon as I finished I'd say, 'Whe-whe-where is m-m-my coat now,' or something like that, you see. There was nothing they could do at all. I had the stammer for ages. But it's been a lot better for months and months and months, where nobody knows about it. If I go into company with people I haven't met, maybe I usually tell them about it, because *they* feel more embarrassed about it than I do.

I was only at that school a couple of years, you see, when my father was killed, and my mother died about a year or so afterwards. She just had a heart attack. I say she died of a broken heart. She was forty. Oh, it was terrible, terrible – I can't go into that because it would upset me. Anyway, the whole point is that – there now, you see my mind has gone a blank now. As far as we know, there wasn't anything wrong with her heart. When people used to talk about all sorts of – broken hearts . . . I used to think of – about you must have taken your heart out and dropped it on the floor, you see, or something like that, when I was a child. But then she had this heart attack. Well now, before my father died she was a beautifully smart woman, upright – a little bit plump, possibly like me, but perhaps a little bit heavier. When my father died she just shrunk and shrunk and shrunk. But, I do remember about – it must have been about a week or so before she herself died that she said to me one day – 'Oh, I feel better than I have for ages, everything is going to pick up now, and be absolutely fine.'

Now I don't know if anything is relevant as to what I am going to say now, but this half-brother, I believe he murdered her. He didn't murder her with intent, but he used to – he was a bit of an alcoholic – or not that, but he used to drink – he would come home in the middle of the night and knock us up, and my mother had to go down and let him in. Well now my father had a very expensive diamond ring, terrible expensive, and of course when he was killed in the War all his possessions came back to her. One night my half-brother asked my mother if he could borrow it just to go out. He went and got into a brothel and of course he came back without the ring. Now, my mother had to go down and open the door, in the middle of the night. Now, I don't know about this, but I am positive it must have happened. He must have told her about the ring at this time, and she came into my bed and she died at the side of me, practically. People said afterwards, that if I had given her some brandy or something – he went downstairs and fetched her some milk, and by this time I was out of bed holding [sobs] . . . Anyway . . .

Well then of course I had to attend the inquest. And the aunt that had brought my half-brother up, she had him off and on – she didn't live with us, but used to spend a lot of time with him – and I heard her telling him, 'Whatever you do, don't you say anything about what happened on that night.' I heard this myself, but I was dazed and young, you see, I was . . . you see . . . but of course after the inquest – you see we had it in the house – the Coroner said to my half-brother, 'Did you tell anything? Did you tell your mother anything on this night which would have upset her?' And of course he did what his aunt told him, he said, 'No, nothing at all.' And the whole thing passed over. I still persist in saying that he murdered her, and of course I haven't had anything to do with him for years and years – I don't know where he is now. Anyway, after that we went to – oh, my mother had some very well-off relatives, and she always said, you know, 'If anything happens to me – you go to your Uncle Bill, he will look after you.'

Anyway, where did we go first of all? There was four of us, you see, and we had a very substantial pension, you see, we had about almost a pound a week each, or something, which is a lot of money in those days, see, so the people were quite glad to have us. They didn't trouble how they looked after us, you see. Anyway, eventually, the first proper home that we were to have was with my mother's brother. He put my sister with his daughter, and this broke her up – I mean she cried night after night, she didn't want to part from us, you see. [Sobs.] She ran away one Saturday night on a filthy night like this, and she walked right over the mountain, and of course now there was a bit of a panic, and I had to go to the Conservative Club to fetch my uncle out to tell him that Rose had run away. Well this was a terrible disgrace on them in this community, that they had a child and she had run away, they must have been beating her or something, but it wasn't anything like that, she just didn't want to live with them, she wanted to live with us. Anyway, they were absolutely fed up with her, so they sent her to an orphanage.

I didn't go to my beautiful County School now, I went to a mixed secondary school. And I had developed now, and I had a bosom, and these boys used to tickle you. Ooh, I used to bind myself with sheets. It's a wonder I didn't have cancer in my breast. I used to bind myself with sheets every morning to try and flatten my chest – ooh, even my own brother – oh, I used to fight with him like hell. Well, I suppose there is nothing in it really, but for me it was absolutely dreadful, I was thoroughly ashamed of myself. No wonder I used to cry to my mother and say I wasn't pretty – I was ashamed to be on earth at all.

Anyway, this period passed. I didn't get on very well at all. I couldn't sort of learn anything, with boys in the same class – you know, it was crude and all that – you know, I hated it. Well then of course they had to employ somebody to do all their work, and on the day that my pension stopped – back in the kitchen, working like hell, and believe me, on a Friday afternoon when she had done all the work and the miners were coming in to buy their stuff, and I was downstairs, I was doing all the scrubbing. It must have been bloody awful, and one afternoon we had everything out in the garden, it was very hot, and I remember my brother, you know, he used to help in the slaughterhouse, which is down at the bottom of the garden – and I came out in this hot sun, and I just sat down and he said, 'Don't bloody sit there – get on with it, you lazy bitch!' he said to me. Well, we had such a fight, my God, I nearly murdered him. I was a wild-cat, absolutely. The thing that used to make me tear my uncle to bits was because he used to spit on the bars of the grate, and I used to have to clean that grate in the morning. 'What's the matter with you, gel?' he'd say. 'Leave me alone.' 'Stop spitting, you pig, you pig!' I used to say. 'You're worse than the pigs in the garden.' And my aunt used to come down – and she didn't take any notice at all. She used to let me just get on with it. This is only just a little incident.

Courtship

'I could always get any boy.'

Well, now then. Then of course I used to go out with boys, off and on. But very – there wasn't more than holding hands or anything – because I was still all inhibited. Then I met Grant Ashton, he was in the RFC – the Royal Flying Corps. I could have met him before I was sixteen, when I was at school, because I used to go to what they call the Parish Hall Dances. And the aunt I lived with now, I mean we weren't very unhappy with them. Oh, we had to work, but I mean they were quite all right, and I had my piano there, you see, and I used to play the piano, and play the piano for hours on end, you know, when I had done my work. They were quite happy about it. My aunt used to be downstairs and she would say to me, 'Well, I don't know anything about music at all, but I can always tell when you play a wrong note.' And they were quite happy about it you see.

Anyway, this chap now came out of the Flying Corps. I may not have been very handsome but I could always get any boy that I was after, if you know what I mean. He looked gorgeous in his cap and his uniform and he used to start to come to the dances, and all the girls were, you know, after him like, and I thought, well they won't have a look in. Which they didn't. But he took it very, very seriously, and now I wasn't in love with him at all, like. But he was very much in love with me, and of course he was eight years older, and he used to come down to the house, and he used to be very nice to my aunt and he used to buy her occasionally a box of chocolates, and she thought the world of him. He used to take me to the theatre, buy me presents – he was absolutely wonderful.

Well, then, when I got a bit older – about – I should think about just over sixteen and a half, we became engaged and, you know, there was a talk about being married. But this to me was miles away, you know, it didn't seem – I wasn't sort of real about it. Then he got a job somewhere and he said that directly he found a house he would come back and we would get married, because, he said, 'I don't think this is a very suitable place for you.' I was beginning to develop and there was a lot of men coming into the shop – oh, and my aunt wasn't a very nice girl.

She used to go – this is very funny – she used to go out on a Monday night, and when there was miners' strikes and all that, and business would be rock bottom, she used to tell me, 'Well, I've only got threepence in my purse, but I'm going to the pictures tonight whatever happens.' She would go out. She'd come back, she'd been to the pictures, and she would bring back with her a couple of rolls of cloth. Now in the middle of the High Street there was a tailor, by the name of Mr Pritchard, and when I got older – it was years after that I realized this, with the help of my young brother Bill – because he used to go with them sometimes, and they used to – they went into the back room, I suppose, and did their stuff. Well, I mean I didn't understand it at the time and she was a wonderful dressmaker and she used to dress me up ever so smart. Ooh, she made beautiful clothes, and I used to go to these dances, and I was the belle of the ball quite often, so I had a wonderful time.

Well then as soon as Grant Ashton went away, about a week, and I began to feel so free, and I thought, oh, this is lovely. I don't want to be going out with him every night, and getting married and all that. What's this nonsense talk? This is going on in my mind, you see, and I still went to dances, but I had to go with my brother. Well I went to a dance one night with Grant and I saw Douglas. Now he used to come to this slaughterhouse when he was a young boy, he used to wear little shorts you know, and I couldn't place him, because he was gorgeously handsome. He is handsome now, he was a very attractive man. At that time I thought, 'Oh isn't he gorgeous.' So I sort of started to look at him, you know, and he came over and asked me to dance, and everything in those days was done so properly and beautifully. He came and asked me, and took me back to my seat and all. When I think of it now I could scream with laughter, as against what it is now. Anyway, we were having a dance – ooh, and he is a wonderful dancer. And of course so was I, I could follow anybody, and he said, 'You don't remember me?' And I said, 'Well,' I said, 'I think I do, yes! I remember you – you used to come down the slaughterhouse in little short pants.' 'Yes,' he said, 'and you used to wear a big top-knot on your hair.' 'So what,' I said, or something like that. Oh, we got on beautifully, we didn't stop talking during the whole dance. Then he took me back to Grant and Grant said, 'Oh, you seem to know that young man.' I said, 'Oh, yes, we're getting on very well.' Obviously he felt a bit jealous.

Well actually, he did tell me afterwards that if we got married he was a very jealous man. He told me this after, but I didn't – this didn't have any significance to me at the time. Because I don't think I would quite know what jealousy was. I hadn't felt it. I think the only time I ever started to feel jealous was when I had the children and Douglas was getting on so beautifully, and I was crushed down and then I was jealous of everything he did! Oh that was awful, because it's a destructive force, you know.

Anyway, then after this Grant must have gone away, and as I said, I felt very free and I went to dances and I met Douglas once or twice, and we sort of danced a lot, but there was a lot of young men there. Ooh, I had a couple of offers to make good marriages. Actually, I was very well developed and looked a lot older, you see, and then of course came the time when I had to – I mean I absolutely fell flat on my face for Douglas. Never have I felt like this towards any man at all. Except perhaps when I was very young, I used to have girlish crushes on the choirboys or something like that. But I mean, this was a consuming passion absolutely, and it was the same with him. It was like as if two magnets were, you know, like that. Anyway, now came the business now, even though there wasn't anything that had passed between us, possibly a good-night passionate kiss. But I realized now that I could never go through with getting married to Grant Ashton. And as the days went on I practically forgot about him, and I thought, I've got to do something, I've got to write him a letter. And I had to tell my aunt and uncle, and that was a thing, they never forgave me. They called me everything. 'You're giving up this young man, who could look after you and provide you with a home, for this! A man that works in the bloody colliery, and has been out of work on the strike, and all that – you must be mad, your mother would turn in her grave!'

Ooh God, I was absolutely alone. I didn't have a friend in the world. I *had* friends, I told them about it, they all said the same thing. And I was very friendly with a wealthy farmer's daughter, where I used to go, and they thought the world of me there, and I could play the piano, and I was – you know, I was very good socially, and when I went there I didn't have a stammer. Because it goes and it comes, you know. It isn't here you see all the time. When I told them, the same thing happened – her father practically blew me up. Well I felt as if I could go nowhere, I was just on my own, but I had to write him a letter, and I must have wasted a whole pad to write this letter, because now I really felt miserable because I knew I had to face him as well as all the others. So at last I sent him a letter, and I got a telegram back:

YOU DO NOT MEAN YOUR LETTER TODAY – PLEASE REPLY

So what could I do? Just say:

EVERYTHING IS MEANT – VERY SORRY – ANNIE

Then he wrote me a letter – oh, it was terrible, oh, it was dreadful! He said that he had a suspicion of something – that I had been talking about Douglas in my letters, that I had said I had been to dances – 'I appreciate your honesty'. Well, there wasn't anything to hide as far as I was concerned. And he said, 'I won't come home at this present time, because I don't think I could bear to see you at this moment, without this in your eyes which I hoped was for me. I will come home at Easter.' I thought, oh thank God for that. That will put it off for a while.

Well you see, now of course having done that I threw myself at Douglas and went out with him as often as he wanted, night after night, dancing and all that. He couldn't come to the house, my aunt wouldn't have him at all. Well then one night we were coming home from a walk, from the place where we used to do our courting, with lovely old ferns all over the place, you know. And as we came down the hill – of course news travels in these small places – about three people sort of came up and said, 'Grant Ashton's home!' 'Grant Ashton's home!' And of course I was having a bit of a flutter. So Douglas said, 'Not worried are you?'

Anyway I went home and Grant Ashton was there. He was downstairs having a meal or something or other, with my aunt you see, and I went down see, and I held out my hand, I didn't know what to say. Everybody looked a bit embarrassed and I can't remember whether he said, or I said, 'Hadn't we better go upstairs?' – to where we used to call – the piano room. It was only a little tiny room but

I had my piano, and where we used to spend a couple of hours.

I remember him coming up, and the first thing he said was, 'Well – I can tell it is over between us.' I said, 'How can you tell that?' He said, 'I can see by your face, I can see how your eyes shone when you came in.' I had been out with Douglas. Of course I didn't say anything, because what could I do? And then he said, 'Oh, there is only one thing I ask.' Oh, and I offered him my ring back – oh, I didn't have it on, I went up to fetch it. 'Oh no,' he said, 'I don't want that, keep it.' And then he said, 'Will you just let me take you in my arms once again,' and he went. I can see him now – he used to wear a little bowler hat – going out to the door. I wept my bloody soul out. I felt so sorry for him. It was terrible. But, he was a lot older than I was, see.

Anyway, that went off now, and I had to face the other bloody scene. Well it got – oh then Douglas started talking about getting married, taking two rooms in another place, and all of a sudden I felt trapped. I thought, 'No, I can't' – I didn't tell him that, but I sort of 'ummed and awed', and then I decided it was time that I went, because I didn't have a friend in the world. I don't know how his parents were taking it, but I don't think – I went up there once or twice, and I don't think they were very pleased.

Work

'Talk about paradise.'

Anyway, I decided to get myself a job, and I thought to myself – oh, what can I do? I can't do anything! I got the *Nursing Mirror*. Jobs advertised anyway, up to eighteen – and I should think I was just coming up to seventeen, but I could easily put my age on. So I got a job now in London. Oh, I was so excited, it was so fantastic. Freedom. I didn't want to be with my aunt, I didn't want to be with Douglas or anything at this time. I mean I hadn't thought any the less of him, but he did think that I did. He said, 'If you really love me you won't go!' 'Well,' I said, 'I can't go on where I am, and besides,' I said, 'my aunt is becoming very fond of Rose, and it would be a good thing for me to get out of the way so that Rose can take my place, and it will be very good for them all.'

Well then, I knew nothing whatever about nursing. They were aware of that. Well then, to crown it all, this young girl that I was friendly with from this very wealthy farm, she wanted to come with me. Now, I didn't really want her. I wanted to go on my own, but I thought, oh well, she might as well come if she wants. This is another incident that will always stick in my mind. We arrived on Paddington Station. It was the first time I had been to London. The porters and the taxis and the trains! It was absolutely fantastic. And she was panic-stricken! 'What are we going to do? We'll have to go all the way back home!' 'Oh, be quiet,' I said – I had to go all the way by taxi, and I had to pay fifteen shillings, to go by bloody taxi. And of course when I wrote a letter to my aunt now, and told her this, she wrote back and she said: 'You're a pair of country bums, paying all that money! You could have gone by underground or bus.' She had obviously been to London.

Anyway let me tell you about it. It was a little isolation hospital, and when we got there I thought that we had come to the wrong place, because there was a tennis match on. So we went in, you see, and we were asked to sit down. Anyway, very soon a very nice matron came up and she said, 'Oh, you're the two new nurses?' I said, 'Yes, are we in the right place?' 'Yes, you are indeed. This is an isolation hospital. We don't have patients very often, only if we have an epidemic. So when we haven't any patients, we play tennis. I'll show you to your rooms.'

Ooh! Talk about paradise, I couldn't sleep with excitement. We had a bedroom to ourselves. And beautiful clean sheets, and three whole pounds a month, all found. Uniform and *food* – the food was absolutely out of this world. I got so fat that I couldn't fasten my nurse's collar. I used to eat like a pig, it was absolutely gorgeous. But the other girl wasn't a bit happy. She wanted to go home all of the time. Her parents were begging her to come home. Sending her money and God knows what. Anyway, at the end of three months the silly bitch went home and that was it. But while we were there we had a wonderful time. I used to play the piano, and all the nurses used to come and sing, and we used to have dances. Ooh, it was wonderful.

It was hard work when we had an epidemic, and this will show you what a responsible girl I must have been. I had a bit of a stammer at that time, and when you go to these hospitals you're not supposed to fetch a patient in until you have been there for at least three months. You are not supposed to go on night duty until you have been there for three months. But after I had been there for a couple of months, or even under that, we had an epidemic, and I had to go and fetch a patient. Oh my God! I was weak with fright. But I went to this house, to see to this child who had diphtheria, and I had to carry the child and the parents were crying, and it was awful but – God help me, I managed to speak and console the parents and take the child. The only way I can speak when I am very bad is to assume another voice, you see, I assume another voice, and I spoke in a drawl, and I comforted the parents and I put the child in the ambulance and I brought her back, and everything went fine.

The next thing, we had to go on night duty, but they always put us together. By this time we didn't have many patients, but we had a good lot, and this hospital, it had wonderful grounds in it, you used to wander over the grounds, and I don't know whether you have been in the middle of the night where there are sort of trees, you would swear that there were shadows going back and forth. Of course she was petrified – 'Oh, look, there's a giant! Ooh!' And I'd say, 'Oh, for Christ's sake go in, and I'll stop here by myself.' Oh, it was terrible.

Then, of course, when we didn't have to do much at night we used to go to sleep on two armchairs, and this is when we used to get this night nurse's paralysis. It's terrible. You go to sleep but you don't sleep completely because you have got to be on the alert. Maybe you have only got one patient in the ward, but you've still got to be alert; and you are seen to be sleeping and all of a sudden people are calling you, and matron comes, and the sisters come, and they come in: 'Nurse, what are you doing asleep there?' You can't move, you seem to be gone – you can't move. Oh, it's terrible, and all of a sudden you wake up and oh, my God. It's a terrible thing which you get once or twice, and you desperately try not to sleep, but of course sometimes you can't help it, you see.

Now what happened after that? Oh yes, this silly bitch, she was one of these show-offs, she used to write letters home to her friends. I was writing to Douglas practically every day. She used to write the letters home to her friends and say, 'We are having a wonderful time – all the doctors, and there are students,' and that we were going out. Well we were going out to the theatres a heck of a lot, because they used to give complimentary tickets. Good God, I hadn't been in London two nights before I went to see Gladys Cooper in *Diplomacy*. I have been going to write to the BBC all these years to ask why the hell they do not put that play on. It was the most exciting thing I have ever seen. Gladys Cooper in one of her scenes where her husband thought that she had deceived him, and sort of locked her in, and she put her arms on the door and cried, and ooh! Her acting was wonderful, you know. This is what my mother did when she received this letter about my father. She put her hands and she clung them to the door and she said, 'Oh my God, I can't stand it!' It's the same thing. I've just thought of that. Perhaps this – perhaps it wasn't Gladys Cooper's acting after all, perhaps it was . . . this with my mother.

Anyway, where are we now? Oh, yes – well then Douglas and I had a bit of a tiff, by post you see. Well in the meantime he had been hearing all this, that we had been having a wonderful time. And of course I obviously had told him that we'd gone to theatres and all, see. All complimentary tickets were issued to the hospital, we used to go out in evening dress and all. I had a marvellous dress. When I went there once – there were seats, you know, in the stalls you see, and when I went there one day, one of the commissioners said to me, 'All right, you don't want to be nervous.' I felt like bashing him because I was walking as if I owned the bloody place.

Anyway we had this tiff by letter. Now this is rather an important incident, which gives rise to people saying that I chased him, because at this occasion I did chase him. We had a bit of a tiff and I didn't send him a letter for over a week, and he was desperate, and writing day after day, 'Why don't you write? Why don't you write?' Then all of a sudden I decided to write, and I mean you know, I could get any boy I wanted, and treat him as I would like. He was the first man that ever said – 'You are a spoilt brat!' He told me that, not very long after we met. Anyway, after this now, in the meantime when I hadn't written, and he had heard all this tale, he wrote back and said he didn't want anything more to do with me, that he had heard these rumours, and he didn't believe them, but when I didn't write for a whole week then they must be true.

Well now, I was desperate now, because there was nothing in it. We had one bloody doctor that used to come to this place, and this is one other little incident that makes me laugh, and the nurses used to run to open the door for him. But *not I*! When I went to the door I stood there, and if he didn't open the door, well, the door wasn't opened. So I didn't say a word, and he didn't say a word either. But ooh! This sort of thing used to make me thoroughly sick, absolutely sick.

Anyway, oh yes, now then I was so desperate – I had to see Douglas, I had to see him to tell him there was nothing in these rumours. So I went to the matron and I asked if I could go home. I forget what I told her, I must have told her that somebody was ill. And I didn't have enough money to pay my train fare, and I asked her, could I have a bit of next month's salary, but oh, she was awfully fond of me, she sort of said, 'You have that money and don't worry about anything.' So I came home and I met – I can't remember whether I sort of told Douglas by post or by telegram that I was coming – and I met him, and he still wouldn't believe me, and I wept and I cried. 'Your tears don't hurt me now,' he said. 'This is all over between us.' I ought to have known at that time what a bastard he was, oughtn't I? But I didn't, I went back to London and my life, as far as I was concerned, was over. Oh, I was desperately unhappy. Ooh, it wasn't only what he had done, but there was no truth in it. I wouldn't have looked at another man, I wasn't interested. He was the light of my life, absolutely. Anyway, that was it.

About three months afterwards, he wrote me a letter. There was nothing much in it, very nonchalant, but I knew that it meant something else. So we started to write again. We started all over again, and when I returned he met me, and everything was absolutely fine. But I was in this hospital, oh, for about – God, the things I have done . . . well – Oh Christ, I've forgotten, I haven't talked for years about this. When I learned to play tennis, you see. Of course I was marvellous at it. I used to play sort of matches with other hospitals. Well, in those days you weren't allowed to work over one year without a holiday. Well I was there for this one year, and I was to go home for three weeks. And they were having a very important match and this matron said to me, 'Nurse, if you are going to have your holiday now, we are going to lose this match. It's no good, we haven't got any tennis players quite up to your standard.' So I said, 'Oh well, that's all right, I'll stay.' Well now it must have been the effort of playing tennis with my arm, and I could have picked up a germ, but when I got back home I had an abscess in my arm – and look, I've got the marks there. Look, you see that elbow is not like the other one, see. It started here and it came like this. And I was in so much pain for a fortnight. Why I didn't jump out of my bedroom window I don't know.

They couldn't lance it until it came to a head, and then my aunt said that there is one thing that could bring this to a head, she said, if anybody would go up at about – in the early morning, it would have to be about four o'clock in the morning, to get white moss with the dew on it. So of course I told Douglas and oh, he went up straight away. He got up early one morning and brought this white moss back with the dew on it in a box, my aunt made a poultice and it burst in four places and I passed out completely. There was my aunt and Douglas now, working on it, and I was absolutely out – anaesthetic. The pain – oh, it was terrible. My God it was all – just like having a baby you know. Like when you've just had your baby. Of course they still sent me my three pounds a month, but of course my aunt told me, people told me afterwards, that I could have claimed compensation from them. In the first place, she enticed me to stay there for thirteen months without a holiday, that could have got her into trouble; and then having all this I would have got compensation. I thought that it was marvellous that they still sent me my salary once a month, three pounds a month, which was great, you see, to me.

Anyway, I went back then – I was supposed to be there for a couple
of years – I went back, but after I had been there for a year and eight
or nine months, Douglas got very, very restless. So I came home and
I was home then for a while, I don't know for how long, and I wasn't
very happy so I thought to myself, I'll go and get another job – and
I didn't want to go into a hospital. So the only thing that I could do
was to look after young children. So I got a job as a sort of nurse cum
mother's help in a very posh place in London. They had three
children, the most gorgeous kids. The eldest one's name was Lucy,
and I thought, that's all I want to do is to get married, have a baby and
I shall call her Lucy. And this, of course, came true. Part of it.

Anyway, I looked after these kids so well. I could look after them
much better than she did. One day she said to me, 'You're not
entirely happy are you?' And I said, 'Well, no, I am not particularly
happy – why?' 'Would you be happy if you had your' – I think they
used to call them – 'your young man.' 'Oh, of course I would.' 'I'll
speak to my husband,' she said, 'and we'll see if we can find him a
job.' Because of course he was out of work, you see. This is another
thing he doesn't like to hear about. So I wrote him a letter and it was
arranged that he should come up. This is another thing I remember –
I went to meet him on the underground, and we were walking up the
steps, just looking into each other's eyes, we nearly stumbled at the
top, because he had never been on an escalator before you see. And I
had a white dress on – oh, with big flowers on it, I remember. Oh, I
must have looked gorgeous, because by now I really sort of blos-
somed out you see. Oh, fantastic. Anyway, we went back to the house
and we went to find a couple – we went to find a room, and he had a
job, it wasn't much of a job but still, he was there. And of course he
never looked back. He didn't stay with this chap very long. Something to do with – radio – wireless they used to call it. And Douglas
was a kind of traveller, he had to go around. Anyway, he didn't stay
at this job very long. He went to work right the other side of London,
which was a hell of a long way.

Well, from now I can see that really things began to deteriorate.
He was terribly sexy, he wanted sex all the time. He wouldn't care
how and where. We didn't have a chance to sort of sleep together. We

used to have it anywhere. He'd even come to the house and he'd have it when the bloody kids were in the back, and I used to beg him not to touch me – he obviously couldn't help his bloody self. Oh, it was murder, I don't know. Of course I didn't know anything about being sexually satisfied, to me it was just a bloody nuisance.

Except now, see – all of a sudden – oh yes, there was an incident: these three children are marvellous, but this – the eldest one was a girl, the next was a girl and the other was a boy. Now this middle girl was very high-spirited. As high-spirited as I was almost. Now I used to get up on a Sunday morning and I used to make the kids' breakfast and make the parents' breakfast on a tray and take it upstairs, and now they used to have fruit to start with, then we had eggs, egg and bacon or whatever, afterwards. So I said to these children, 'Now are you going to have an egg now, after you have had your fruit?' I was always very sensible with children. They all say that. The other ones said that they would have an egg but the little girl in the middle said no. I can't remember her name. No, that she wouldn't have an egg. So we were eating our breakfast now, and when we started our egg she wanted an egg. And I said, 'Well I'm not going out to cook you an egg now, you'll have to wait.' So she said, 'I'll go up and tell Mummy.' 'All right, go up and tell your mother,' I said. So her mother came down the stairs. 'Why don't you cook Pamela an egg?' 'Well,' I said, 'I asked her did she want an egg before we started and she said no, and if she wants an egg now she will have to wait until I have finished my breakfast.' 'Oh, well, I think you should cook her an egg, now.' 'Well, I won't cook her an egg now,' I said. 'Oh well,' she said, 'that's quite enough chat, I think you'd better leave.' 'All right,' I said, 'I give you my notice now, would you like me to go now?'

I knew that they didn't have much money, you see. And I was going to catch her now, because I had worked hard enough, and with those kids. 'Would you like me to go now, or will I hang on a month?' She had a conference with her husband and she said that perhaps I had better stop the month. So I stayed the month. But I always remember on the last day I was there, he said to me, 'There's still time to change your mind, you know. You could stay here, and you could stay with us.' I said, 'Well, you have arranged it all – and in any case I can't.'

Now you see Douglas and I were going to spend a couple of nights together. We had never slept together you see, and we were going off, not very far away, and that was very nice actually. I thoroughly enjoyed it, completely relaxed you see. We went as a married couple with our own bed, it wasn't very clean or anything, but what did we care about that! I didn't feel guilty about it. I have only felt that when I have had to have it and didn't want it. I thought that I was prostituting myself, which of course I have done – Christ, I would *still* prostitute myself, now.

Well I mean his sexual powers are beginning to fail, you see. And he is terribly inhibited, you know. I mean I'm not a bit inhibited, now I mean I've had one or two little incidents, and I mean – oh, I've had a whale of a time. I haven't got any inhibitions about it at all – but I have never had an orgasm, you know. I've nearly got there sometimes, but I've never actually had one, and I can't discuss it with Douglas. He thinks that it is a lot of things that are coming out of Women's Lib and all that. There's a lot in this, I suppose, because if you enjoy it and you go to sleep afterwards, what does it matter? This has happened to me lots of times. But *now* he is beginning to fail, and he says in such a – 'Do you mind if I put it in directly it's erect?' What a way to talk when you are having intercourse! Isn't it terrible? It makes me sick, and makes me feel a little bit guilty, but then again he's so fond of me and he thinks the world of me and he buys me all these presents, and he comes down and is thrilled to bits, it's like meeting a long-lost brother – 'Ooh, lovely to see you' – which it is, lovely, because we talk. I talk to him about politics, he talks to me about it, I'm still fascinated with his politics. I am now, because I think he's sound. He prophesises things and they nearly always happen, and I admire him for it immensely.

Well now of course Douglas didn't want me to be tied in any house. He wanted me to find a place and get a daily job. What could I do? Housework! This is the only thing I could do. This didn't seem to bloody worry him, the sod! I have been to some *terrible* places, and wherever I went the men were always nice to me and the wives were always bitchy. One woman came in one day and her husband just called me Ann, that's all – she absolutely flew – I had to leave straight away. That's all that happened. I mean I didn't want anything to do with these men, but I was friendly with them. I get on well with men anyway. And I went to one place – oh, my God, if that place was there I would call in, but it's years ago now. It probably isn't there anyway. But it was a gorgeous confectioner's, and I used to have to do the scrubbing and the cleaning of the shop, and I had to do a bit of ironing one day, and this woman was horrible, she used to make me feel a little bit nervous, you know. One day I went to put the iron on and she said, 'What's the matter with you, are you cockeyed, why don't you put the iron straight?' And I went back to Douglas in the evening and I said, 'I've packed that up.'

Then I got a job as a kind of a mother's help. There was an actress there – a would-be actress – and heaps of the people used to come. Anyway, I think Douglas used to come back every night. And we spent a couple of nights there, because I used to sleep downstairs, and I always used to lock the door because there were sort of men in and out, so he would spend the night and go out in the early morning. And he used to say that I was the hot bitch then, because I used to plead with him to stay – I probably did. Anyway, they used to have these actors to sort of stay there – the, like, woman of the house hadn't got a husband – and she used to go to the shop in Hampstead, there is a big shop in Hampstead – John Barnes, isn't it? And she used to buy halfpenny eggs and scramble them because she daren't boil them, because the bloody eggs would be bad anyway. One day she was scrambling these eggs, and of course I was an expert at it, and I was watching – I thought to myself, the silly bitch. She was called to the phone, I think, so I did the eggs before she came back, and she looked and she said, 'Who's done this?' I said, Who do you think? I have.' 'Ooh!' she said – she knew bloody well that I could scramble an egg.

Douglas came back one day and she went in to her mother and she said, 'Oh,' she said, 'Annie's young man is awfully good-looking.' And her mother told me this the next day, and before I could stop myself I shouted, 'Why shouldn't he be?' I said. You know, as if it

was – 'Aren't you lucky having such a good-looking young man.'
'Why shouldn't he be,' I said. 'All right,' she said, 'I didn't mean
anything.' Well she didn't, obviously – it's just me being a bit edgy
I suppose.

Marriage

'My ambition had been fulfilled.'

I was over twenty when I got married. I don't think Douglas was
particularly keen to get married, you know. I really don't know this,
he has never said so, but I had got an idea at the time – I couldn't go
on as I was at the time you see. I didn't issue an ultimatum or anything.
We just decided, we seemed to decide between us. I had a job doing
housework, but in a very nice place. They thought an awful lot of me
and when – I mean they used to have Douglas in and I used to do the
cooking and all the rest of it. I often used to make him a meal. Then
when they knew I was going to get married she made me a nice little
dress, you know, and she actually came to the wedding, which I
think was awfully nice of her.

Anyway we got married. I felt I had to – well, I was afraid I was
going to be pregnant you see; and he was practising withdrawal all
the time. Well, how I didn't get pregnant I can't imagine! Because
we had been having intercourse for years. But in awkward places,
and except of course that weekend that we spent together in bed. I
can't understand why I didn't get pregnant. Every month it was
murder, I was watching for my periods and all this, and I thought the
only thing to do is that I'll have to get married, you see. So we got
married and we had one horrible little kitchen and a living-room,
practically underground, in the basement, and we had a bedroom
upstairs. We had a table, three chairs, and I think there was a built-in
dresser, and that's about all we had. And out of this basement sort of,
there was a window with a big window-sill which I used to scrub,
and put this polish on it – not polish – I was going to say 'grimestone'!
– limestone, yes, before I went to work in the mornings. Well now I
wasn't very happy, I was miserable and quiet. Douglas used to com-

plain about this, the fact that I . . . I think I was . . . I think I was having intercourse too much and not getting anything out of it, and oh Christ, it was terrible.

Motherhood

'Well he wants babies, he might as well have them.'

Anyway, my first child now. We had a top flat which was very nice actually, and it was there that I became pregnant. And now this is true – Douglas takes great joy in telling people this – we decided we would have a baby you see, so he didn't practise any withdrawal, and I thought, well I won't get any more periods; and I got a period, and one night when he came home I was down on the doorstep meeting him in tears: 'What on earth's the matter?' 'I know I'll never be able to have any babies, I know I won't! I've got a period!' He tells people this, and he's thrilled to bits to tell them that. Oh Christ, how innocent can you get?

Anyway, of course I didn't have a period after that, and I had Lucy and of course he was thrilled to bits, and we were very happy now, you see. Because he didn't have to withdraw or anything, and I expect he was all right having intercourse, and ooh, when I had Lucy, talk about walking on air! Goodness me, they couldn't keep me down in the bed – 'You must lie down, Mrs Williams, you must lie down.' Anyway, and of course he was thrilled to bits as well, he said that when he came from hospital. I think I had her at four o'clock in the morning.

Oh Christ, none of them have been an easy birth. Oh God! Five or six hours really hard labour, really hard labour. But mind it's disgusting sometimes, these women were screaming; I could never scream, and of course the trouble is you see, that because I would bear pain as somebody once told me – 'You must bear your pain with fortitude' – because of this, I think they didn't have time to scrub up in the end because I was – you know, I didn't tell them early enough. You see I couldn't bear them to come along and say, 'Oh, you are miles away.' Oh, and I – this is where I played a trick on them when

I had my other one, because I did think the head was coming a bit low and I called somebody and she said, 'Oh, you're miles away!' I thought, right, you bitch, I'll have it on the bed, and I almost did, and when they came and complained I said, 'I called you!' Even in my blinking pain – oh, the bloody nurses, and I know what they are because I've been on two sides of the fence. Anyway, where are we now?

Yes, and Douglas came to the hospital about half past eight in the morning, and he told me afterwards that when he went home, like it was – no, it must have been earlier than that, I don't know whether he was allowed in or something – but he said that he was out early in the morning, and somebody came and asked him the time, and he had to tell them that his wife had just had a baby! He was so thrilled he had to tell somebody. I thought it was lovely. Anyway, we had her home, but do you know – this is something that *kills* me – it was nothing except . . . I think we had my aunt with us – I don't remember why we had her, but I think she was with us – she must have been, because what I am going to tell you concerns her. Now we had this very nice flat, it had one bedroom and a very nice living-room with a tiny little bedroom leading out, and when I brought Lucy home – but I've got an idea this incident took place when I was just coming out of hospital with my second child, and yet it can't have – anyway, there was an incident when my aunt was in the living-room, and directly Douglas came in I had to have it on the side of the bed with him, with her there, and I was trying to fight him off, but it was no good – I mean, he must have had it in his mind while I was away. Just ten days! Just coming out of hospital.

You see I wouldn't like the girls to sort of know about that. On the other hand I am a bit jealous of their affection for him, but I don't have to be, because it is a hundred-fold to me; but this is my little bit of jealousy, which I am aware of, and I wouldn't like to tell them that because he's their father. Anyway I begged him, I said, 'Douglas, they told me at the hospital it's so easy to have another baby.' This makes me think it must have been with only Lucy, because I was pregnant again within six months.

I was feeding her myself on the breast, and all of a sudden there was nothing wrong with her, but she was listless, she had no life in her at all. She was as good as gold, she was a lovely baby, she didn't cry much, but she was absolutely . . . I was going backwards and forwards to the Welfare, and the silly buggers – I kept saying, 'I know there's something.' 'There's nothing wrong with her.' 'Look, I know my own baby, she was always alive, she used to wake up in the morning and she used to clamber up to the cot before she'd open her eyes, and she was able to stand! She doesn't do that now,' I kept telling them. And all of a sudden one bright little spark said, 'Do you think you are pregnant again?' And I said, 'I must be.' 'Oh well, Mrs Williams, just in case of anything, take her off the breast immediately. Put her on something else.' She picked up marvellously. Oh, and she didn't gain any weight. That was it, she didn't gain any weight. You know, in those days you used to take them to the Clinic and they had to gain four to six ounces every week and all that.

So then I had poor Patrick – now this is another thing that I feel guilty about. I was pregnant again, and I had Patrick within a year and three months, there's a year and three months between Lucy and Patrick. Then I had a nice long gap; then there's a year and three months between Gillian and Mark; nice long gap, Jane; nice long gap, Ben. Jane was on her own and so was Ben. The other two are together.

Now then, what I – the question I would like to ask, you see – they do tell you that directly you are pregnant you should begin to love the baby. Well I mean, I didn't want another baby – I wasn't hostile or anything, but I just was . . . I had – my ambition had been fulfilled, I got married to the man I loved and had a baby, and I didn't want to be bothered by any more. Anyway, Douglas was marvellous. Oh, he always loved me to distraction when I was pregnant, he would have eaten things out of my shoes, absolutely marvellous when I was pregnant, he loved it. He would make a fuss of me, buy me anything. If I had any fancies, walk to the end of the earth to find it, you know. Anyway, I had Patrick and I wonder, you see, how much influence this has got on him. You can't answer that question, I suppose nobody can. I mean is he as he is because, you know, it was contrary to what I wanted? Or is it just chromosomes, or what is it? I don't know.

Anyway, he was a miserable baby, cried a lot after – he cried before I fed him, and he cried after I fed him. But then you see, he didn't cry so much as Gillian, and I was quite happy to have her. I had a five-year gap and I could see that Douglas wanted kids and I didn't want to go out to work anyway. I wasn't a career girl. Whatever I do, I would have to speak, and even though my stammer came up every now and again, it would come out at a crucial moment and when people may say, 'Oh, we just can't have her here,' you see. So I didn't go out to work. Douglas went to work and he went up, and up, and up, and up.

We didn't really have any money until in 1937 when he left the factory and started a clean-clothes job. And the poor chap, then he really had to pull up his socks, because he was very uneducated; and I think he had to do a bit of typing, which he did. And, of course, there were times when I felt very, very sorry for him and have done my best to help him. Then he did get a good salary and he got expenses and of course he would always cheat a bit on expenses. He went off to Paris with another chap and of course he had a hell of a lot of extra money, and I had plenty of money to spend while he was away, which was glorious. But I was as jealous as sin that he was going off to bloody Paris and I was there stuck with four kids.

I used to go to Marie Stopes Clinic before the bloody thing was opened in the morning, and I used to be there, I went there with Lucy in my arms. And I used to wear a cap, and this is another thing – he wouldn't have it. You know, he used to rip it out and – 'I can't do anything with this in.' But then of course he would. Then he wouldn't have it, he would withdraw, and then of course there were times when it got really bad and I wouldn't have intercourse unless he wore a sheath, which he had to for ages and ages, you see. Well then of course the time used to come when he used to try to get things to make me in the mood like, you know. I was over forty, I think, before I had my first taste of alcohol.

Then I must have become pregnant again, with an accident, and of course he didn't seem to mind and I was easy. I thought, 'Well, he wants babies and he might as well have them.' And of course these two kids were gorgeous, and when they got a bit older they were, ooh, Lucy and Patrick! And of course – ooh, I looked after them so well! In those days you know, young children used to have red eyes and all the rest of it. But ooh, my kids had eyelashes that were gorgeous. Well of course I used to study diet, it was a science to me.

Of course I loved the children and I loved looking after them and I loved preparing Douglas's meals and all the rest of it, but I think I used to spend a bit more time on the children than I did on Douglas, which caused him to be insanely jealous you see. I mean, when I had a breakdown after I had Ben, Patrick was there – and in a way I was glad that he made this particular statement in front of Patrick and the children, because Patrick said to him, 'There isn't anything wrong with Mum that you couldn't help! There's nothing wrong with her mentally or physically, but you are dragging her down.' And Douglas said, 'Your mother has never loved me, she's only ever loved the children.' He said this in front of Patrick, I felt a bit ashamed that he would have said that. That's what he said, anyway.

Anyway, I had – by now I had Lucy, Patrick, Gillian, Mark, and then the firm sent us – sent him to Newcastle, and while we were in Newcastle I became pregnant again, and I decided I wasn't going to have it. Mark was very young, I would have had another one in about a year and three months again. So I decided to have an abortion. But Douglas wouldn't have anything to do with it at all. He didn't want to know, but I had to ask him for the money. I found a back-street abortionist in Newcastle – mind, it was healthy enough, we had looked after ourselves and I didn't have any fears about it. And of course she did it beautifully, she had – what is called a silver dilator, which was made for her by a doctor to do this very thing, and she used to get a lot of warm water and she'd just dilate the womb, and I had to go down to her nine times before she really got the baby away. All this time Douglas didn't want to know.

Oh, and I had a lovely little doctor in Newcastle, that was very very sweet on me – [whispers] he spent a night with me actually when Douglas went away, it was wonderful. And he said to me, 'Well my dear,' he said, 'you'll never be right now until you have another baby.' 'What do you mean?' I said. He said 'I'm telling you, you should have another baby for you to be complete, because when you have an abortion . . .' – this that and the other. Of course I believed him, and then of course when I became pregnant with Jane, which was a very long time afterwards, I thought, well, no more about abortions, anyway I'll have to have her. And Douglas being quite thrilled about it, we had her, and of course, as I keep telling you, we have been so fortunate.

Now it's a very nice thing, Douglas always maintains there's no mother in the world like me. 'Absolutely marvellous. Any child, just give it to her, she'll bring something out of it.' This is partly true. Any child that used to come to the house a little bit inhibited, I'd talk with them, you know, and draw them out. Anyway he still maintains that our kids are as they are because of my mothering. Now up to a point I suppose that's true. But we have been most fortunate, because all these kids have been born and there has been nothing wrong with them. Mark at one time had a bit of a shock when he was very young, and before he started school, and I thought he was beginning to stammer. And I was petrified and I thought to myself, now what do I do? So I did take him to the doctor, and the doctor gave me a note to go to the hospital which I steamed open, and it said: 'This boy stammers badly – can you do anything for him?' So I thought, shit! – and I tore the bloody letter in half. I put him to bed. I went up and I talked with him, and we read stories and we did that and the other, and I did this for a couple of days, I kept him away from the other kids, and he hasn't had it since.

Anyway, what's after this now? The War, of course. Jane was born after the bombing had stopped, you know. Douglas was in a reserved occupation during the War, and did very well, and he made a lot of money out of it. I don't know whether I ought to tell you about it, how he started his business, because I mean I could go on talking for twenty-four hours I imagine. By now Douglas was in a very good position and he used to have to go away on trips you see. He never went away on any business trip without he took me, we managed in some way to get somebody to look after Jane, because at this time she was the only one that really counted. I mean we always had a wonderful time on our trips. I suppose we decided, this is a trip now and we mustn't have any arguments, you see, and I mean when I used to get into the car, I was so exhausted I would just sit there and be driven. I'd never give anything a thought. Whatever went wrong now, I couldn't do anything. I was away. And of course it was a long time before I came to, and this is how he used to say it, he used to say, 'You're talking so much, I can't get a word in edgeways!' – or you know, and he'd say, 'You still there? Oh that's good!' This was always the start of the holiday, but don't get me wrong, I was thrilled to bits. I loved going away, I still do. When I have to go away anywhere I never can sleep the night before, with the excitement. It's not only excitement, it's getting everything ready, and wondering if I've got it all taped and do this, that and the other – but I love going away, there's no doubt about it.

But we had bitter quarrels, oh, bitter. Now you see young Ben told me the other day, about when he said the first incident he remembered. He said that one day I was out in the kitchen and Douglas went in to where he was in the other room, and he was carrying a glass of water or something or other, and I think Ben should be about ten, and he said to Ben: 'I should throw this over the daft bitch out there!' *Me* – and I said, 'Oh, Ben, you never told me that before!' And he said, 'I've never been able to speak of it, Mum, because I was prostrate, I was so upset.' Just fancy, this shows what a bloody bugger he is.

Oh and – oh I'll tell you one incident, my God, when . . . and he's always managed to come home for lunch every day, and this is terrible, I used to think, when you've got a lot of bloody kids around. The only times he didn't come home for lunch was when he got this very good job in London. He used to go out all day, and would have to have his lunch out, so I didn't have to prepare much in the evenings, and oh – and of course the other thing you must get down is to go back a long way, when I was pregnant with Lucy, and we lived in this flat, and you know you can be so lonely in London, and he was *determined* now to educate himself. This is why he put his parents out of his mind, because they didn't do anything for him – and they didn't! He was determined to educate himself. So on these nights, he used to go out at seven o'clock in the morning – I had to cut a pile of sandwiches – and he never got home at night until eleven o'clock, and

I was there all day by myself. I even got a letter from his father, who I got on with very well: 'I don't like this idea of Douglas leaving you alone then when you are pregnant in London, he shouldn't do it.' But that wouldn't make him – he was a determined bastard, he was going to bloody learn. I say he's done everything on my bloody back, and so he has. Women's Lib coming out.

Anyway I was forty-five when I had Ben, and I thought that it was the change, and Douglas said, 'Yes, of course, of course.' 'Look,' I said, 'I've had five bloody kids before, don't you think I know?' The first thing that always happens to me, I can't drink coffee. Look, this is fantastic – I have coffee, I am very fond of coffee, I make myself coffee when I'm on my own a hell of a lot. I could have a cup of coffee, and I'd take one mouthful and there's something wrong with it, and I *know* I'm pregnant. No, it's never gone wrong, absolutely positive. And he said, 'No, you're not pregnant.' 'All right!' I said. 'I know I am – we'll wait.' So I went up to the doctor. I didn't want an early pregnancy test, I knew bloody well I was pregnant. I'd get sick in the morning – I know all the signs. I went up to her after about three months and she said, 'Oh, Mrs Williams, you are well and truly pregnant.' 'Good God, I'm not am I?' I knew I was, but you know . . . 'Yes, my dear,' she said. 'Don't think you can drop birth control,' she said. 'You and your husband are both young and healthy and useful.' She said, 'I've just come away from a woman that has had a baby at fifty-one.' 'I don't believe it!' I said. 'It's true,' she said. I said, 'Oh my God!' So I went back and I told him. Of course he tried to hide his pleasure, but there was no doubt about it. Then he said, 'Look,' he said, 'I'll buy you the earth, I'll buy you the best pram that's ever been bought.' He said we'll go out and buy this and do that.

He's like that because he is – because all of them are so bloody marvellous, I suppose, and they were – oh, they are wonderful children really! I had a terrible lot of trouble with Gillian – oh, she was really a bitch of a girl, still! She was high-spirited, highly sexed, like her bloody mother – what I call 'a sexy bitch'. Christ! The men I could have here, if I wanted them – oh, it's fantastic, it makes me laugh. Actually, if they only knew how old I was – that's neither here

nor there. I wouldn't mind having a love affair, mind. Of course I do
fancy young men – obviously I don't want a man of my own age,
they'd be useless. My husband is getting on, he's as useless as any.
Not that I want the blinking sex thing. It doesn't matter, you come to
it gradually, don't you?

Anyway, where are we? Oh yes, young Ben. I must tell you that
when I was having Ben I was petrified, because they say if you have a
child when you're on the change, he's going to be a genius or a
moron, and Douglas used to say I've got a pessimistic streak in my
nature, which I have. I wouldn't say it is pessimistic, I would say that
it is realistic, but I used to be worried about him, very worried. But
now of course, not only was Douglas very thrilled about this, all the
kids were. I couldn't have done anything about it anyway, at that
age I couldn't have had an abortion.

The kids were thrilled to bits. I only had to move awkwardly –
'Are you all right Mum, are you all right?' I was going to have it at
home you see, and I got everything ready, the bed. So in the end I
decided that I wouldn't move, I wouldn't say anything, I wouldn't do
anything – even if I had indigestion or I was sick, I wouldn't say
anything to anybody.

So I let this go on and on, till one Sunday afternoon – I can see it
now, we had a bed downstairs so that I could have plenty of rest,
and Douglas and Mark were outside on the balcony doing something
or other – the pains started. I got the clock – to really time it. I thought
I won't say a word now till I am positive. So I had these pains for a
couple of hours – of course the first couple of hours isn't bad, but I
knew it was on the way – and then I thought, oh, now for a bloody
rumpus! So I said – I called them – I said, 'I think the baby is on the
way.' 'Oh my God!' Good God almighty, all the running up and
down stairs and everything, and we had a nurse that came, a midwife
– she was marvellous – and of course it came a bit quicker than they
imagined because I did go on and on, I was determined there wasn't
going to be any mistake. And I must tell you this, we had a beautiful
big stainless steel bath that we had, it's fantastic, and when this nurse
came, she said, 'Oh, it won't be for a couple of hours yet' – they all
say that, they haven't got a clue – and it came quicker and Douglas

was in the bath and she had to go in to get hot water. [Laughs.] Lovely, I think!

Anyway, he came to watch the birth, and you know this was another thing, that makes me *sick*! He didn't have a thought about the pain that I was going through, to him it was wonderful! And this little boy came out, and he peed over me – marvellous! I mean I could have been an iceberg or a bit of bloody stone! Oh God, Jean, he's got no heart you know. He's emotional, but this is a different thing from being deeply sensitive. He hasn't got a sensitive bloody bone in his body. He's very sensitive to me and my moods. When he comes in, he can see straight away if there is anything wrong you see. But other than that – oh, he seems to be like bloody ice. He's got cold blue eyes. And he's very blond, and I think blond people are inclined to be a bit cold, but he's like bloody ice, he really is. Anyway this was the first time he'd ever watched a birth, and he was thrilled about it, this wonderful boy came out you know, and of course I didn't know. First of all I was glad to hear that he was complete, that there wasn't anything wrong with him, but what he was going to be like I don't know.

Oh, he was the most wonderful baby, that boy was a joy to us, for years and years and years. He was *brilliant* at school and he was so good-looking, and oh, I've got his pictures and the computer that he made when he was in public school, he was absolutely marvellous. All the time there was this little pessimistic streak that said to me, this can't go on, one day it's going to stop, and by God it did.

Ben's Illness

'It's a wonder I am here to tell the bloody story.'

I went to look after my granddaughter and while I was there I had a telephone call from Douglas. I had just cooked the lunch and I was starving and it was in the oven, beautiful liver and bacon and onions, my favourite lunch, and Douglas phoned me about half past eleven – a quarter to twelve, twelve o'clock, I don't know – and he said, 'I'm afraid you'll have to come home, Ben has completely lost his mind.'

The shocks I've had in my life, Jean, it's a wonder that I am here to tell the bloody story. So I nearly passed out, I went all to pieces like, and Mark put me on a chair, gave me some whisky, and I said, 'I'll have to go back.' And oh, I was terribly upset.

Anyway, I went back in the afternoon and managed to eat something. I couldn't go straight away because – driving myself and everything you see. And I went back and I got back about half past three to four. I telephoned the office and Douglas came home, and he said that when he had come back that morning, Ben was there. A lot of things had happened before, and he came in apparently when Douglas was preparing a bit of lunch and he said to Ben, 'Will you have a bit of lunch?' And Ben said 'I don't want your fucking lunch, keep your bloody lunch!' And he went out, you see. Douglas told me that this was what he said to him, but he doesn't say 'fucking', he says 'effing', he's too much of a gentleman. So then Ben went out and he didn't come back.

Well, it was getting on half past four, five o'clock. I said, 'Look, we'll have to go to find him,' and he said, 'Well where can we go?' 'The first thing we can do – is,' I said, 'we had better go down to his digs.' So we went down to his digs and his papers were on the stairs, and I asked the people there – they didn't know where he was. So we came back home and I said, 'Hadn't we better telephone the police?' So Douglas said, 'Perhaps we'd better.' So Douglas phoned the police, and I could see he wasn't getting on so I said, 'Let me have the phone,' but I was inhibited because he was there, you see. You see I always get on well with people, all the awkward phone calls I usually make. So the chap said – I told him about Ben and I said, 'I was just wondering, if you came across him, if you could pick him up or something.' 'Look, my dear,' he said, 'Look, my love – we can't pick him up, he hasn't done anything.' 'No, but,' I said, 'he is wandering around, he must be, he's got no money in his pockets or anything.' 'Well,' he said, 'I can send a panda car out, but I don't think there's much we can do.'

In any case, after a while Ben came back – poor kid, he looked terrible and I – [sobbing] and he was hungry. He looked so bedraggled and oh God, he was awful. Anyway, he was hungry and I cooked him a lovely meal, and he ate it all, and I said, 'Now look, love, will you go to bed now for a while?' And he said, 'Yes, all right.' I could do anything with him, anything at all. So he went upstairs and he went to bed, and he'd been up for about a quarter of an hour, and I said to Douglas, 'I better go up and have a look.' He was dressing himself. 'Oh, I can't stay here,' he said, 'I've got work to do.' Well he didn't have anything to do, and I couldn't stop him. I think now I'd been down to our doctor, who also thought the world of him. Everyone loves him, and we never called a doctor, he was hardly ever ill, you know. So, I can't quite remember what happened, but anyway, he wouldn't stay in bed for the doctor to come, and he went out, and I think I had to telephone the doctor to say that he's out now or something. Anyway I went down to her and I told her all about it, and she got on to the hospital and said we must get him in at once – and she went – she must have spent an hour phoning around, she was absolutely marvellous.

Yet she seems to be a very strange person. She's got five children – and her house is like a pigsty. She can't put anything on her desk, it's all piled up with papers, you know – I can't understand how people can live. Nevertheless, she spent an hour trying to get Ben a bed. And I think he was in – I can't remember it all. Oh, and he told – oh, my God – oh Christ – when he became ill first of all, it was over a girl you know, but he was – he had a lot of conflict when he went to the university, because when you go to university you are thrown on to a heap, aren't you? Public school he was something. He was in everything; his housemaster practically wept when he left, he said he'd never had such a responsible Head Boy, and he was Head Boy of the whole school for a year. He had never had anybody so marvellous in the House. When the sort of young ones came – he wouldn't have any fagging and he wouldn't have any corporal punishment, he was absolutely marvellous, and he is wonderful with kids. He's like Christ, if you know what I mean. He is absolutely wonderful. Anyway, where was I in my enthusiasm over him?

Oh yes, and Ben – here's the part I want to tell you. It started off over a girl. He came home from holiday once, and I can't go into all this. We were having a drink, he wanted to tell me all about it, which he did, and in the process of this he said to me, he said, 'She's never had an orgasm with anybody else, only me – it's because I take so much pains and so much – have you ever had an orgasm, Mum?' And I said, 'No, I haven't.' And he told Douglas this, in his wildness – he said, 'It's a bloody disgusting thing, you've never looked after Mum. She's never had an orgasm with you, you selfish bastard.' This is what he told him in his madness, and of course Douglas has been holding this up against me ever since, and I try to tell him and he says, 'You discuss my affairs.' 'I didn't discuss it, I didn't discuss it,' and I wept about this. But it's no good, you might as well talk to the bloody wall. Anyway, I don't care a bugger what he thinks anyway. I just wanted to get that bit in, because I think it is rather important.

Anyway we managed to get Ben into hospital and he went back into the ward that he was in before, and while he was there – anyway I'm not going on about that. Oh, the other thing I want to tell you is that I had to go up one evening, on this night that he was taken ill. I went to talk with a young student doctor, and I was in this private room with her, but I had come up to the hospital with Lucy. Now after I had been in there for about half an hour, Lucy came in and she said, 'Do you mind if I come in? Because,' she said, 'I feel as if I have almost brought him up.' Which she had. And the first thing she said to this doctor – I'll never forget this – was 'Well,' she said, 'there is a lot of trouble in our family because my father tells lies.' This is what she said to the doctor. I was thrilled to bits, in a way – I mean because, I didn't want to tell this student doctor too much about Douglas, he wasn't there to defend himself – and even in the blasted court the wife can't give evidence and I agree with it – because after all he wasn't there, but she said this about Douglas and I was glad she did.

But they're bastards at the hospitals and all, you know, they want to probe. I had to go up there once to have a chat about Ben, and when I went they had heaps of people around, students, so I wouldn't say anything, wouldn't answer the questions. When I came out I wrote the Professor a letter and he answered it very nicely and said he didn't know that I would object. 'Oh,' he said, 'I hear your husband and you are parting,' in front of all these people. I said, 'This is a lot of nonsense, we're not parting.' It's disgusting, it's bloody disgraceful. Anyway this was the thing that caused a rift between Douglas and me, with Ben. Now my mind is going blank.

Living Alone

'I just danced around the room.'

For years I have thought to myself, good God, I hope this man will die before I do, so that I have a few years without him, because you think of the years that I have been with him, and what could I have done? This is the bloody guilt that I felt, that I should have done something and gone, but how could I have left the kids, anyway? And what am I capable of? I can't take a job, I can't do anything very much, I have had no particular training. I can play the piano. I could have done a lot, I expect – you've got to have a bit of a sponsoring, you've got to have somebody to give you a bit of a helping hand, and he wouldn't have – I've taken a couple of jobs while I have had them, and it's been murder! I mean he has made my life a bloody hell.

Anyway, wait a minute now, coming down here. We'd been having – oh, we'd been unhappy for a long time, we've had a hell of a lot of rows and Douglas won't argue a thing through. Now when it gets to a point where he's stumped and he's nothing to say – I'm pretty articulate you know – when it gets to that point he says, 'Well, the best thing to do is to part.' Then I will say, 'Well how can we do that?' Now I don't want – I am a scheming bitch, you know – I didn't want to do too much on my own, I wanted him to suggest things. So we would go over this carefully and then I said, 'Well, if I part the first thing I'll have to give up is my car.' Now, well he wouldn't have that – which is a good thing – he says, 'Oh no, you can't give up your car, you've been used to a car for so long. You would be very unhappy without a car if we're going to be parted as well.' I said, 'How are we going to have the money?' *'Don't* worry about that, leave that to me. Where would you like to go?'

All the time Southsea was in my mind. I don't particularly know why, partly because I love the sea, and I've got lots of friends and lots

of relatives around here. This is another thing, I *hated* Newcastle, all
the time I hated it when we went there, and he knows this, and there
was a time when Douglas used to say: 'Well when we get a bit more
money, we will buy a house or a cottage somewhere.' He wanted to
buy a cottage in France. Can you imagine it? This is the first thing I
think that gave me the idea, well if he can afford to buy a cottage in
France, we can have a cottage somewhere else in England, but I
wanted to manoeuvre him, I didn't want to put things – I wanted
him – he is the one that's going to pay, and I wanted him to pay me
well after all the time I have worked. I think I deserve to live in – not
luxury, but comfortable, so between one thing and another, I got
him round to saying, 'What about Southsea?' 'Ooh, yes, that sounds
very interesting.' Oh, I was loving this now. 'Yes, I wonder could I
find a flat down there or something?' 'Well why don't you go down
there and see?' We were getting on beautifully now, so he came
down here once or twice and I came down and found this flat.

I was thrilled to bits – paradise! Absolute paradise! I mean, well,
as I told you yesterday, when I came here, and when I paid the chap,
paid him off, he went down and gave me the *keys*! My *keys*! I came
in here and I just danced around the room, sang and – oh, I think it
was wonderful. I didn't have a piano, I did the can-can, I did everything all around this empty room. And then I furnished it in my
mind, with all the furniture we had got at home. This red carpet, this,
that, that – no, I didn't have that in my mind – I had already bought
this on offer, and these are the things I bought at a sale, these chairs
all came, and then we went out to buy a piano, then this colour
television, which is the best one in Great Britain, I swear it, it's
gorgeous – it was at home, and Douglas said I could have it, which I
thought was wonderful. That was three years ago.

3.   Annie Davison

Annie Davison was born in Belfast, Northern Ireland, in 1908 but has
lived in Glasgow since she was four years old. On her father's side there
are Irish connections which go back to her father's great-grandfather,
an English soldier in the King's Yeomanry sent to quell the potato
rebellions in Ireland. He was offered a small farm in Northern Ireland
as an alternative to returning with the army to England, and, since he
had met and married an Irish girl, he accepted this offer of land. They
had numerous children whom the farm could not support, and so some
left Ireland for Glasgow to look for work. Annie Davison's grandfather
settled in Partick, a working-class district of Glasgow, and became an
unskilled labourer in a saw-mill. He and his wife had eight children and
brought them up in a one-room-and-kitchen tenement flat.

Annie Davison now lives with her husband, Charlie, in Glasgow.
They have two grown-up sons and five grandchildren. After the interview she wrote to us asking us to include the following passage sum-
ming up how she feels about her life:

*My husband and I have evolved through the years, by understanding,
consultation and debate, an equality of life together which greatly satisfies us.
He pursues his trade-union activities and the many facets of being a district
councillor. We often go on separate holidays – he to various conferences –
and sometimes we have a relaxing holiday together.*

*I have my interests and attend two painting summer schools each year. I
also have the interest of the Co-operative Women's Guild and Labour Party.
We are both very interested in the arts and drama. We spent our pre-marriage
years acting in Glasgow Clarion Drama Group and Workers' Theatre,
specializing in the plays of Bernard Shaw and European and American plays
with political content. Charlie looks after our smallish garden and helps with
home decorating and is not averse to housework as required. An abiding joy of
our lives lies in the love of our grandchildren, all under seven years of age,*

the youngest boy being nine months. . . Our two sons and our daughters-in-law
have our love and respect. We are lucky in having forged the type of marriage
which suits our personalities and does not conform slavishly to outside pressures
except where we choose to consider the susceptibilities of friends and family.

Childhood

'I think, without boasting in any way, that we were an unusual family . . .'

Now my father and mother were both born in Glasgow and both
attended the Episcopalian Church when they were young. At six
years my father attended a school in a hall and brought one penny per
week and a lump of coal for the stove during winter. Later a school
board built the first school in the district and father and others
marched into the new school on its first day. This was the start of
free education.

Well actually at eleven years of age he left school to help the coal-
men carry coal up the tenement flights of stairs, they used to carry a
half hundredweight up the tenement flights of stairs at that age –
that was before he went into the shipyard. He went to work in the
ship-building when he was twelve years of age, his people changed
his birth certificate. Boys had to go to a doctor to be examined to see
if they were old enough and in good enough health to take a job in
the shipyard. My father said he was fourteen and the doctor winked
and passed him as fit, knowing that he badly needed a job. I think a
lot of children got in that way; long before their time they were
stuck down to this hard work.

He was very keen on music, my father, he just loved music. There
wasn't an instrument he picked up that he couldn't get a tune out of.
As Dad grew up he learned to play the organ in the church; he
practised away until he became the organist for the Bible class and
then he joined the church choir and that's where he met my mother.

After they were married a few years they changed from the
Episcopalian Church to, of all things, the Methodists. My mother's
older brother, whom she was very fond of, married an Englishwoman
who was a Methodist. I always think of Methodists being very

strictly brought up – I believe it's English but it's a sort of Scottish way of living too. This older brother of my mother's was a little bit better in life than we were. He became a pawnbroker in Bridgeton where all the poorer people lived. They had to pawn their clothes every Monday and get them out again for the weekend, but my uncle was a very kindly man and all the women in the district called him Uncle Davie. So that is the background we had.

When my father was just a short time married he found he couldn't get work in Glasgow, so they finally went to Belfast for work, because he being a boilermaker was told there was a ship being built over there. We lived for seventeen years there, and all of the family were born in Belfast. Although we lived there for seventeen years my father was keen to get away from it. He said it was so full of bigotry and hatred. Yet that is the place where he met a man, Tom Henderson, who was in the newly formed Belfast Co-operative, and he was a socialist and he gave my father a lot of literature and books to read and it wasn't long before my father left the church. My mother, who had been brought up even more tightly to the church, found it difficult, but as a very very intelligent woman – in fact I think she had a better brain than my father – she read a lot and took a long time to consider changing.

Well, as soon as he could get a steady job in Glasgow he took us all back and I was only four when we came here. I still have a wee bit of Irish about me, about my speech, and I can't help it. For instance a Scottish 'r' I can't say very well. I say 'turn' instead of 'turrn'. Well anyway, I've still got a wee bit of the Irish left.

I remember our Belfast house, I could describe it – in fact I went back fifty years later with a friend to stay for a week in Ireland and said, 'Would you mind if I go to Bryson Street, Belfast, and have a look at my old house?' I thought it was a big house – it had four rooms and a downstairs and an upstairs, with a little back garden and a lane at the back. When I went back there was an old couple in the house and I said, 'I used to stay here. I was born in this house and I haven't been here for fifty years. I hope I am not disturbing you, I just wondered if the house was the same as I remember it.' They said, 'Come away in. I know the man that got the house after you and we got the house from them.' So anyway I went in and had a cup of tea, but before I went in the door I stood in the hall. I said, 'If you'll excuse me I just want to see if I am right,' I said, 'to the right-hand side is the front parlour where the piano used to be, and the next door on that side is a big kitchen with a scullery off it and a great big boiler for doing the washing. Then the stairs go straight up here, but there is a little half-landing where there is a small back room. Then you come up on to the main landing where there is a back bedroom and a great big front bedroom which takes up the whole of the front of the house.' He said, 'That's exactly right.' I said, 'Well I was four when I was here last.' I remembered that house so well – all fifty years ago. Anyway, I don't remember a lot about it except being taken by my mother to see Auntie Thomson; we called her Mrs Far-out-of-the-road because she was away at the end of the tramway lines and that was a far far distance to me.

I am sure that I had a different background from the average child round about me. I think, without boasting in any way, that we were an unusual family – considering my parents had little education – but both were determined to give us the best education possible. We were allowed to think for ourselves, so we were known locally as 'bolshies', the epithet for all who did not conform to the pattern.

My father, as I say, was musical in every way; he joined the Socialist Choristers' Choir, he was in the Independent Labour Party – he played the flute, the ocarina and the concertina, he'd take a shot at anything, at any musical instrument, and he was keen. He was one of the back-room boys in the ILP; he never had the education to be a speaker, but he read a lot and so on. He was very keen on his children learning as much as possible, even though he hadn't the money really to educate them very well. He never did drink, or gamble. He did a little smoking, a pipe and that was all. My father went occasionally to a music hall or play – he was a great man for dramatic plays – so he used to take me; in fact mother and father took me to all the halls and we used to go to the Alhambra Theatre.

We had five in the family. My elder sister went out to work as soon as we arrived in Glasgow. Her first job was in Bailey and Ferguson,

the music-sellers in Queen Street – it's away now. She had learned
the piano when she was a young girl over in Belfast. That was the one
thing my parents bought that we paid up – no, two things, there was
a sewing machine as well. My mother didn't like to buy anything
unless she had the money for it, and if we didn't have the money we
did without. But the sewing machine was paid up and the piano was
next. My father found a teacher for my elder sister, and he advised
Dad for Nellie's sake to get a piano, because it would be the instrument of the future. Nellie became a good pianist and she used to do
the transposing of music for customers in Bailey and Ferguson's
music shop. But at the end of the First World War she went to
Australia. She married an Australian soldier and that was the first real
break in our family. My father was absolutely against the War and
hated soldiers and soldiering and he wouldn't speak to my sister because she was going away. My mother of course, being a mother, you
know, was on Nellie's side. If she really cared for Reg, her husband,
she would help her.

The upset spoiled our family life for a number of years until my
father got over it. He was too proud of Nellie because she was a good
pianist, bright and clever, and had then started to play for the Co-
operative Choir. She went from that to play to the Clarion Choir,
and was pianist there until their old conductor went sick and gave up.
She was asked to take over the conductorship, and did very well at
music festivals with that. She only had that two years with the choir
when she went off to be married. Father said, 'Going away to the
other ends of the earth and marrying a man,' he says '– not a man, a
hired assassin!' Oh that was a terrible time! Then when Nell's first
child, a girl, was born he relented when mother said, 'You've got a
wee granddaughter.' There was a wee boy after that and he sent them
a railway-train set, so he was a bit mollified by that time.

After my sister there was a boy, my brother Robert, who went to
America at the time of the – just about the end of the American boom,
in the 1920s when we were having it badly here. Robert worked in
the shipyard too in Glasgow. He started off first by working in an
engraver's – brass engraving – because he was quite a good drawer in
school. He went to night-school and did etchings and drawings that

were popular in those days, and so he thought he would like to learn engraving. He was apprenticed to a shop-fitter's place in Glassford Street – Hamilton's it was. He had nearly finished his trade – I think he would be about seventeen – and it was coming up time for him to be called up. It was during the war, about 1917, there was a foreman in the place who said, 'What about you, son? You're nearly eighteen, what are you going to join when it comes your turn?' My brother Robert said, 'I am not joining the army,' he said, 'I am a Conscientious Objector and I am not going to join; when they call me up, I am going to prison,' he said, 'but I don't think they will call me up yet because my time's not out.' Robert went home and told my father and my father said, 'That man's got it in for you; he could keep you on because of what you are doing, work of national importance.' He was engraving plates for warships and things like that, so he could have been kept on.

He was in the SLP by that time. That was the Socialist Labour Party, it was a very left-wing organization. They were connected with Eugene Debs and connected with American people. I remember once he came home in great excitement to my father before he went away to America. He said, 'Dad, if I could just get enough money,' he said, 'I was at the meeting tonight, the SLP up in Renfrew Street in Glasgow. If I could just get enough money, I would like to buy Eugene Sue's novels about the history of the working class in France* – I was offered the complete twenty-one volumes at the meeting.' This was a huge work Sue wrote taking a family from the early days in Brittany – I think Gaul they called it then – anyway, from those early days the novels built up history through the eyes of a family in the olden days when families were tribes, and it took them right through the period of Christ coming, the Middle Ages, famines, Huguenots, French Revolution, right up to the present day. They were novels but the whole work was a family saga through the ages. I can tell you this, my father gave him the money, two pounds. It was an education to me, because I had them all read by the time I was

*Historical novels in twenty-one volumes, *The Mysteries of the People*, or, *A Proletarian Family across the Ages*.

fourteen; I had read them twice over by that time. I can still remember lots of it. We had them in the house for many years, and many friends had them on loan from us, but we finally sent them to some Labour Party sale of work or something like that. Oh, I was a terrific reader. I was never any good at mathematical subjects or science, I just hated that, but I was always good at English. Not so much history, although I like history, but I like it to be a bit more romantic – I liked historical novels best, because it is a bit boring, all the dates etc. I can remember better when it is in story form. I used to do a lot of reading.

Socialist Sunday-school

'This Sunday-school was just like the church to me.'

My father was a strong socialist by that time, with the reading he had done in Belfast. He was a Co-operator and he was an atheist as well. First thing he did, he kept up with this man, Tom Henderson – he became an MP for Tradeston, Glasgow. My father didn't care much what you were; if you were a socialist that was all right; what your beliefs were it didn't matter, as long as you wanted a fairer share for all. Dad sent me right away to the Partick Socialist Sunday-school. Partick ILP is what he joined because we lived in Overnewton, which is only about a mile away from the hall. I was taken down at four years of age to the Sunday-school and that was the happiest time of my life right up until I was fourteen. I went through the whole of the Sunday-school, learned all the songs, and then later on I played piano for the children.

It was discovered after I had, you know, done a few little readings in the Sunday-school and so on, and in the school I was quite good at these things, and father said, 'I think I am going to send you to elocution.' So he sent me with his hard-earned money again; my mother couldn't afford to do it off his wages, but the odd bits of pennies that he saved – he didn't drink – he used it to try and educate his children, and he said to me he said, 'Would you like to go to elocution classes?' So I went to the – what was then called the

Athenaeum in Glasgow, and it's now of course the Scottish Academy of Drama and Music. I went there to classes and of course, once Dad saw that I was quite good at this sort of thing, he started hunting for socialist poems. I wasn't to just – to do ordinary elocution, it was to be socialist poems and I was sent round by him.

Eventually I became well-known in the socialist propaganda meetings as a reader, especially of poems with a message, and was asked everywhere in the city. 'Your wee girl does elocution – she does readings?' 'Yes, do you want her to come along?' he'd say, and, 'Oh, Annie will go along.' I went to the BSP Sunday-school – British Socialist Party – and I went to the Anarchists – they had a Sunday-school for children – and of course all the other Socialist Sunday-schools in Glasgow – we had a great number then. There must have been about thirty groups of Sunday-schools, all socialist. I went round them all in turn doing all sorts of things. There was one poem in particular that I used to be asked to do because it is a real old rousing socialist one and my father found it in the weekly socialist paper *Forward*. I never found out who wrote it, it had eight verses in it; I can't remember some of it now. It was real socialist propaganda, you see, and I gave it full throat.

The Socialist Sunday-school was only called a 'Sunday-school' because that was the only day the children were available to go. They were at school other days, and these were mostly children whose people were thoughtful of the future and they were really socialists and they didn't bother so much about religion as the average person did. But this Sunday-school was neither religious nor irreligious, it was to teach children the principles of socialism, and from the earliest days you learned the precepts and declarations in which you were asked a question and you gave the answer. This was the form it took, but apart from that they had a wonderful collection of songs. I have the song-book somewhere about the house and the songs were – quite a lot of them were written by people like – William Morris, and one of these other poetic type of socialist of that period – Carpenter, Edward Carpenter is the one I am trying to think about, and Bruce Glasier, some of his pieces were in the song-book. We sang them to hymn-tunes which were taken mostly from ordinary religious Sunday-school hymn-books. Of course we learned the 'Internationale' and 'The Red Flag'. You had little things for younger children like – carrying mother's parcel for her, guiding blind men over the street – these were the little things we would do. They taught us a simple moral attitude.

Then we had a Superintendant who asked all of these various questions each week, and each child got a chance of saying if he knew them, such as 'Love your school fellows, who will be your fellow workmen in life.' And then another one was 'Love learning which is the food of the mind; be as grateful to your teachers as to your parents.' A couple of precepts I remember are: 'Remember that all the good things of the earth are produced by labour – whoever enjoys them without working for them is stealing the bread of the workers.' 'Do not think that those who love their own country must hate and despise other nations or wish for war which are the remnants of barbarism.' 'Look forward to the day when all men and women will be free citizens of one fatherland and live together in peace.' There are ten of these. I am trying to remember the question-and-answer ones. 'What is socialism?' – now I am not sure if I can just get the right words – it is all just pouring into my mind. 'Question: What is meant by socialism? Answer: It means common ownership of the production of all things necessary to live happily and well.' 'Question: What are the three great principles? Answer: Love, justice and truth.'

Anyway, that's the sort of thing we got in the Sunday-school and we had a speaker each week who came and talked about things. Mostly interesting things about the world, stories about people who had invented things. Our speakers made them interesting, talking about way back in the past history, not of kings and queens, but common people. We were told quite a bit too about the early days when children had to work in the mines and all this sort of thing, and down in the Midlands when weavers had their heavy work and their children were sent out to work early.

In my early days in Glasgow my father was so keen in the Movement – he used to go to John Maclean's meetings, which was the BSP, and he had open-air meetings in the street up near the centre of

Glasgow – Brunswick Street – and I remember on a Sunday night my father and mother would take me there. There was another little girl whose mother and father came and brought her and we used to play tig round-about and shout, but we felt the atmosphere – we were at something special that other children didn't go to. One day this little girl was standing beside me at the school and I realized it was my little friend; I was so pleased. I just happened to turn and look at her: 'Oh Maisie, I didn't know you stayed here and came to this school!' She said, 'Yes, I just live across the road there.' So I said to her, 'You must come to my Socialist Sunday-school', and she came to the Socialist Sunday-school from that Sunday on. I used to go for her and take her to the Sunday-school. We were good chums for years. This is the sort of atmosphere I was brought up with. This Sunday-school was just like the church to me.

The Socialist Sunday-schools were a large movement. We had them all over Britain; they were in England – London had dozens as well, and we sometimes got in touch with them and we had annual get-togethers and even Glasgow district held their annual gala. We used to come together in the City Hall; also we produced little plays and did action songs. There was also for many years a Socialist Music and Drama Festival in Glasgow, and many young people learned a lot about music and drama in these annual competitions. These children are now mostly the backbone of our Scottish institutions, like in trade unions, acting, orchestras, writing, poets, CND, Women's Lib, etcetera.

It was very well-organized in Glasgow and all of the socialist – the Labour voters as you would call them nowadays – they were really early socialists who wanted a change of society and their children to learn as much as possible about these things. They didn't want to have to – they didn't want to just vote Labour. They wanted their children to learn that socialism was a good way of life and what was good for one was good for all, and so this was a moral attitude they had. What I call myself is an 'idealist socialist', and it's laughed at nowadays because the world has become so complicated. Idealism is not very popular nowadays because there are so many practical things that have to be decided where your ideals have to be pushed aside to some extent in order to get a result now. But I feel that a long-term result must be the real goal of socialism, and in the end the best rather than trying to do something as a short-term measure. If the short-term measure becomes permanent then it's no use, because the short-term measure is the wrong measure to me. That's not very well-expressed but that's what I have a feeling about.

My Mother

'She was always working hard.'

My mother was a 'family' woman, she was essentially looking after the family, but she read a lot. She listened a lot to the radio, she read a whole lot of political books and pamphlets. She became quite knowledgeable along with my father, but she couldn't spend the time to go out and work in the Movement. The only thing she ever joined, became a member of actually and did any little thing she could, was the Women's International League. But she didn't take an active part in it, because she just hadn't the time.

As I was thinking about it, I feel that the women then didn't have the chance that women do have nowadays; and yet the women today, so many of them really don't take advantage of the freedom from work that there is. What I mean is the gadgets that are here nowadays to help you get through your work quicker. When I think of my mother's washing day for the family once a week, that was a day's hard labour, and then she had a day drying the stuff indoors when weather was bad. We went down two flights to a horrible dark backyard washing-house. You had to light the fire in the boiler to get the water boiling for the washing. There were horrible old tubs and a grimy old wash-house that nobody really cared about because eight families used it, and there was no upkeep of it really by the factor.

I do sadly remember one occasion when I was going out to recite somewhere. My mother had this old black fireplace, she was trying to clean it up – I think, you know, it was for the weekend or something like that she wanted it – and she said, 'Are you going out, Annie?' and I said, 'Yes, you know I am going to–' – whatever it was, some place – and she said, 'You might have stayed behind and taken the emery paper over the steel for me. I am doing all the black-leading, you might have done that for me.' I said, 'Well leave it until tomorrow and I'll do it.' She said, 'No, I must have it done tonight.' And I said, 'Well, I can't do anything about it.' I said, 'I promised to go out and I am going to the elocution.' And she looked up at me and you could see the tears in her eyes, she was tired – oh that hurt me! Afterwards I felt terrible about that, and I've never forgotten that, I just thought, 'Oh, what have I done to her?' So later on when I came home I said I was sorry, but she was so forgiving always. It's a small thing to anybody else, but for me I was so stupid not thinking of the work she was doing, always working hard, that's why she never had any time for things for herself. Being the youngest I guess I was spoiled, and my sister was in Australia by then.

My mother had rheumatism when she was in her fifties, and it gradually got worse and became arthritis. My father was very good to her in these later years. He was idle for so many years after the Second World War. He always said, 'I am doing this for your mother now; I wish I had realized what women did, what they went through. I realize now housework is a continuing thing and it is something that you don't realize when you are a man, the continual work.' He said, 'I am always so glad I can do so much for your mother now.' And my father did everything for her. When I married he did all the washing and cooking himself, and he did look after my mother; they were happy together.

My mother's legs began to stiffen, the knees were blocked, and he used to take her out in the summertime in a wheel-chair. She couldn't go out in the winter, but in the summer he took her out in a chair, and the first time she went out in the chair she felt it was terrible that she had wasted a year and a half staying in. She was finally so dying to get out, she said, 'All right James, I'll go out in the chair, but I hate people seeing me.' And he said, 'I'll take you over to the bowling green and you can see all your old friends and talk to them.' And a crowd of women began to come around my mother. My mother was a great talker too, you know, and never forgot to tell the women about the political events of the time. A sweet gentle character!

Work

'Where do the capitalists get their money from?'

I was looking for a job – when I was leaving school – I wouldn't go back to the third year of my secondary education, I said no. My father was on the Bureau (Employment Bureau, or Labour Exchange – in Glasgow folk pronounced it 'broo') and my brother was still serving his time and I thought it was time I was off to do something, so I was looking for any kind of job to start me off, and I saw this one that said, 'General good writer, personable appearance, required for shop – Partick district.' There was a shop in Partick, there where I stayed, and it was an old-fashioned shop run by this old fellow and his daughter, I think, and his wife. It was a big double shop and he sold all sorts of cloth and blouses and dresses and things like that – in a very old-fashioned sort of way. And I thought – well it won't be too expensive to travel there, to walk to that – so I wrote in my best handwriting a nice application. I got word back right away to come down and see the gentleman. I went down to see him and he told me all the duties, he asked me to add up a column of figures – I was never very good at that, but I managed to do it correctly – then he looked at me – I was clean and tidy and so on, and I seemed suitable – and he was pleased with me and he said, 'Well, you're a nice writer and I like your appearance and I think we'll just take you, Annie, we'll just start you. Can you come on Monday morning?' 'Yes sir,' I said, 'but what are the wages?' He said, 'Oh well you start with seven shillings a week . . .' and I said, 'Seven shillings a week?' and he said, 'Yes, you see you're just beginning, you'll probably get eight shillings next year.' I said, 'My father is unemployed and I am only leaving school to help him; I am afraid I couldn't come for seven shillings or even eight shillings a week – that's far too little to pay anybody.' And the man looked at me in amazement and he said, 'Oh well, that's it; take it or leave it!' I said, 'Well I am sorry, sir, but I'll have to leave it. I'll have to get a better-paid job than that.'

I walked out, and it was just after my father had told somebody in the ILP about Annie saying this to the employer and this man knew the old fellow, you see. 'Oh,' he said, 'he's an old miser that one anyway.' One of the members of the Branch was there; he had been a printer and reporter, who became Lord Provost of Glasgow later on. He was given the job of being the Manager of the ILP Press and to run the paper. Of course he wrote many of the articles for it. He asked Dad, 'Is that your daughter you're talking about?' and he said, 'Yes, you know she's leaving school and we wanted her to stay on, but she says she would need to stay on too long to get a sort of decent job and she wants to leave now.' He says, 'You know, I could do with a girl starting in the Pilot Press,' and that's how I started there. I was there for four years, working for the Partick ILP's little weekly paper. I was taken on there as a printer to learn the printing trade, to be a letterpress feeder. I had to leave there when they stopped running the paper – they couldn't afford to keep me any longer. At that time I was getting good wages, I was getting thirty-two shillings a week as a journeywoman (four years' apprenticeship).

The printing trade has always been well-paid, they've always been well-organized in their union. Them and the journalists have been very well-paid people compared to the average working-class person. I got twelve shillings a week to start off with, the trade-union wage, because the Pilot Press paid trade-union wages although it was such a small business. When I went to get a job as a printer I wasn't quick enough at the machines – I was working with old-fashioned machinery before – it was all modern and in the four years I had been doing this all the modernizing had taken place and every place I went to they said, 'Oh you're too slow.' I was spoiling more pages than I printed.

I didn't know what to do, and I was really desperate by this time because my father was then on the means test, you know, things were worse than ever. I saw an advert: 'Girls wanted for office or bakery work in James Craig's' – in Glasgow – big bakery. I went there and saw the boss – he was a big bull of a man – there was a long queue of us, about thirty or forty standing outside waiting on a job – and so it came my turn and he said, 'What is it that you want to do?' I said, 'Well, I'll take any kind of job – I think I would like office work.' And he said – and this was my failure in life – he said, 'Well what's 5 per cent?' I said, '5 per cent of what?' He said, 'Of a pound.' And I floundered – 'It's either a shilling or sixpence.' You see, I was just no use at maths or – I was thinking, 'It's either a shilling or sixpence.' He saw I was not quick at figures. So he said, 'I think we'll put you in the despatch department.' [Laughs.] So I never got into the holy of holies, into the office, and I'd have been good at office work, I know I would have been, but anyway. Evidently you put out the bakery accounts – it was 5 per cent off that people got for something or other, I don't know what, but you had to know your 5 per cents right away. It's the way he shouted at me, I was so frightened.

Do you know what? From the thirty-two shillings a week as a printer I was taken on in Craig's in the despatch department for twenty shillings a week, and after a year I got twenty-two and six – and my second year I wanted a rise, and was told, 'Oh, we're not giving any more a rise.' And I said, 'Well there's girls here . . .' Because I was the one socialist in James Craig's – I discovered I was in a non-union place. He was the man who helped to break the dockers' strike in January 1920. He got the university students who were doing the black-legging there, and he got his bakers to stay in all night in his baking factory and they baked for and got special vans to run down to the docks and feed the strike-breakers. These lads were kept down at the docks and they didn't come out of the docks while the strike lasted, and the dockers were defeated. So James Craig gave his men and those who worked for him a big rise of wages, he gave them more than the trade-union wage, but he was a 'fly boy'. Everybody else he took on after that were *under* the trade-union wage, and by the time I came this was an old story about these men. The only well-paid people were these old-timers who had been there from the beginning, and had been guaranteed a job for helping the strike-breaking. I know I heard this from an old chap in the place who was a Labour man, and he was able to tell me about it. And he says, 'I came on after that and I am getting a lesser wage than these people here;' and he says, 'I had to come in here when I couldn't get a job elsewhere, I am too old to pick and choose.'

They didn't know for a wee while I was a socialist, it took a few months before that became known – the other girls really thought this was terrible, they had a Communist among them, you know! I was there during the time of the first Labour Government when MacDonald came in, and you should have heard them the next morning: 'What do you think, Labour's in! That's the end of things – the system will be finished!' And I'd say, 'Why should it be finished? We're still working; it's the workers who produce the wealth of the country and so why should we be finished?' 'Oh Annie, it's the capitalists that have got the money – they've got the money and where will we be if we haven't got the money?' And I said, 'And where do the capitalists get their money from? They get it from our labour!' 'How do they do that?' Oh, and I had to start away – they were like five-year-olds, you know, they knew nothing – and of course I had to argue the case all round. I nearly lost my job in arguing because of that.

I started at seven o'clock in the morning and I finished at six p.m. at night. At ten o'clock we got half an hour off for breakfast because we were in at seven a.m., at one o'clock we had an hour, and then we finished at six p.m. at night. On a Saturday we started at six a.m. because Saturday was a busy day and the goods had to be in the shops early. So it was six a.m. till five p.m. on Saturdays. I had Tuesday off for my half-day and for these hours I got a pound a week for a year and then twenty-two and sixpence.

Finally I was really getting a bit cheeky. After the second year when I didn't get the twenty-five shillings, the forewoman said, 'Oh I can't ask the boss for another rise for you just now, Annie.' And I said, 'Well, you can just tell the boss that my father is unemployed and he would like to be able to work but he can't get a job, and there's millions of people without jobs,' I said, and, 'Why should I be working for twenty-two and six a week, I am doing more than her across the road there. But she's been ten years here and she's got the big pay at the time you broke the strike.' I told the forewoman this. I said, 'I am working for twenty-two and six and I have two years' full time; you don't need experience to do the hard work that's here.' There was a printed list of over two hundred different cakes and bread and biscuits and each branch shop marked down their order for the day. I was doing packing for a smaller type of shop at first, then on to a larger one, and the girls who were packing for the big shops like Sauchiehall Street, they got special treatment. We others had to fight with them for our share of the baking. It was hard work and badly organized. The forewoman said, 'Well I'll tell you what I'll do. I'll speak to Mr Craig and see what can be done; I'll tell him that your father is unemployed and you're the only one working.' Anyway she called me over one day; she tapped the window – she could see everybody in the place, she knew what they were all doing, she tapped the window and we would all look up – and then beckoned to me. I went over. So she put an order book in front of her mouth and she said, 'Just nod your head now and again and I'll point to this book as if I was telling you something else. I don't want anyone else to know what I am talking about, because Mr Craig is giving you a half crown a week more; you are getting twenty-five shillings a week now, and that will start from next week.' She said, 'You can be very pleased that I put a word in for you.' I said, 'Oh, thank you very much; I know you've done your best for me, Miss Dempster, but I thought I was due for a rise, it is overdue.' Anyway she says, 'Nobody else is going to get a rise and if a girl comes to me and asks for one I'll know that you have told her that you got that.' So I had to keep quiet.

I got to the stage then, I was fed up. So the next week I was telling this story in the Clarion Players, and the antique dealer who managed our drama group had started on the philatelic side – stamps and coins – and sold antiquarian books and coloured prints, heard me talking about the horrible wages that I was getting in Craig's. He says, 'I need a girl for my shop, could you come to me?' I said, 'And what's your wages?' He said, 'I'll give you what you're getting there,' and he says, 'And I'll give you a rise as soon as I can afford it, but there's a lot to learn in our shop.' I said, 'Well, it sounds very interesting.' So I went there and I was there for five and a half years until I was married.

I stopped full-time work when I married and only went a half-day to the shop. While Charlie was unemployed I decided I wanted to learn hairdressing. If Charlie couldn't get back to his own trade he would have a bookshop and I would have – next door if we could get it – a hairdressing shop, that was what we planned, and I paid twenty pounds at one of the schools of hairdressing, and I went there every night but one during the week. I went there four nights a week and I did my whole half-day at the shop. Then I spent my afternoons learning hairdressing, hair-cutting, Marcel waving. I didn't go in for any of the beauty things because I can't be bothered with all the beauty stuff about your hands and face and things, but I liked the hairdressing.

I heard there was a Eugene Waving Machine up at the Crown Hall Saleroom. Of course they were a terrific price in those days and, do you know, nobody wanted it. It was a very old one, it had funny old-fashioned legs, but there were good curlers on it and we got it for thirty-four shillings. I put it in my flat and I worked in the flat doing perms, which at that time took about four hours at least to do a whole head of hair. It had to be cut and washed, and it could be much longer according to the type of hair it was. For that I earned from five to seven shillings, and used electricity and gave a cup of tea. We did water-waving, finger-waving. The Marcel waving with the irons was all corrugated, but the finger-waving was what I was taught to do – you know, you wet the hair thoroughly and set and dry it. Nowadays they curl it up with the softer wave which is more natural; anyway, it was 'the style' then.

Courting and Marriage

'*Our people trusted us.*'

I was always considered a bit prudish among the Clarion Players drama group. Those I got I could immediately sense were playboys – well, I had no time for them, and I think also because I was also rather a plain person myself. Not a sexy type of person. I was more inclined to be intellectual than sexy. I'd like somebody – the look of them – but I didn't go all gaga, the way some of the girls did. It wasn't a way of life to me, that 'Oh, when will I meet the next one?' – you know. With my socialist upbringing – it was almost like a sort of Methodist upbringing – it was a tightness, you know? And I think it had that effect, but I am really glad now that this happened. I am quite pleased about it, and yet I consider myself a very broad-minded person; I am broad-minded even for nowadays. Except that I don't think being broad-minded means leaving people to do what they like whether it affects other people or not, I think a certain morality must go in with the building-up of your character when you are young in order to keep you on the right rails, and by the right rails I mean not doing things that hurt other people, thinking of others as well as yourself, learning as quickly as you can how to judge people, find out pretty quickly if they are trustworthy – I mean that's it.

Oh, there was a wee boy I was very keen on when I was young and I was really . . . I was terribly hurt because he liked a girl who was a little . . . horrible wee sponger, and I didn't like her at all. She was so pleased with herself because he was all for her, and of course I made a bit of a fool of myself, making eyes at him and that, and everybody knew I was keen on him. I'd be about twelve or thirteen. I remember he was a nice lad, I liked him, he was in the Socialist Sunday-school – he was about the only one in the Sunday-school that I really fell for in a big way in my younger days. Later on there was a girl I went chums with – a girl with one leg that I got pally with in school because she didn't have many friends. Although I was a socialist and she was a keen church-goer, there weren't many church people who did much for her and she thought a lot of me and we got on great together. Well, her cousin was very keen to take me out and I wouldn't. I liked him, he was a good-looking boy and that, but he wasn't a socialist so I knew we would not be suitable for each other. The other socialist lads, I don't know why I never seemed to . . . I felt I just was a big long skinny drink, and that was it. I was very tall and thin. I had to depend on my personality rather than my looks throughout my life, I have always had to do that. I suppose that . . . everybody has to use whatever they've got at hand and make the best of it.

.   .   .

Charlie was my first and only real big emotional experience. Anyway he was the first one that I really fell for in a heap. He looked thin and was a poorly dressed lad, but exciting personality. He always wore tartan shirts because 'they didn't show the dirt', as he said. You didn't need to iron them, you just washed them and smoothed them out with your thumb while they were wet and then you wore them. He had no mother at home to keep him – had to do his best by himself.

We met at the Esperanto Society in Glasgow – Workers' Esperanto – there was a non-political Esperanto society but this was the Workers' Esperanto. His brother was the first person I met, and his wife, then Charlie came along to the meetings. He had learned the language so quickly, he was good at teaching it, and I went to a beginners' class which was held in College House off the Great Western Road – it had been the College Socialist Sunday-school premises – and Charlie was the tutor. We got chummy that way, me asking him questions, and we would walk down the road together and that was it, you know. Then we went rambles with the Esperanto Society and we started a camping club out at Carbeth about ten miles from the city. There were two tents along with others in the field, a girls' tent and a boys' tent, and we slept there the Saturday nights and we would go on rambles and all that sort of thing, and most of the time we tried to talk in Esperanto and we also learned to write to people in other countries and so on. Our people trusted us, but to the neighbours it was the talk of the 'steamies',* as they say.

When Charlie started going with me, he'd come to the house and we'd go out with our packs on our backs, a big pair of boots, and a pair of socks over that, and long stockings folded down here like golfing hose, you know? We had riding breeches, that was the style then, at first; later on we went in shorts – long shorts to your knees, sort of thing – and we thought we were really something, very daring at that period. But it was the riding breeches before that, with the long stockings pulled up, turned over, and then a little pair of socks round the ankles to keep stones from going in your boots, you see, as you are walking along. We would go away to Carbeth to the

*Council wash-houses, noted for gossip.

Esperanto Camp, you know, for the weekend, and later on we went
to the youth hostels, but as we went along to the end of the street
all the kids followed us shouting, 'Aw, the funny hikers! Aw, the
funny hikers!' And, you know, we were all embarrassed but we
laughed and soon didn't care. Another thing we found very amusing
when we went hiking with the Esperanto Club, we all had a green
badge shaped like a star with S A T on it, which was the International
Workers' Esperanto Association, as we went along the roads we
would pass people and say, 'Here's people coming and they'll wonder
who we are wearing this star.' So as they came nearer we talked in
Esperanto and not a soul could understand what language it was and
we had a real laugh; we overheard some odd guesses after they went
past.

So that was the fun and interest we got out of the Esperanto
Society, but we really worked hard during that period, to find a
common link between people. I was so terribly keen. We felt that an
international language – and I still feel it – would do an awful lot in
the world to help people's understanding. It was very popular to
decry that; you get people who had been well educated at university
and they'd say, 'Oh but the English language is the best international
language you can have, it's talked all over the world.' And so on like
that, and, 'Esperanto is a very cumbersome language.' In fact Esperanto has a lovely-sounding tone about it and you build your own
words as you go along; there's a way of building the words by
putting bits on to it to get the meaning of what you are saying. And
so it was a very interesting language, and what I always feel about it is
it could be commercially and socially useful. It doesn't have to be that
everybody speaks the international language all the time. What I
mean is that you don't speak it in your everyday life. Everybody
could have their own national language but they could learn an
international language as a secondary one, so that they could converse
anywhere.

When we met, Charlie was still an apprentice. He became unemployed
the very week he became a journeyman, he was given his cards along
with his first journeyman's pay. He was in a very unusual little trade –

he was a brush-maker. The boss said, 'You know, Charlie, we would like to keep you on because you are a good worker, but you are the only unmarried man on the floor.' He was not really making brushes, he was a bristle-mixer – he blended hair so that you could put some good-quality amongst some poorer-quality and make it better for brushing certain things than others. That was his trade; every kind of brush – any kind of brush under the sun – he could do the mixing for all types of brushes. Of course machinery has done away with a lot of the trade nowadays. As I say, he got the sack because he was the only unmarried man. All the other men had families. They had to keep them on. So that was him on the scrap-heap right away.

When he left school his father changed his birth certificate to get him into a trade at fourteen and a half instead of sixteen, otherwise he was going to be running from cheap job to cheap job and his father had no other way of seeing him in a steady trade. So he got him into this by changing his certificate, you see. He was warned not to tell anybody by his dad. I said, 'Well surely you could have told me after we had gone together for seven years.' Just before we were married he told me. It was nearly a break-up that, I was mortified – not because he was a year younger than me, but because he could go for all that time keeping a secret like that and not saying anything to me. I said, 'How can I trust you, if you can keep that to yourself all these years? How could I trust you – or believe anything you say is true?' and so on. That was a difficult time.

I did hairdressing in the house for two or three years before I was married, and it helped just to build up a clientele and a little money to save towards getting married, because we didn't have much, my father being unemployed. Also Charlie was unemployed for years until he managed to get a small job doing part-time work. He finally said, 'Look, we're not waiting any longer to get married, we've waited far too long.' But of course we were of the old school, and we didn't believe in living together. We felt that it would hurt our parents and hurt their attitudes with their friends, and so we always decided that we would just wait until we could be married. He said, 'Well we're not saving up anything, we're just going to get married now if we've got an income at all.' We would just have to manage, and we were very lucky in being able to get a room with kitchen and a bathroom up in Overnewton, the district of Glasgow where the children's hospital is, now named Queen Mother's Hospital. It was a nice little house. The rent was twelve shillings a week, and Charlie's wage was forty-four shillings a week.

A few months later, in 1936, when we had saved three months' rent in advance, we got married. Charlie was very lucky. A man that used to work with him got the foreman's job in a small brush factory and Charlie had gone up to see if he needed any help, and he said, 'Well look, this hair department is in an awful mess, I could give you a fortnight's work.' Charlie said, 'Well, it's always a fortnight, I'll be glad of it.' And when the fortnight was up this foreman was so pleased with Charlie's work he suggested to the boss that he could maybe keep him on part-time until things got better; and so he was kept on part-time, for which he got about thirty-six shillings; but when he got married he was getting forty-four shillings.

I went to the doctor after I was married, saying that I was coming on – coming up to thirty – I was twenty-eight when I was married, we met when I was twenty and he was nineteen – and so I went to the doctor a year later and I said we had wanted to wait until we thought we could manage to start a family, but we thought we could manage now and we'd like to start a family, but nothing had happened in the last six months since we had been trying. He examined me and he said, 'Your womb is out of position; it's too far forward and you probably would lose a child if you were pregnant.' So he said, 'Come to me immediately after your next period, write me a postcard saying "my period is finished today", and I'll get you into the Western Infirmary.' He had a bed there he was allowed to do a specialist in that line, and he said he would do something about it. Well, as it happened, whether it was something to do with relaxing or what, but I never had that other period. The unfortunate thing was that after I had passed three months quite safely and he thought I would be all right, then just on the fourth month I – you know, I started to – I miscarried. And he said, 'Now take six months of a rest before you think of starting again.' So we were all that time wasted, you know,

a year and then six months and then four months' pregnancy and
then six months of a rest, so Ian wasn't born until we were three
years married and I was then thirty-one years old. I never worked
part-time again outside.

The War

During the War the children were young; Charlie had stomach
ulcers and he was C3 category so he wasn't called up. We lived in
that house in Overnewton. In 1940 a bomb fell down the funnel of
the *Sussex*, a cruiser, and it was full of ammunition right in the docks.
Our flat was above the docks, so if it had blown up we could have
come off badly. They cleared all the people out from the docks right
up to where we were, and we went out at four a.m. that morning.
The first thing we did was to go right through the West End Park to
our comrade Annie Gordon's* house; she had a good-sized flat, and
we knew she had spare room. Ian was a baby, ten months old, and
Charlie and I took the pram and walked right through the park, and
she put us up for that night and the next night. And then our friend
who had a hut out at Carbeth, ten miles from town, and we went out
there and stayed for the next six months. Ian learned to walk in the
snow out there. And in this hut of course there was no water, just –
you had to go up the road to a spring, and carry your water up and
down over the field. There was of course no lighting except oil
lamps.

After six months there we heard about a house that was going to be
let near by, and we went up to the man that owned the place and asked
if we could have it. He said, 'Do you think you can afford it? Because
I let it as a furnished accommodation, because I have one or two things
in it, although it's not fully furnished,' he said, 'but it's because I
might want the house, and I could only give you a three months' let,

---

*Annie Gordon was a Glaswegian anarchist and feminist, rather older than
Annie Davison – she could remember the suffragette campaign. Her father
used to book rooms for Maclean's meetings.

from quarter to quarter.' We said, 'We'll take it.' It was during the war and we were glad to take anything, we didn't want to go back to the city. We still kept on our own house in Glasgow, you know, although we went out to this hut, because our own house wasn't blown up, they managed to get the ship clear. The whole area was evacuated for several days. Charlie wouldn't let us go back because he said with a baby we're not going to take a chance like that. We stayed out there for five years until the end of the war.

Well, what happened was that a cousin of mine got married and had no place to stay, so I let her have the house; we didn't tell the factor and later on she went away some place else. By this time Charlie's brother had been staying down in Kent and he came up to get away from the V bombs, you know, the worst ones. He came up because their nerves were all to bits and we gave them the house and he stayed in it from then on – it was the same name – and he stayed in it right till just recently. So I was five years out in the country in the rented house. It had four rooms, but my mother died just about that time, and we took in my father and Charlie's uncle, and we had Ian as a baby, Charlie with duodenal ulcers; but I had my usual good health, fortunately.

Painting and Acting

'I felt lost.'

When I came back to Glasgow after the War I taught elocution classes for children, Co-operative children. I had a class at George's Cross and one in Partick for some years. I gave it up at the time when my father was getting very old. He stayed with us until he died at ninety. My father was with us for seventeen years of our married life, and he took ill with heart trouble, and after three months he died, so that year when he wasn't well I gave up the elocution. Then my boys were getting to the stage when they were going to university and so on, and they were busy and I felt a bit lost, because Ian got married and Alan was still there, but four years later he married also. I felt lost.

I said to Charlie, 'You know, I don't know what to do, I feel I have lost all my creative abilities.' So I went to Edinburgh in a nature-cure place there that we know. I had a holiday there by myself, just a rest, because I had a few worries at that time. I said, 'I am going to start painting.' So I went down to a shop there and I said, 'Give me a book and a box of paints, not too expensive, please, but just a variety of colours and a couple of wee boards.' The whole thing cost me about thirty-five shillings or so. I went back to where I was staying and of course it was an open-air place, with plenty of trees to look at, and flowers. I picked a few flowers out of the garden, put them down on the table and started to try and paint the flowers in colour. I didn't bother drawing with a pencil or anything because I can't draw, and ended up by doing my first 'masterpiece'. So from there on I just enjoyed it, I became engrossed.

At one time I was the Chairman of the Scotstoun Women's Guild, and I found that many of the younger women wanted something sort of exciting to do. Something more interesting than just the meeting – and they weren't very good even at talking at the meetings. It was only one or two people that did the talking all the time, and as I had done a bit of elocution training with children I said, 'Would anybody like to do a little play? I could get a one-act play and some of you ladies could come forward and learn the parts; we could have a day – a special afternoon we practise – and then we could put a show on for the Guild.' Well, at first they said, 'Oh no, I couldn't do that – I never did anything like that in my life.' I said, 'Well look, we could maybe take a couple of plays, read them, and everybody just hand the book round – you do the next speech, you do the next one – and try and do it in the kind of voice that you think that character would do it in.' And after we had done that a couple of times they felt so enthusiastic about it that they said, 'Could you be the producer and teach us, and let's start this?'

I ran that for three years at the Guild, but I told them at the beginning, I said, 'Now the bad thing about starting a club like this – and it happens in every club, not just here but every place all over the world – in a little while you become discontented, because if you have a little success and people say, "Oh, you did well in that part", your head begins to swell. You begin to think that you are special and that you are quite a Sarah Bernhardt or something like that. So in a little while if you start not enjoying it, and if I start not to enjoy producing the plays, I am going to say, "That's it, girls, get somebody else, I am finished."' And that is why it lasted; it lasted three years, but at the end I was just getting too much else to do and I was beginning to get a bit tired. But if these women had somebody like that helping them, it's wonderful what they could do, and they were able to do – speak up in the Guild after that very much better, and we did some very interesting little Scottish plays, one-act plays, and we got a lot of humour out of it – we dressed up, we had all the fun of setting the stage and everybody – 'I'll bring in a cushion' and 'I've got a wee chair' and 'I've got something else' – and everybody would come the day of the show and we would bring friends and family along to hear it and they really enjoyed it.

Politics

'We always have kept interested in every side of the Movement.'

We were always in the political scene – Clarion Scouts, the Labour Co-operatives. But during the war I was too busy with the family, I had too many people to look after. I had two old people and two boys, Charlie and myself. After the war, back in Glasgow again, we went into the Co-operative Movement and joined the Labour Party, and of course Charlie was very keen in his trade union. His union is ASTMS, and he is now the Chairman of the Scottish District of his union. I was always in the ILP, I was in that from my early days; it faded away; we decided: 'Well, what do we do? It's the Labour Party or the Communist Party. No, we don't want the Communist Party, we'll join the Labour Party; we'll get to the left-wing side of it and push that on a bit.' We felt that the 'upper echelons', as they say of the Labour groups or the Labour Party, mostly now they have all changed from the working-class ideal they had before. They are nearly all well-educated middle- or upper-class people or working class who have been educated now. I think they tend – unless the rank and file remind them enough – they tend to forget that we're looking for a socialist state, not just a capitalist state run in a sort of social democrat way: this we don't want.

We always have kept interested in every side of the Movement. I'm a member of the Labour Party only because I couldn't accept the Communist point of view. I couldn't accept it because I felt I didn't want dictatorship – I didn't want someone to tell me what I must do and think. Why must I do it? I wanted it to be talked out amongst all of the members, not just amongst a small conclave who decided what you were to do, and that was the reason I didn't join. My early Sunday-school precept comes to mind: 'Observe and think in order to discover the truth. Do not believe what is contrary to reason – and never deceive yourself or others!' As a matter of fact, my eldest son has gone through all this Labour Party thing and probed all the rest of the various parties and he has now joined the Communist Party. I have conformed because my way of life has been conforming, and I am married and I have had a family and a happy marriage, but always with the ideals in the back of my mind that I wanted my children brought up to think for themselves.

People that I met like Annie Gordon and some of the women in the Socialist Sunday-school were rather inclined to be in favour of women. In fact we believe in equality for everybody, never mind just women – equality for coloureds, and equality of every kind. I myself have certain reservations about Women's Lib. in the way that it has been presented to us with the media. I feel that it hasn't always been good propaganda, and I think the media are to blame that they take the side of it which will appeal to sensation-hungry people – they try to make of it silly things like burning bras and stuff like that. That is a symbol to me, it was used and taken up and has created a certain attitude with older women.

I do think also that women who are housewives like myself, they have a sort of 'can't be bothered' attitude to it. We applaud women in industry who are working for equality. I think women have quite a lot in their daily life that is tiring. I think also that changes in the law on women's rights are long overdue; and on top of that there is the demands of a husband which in some cases are quite strong, and women can't always cope with all the physical work of the house and tiring things of looking after children and the demands of a husband as well, and they just want to be quiet and don't bother with it. I suppose women who have a good marriage become thoughtless of others less fortunate. I think there is a lot of that. I am talking generally, I am not really saying that everybody is like that.

There are many women who nowadays may want the freedoms the men are having, and good luck to them. But I sort of feel that they must remember a woman is the bearer of the children and she must look after these children to her best ability while they need her, while her husband is working for their common good. I think quite a number of women have opted out of that. They are looking for places and other folks to do the job that they should be doing. I feel many wives go to work to supplement the family income, but it is not always spent wisely from some I have noted. Unless we look for long-term results, short-term results won't work. Now the long-term attitude is to my mind the ideal attitude. At the same time, if women don't work in their organizations to change the system, this business of getting equality, that alone won't do the trick – that alone won't bring what we want in the long term.

4.   Catherina Barnes

Catherina Barnes was born in Rotterdam, Holland, in 1917. She had
three brothers and two sisters. Her mother helped her father in tailoring
until the Depression forced him to take up labouring jobs. Catherina
Barnes worked in a stationers' shop, then in a Co-operative Society
office. At twenty she started training to become a missionary, but
settled for social work in a children's home. She was twenty-three when
the war broke out and Holland was invaded by the Nazis. She worked
in an old people's home during the War.

In 1944 she met Jim Barnes, then a sergeant in the Black Watch,
during the liberation of Holland. They were married in 1946 and went
to live in his home town of Carlisle. She has three grown-up children
and now works as a nurse in a mental hospital.

Childhood
'People build a shell around the kids . . .'

I was a typical big-town kid. I was brought up in Rotterdam, that's
a docker's town and very much a metropole. I was still very protected because my father and mother were very religious in a kind of
Salvation Army kind of Methodist way. Their religion was a very
practical religion but also a very alive religion. So in a way she
brought us all up to be like in the world but not from the world, so I
did accept to be prim and proper really, and now I often think back,
I was a bit of a prude.

I was one of six at home and there was eight years between the
oldest and the youngest and I was the middle one. I was always
average middle one. I didn't get the privilege from the oldest or the

privilege from the youngest and so we did grow up like that. In a big town religion really did protect you from a heck of a lot, if it is protection. Maybe it was making you blind for a heck of a lot of things, what other young people did.

My father was a tailor, a good tailor, but in the Depression nobody could afford to have private-made clothes, you see, and then he did start a lot of things to do. He was a tailor and he did like to play the violin and then he did get a job as a demolition worker, and that did play havoc with his hands, because it was so opposite to what he was used to, but he did do that for the family – snow-clearing and all them kind of jobs he did do. I can remember vaguely that when we were very small we were very well off, because he had his own tailor's business, and then the Depression came and he did take all kinds of jobs. I can remember that I was so very upset because his hands – he tried to play the violin and his hands were so torn because he was not used to it with demolition work and so. Then he got a job, because my mother was always very strong in the Co-operative Society, he got a job delivering milk – you know, the milk round. He had that for the rest of his life nearly except when the war was finished, and he got a job back at tailoring when he was in his fifties. He died when he was seventy.

If you have got parents what are prepared to sacrifice and live for the family, really I think it is the caring that is the most important, no matter how poor. For although my mother had nowt and my father had nowt, when I look back, we were very close. The bit of pocket-money we had on a Saturday we would all give threepence and buy some flowers for my mother. We did spend our pocket-money on her, and she did spend nearly all on her kids, and that was the way we did live. We were very very close and living for each other, we did thrive on each other's talents and things like that – that was the light that was shining back on us. And I was more aware of it when I met my husband, and I got closer contact with him, because he was from a broken-up home, but his father and mother could have been well off. You can be brought up in a town like Rotterdam and in a district, a working-class district, and very near it there is Amsterdam with the red lights and things like that, and you know nothing about it. You can grow up and know nothing about what goes on there, because you are living in your . . . you've built a shell. People build a shell around the kids, and that's possible you know.

I can remember at fourteen, I was nearly fourteen, my mother took us to a careers office. You know, my mother was ambitious enough for us to take us up there, but the background, at fourteen you was aware of it even if you did not say it. All I really wanted to be was a nursery-school teacher and when I was sitting there the first thing the woman careers officer said, 'Well of course she won't make any money before she is twenty.' She spoke to my mother, over my head – of course, at that time children were not asked, you did not come into it yourself. You see, your parents had to keep you till you was twenty. 'Oh,' my mother said, 'well, do you know any other jobs?' And she did mention a few, all of them kind of jobs that were all for rich girls whose parents could keep them. She did not put it so bluntly as that, but the woman did know, she showed the people, of course, that did come, and she did make clear from the start before she wasted any more of their time the things that were open for people who could afford to keep their children. So I was sitting there and I saw right away that that was out for us, so my mother said, 'Well, what do you want then?' And I of course said 'Well . . .' and then she mentioned a few things; there was one job open as a shopgirl, and at that time a shopgirl was a somebody – it all depends in what kind of shop it was. So I worked in a shop, that was when I was fourteen to eighteen, and then I went to evening classes for three evenings in the week because I was aware that without education you didn't come anywhere, but academically I had never been very bright.

I followed a course to become a nursery-school teacher, you know, working at the same time. That means that very often in the evening you were doing your homework; you were from seven in the morning until ten at night, one evening in the week off and one weekend in six off, for ten bob in the week and your keep. But of course that was nothing outstanding because everybody lived like that. My father's wages was two pounds, fifteen shillings – that was a man's wages, approximately the same as in England. I had to work hard for any qualification that I did get, and at eighteen I got to the training college for a year, that was nine months really; when I did come out I worked. I had the intention to become a missionary, a Salvation Army officer in the colonies.

I sincerely did believe, like my mother – though maybe my father had a bit of a different idea – I did believe that because the Dutch Queen was a religious upstanding woman and the Dutch people were religious, we had not that colour prejudice like the Portuguese and the Belgians, and that we did go to India not only for our own profit but we did educate them and did bring religion to them poor niggers.

Because of that the Lord God would never allow Holland to become involved in the Second World War. We were all convinced that the Lord would look after Holland because we were so much better. We were not frivolous like the French, we were not bad like them Germans were and we were not daft like the English were.

The War

'The real live Englishman . . .'

Now when the War broke out in 1940 they bombed Rotterdam. You know we had built up our defence material, but all that they had to do was twenty minutes bombing Rotterdam and the whole city was bombed out. There was nothing that a country like Holland could do against a military power like that. I was working in a home for old people and every time the Germans had their eye on the building you was moved; we were six times moved in a year to another building. At that time we were in a big school in the south of Holland, and Holland was cut in two, the last half-year of the War.

I had never seen an Englishman yet, because we thought all the time, 'Oh well, the English will not leave us in the lurch' – we had signed so many pacts with England before the War and all that kind of thing – but we called them everything of course, because they did not. And there were jokes going on, like – Hitler had caught the English Prime Minister and he had said, 'You are going to be executed for your part in the War.' And he said, 'Which part I had in the War?'

And he said, 'Well, you fought the Germans,' and the English Prime Minister said, 'I fought the Germans, where?' And he said, 'Well, in Africa,' and Churchill said, 'In Africa, there were Russian armies, American armies, Canadian armies, but not English!' And Hitler said, 'Well, you fought the Germans in Scandinavia.' And he said, 'The Norwegians, the Danes and the Swedes, but you didn't find an Englishman.' You know, because we felt bitter about the English did not come to our rescue before, all them kind of jokes would go around.

We were aware that was not really true of course, but that's how you kept yourself going. You did listen to the broadcast – that was not allowed of course, but you still did listen – but you still did not realize how they were coming. We did not know that they were coming from Brittany up to Belgium and fighting there and in the Ardennes, etcetera, etcetera; but we did still not know and the last week we were there, there was a curfew all the time and there was not a window which was not broken with the shelling. For a week you could not come out and all that we had was one big pack of dry peas. We had three people that died and we could not even bury them, you know, they were in sheets, wrapped up in sheets somewhere there because of the fighting and that. All that we had was the dried peas and did serve them; you had to steep them and cook them and serve them for breakfast, for tea and for dinner. And then there was hell of a lot of shooting. We saw great big tanks through the narrow streets going, and there were wounded laying on the tanks; there was one German and he had his whole hip shot off and his arm it was laying bloody, laying there on the tank so it was really like a butcher's shop. But we still did not realize that the English were so near.

Then early one morning I looked out – they were still shelling all the time – and there was a very handsome lad standing there, and oh, he was very handsome – a little red moustache – and he was obviously in command, and that was an Englishman. And so I looked out and shouted, 'Oh, you are much too late!' – it was a little bit of English that I knew; and he said 'Why?' and then he did come in. They literally liberated us from the Germans. Well, he was literally the bloke – he was in command, standing giving you orders – he was literally the bloke that liberated us. That was in the October of 1944 and the War was finished in May 1945.

Anyway, the real live Englishman, that was the first one what I did see standing there, and he did come back in the evening, and we had Battery cocoa and one of them played the organ and it was a broken organ. The nurses were all there you know, we were with ten to twelve, and then they played the organ and there was one that had to lay on the floor because there was something wrong with the bellows, and he had to do that, lay flat on the floor and doing this, and so it was great fun.

But from the twelve lads who came in there then only he and two others came back. If you had been sitting drinking cocoa, and being the liberators and all that, and there comes three back. Even if you were used to the bombing and shelling and shooting, only then do you realize that them lads did give literally their life for it. You know, you did get much more aware. People in England don't – if you hadn't really seen it you don't know what a hell war is, literally bits of leg you find in fields and things like that. He did say that his grandmother – he was always on about his grandmother because he lived with her at that time, and he said that she – showed us letters from his grandmother, she had sent him socks and a scarf '– and be very sure that your feet keep dry and don't catch cold.' Well, if you saw Holland, it is marshland; well they did dig ditches to hide in, and so soon they had water in their feet and they were laying in it practically. English people had not a clue about how it really was, and I don't think that you can understand anybody coming out of that unscarred.

We got the most friendly with them three, and a girl out of the village went with one of them, Tex – he was a lot older than Jim. Jim was only nineteen at that time, he was one of the youngest sergeants in the British Army. He never went to school much because he had appendicitis and an appendicectomy and at that time there was not much of the antibiotics and for four years he was dying and better and dying and better; he had seven great big scars over his stomach. When he was fifteen he enlisted. Jim's mother and father – his father and mother had broken up. He found he was a strain on his grandmother because his grandmother had him and she was well in her sixties and a real country woman. He had not had any schooling really because he was so ill – he had read, he knew all Dickens by heart, and Chaucer and Shakespeare and things like that – but he couldn't do the table of five, practically. In the army they educated him a lot – he is very academical, very clever – but he was very bitter, because of the breaking-up. His father had promised, 'If you choose me in court I will send you to Wiston Grammar School.' But he never did, of course, he just left him.

On the last day of the war, fifth May, the day before the peace was settled, he got shot in his foot and they sent him back, and his friend did write me a letter right away and he was in Hospital 109. The addresses of hospitals was not allowed to be known, it was just by numbers. Well, by the time that I got all the records and by the time that I did find out that 109 was in Brussels, the day before Jim had just been sent to England by plane. He was still in the army, he was wounded. Well I did picture of course his leg shot off and, well, if his leg was shot off and he was an invalid he needed me more than anything, in my opinion. What happened, a bullet went through his foot and it was taken out and it had to heal maybe for six weeks really. But of course my picture was different, and I was then so determined, and that was the first time in May that I could go back to my parents because Holland had been cut off for half a year, in two by the Rhine, and I went back to my parents and told my mother all about it. My mother was making objections because of the difference in age, a great objection. But she did know that she could not object really by then – I was nearly twenty-five in August – and my father was all for helping us as much as possible.

I've later thought about that; if I had met that lad – in the first place I was a few years older than him, but that is a big drawback for a girl and his whole background was so different – if I had met him under ordinary circumstances he would never have looked at me and I would never have looked at him. I can remember my mother putting me off a lad once, when I was seventeen or eighteen, with just saying, well, he couldn't be any good because that whole family was dragged up, you know, his mother had left him when he was eight or nine, between them all the sisters and the father had looked after them. Well that was just . . . and my mother was very – maybe I am the same myself – typecasting them and dismissing them, and that was that. Maybe she did not mean it at all, but to me it had to – oh well, he couldn't be any good so that was that. Well, by then I was older and nothing would have put me off any boy, you know, but when you were in your teens . . . A word, like, on the right place, can do a lot of harm or good, you know; and with that I have always been so . . . I have been aware of it and scared for the power of my words to our kids. A parent's influence can be just so strong. Now no parent is able to say 'no' any more really, but in that time in Holland you just couldn't marry without your parents' permission when you were under thirty, without going to court.

Well, the Dutch Government were very reluctant to let girls go out of the country and marry because of – well it was a protection for their own citizens, their own people. I had to have at least twelve papers, from his officer, from his father, that he was not married, etcetera. Anyway, he was an instructor then and he did write and ask us to come and make arrangements for us to get married in the beginning of January, so I was determined to get to England.

I got all them papers except for one paper the clerk was not going to give us, and that was very difficult. I landed in The Hague and there was no transport, and I got a lift and I landed at the office at five o'clock and they were going to close it, so I made a carry-on. I got in and he said, 'Well, you can't get permission for getting married.' And I said, 'Don't you understand I have to get married.' When I was saying it I did not really realize what I was saying, but he took it right away and he stamped it and that was that.

Grandmother's House

'It was as if time had stood still for a hundred years.'

So I went over to London and Jim did come and fetch us from London. That was another thing I had not realized, that from Carlisle to London was such a very long way, and he had to travel up and down from London; it was a hell of a lot of expense and time. Then I did come in his grandmother's house and I had never seen anything like that in my life. There were villages in Holland of course, but I had never realized that there were villages in Britain. Time had been standing still for fifty years. But his grandmother, she was born Scots, and she had very beautiful skin, she had dark blue eyes and beautiful white hair and she always had a knitted cap on her head, and when she did come in she did look like a fairy godmother. Because in that house there was a great big black range and that was the only cooking facility, a cement floor, and there was some hooky mats – that was a mat made from old clothes, you know, hooked – and that was all. And a table, a varnished table, and on the table legs there were socks to protect the varnish from being kicked, and a big oil lamp on the table. There was no electricity, and the water was outside, and the lavatory was a half mile in the garden.

Jim always had only talked about his house in Cumberland and his dog and his grandmother, and his house and Cumberland was absolutely like a fairy story, it was like Disneyland because – well Holland is flat and I had been to Belgium and to the west side of Germany where there were hills etcetera etcetera, but I still had never seen anything like the Lake District. When I did come there everything was in frost; it hadn't snowed, but everything was white from the frost, the trees and so, and it looked very beautiful. And you know his mother lived in Watch Hill; it was on the hills of course and you did look to that valley. It really did look like a Walt Disney film. The little church was there, it was over two miles further, but you could see it. His grandfather was a carpenter and a wheelwright. And, well, in Rotterdam if you did get married you most likely got married with twenty couples on the Register, and in the church it was the same, you very seldom got married alone. His grandmother had saved the Christmas cake as a wedding cake.

That house, I have never seen a house that was so – I had seen very much poverty in Holland in town flats, you know, town poverty, but it was so very different as this kind. They did not think themselves poverty-stricken, but you know there was that kind of furniture, it was as if time had stood still for a hundred years. And she walked about and she cried when she saw me, and she said 'Jimmy's lassie', and I had learned a bit of English at school, but the Cumberland dialect was of course a very different language from the English language, you know. She was very pleased for us; the house was my house and her food was my food literally, you know. And she was very good to me; I was not allowed to clean up for her, because me not being able to speak proper English I wouldn't be able to cook – I wouldn't be good at doing the washing or the sewing machine either. Over your head she talked to the neighbours – 'She can sew, and she can . . .' – oh, she was very proud of me.

That was all that she had – good bedding and so, and a grand-father clock, very beautiful grandfather clock, and hooky mats on a cemented floor; and all the cooking could be done on that big range; she got up every morning at six o'clock and she did do that big black range, it had the brass shining. Every day she did do that, she was a good housewife. She had brought her own kids up, she brought Jimmy's Aunt Agnes up and she had brought Jim up most of the time, and never thought anything of it, and we would think very much about it. Jim's grandmother had never been out of the village for the last twenty years. She had married when she was nineteen from Motherwell and she had never been back there ever. You know, in that time the distances were that big, she had never gone back. Mind, she would have relations stopping with her, and she had had quite a lot of relations. His real mother – well she was a waitress in the Isle of Man for the summer season and things like that, and in the winter season she always stopped with grandmother, she did use that as her home. She was a very small, petite, quite good-looking woman, and first she had beautiful red hair, wavy red chestnut hair; by now it started to be white hair, but she was always quite – as a waitress she had standing, because she could do the job good.

Child-bearing and Housing Problems after the War

'I did begin to start feeling very bad about putting kids in the world.'

I married in January 1946, the first day of the new year. Now I got

pregnant in April, and Jim was very keen on a family and I was so
aware that my childhood was so much happier in a big family, but
when I was living in Cumbria I was – it was a village like that – I
said when I was pregnant, 'Oh, I could shout it from the roofs!' but
Jim's grandmother wouldn't even let me give the milkman the milk
tokens for expectant mothers because he had not to know. Oh she
was very annoyed about that – you did not let people know that you
were pregnant. Kate, the daughter, she was seven months pregnant
before her mother knew it. I had gone to the clinic; that was dirty,
you know – she was very Victorian. She didn't let the dirty milkman
know that you was pregnant, oh no, and you did not tell people – it
was just not done.

I was trying to find what you did do – so the first thing I did do was
to go to Carlisle, and I went there, and I did look round for the ante-
natal clinic and the post-natal clinic. When I did find out where it
was, I went for an examination, and they did say I was pregnant and
what I wanted. I said I wanted to think about it, and I went back and
I told mother. I said to mother, 'I have been to the clinic', but she
thought I was too forward in a way – that her daughter and the girls
in the village did just accept what their mothers did say and they would
take them to the doctor, and somebody would call for the doctor.
I said I was going to the clinic in Carlisle and mother – 'You know,
Catherine . . .' – and when she could not get at me, when she did
realize I did not listen, she had more stories and she said: 'Do you
know, Catherine, there was Susan Bell and she went to one of them
clinics and the doctor – Doctor Willie – had sent her to the clinic,
and do you know what happened? In two days she was dead.' You
know, and them kind of stories did come repeatedly to me – the thing
to do was not to go to the clinic; they did not see that the doctor had
only sent people to the clinic when there was really something wrong
with them. But they did not see the context of it, and I couldn't
make them understand that that was absolute baloney.

So by then I had got a few friends in Carlisle. I had made friends
with some kind people. Jim's father was friendly with a man that was
a coach-builder, he had his own business, and his wife got very
friendly with me. And then I was looking for rooms, I did get that

mad – oh, I had to get out of there; it was all right living there, but I was living off mother, you know, and that was not right of course. So I was determined to get out of there. Jim was still in the army. I had looked round, and I did realize that there was never any work for Jim when he did come out of the army, except as agricultural labourer, because everybody else was farm labourers there. One of Jim's uncles was a fireman, he was in the Fire Brigade, but I thought, well Jim was never in agricultural work; so I thought, well if I stick with her, he would come out and there is no job for him. So we did believe strongly that the army would give us a house and a job, but I was getting my doubts by then a bit. So I was very sure that I could not have my baby in mother's house. It was impossible there and the hygiene and so – I could not see that millions of babies had been born like that, and it went all right.

I got some rooms in Carlisle. There was a family – he was a printer and he had a house in the north of Scotland and he was there in the summer months, he was most nearly always there – so they let us have two rooms in their house. It was a council house. They did really do it because they did like somebody in the house when they were away for a few months, and his wife felt happier about that. So I got rooms in there and I started to live in Carlisle, and mother was very upset because she had like me to stop because of course to look after father. She had found that father was going to be a bit much for her, and because he got a few times another stroke and he had cancer in his neck and his throat, and he was getting an old man; but I was frightened to get a baby there that I did move and I did not see any future in it. Jim's aunt was living round the corner, you see, so there was not really any need for me to stop there, because of course she was not working. But Jim's aunt was a woman that for instance she could not change father's bed when he wet his bed, she could not bath him – but that was a problem that she had to do when I was not there, so it was better that I did move. There was not any hard feeling. It is better to go anyway, when you were sorry to break it up. Mother was always very fond of us still, and I of her. I thought she was just like a fairy godmother and I never could get over that anybody could be such a good woman, and so wise.

I did live a long time on the fifth floor. I still don't know how we did do it; it was a fifth-floor flat with eight of us. Them people were very nice, mind. But they did not like a man in the house, men in the house. There was a lassie that was fourteen, that was very friendly with me, and when the baby was born – you know how it is with lassies of fourteen, they don't play with dolls but they do take babies out. Oh, they were very good to me, before the baby was born, and when the baby was born, but we had to go through their sitting room to go to the kitchen – you know, the door was in the middle and that was my sitting room, and the bedroom was upstairs. There was no door through my room to the kitchen. I always could play that very well when I was alone, but when Jim was in it was always much more difficult, you know, much more imposing, and it is different if you have got a woman in the house that is friendly with the wife. But anyway then they did decide to pack up; the baby was born and Jim did come home and then they did decide to close that house and give it back to the Council. The Council wouldn't allow us to live in it, you know, there was such a housing shortage.

I was just pregnant with the other baby; so then we were looking out for another place and then we were a family you know – well, that was practically an impossibility. Then we did get in with a man. His wife had left him during the war, he was an ex-soldier; and that was a small house that was only a sitting room and two bedrooms, and he had a boy of twelve. I was going to be house-keeper and looking after him and looking after the boy. That was very crowded. He was a very demanding man, but, like I said, any man what had been through the war, you can't understand them coming out sane of it.

Jim worked as a cleaner, that was the first time he got a labourer's job. The other men had come back a year earlier so the whole market was flooded with people coming back from the war, and by then people was very sick of people what had been heroes, because the biggest heroes had been the ones that had stayed at home, and had looked after the women folk, and that kind of thing. You know, there was such a battle, and that was because there were not enough jobs, suddenly, for everybody, and not enough houses, and there was a heck of a lot of carry-on like that, and very bitter ex-servicemen. A lot went right away back, because they saw that there was nothing for them, and people who had been somebody like Jim – he was an instructor and a leader of men and suddenly – well, he found it very hard to take, although he had no academic qualifications whatever. And then he had quite a few jobs before he got on the railway as a cleaner. He always collected *The Times* and the *Guardian* newspapers and he would come home and read them all. Once he had seventeen jobs in one year. He was out of work very often. He is a very intelligent man, and he reads a lot, so people thought he was a bighead. He was not really, you know, but he could take anybody on, he could defend himself, with words, and that did very often not suit people.

We were having the second baby, and then of course things became all the time more difficult. We went into a house with a family with five children, and she was a widow and them children did thieve like blazes. You couldn't put the insurance money on the radio, it would disappear. And I had a little clock given by the nurses when I left, a nice little clock, and that walked out of the room, and it was standing on her mantelpiece quite blatantly. The pillow cases disappeared from the line and the next day they were on her bed, even that. Well, you had to put up with it because there was not a thing you could do about it. At that time he still wanted a family, but I did begin to start feeling very bad about putting kids in the world. We hadn't an outlook for a house; you know, we had our name down for a council house and we still did believe that ex-servicemen, they could get a house, but it did become airier and airier. I thought, oh it will go on and on and on, every time when we were near on the list, something else will happen and we will be put back – it will be taken off us.

Birth Control and a Council House

'I was pregnant again.'

Because we had two in a year, the doctor sent us to a birth-control clinic, but in that time that was whispered about still, you couldn't speak openly about that, so I did land up at that clinic and I was – when I mentioned birth-control clinic I was whisked away to another room, that was the post-natal clinic really. And there was a very beautiful young woman doctor, a very beautiful girl, and she was very haughty and she asked me a lot of intimate questions, and because she was so beautiful and so haughty I did get much more upset and flushed and I didn't know what she was on about really, and because of that, if it had been an older man I think it would have been easier, but with a woman that was so obviously out of my reach. Then she did explain a few things and give me the Dutch cap that she fitted in, and said over my head to the nurse what was assisting her, that was a rather sensible woman, 'She has not got a clue what it is all about.' But of course I heard that and I was very hurt and upset and angry about that, and I did not listen to her at all what she said any more, really.

Now I would definitely have made her do the job properly and explain to me properly. I think if she had not been so beautiful I don't think I would have been so . . . but I felt so poverty-stricken and slummy in comparison with that exquisite creature, that I slinked out of that place and of course we made a mistake. I don't think that the birth control fail us, I think we did fail that, because I was too stupid to understand what it was really all about. I just did go home, and we did practise birth control but it is – it was not a very efficient method in that way, that . . . well, if you ever feel like making love really, just on that moment; you very seldom go to bed with the intention for starting to make love, it most times come after, and then you have to say, 'Oh just a minute', and start to fiddle about with bottles and carry on like that. So that was that, and I suppose we did make the mistake.

I was pregnant again after two years and that was a very terrifying thing; in the first place because we did not have a house yet, and the kids, because the doctor was . . . A woman doctor what was in the baby clinic was very sympathetic to us, and she put the children in a day nursery because Jim went to sleep in the day when he was working at the railway and we were sitting in that one room. Tiny was one and Beatrice two – and then I found myself pregnant again and I knew I had just used the Dutch cap with this gelatine which was specially given for that, and there was 'poison' written on, it was poison, you know, on the tube, so I always had to hide it away from the children. But it did worry me very much because I thought – oh, I was pregnant and I had been using birth-control articles at the same time, and we had slipped up somewhere and I was very worried that it would have affected the baby, and the more I thought about it the more I was convinced that it would affect the baby.

Down at the pre-natal clinic was always so mechanized that you had always – you was first examined by a couple of students, and then by the doctor himself. But they had the report of the students and there were always students around. So I went when I was sure I was pregnant – I was sure, three months or so – I went to the doctor and he sent me to that clinic, and I was very anxious about would the baby be born affected by that. There was nobody that you could talk to about that, a woman worries about that. I had not my mother here – well maybe if I had a mother that you could talk with, that would be different – but it was not so; you could really go to nobody and talk about that and say, 'I have used birth-control articles, and I got still pregnant. I used them and after that I was pregnant because I did not know that I was, and the poison, will it affect the baby?' But of course I got pictures. I pictured a mentally or physically handicapped child because of that, and it was no picnic to go to the pre-natal clinic and sitting there waiting until it is your turn. It was such a drag every time, with the two children, to get them ready, and especially lifting and carrying them. So I got myself to it, until I was six months pregnant.

Then one morning I got my courage together and I said to the doctor what was examining us, 'Can I speak to you in private?' And he said, 'Yes, you can say anything to me – there are just my colleagues.' I insisted on speaking with him in *private*, I was not going to say anything in front of all those snotty-nosed students, and student nurses. So he sent them away, and he said, 'Well, mother, what is worrying you?' And the two toddlers were still standing beside me, you know, and it was never any joke to have them standing there when the doctors were examining you, and I did ask him, and I said, 'I am very worried if this baby is all right because I was using birth-control articles, I was using the Dutch cap and the gelatine that I was given in the birth-control clinic. I must have slipped up somewhere and I am very worried, because, this baby, I am sure it is affected by it, because there is 'poison' on the tube. And then he said that was not strictly true at all: there was 'poison' written on because that was the law, but this poison only would do away with a lot of germs that were streaming away anyway, and it would only affect them, it would never affect myself, and it would not affect the baby that was conceived anyway, so that was absolute nonsense, then. I could put that right out of my head. He was very very assuring and nice, and I was only sorry I had not asked him a long time before.

In 1950 the Council had promised me a house and I didn't believe that very much, I thought they would put us off again. Jim had to sleep through the day and I had to go out with the kids and some-times it was pouring down with rain and I did come in. I went to Marks and Spencer, in the café, and got them a pint of milk with a straw; that made it a treat for them, and it used to keep them quiet really.

One Sunday I was so very worried about it and so fed up that I really thought that it was not right that – I was so guilty about bringing kids into the world when I hadn't really a home to give them. And Jim, he was first of all at home, his grandmother was very good to him but he was still always really very neglected, and what could I give him for a home? Nothing. Now it's nappies, and now I was pregnant again and that was only because of my own fault, because not understanding and listening proper to the woman, that any sensible girl could have done. So I went to the river and I was standing there and I thought well it was much better not to go on with them kids because what could I give them? Nothing. There was a very bad atmosphere and that . . . atmosphere arose because of money, bad conditions, and I was not right. So I was standing on that bridge and I was trying to lift them both over at the same time and I couldn't possibly manage it because that bridge was so . . . the walls on the side were that high. So I thought, well, we find another method, and I just went back home and then Jim that evening he said he was very sorry if he had shouted to me, it was just because he was miserable that he had not been to better schooling, that he had not a better job – the cleaning on the railway he felt so bad about, because it wasn't very manly, and an odd job that anyone could do better than he did.

Well, we made it up very much together and we were some of the lucky people because in that month we did get a house, and it was looking like a palace. It was semi-detached, three-bedroomed house with a very big bathroom and a good-sized back kitchen – a front room where we had only one easy chair in, and a stone floor, but that did not matter – we had a house, and it did look like a palace, you know.

It was very beautiful and very classy in comparison with what we were used to because the Council had never built houses like that before; it was one of the bigger and better ones that they had ever built, and the drawbacks did only come out later. The walls were very thin – you could hear the neighbours changing their mind – and the shops were . . . the roads were not made yet so the shops were still a long way off. I had to walk a mile and a half – pregnant, with two children because I had nobody to leave them with, of course – to go for some bread. The only thing that was the beauty of it, I could shift them all in the pram; I had a big pram and could get everything in. It was on the outskirts from Carlisle, yes, in a new council estate. It was an isolated council estate, so it was hard to reach and there was nothing – they forgot to build the shops and they only built the pubs and the churches. We were surrounded by the Mission Hall, the Catholic Church, the Catholic Mission Hall and the Methodist Church, and the pubs were there, but that was all. At first there was no community life – the schools were not built either – but it did become later quite a strong community because of the isolation.

When we got it, the house was absolutely a palace, and then a few months later our boy – the baby boy was born. Well, can you have anything nicer? Three kids in three years and two girls and a boy, especially the girls were practically twins, and they did grow up equal. Tiny was just that wee bit cleverer, quicker. Beatrice had to always – everything she did she had to learn: she made a job for

learning to walk, she made a job for learning to talk; and she was very
funny when she was – she never was a baby, she was always a little
girl, if you know what I mean.

The learning to talk was very different. Tiny did pronounce the
words right away very properly, she used to say one word. Beattie
did always talk in sentences, you know, she was laying beside you on
the floor – 'di di da di da di di' – you know, that kind of thing –
she had copied the way of talking. But I never forgot the first thing
that she said: I was pushing the pram up and the baby was laying in
the pram and Beattie was sitting on the front and it started to rain,
and she was on the front of it and I had to put the hood up and she
was sitting in the rain and it was getting cold and dark and miserable,
and I said, 'Never mind, we are going home now, and we put the fire
on and . . .' And she suddenly finished the sentence and she said, 'And
mummy make some nice cup of tea.' And I started blaring round the
road because suddenly one thing, that did belong to me, started to
talk – you know, instead of just in sentences, she pronounced the
words properly.

Tiny was very much a baby and had very short arms and beautiful
long eyelashes and big dreamy eyes, and she always did talk like a
baby as well. Every child was so different, even if you get them so
near each other that you think they were alike, but they did grow up
very easy together because they had each other. They had the company and rapport between each other, and they still hang very much
together, you know, all three of them, but the boy was different
altogether. He had it so much easier because he had the lassie to help
him; and I was a lot better by then, of course, and we had the house.

I know when we got the house that was twenty-one shillings the
social worker did come and ask if we could afford it, because Jim
had ninety-five shillings on the railway at that time. So I took sewing
in at home, and at home it did make you even more housebound. I
remember I did make between fifteen shillings and twenty-five
shillings for the sewing for the Town Hall. I did it when the kids were
in bed. I could do a bit of sewing, but I still have never been a dressmaker, so it was difficult work for me as well. It did not come easy
to me, you know, and of course then I made all the clothes for the

girls myself as well – the coats and everything – because I could not afford to buy them. I did like to make the girls' clothes, you know. You get a heck of a kick out of making a nice little frockie for a yard of material for two and elevenpence and thinking that the kids look much bonnier in that. Jim was going off on a Government's course for half a year to Birmingham and that time I took sewing in because I think we got four pounds in the week.

He did come back on the weekend suddenly, and on the Saturday I did discover that the Dutch cap that I had got from the birth-control clinic was really – the rubber had deteriorated; and I asked a neighbour if she minded very much to look after the children for an hour and I went to the town to a chemist and I had the box for the size with me. I walked into the first chemist and said, 'I want one of these.' It was easier to say 'I want one of these' than explaining. And he looked at the numbers and the figures and he said, 'Sorry, not in stock.' And so I went to the next chemist and they did phone – they said they had none in stock, but 'just a minute' – so she phoned and she said, 'Oh very sorry', but that was not in stock. So I went to the next chemist and she was very sorry but she did not have it in stock, and she phoned, and I went to the next chemist. It was a gentleman that phoned. I was getting desperate; I thought, what can I do? He said to me, 'Are you the lady that has been in Boot's and White's the other chemist with that as well?' – over his glasses, as if that was a crime really. I said 'Yes' and he said, 'Well I have just phoned the Central Dispensary.' All the chemists' shops get it from the same central chemist and the central chemist had told Boot's that they didn't have it. 'So,' he said, 'we don't have it either because if the Central don't have it, there is not anywhere in Carlisle where you can get it. The only thing I can help you with, we have one a size bigger.' So I thought, oh well, I'll just have to have a size bigger, and I said, 'Just give me that,' and I thought it was a very embarrassing thing to have done. Why I don't know, really, but at that time it was very embarrassing to go in a chemist and ask for that, and especially the way it was done. So I did come home with the thing. And of course we had to use it in the evening, and we couldn't manage at all because the thing was too big, and the fumbling about that there was, you have no idea, and the putting off. Of course it did put him right off and that was the end of that.

That's the kind of thing women can be up against. Maybe you ought to be better prepared, maybe you ought to be better organized, but I think there is a heck of a lot of very poor service for a woman in that way – maybe just because it is a small town. But that kind of thing did make me so much more determined that if I ever was able to do a lot more for a woman in that kind of . . . in that part of it, because that was very . . . things that were so important, and what you can't talk about with anybody and cannot be written about, and what cannot be done about. It is only the people what have got the power what ought to be much more aware of the need for women in things like that. It slipped up – it was not only my fault for being badly organized. I think things like that ought to be much more easier available, and you ought not be having to go thinking about being up against it. I think there is nothing worse for a whole district of chemists' shops to be without essential articles. It is their duty to be prepared and not letting get a woman in such awkward positions. Maybe there is not the need for it now so much any more, maybe all them kind of things have been sorted out, but I still think that they ought to be much more brought out in the open, like Women's Liberation says, that you are not pushed in things like that. A lot of women were involved exactly the same and made the same strange mistakes as I did. It is very easy now to look back and think, how can anybody be so stupid? But it is the atmosphere. I think nowadays the young people are much more honest; everything is much more clear. I don't think they will make the same mistakes, even though still a lot of girls still have to get married, especially here in this district.

Politics

'It suddenly did fall into place.'

Just after the war there was such a scare. The idea was to continue the war and smash Communism right away. In 1948 the Government

started the Z Brigade. Any ex-serviceman was still in the army – you
know, whether you like it or not you was in this Z. That was the
thing that made Jim politically conscious. He saw all the implications
of that, and he did start to get a great movement going in Carlisle
and district. But the Anti-Z-Brigade movement was made illegal by
the Government. We all voted Labour at that time, and we all really
voted for socialism, but we did not get what we voted for. We just
got some social democrats, a bit of reform – but never really socialism.
And the movements were cut up everywhere. That did teach Jim a
heck of a lot about politics, organizing and that kind of thing. He was
a member of the Labour Party, but he organized the Anti-Z-campaign
very much on his own, with people that he knew that had been in the
army the same time as him, and what had been in the war. There were
a heck of a lot of people like that in the town. They all felt very bitter
about the Z Brigade because you had fought the war that was the
last war to end all wars and so. The propaganda went suddenly very
much against the Russians and the East because I think Truman and
Churchill had set it up between them. Now they had won the war
against Hitler they were going to have a go at Stalin and the Communists, and so they did – there was a heck of a lot of anti-Russian
propaganda and a heck of a lot of that propaganda did stick. Eventually he began to go to Communist Party branch meetings and he
finally signed for the Communist Party.

I did not fall so much for the anti-Russian propaganda. I did start
to think a bit more about it. I did not join the Communist Party for
a long time after Jim joined because he is a domineering man, and he
is a very intelligent man, and there are sometimes things what I
thought that he was not right, but he was so much more eloquent
than me that I couldn't argue it out. And with my religion, he had
always the greatest respect, he would never ever sneer or talk it
down. I respected his religion and he mine in a way, and we did agree
to disagree, except that I – it couldn't help but rub off sometimes,
you know – of course we did read the *Daily Worker* every day. Before
I joined the Communist Party even, I went to women's meetings,
but the Communist Party in the early 1950s was 'industrial comrades'
– the industrial and intellectual were in the lead. Because the Com-

munist Party in the early 1950s were given such a bad name, the propaganda was so much against it, especially in the Labour Party, that the comrades had started to isolate themselves as well, you know they did become in a way more self-righteous and isolated, and because of that I felt I could not join.

There did become a bit of inflation, they started to put the rents up everywhere very much, and suddenly the Communist Party did get the lead against the Labour councillors. The rent was put up mostly by Labour councillors and they were pushed into it because of the bank loans, the interest was much higher. Tenants' associations rose up and we did form a tenants' association in our district and that was suddenly driving very quick, but the propaganda against it was that it was Communist propaganda. There were quite a lot of people what did not fall for the red scare, but the majority of the people did and the majority of the people did still want to back the Labour Party.

I organized meetings, that was the first time I really did start. Then I did start helping to organize the *Daily Worker* bazaars, and the two girls had started school and it was a bit easier just having the boy at home. There were fifteen women that worked for the bazaars and most of them were in the Party, but it was really just a bazaar group and we did talk about – there was one, Sadie Halfred, and she did agitate a lot for birth-control clinics. She was much more aware than the other ones of the necessity for women's clinics and birth-control clinics and I backed her up with that. We did try and do something about it, but I found that a woman got quite bitter about that – it was a combination of things really, the women felt bitter that the Party did use them just for women's bazaars, and there were a few women that were more Marxist and conscious of it, and they felt bitter that you were by-passed when the District Committee was elected, but I did not really – it did not bother me. I joined after 1956. That weeded a lot of comrades out, a lot did fall by the wayside.

It is my opinion that it was the infiltration of foreigners, agitators, in Hungary that caused the uprising, that it was a real Hungary uprising, I still do not believe. I think the leading Communists had made mistakes, like they had made here. I think they were – when

they had taken over in Hungary after the War they had not considered the people enough and the mood and the feelings of the
people, they had tried to be too much demagogues in slamming
Communism through instead of explaining to the people properly.
It was what Lenin said, that 'you cannot get socialism before every
cook in the country knows what it is about', and that's true. I think
that if people don't understand what it is about you cannot expect
them to act accordingly. It has to come out more from the people
than it can come out from the leadership.

I read *The Grapes of Wrath* of Steinbeck. I like reading stories or
novels and I read a few of Steinbeck's books. I think if I had read
Steinbeck before I met Jim that maybe I just would think that it was a
lovely story, but because I read it that time, when I had been indoc-
trinated with Communism and had to resist it for so long, suddenly
that evening that I finished the last page it suddenly did fall into place.
I could suddenly remember things from Holland at the time of the
Depression. They sent young people to labour camps instead of
giving them work. They did use them as cheap labour really, but I
had never seen before. Suddenly it fell like a jigsaw, all into place. It
was exactly like Steinbeck did describe, and that's what capitalism
does to people. And I thought I had to join the Communist Party and
work as much as I possibly could, because otherwise we would never
get socialism, because I could not see any other way.

Work

'The word went round: "She is the wife of that Communist."'

In 1956 I started at the Garlands Hospital because that was the only
place. I could not work in the children's school because of my accent.
Garlands is a psychiatric hospital. They had trouble getting people so
they did really take anybody on, and I had a bit of nursing experience
in the War, so they did take us on there and they did train us at the
same time. I worked mornings. I lived on the other side of the town;
I had to be there at a quarter to seven and I had to leave the house at a
quarter past five to get there. I worked until half past one and I could

be home by half past two, so if the kids were having their holidays a quarter past two I could manage it, in the holidays when the kids were off I could make them the dinner when I came home. When I started it was much more like the workhouse still; now the hospital is immensely improved. We have got the holidays. They started first ten years ago and they got a bus-load of people from our hospital went to the Welsh hospital and brought the Welsh people back to our hospital, and then they . . . for a whole fortnight they did give them outings to lakes and to Gretna Green and around the cars factory.

We were never very well-paid, but of course by that time – that was ten years ago – we did follow courses and we were made Enrolled Nurses. We did get on the register – enrolment anywhere – so if you was an Enrolled Nurse and a State Enrolled Nurse you got more money as well, but nurses were never very well-paid. When I did start there was a union – the Confederation of Health Service Employees. It is a nurses' union. It is more for the ordinary nurses than the Royal College of Nurses, which in our opinion is always more for matrons and the higher grades, and they were very very conscious of nursing as a profession and that you really don't work for wages, but you ought to be properly educated – it is a middle-class union, very much. They had started in our place with COHSE in 1935 and it had worked quite well, there was still quite a lot of people in when I started at the hospital. Of course I joined the union, and maybe half of them were in the union and half not, or maybe even less. In that time I was classed – you know, before I was ever started, in the first weeks that I was there – the word went round: 'She is the wife of that Communist.' Because Jim had very often stood talking at the Town Hall, you know, and even if I was a Communist or not I was classed as such.

The sister from the ward there was very much a Tory and the régime was a spinsters' régime because nearly no married women could come. The hours were very long; we all worked half-time, you know – we worked thirty hours and that was half-time. The full-timers worked fifty-six hours, so very few could – only spinsters could really, and at that time it was spinsters who could do the training and become a sister, a charge nurse or . . . and then go higher to assistant matrons or the matron. And because of that they were nearly all . . . most of the time they were Tories that were in it, and most times you were very narrow – the people there. There was a very strict segregation between the female and male patients and also between the female and the male nurses; there were a few couples, but there was not much social life in the hospital at all.

But the unions started to work for less hours. So then I started – well, I had my say about a few things. I went to the union meetings quite a few times – if I possibly could I did go to the union meetings – and the union did get shorter hours. That was a big breakthrough. First it was forty-eight and then forty-four hours. And when I started, the woman what was doing the union, what was really only the collecting and the recruiting, she did ask if I would take it on. I said, 'Oh, I am a Communist'. I went to the meetings and they did say, oh, it did not matter if I was a Communist or not. That was with the Labour Proscription time, it was very difficult because the Trades Council did not let anybody . . . it was forbidden in the Trades Council to have any officers that were Communist. So I was asked. I think it was Hobson's choice, nobody was there to take it on, because it was a union and it was still not a done thing to work in the union. The nurses . . . it was not dignified and it was not really done, so I was asked to do it, and I started to work.

I did never make a lot of propaganda about it because I had the drawback that not being that eloquent and able to say . . . and in a hospital you can't if you have got a Tory sister. She can blare her politics out and say, 'I can't stand Communists, he's been standing speaking at the Town Hall again,' you know, 'If I had my way I would shoot them all, I would shoot the lot!' And you have to stand and take it and not say anything because anything that you would say back would be propaganda – *they* could say anything and everything. But by then I had learned to do my work properly and do it as good as anybody, and because of my training what I had before I was married, in social work and wanting to be a missionary, I could use all my training in that way and I could hold my own very much.

I have had quite considerable influence in the last years because then we started the Joint Consultative Committee. In most places a Joint

Consultative Committee had not been working so good because you very often get the bosses' opinion is being laid out to the underlings and they have to go and spread the gospel, and it has only been in our place the opposite because I have been able . . . and I think it has only been because I had Communist training in the last years. I have been able to bring a lot of – what is the word? – anomalies forward to the Committee. I have been able to bring them forwards and the Management Committee has been willing to listen. A year ago the management had brought forward that the night nurses had to have half an hour break in the middle. That was very nice but it meant that the night nurses got half an hour less pay, so that's two and a half hours less in the week she got paid.

The conditions on the male side were always much better than on the female side. Granted the male side did work with less people, the female side was much much cleaner because of good husbandry, their wards were absolutely spotless. When I started they were Ideal Home Exhibitions. That floor was polished every morning at ten o'clock because then the doctor did come round and, you know, the whole rigmarole for that. On the male side they were always much easier with that. We did say that the male side was filthy. The male nurses did say, 'It is not a job for the nurse to lay on their knees to do that,' and they did definitely make it much more homely for the men, you know. They were more homely, it did not seem to matter so much to them, so – but the males would always get away with having no dinner-times, no meal-times, taken off them, they did work an eight-hour shift altogether.

As soon as you start training people, you get a better standard of nursing. I don't say that the trained nurses were better than the untrained ones, the only thing I am saying is that a good nurse what gets training is better after the training than what she is before, and that's what I have always tried to influence.

I started to do the union and I worked very hard in it, much more because – well, that sounds boasting and I don't know how to put that different – but it is because I, from my own personality and because of my integrity, how I looked to my work – they did see that Communists did not eat the babies for breakfast, and that you could be as good a worker as anybody and as good at understanding people as anybody and still could fight for the rights of nurses. And I had made it clear through my own example more that fighting, that the more you fight for the rights of nurses, that it is a good thing for the patients. I think that's one thing I have achieved in the twenty years that I have been there.

5.   Maggie Fuller

Maggie Fuller was born and brought up in Leith, the dockland area of Edinburgh, where her father worked in the docks. He was injured in the First World War and received a small disability pension. There were nine children in the family, two girls dying in infancy. When her father died, her mother went scrubbing in the local school to keep the family going.

Maggie Fuller has lived most of her life in the country, where she now lives with her husband, Tom, a retired farm labourer. They have two grown-up sons and four grandchildren. Before her marriage she did a variety of jobs – waitress, housemaid, machinist, and working in an engineering firm making parachutes during the War. Since her marriage her jobs have been mainly connected with farming – picking potatoes, making butter, and helping in the kitchens of the local farmers.

Childhood

'In those days a lot of kids got the stick.'

My father was a docker in Leith Docks, he oftener didn't work than worked. He had a gammy leg which was something from the war. He was an awful man to bet and a terrible man to drink. He was good to people that never gave him anything, and when he needed something he got nothing, this kind of thing. It's the same old story of a very poor family. If you got good clothes they went to the pawn on a Friday and if your mother was lucky she would pull them back out on the Monday, because the money didn't go to feed us, it went for drink or for horses or dogs or something.

The only thing I will say and I have always said, we never went without food. It might not have been the kind of food that everybody would be getting, but we never went without food. He always got us food from somewhere, you know. Sometimes it was brought in his belt from Leith Docks. I am not ashamed to say it. It was fish, and we were all so much like fish it's no wonder we all swam. I think it was yon salt fish. Anyway we didn't like it as kids and my mother never had so many 'please could I leave the table?'s. He even brought home cod heads one time and my mother cooked this and she was sorry for us. We used to leave the table and spat them out into our hands and hid them, or tried to put them down our stocking and off to the bathroom. I think my mother knew something was going on but my father didn't really notice – and it was in the days when if you laughed at the table you were collared for it. I will say this, you were brought up mannerly enough for all you didn't have then.

We lived in a room and kitchen and a lavatory in the middle – you know, up one flight of stairs. And my mother had to scrub the floor which was scrubbed every day, scrub the table, six wooden chairs. She had a dresser, and I am not sure if her bed was iron or not, but we had iron beds. Four of us slept in one bed and two boys in another with a very young one, and I think one slept in the room with her. I remember four of us in a bed, and eventually there was two boys and a younger child in another bed, but that was all there was. You didn't have a wardrobe or anything. My mother had a big chest of drawers, and everything was beautifully folded into papers to be preserved because of the pawnshop. Sometimes when she washed your clothes you couldn't get out because you had to stay in till she got them dried and ironed. We didn't know anything about this being hardship.

We never ran barefoot – if we did it was out of choice. We didn't need to run barefoot. My father was a good cobbler, and he cobbled all our shoes. We did go without stockings, but my father used to knit them too. He knitted long black stockings. When he wasn't having a drink he wasn't a bad old spud you know. He never hammered any children, he never lifted his hands. But drink! Oh God – with his gammy leg! He used to bring in a fish supper and we'd pinch it from him, because he was full, you see, he was drunk. He used to sit on the top of the stair – 'Annie, open the door, here's your supper!' – and my mother used to bring it through and give us all some out of that one fish supper, give us all a bite. That's true now, I remember that.

We got a halfpenny a week to spend and it was my father's pension day – I think he had a pound for his war wound, you know. Really, in these days if my father hadna have drank as much we would be quite well off, because a pound is a lot of money, and my mother could have had a lovely home and everything. I think we got a halfpenny and we used to spend it as you liked. When my mother was hard up she would slip my brother a penny or something and say, 'Go up and see if you can win anything at the show.' I remember this time I won sixpence on this thing, I took it home and she took it off me. I nearly broke my heart, I only meant her to have some of it and she took it all [laughs]. We spent a lot of great time up on that fairground, you know – we had to go home by seven o'clock of course.

My mother was a good-living woman. At first when she was very young she never swore or anything, you know, because my grandfather . . . they were brought up with the church, they were . . . their people were quite well off actually. I think maybe she'd been sheltered. It was only her and her sister and there was seventeen years between them.

As I say, my childhood, if you look at it in some ways, it wasn't very happy, but we didn't know any better so therefore we were happy. I can remember my sister once pushing me in the fire, and I got all my hand burned – you know, just out of spite – my mother slapped her for that. I can remember going to Pilgrim Park on a terribly hot day, and I was all bandaged and I remember taking all these bandages off – I remember doing that distinctly – my hands were so hot and sore, and there was a great big water bit and I went and put my hands all on these waters until somebody come and said to me 'What on earth are you doing, child?' I remember this old lady saying that to me, and I said to her, 'My hands are hot, quite hot.' I can remember that, I was very small, mind, and she said to me, 'You know you are a very naughty little girl to do that,' and I said, 'My sister was naughty, she pushed me in the fire.' I remember saying that, and she dutifully put these things on my hands, and I remember going home and my mother at night saying to me, 'You had these bandages off,' and I swore blind . . . Oh, I remember what a thrashing I got because I told her a lie. I got a terrible thrashing. My brother said I'd had them off and I had my hands in the pool. He just said I'd had them off – aha – I got a thrashing for that day.

Sometimes she'd lift a stick. Well you don't blame her, when you think about it. It didn't do me any harm, does it? Probably made me a better person, you know. I mean we are law-abiding. In those days lots of kids got a stick, and if you didn't get that you got a belt, so I mean . . . She didn't often use the stick, it was just that it was handy that time, it was mostly the belt she used. Sometimes she used her hands, but she just didn't know when to stop when she started. We tell her even to her face – 'A cruel old bugger you were, mother!' She'll say, 'Oh aye!' But she wasn't really, truly – it's a funny thing having all these kids.

I don't love her, as I say, I couldn't, but . . . and even to this day I am no the girl who'll go up and kiss my mother. I won't kiss my mother if you give me a pension. I wouldn't honestly, and even when she was ill in hospital I had to turn my face away. I can't help it, honest – it's one of these things, you see. Tell me what causes that, you see, I can't. I don't know, people say 'the Good Old Days', well I am going to be honest with you – where the hell were they? You show them to me. They were only good because we didn't know any better.

My mother was a whacker – oh my God, you didn't ask – you got punished, it didn't matter. Do you know what I really think it was? I hate my mother – I respect her now but I don't love her – but I think it was because she had too many kids and she was so work-worn, the poor beggar. Oh I hate my mother – not now as a hate, but I don't love her. I respect her and help to keep her, I've always said that, and I'd take her for a month's holiday. But you know, now when I am grown-up and I see the life she had! I remember she once nearly killed me.

My father had an accident at the Leith Docks, they took a kidney away. He had just one kidney and he had a wound. My mother – I used to stand and help her, you know – she put her hand all in it to clean it, it was never closed, you see. He was an invalid for about two years. He wasn't a very good man after that, poor fellow. That's where his friends should have come and helped him that he helped. I had a sister, she is older than I am but not as strong as I was. I got left with most of the work, and she wouldn't even run and go and get a book for him. You know, he was an awful great reader eventually, he was a clever enough man – he was an army man by the way.

I got away from school early. I got an exemption because my mother needed me, because she had to scrub the school. I left school at thirteen and a half and I had to go to night school to make up for it. The reason I got away was because I had to take a young child with me to school. There were no nurseries or you couldn't get them in at all and my father couldn't do anything. So I started to work at six o'clock in the morning at a Co-operative Store Bakery, and I'd come home early in the day to prepare meals for the kids that came home and to wash the stair if it was my mother's turn at the stair. One thing I never did was washing. My mother lifted big heavy pots on to a great black grate, because she only had cold water, and you'd help her, but she did all the main washing. One night, och, I had a rough time with the kids, and I couldn't cope with them by the time I came home. You're young, you're fourteen, what can you do? There had been a right fight and I was a bit late with the tea and we always had somebody looking out the window for mum coming home because she was so tired. My mother was scrubbing for the school; we used to look for her and somebody would say 'Here she's coming' and you ran to make the tea. Well this night there was only a wee drop of tea in the pot – I forgot that – and it stood up on this big high mantlepiece, and one of the kids came up against me and I just dropped this tea and it all went over the floor. And by then she was up and into the house and she nearly killed me for that, somebody pulled her off, she was choking the life out of me. Mind, I don't hold it against her, as I say, you've no idea what it was like with all these ruddy kids.

School

'I hated that ruddy school.'

I hated the teacher. It was alright until I got a Miss Melville. She knocked the bloody daylights out of me. Mind, I was stupid at school, I wasn't very clever. I was quite clever at the start and I don't know what took place. I was stupid, I truthfully was stupid. This teacher was always hitting you. I hated that ruddy school. I wouldn't cry for her, and she used to say, 'I'll make you cry,' but she never ever did. It was a horrible school. Of all of us I think I am the stupidest in our family, and that's true. At the start mother said I was quite bright when I went to school. I got stars – you know, they used to give you them – and she said I was quite bright, but she said it was just after I got that teacher I went back. I was in her class so long, you know, until my grandfather took charge and went up and said I'd have to be shifted and I went into my brother's class. He's a much younger brother and they thought it might egg me on, but it didn't. He left me because he was clever [laughs], left me standing. I didn't get through my qualifying, I never passed – I am the only one in our family that didn't – but they put me into a pass class and I got on fine in the secondary school, never had any trouble. I managed to be top for some things.

Mind, I feel I should have been educated, that I do feel; and if I had my life to live again I would, honest to God, do something about it – if I had the sense then I've got now, but you don't have that. I couldn't spell for nuts, you know – ach! I spelt occasionally, but every other word's wrong, but I was like that at school. Now I've read and I've read and I've tried to be able to spell, so don't you tell me to take a book up and read and you'll spell – that's rubbish, you won't, I've done it. I can read and write, anything like that, but . . . education, I am hopeless, that's honest. I don't know why, you know; I've got three or four sisters and they are all really bright girls, you know. The boys went to university because there had to be money for them, but there's nothing for girls – in those days you know. And before my father's money got settled we were two years with nothing. True, we had nothing. After his money got settled, well, there was some money, but it was no use to me anyway because I wasn't clever enough. But my other sisters, some of them got their Highers, you know. It's just one of these things. I have tried. I've never gone to night school, I am more use with my hands. I'd rather go out and do brawny work, something like that. If you give me something dirty to do, I'd do it, but you would all go 'ooh!' Well I thoroughly enjoy doing that, you see.

Adolescence and Courting

'She didn't tell me anything.'

When we were quite young, you know, I was fairly heavy. I had a period before my sister, you see, and I dutifully tried to wash these things. Anyway, I had an awful good aunt, you see. I got a hold of my aunt and I said to her, 'Do you know, I don't know what I am going to do.' Well, she said, 'You've told your mother?' 'No,' I said, 'I am frightened.' 'Oh,' she said, 'you'll have to tell her.' I never said anything more, she told her for me. She gets me into this room, and I'll never forget it, and she said to me, 'When you're like that,' she said, 'you just keep away from men.' I think now it's an awful horrible thing she done; then I don't know what I thought. She got a bairn's nappy and she showed me how to put it on! [Laughs.] And do you know what I used to do when I was like that? When I saw a man I used to run like hell – I did! Do you know, I've never forgiven my mother for these things that she's done, it was all wrong. 'Well you keep away from men,' that's all she said, and when I saw a man I used to run.

Do you know how the running stopped? I met my sister one day, I was going like the hammers, you know, and I was getting on, I might be about fourteen at the time, and she said, 'Good God, Maggie! Why are you running like that?' 'Well,' I said, 'I've got yon in,' I said, 'I've got–' So she says, 'What? Oh!' She says, 'Come on, I am going to see Aunt Ella about this.' And Aunt Ella says, 'Did your mother no tell you anything? Well,' she says, 'she should have done.' And I was left hanging like that too. No, she didn't tell any of us anything. Somewhere my sister Annie managed to learn – oh well she worked in a factory, you see, she may have got it there. Aunt Ella said, 'Well I'll see your mother about it.' That was all that was done. I never knew. She didn't tell me anything. It was all whispered. It's wrong! I always said if ever God spared me to have a girl she would know from a very young age, and it wouldn't be a shock to her. I mean, they talk about girls no being right – how the hang do they know to be? Imagine a mother telling you, 'Keep away from him.' Well, naturally, you got to your bloody feet and you ran, didn't you? [Laughs.]

I'll never forget that day at the Calton Hill. I remember going out with a boy one time. I know what he wanted now, but I never got round to it then, and it was when the Welshmen used to come over, and I was going about with Jimmy White and I went up the Calton Hill, you see, and we sat down, but the others went away, a good bit away, her and him, and left me with this one, and I am pushing – I'll never forget it. It's a shame, do you know, it's wicked, it really is, now when I think about it. Years ago this fellow saying, 'Isnae it all right? Well tell her.' And this one said, 'Oh, aye, it's all right.' I was down on the grass, I was horrified, I kept pushing – you know, pushing him out of the ruddy way – and he's rolling over to this fellow and telling him it will be all right. And you know, I had no ruddy idea what it was all about, and that's the God's gospel truth. I never knew for years and years what the hell he was meaning. But I mean, if he thought he was going to get anywhere, I wouldn't have known to say yes or no, and that's the God's gospel truth, do you know that? It is, the God's gospel truth. I mean, how many people were like me? I often think, well isn't that shocking? That my mother . . . surely she should have told us something! But she said, 'Keep away from men!'

First Jobs
'I kept myself on a pound a month.'

At thirteen and a half I worked in a store in the Co-operative Bakery.

I quite liked it but I wasn't getting on awfully well at home, getting too much to do, and my sister and I weren't seeing eye to eye. She was my mother's favourite. I don't blame my mother again for that and I'll tell you why – my father thought a lot of me. I said once to my mother she shouldn't hit me, and my mother said, 'Well when your father lived, he took your part, and now it's my turn to take hers.' And I hated her all the more for saying that, and I decided I'd leave home, so I went and I worked in the Girls' Friendly Society, it was in Rutland Square in Edinburgh, just off the station yard. I got a job as table-maid there.

When I was sixteen working at Miss Philipps at the Friendly Society this girl got us a job – a – what did you call it then? Up the top of Lee Street and we got one and six for a Friday night to wait the tables – fish and chip shop – and any tips you like. The first time I was there I turned in all my tips with my money because they said you shared it – course like a right ninny I turned mine in. When I came out the cook said to me, 'Where's your tips?' 'Well,' I said, 'I turned them in.' She said, 'You're a great silly,' she said, 'you only give her a few bob, you keep the rest.' So I learned to just give a few bob. You made a lot of money that way. You didn't get much from her though for actually doing it, but your tips, twopences and threepences – sixpence was a lot of money to me. I started to work for ten shillings. In a month I got two pounds and out of that I gave my mother a pound and I kept myself on a pound a month. I got my own clothes, all my sanitary stuff, and gave my mother a pound, and I had myself to keep.

I moved on. I went as housemaid to a place in Churchville, private again. You see it was Mrs . . . I've forgotten her name. She was left a widow and she kept her big house on and kept boarders. That's when I first met the most horrible people ever you imagined. I met a man, he was a boarder in this place. One day I dutifully cleaned his shoes for him, I'll never forget that, and I dutifully did all these shoes – my, I spent ages on them. I put them down at his door. Oh, say an hour after our breakfast, the cook said, 'You're wanted.' I went away up the stairs. Mrs whatever-her-name said to me, 'The Major's complaining you didn't clean his shoes.' Like a great ninny then I said, 'I did so clean his shoes!' – never thinking we were supposed to say you didna clean the shoes, you see. But I said, 'Oh but I did clean the shoes.' Well she says, 'You can go and tell him that,' and I said, 'I jolly well will.' And I went and I said to him, 'I know whether I cleaned your shoes or not,' and I said, 'I did clean them.' He said, 'Well you'll go and clean them again.' So I took them downstairs, walked round the table with them, gave them a wipe with my pinny, took them back up and he said, 'That's much better!'

I'll never forget that till the day I die. He periodically did this. You just said, 'Oh, I am awful sorry.' I wouldn't do that now but I had to do that then, I had to say that I was sorry. I used to take a walk downstairs and take them back up. Sometimes I didn't clean the damned things at all and he never complained. You know, these were the kind of people that you would meet. I loathe folk like that, I loathe people like that.

I went from there to a minister, to St Katherine's Gardens – it's just about at the Zoo in Edinburgh there – a minister and his wife, and they rationed everything you ate. I didn't do a terrible lot of cooking, I just did the vegetables – there was this horrible great big ugly black thing that I hated – and she wanted me up at six o'clock to scrub down some steps, but my mother said no, that day and age was done. She said, 'you can go down and give them a brush, but she's not doing that.' So my mother came another time and I was out. She was waiting when I came back and she said, 'Am I not going to get a cup of tea?' I said, 'I'll see what there is,' and there was a slice of bread with a wee drop of jam and butter on it and one dry biscuit and that was my tea. And my mother said, 'Is that your tea?' And I said, 'Yes.' 'Take me to her,' she said. 'No lassie of mine – you canna work for that.' But he was a perfect gentleman, this minister, he really was, he was a gentleman.

I went from there to work on a sewing machine in a factory. I didn't like it at all. Too many people and too many fights. Well it was terrible – you're going too quick or you're going too slow. Good Lord, I never met anything like it in my life. It seemed that people made what they call 'pace-makers' and you weren't supposed to do more than they'd done – oh, it was just terrible. So anyway, to cut a

long story short, this is when the war had come out, and I got moved.
The men had to go away and they come and asked if I would like to
learn to fold blankets, quilts and things – 'Oh,' I said, 'I'll have a go.'
And before that I had been on parachutes – you know, the things
the men come down in. Then they came and asked me if I'd do the
quilts, so I stayed there for quite a while.

I was going to be called up so I went into Simple Street after that,
to the garage, and they did tractors. They called us paraffin-oil
workers, if you like, we used to melt hot stuff and pour it . . . well it
was motors as well mind, not just tractors but motors – engineering
things – and you'd pour the boiling stuff on and it fitted into these
things and you shrivelled them up and then you fitted on pistons and
things. I could do that. Yes, I did my son's motorbike for him by the
way, och aye.

I turned ill again and I got an exemption and I came to the country.
I came as a kind of housekeeper, everything combined. And I loved
it. And I met my husband, and I married him. That's it.

I worked as a housekeeper – well I was general cum everything,
let's put it that way, don't get airs I'm a housekeeper – but I had
everything to do, aha. He worked on the farm there, he was on the
threshing mills, and I met him there – farmworker, he does anything
on the farm. He's herded, he's tractored and he's . . . well, he's retired
now, you know. I married him there too, and I worked after I
married until I was expecting my child and then I had to stop.

Sexuality and Childbirth

I never knew when I fell with my first child, I never knew I was having
it – I never got any feeling, I got nothing. I did in my second, and I
think in all the times in my life I could count how many times ever
I've got anything out of sex, now that's God's truth. I hate the ruddy
thing, I'll be very frank with you. I think it is a disgusting horrible
thing, I really do, aha. I didn't use to feel like that, I just did it, but I
never got anything, except with my second son, and an odd time
since – not now, mind . . . damned thing. But no, I could count all
the times . . . I never had anything before it, I can assure you, but I

knew when I was having – well, if that was what it was I had – a beautiful . . . I knew that was nice when I had my second son.

I'd rather do without it, it's been left like that, you know what I mean. My husband is older than me, and this is where I think sometimes . . . mind I don't know if it's right or wrong . . . as regards a stable man, you'll not get better. I've been allowed to do exactly what I like, but as regards sex, it's no use – if I hadn't been a kind of stable person I am sure I'd have gone off my ruddy head. You know I'd rather not have it, all that carry on, you know. It's maybe me that's cold, I don't know, I never talked about it – too late in life to talk about it now.

I went down Mrs Langland one time and I hadn't been feeling . . . I'd been doing too much work at the time, and when I am nervous I work a lot, you see, and I rush around, and I've always been nervous, and she just happened to say, she said, 'What's your sex life like?' [Laughs.] 'Now look,' I said, 'I've never had any.' 'Och!' she says. 'No, I don't,' I said. She said, 'How long has this went on?' I said, 'I hate the ruddy thing, you see,' and she said, 'Come on now, why? How? And how did it ever start?' 'Well,' I said, 'I might have had something if he'd waited, but he was always off and on style – you know, never had any time, just there and away. Well, how could anybody?' And I told her, I said, 'Well, when I had my second son, I can remember that, but never again but I think, oh, maybe twice.' I tell the God's gospel, as sure as I have my God to me that's the truth, you'd hardly believe that. She said to me, 'Did you ever feel like it?' I said, 'Oh yes.' 'Why didn't you ask for it?' I said to her, 'Well, I am going to say something,' I said. 'It's an awful thing but,' I said, 'I am not [laughs] a whore.' And she looks at me. 'Well,' I said, 'that's how I feel. I would have felt belittled if I had to . . .'

I am going to tell you, it is a ruddy shock – maybe because I didn't know enough, maybe it was because it was such a shock when the child was born, I don't know. I got a terrible shock when my first son was born. It was agony, it was terrible, maybe due to the fact that I never got any sex life. I didn't want it – I don't know. Well, my husband is quite a bit older than me, and as a man for a marriage – it works all right that way and he gives me every penny God gives him to give. You couldn't fault him that way, you get every little thing. Now he'd rather sleep. Well, I've never been a . . . I love walking these hills, I'll go out and I'll walk for miles.

My aunt told me – I talked to her, she was on about it one time – and she said, 'No, Maggie, it's a beautiful thing.' 'Well,' I said, 'I fail to see it.' But my own common sense tells me as a child's born from it – it must be beautiful to bring in a child, I know that, but the other thing appals me. I have a sister exactly the same now. We've got this old-fashioned streak in us. She's a clever girl, but sexually she's like me too, the very same – yes, the very same.

Once she said, 'Could you tell me truthfully, could I ask you?' And she asked me then about it – she said, 'How do you feel – it's an awful thing I am going to ask you – with Tommy?' Well I told her exactly, well I said, 'To be quite honest,' I said, 'I have had a feeling, I might get a feeling if he would wait for me.' 'Of course, it's the same with me and Willie, you see.' And we talked it over and she felt better, because she knew then she wasn't unusual, you know. She's never had a child, they said she was too nervous. She always wanted one, she even went to see about it. I think she once had a false pregnancy, yes, aha, but she's the same though with her husband as I've been with mine – we've talked that over.

But mind, I wouldn't change him, don't get me wrong, he's given me good years, make no mistake, and he's looked after my sons for me as well, and he's looked after me. I know I've helped, but I mean, if I hadn't he'd still have been happy to take us all, and if there had been any more he'd have taken them as well, but we decided that two was enough, you know. Well, I knew I had Michael. I'll be very honest with you, I didn't know about Sandy, I didn't know what the heck was wrong. Didn't have any feeling there at all, nothing. Well, it doesn't matter for that. Aha, but it is an awful shock, it's a bigger shock when you are having a child and you don't want to go to a doctor, you don't really know, you know it's a terrible thing, you . . . I'll never to the day I die know why my mother was like that. I always vowed that if I had a girl mine would know.

Women are soft, let's face it. Let's put it this way: I think if I had had a daughter she would have had a lot of love that I didn't get and she might not have been as aggressive as I was, and maybe through that love she wouldn't have needed somebody else's attention and love, you know. It's an awful thing to be lonely – have you ever been lonely? I have, and it's an awful thing. I got aggressive instead of the other way – you see it's wrong. Maybe I'd have been better had I gone the other way, you know, but I went aggressive, and I didn't understand what kindness was, you see. Therefore I didn't make friends easily. I think if I had a daughter they could have come and spoken.

When I had my child I didn't know where the hell it was coming from, do you know that? And that's the God's truth. And I nearly flattened my husband, I did, I'd push him away.

Married Life

'When a man comes home . . .'

The first year I was married I wasn't so much at the cottage because I didn't have any children. After the first year I was having my first child, so I had to get down to the house more. These old neighbours used to come to the house – oh dear, dear, dear, oh yes – and the first time, I remember, I hung washing out, they were all out looking at it, I remember that. And it was discussed whether it was clean or not – oh, I remember that, and I remember putting a towel out that had a stain on it, I've never forgotten that. They were 'yap yap'. First comes Mrs Haye with a jar of jam for me, and she was in and she brought down a packet of tea. I was astonished, I didn't know anything about this at all. So anyway, she said to me, 'Ay, Maggie,' she said, 'you ken,' she said, 'I think maybe if you were to take that towel, aye,' says Mrs Haye, 'and rub some sape on it, and pit it doon for the frost, y'd get the stains oot it!' This is how she spoke, you see. And of course I was quite indignant to her, it was awful silly, and I didn't say anything; inside I am quite sure I'd be seething, you know, because I was awfully quick in those days. That's what the jam and tea was all about. So then Mrs Snail says, 'Well, are you no making us a cup of tea?' So the two of them got sat down, you see.

I went away through and I could hear them, 'yap yap', and I am damned sure they were discussing me. Then Mrs Snail said to me, 'Now here,' she said, 'Maggie,' she says, 'when a man comes in he likes his (thump!) table in the middle of the flair!' says she – you see – and I had my table over at the window, so that was the next go. Anyway, they got their cup of tea . . . 'Did ye no make a scone?' she said. 'Well,' I said, 'no, I haven't baked.' 'Oh, a man likes a (thump!) scone!' she said. Well this is how it went on, you see. So when my husband came in, 'Oh,' he says, 'never pay any attention to them.'

So the next washing – I used to wash on the Monday, so the next Monday – I hears the rat-rat-ratting at the door, you see. Tom was away. I used to go back to bed because I was expecting the bairn, you see, and I just went back to the bed, because he worked on the mills, he went away at half past five in the morning. So just got back into bed, and the rat-rat at the door, so I thought, 'What on earth?' So I went to the door and I said, 'Who's there?' 'Mrs Snail. Well,' she said, 'come on,' she said, 'are you no getting your washing put on, I hadna heard you at your fire.' She hadn't heard me lighting this ruddy fire. Oh, really though – it was a race to see which of these two could get their washings out, you see.

Anyway I had a friend came to stay, because I was getting very near, and she came to stay, you see, for a while with me – I already had had this fall, that is why she came. And she said 'No, Maggie, you're not half fly enough.' I asked, 'What do you mean?' 'Aye,' she says, 'wash it out on a Sunday night and then put it out,' she says, 'like a fairy.' I'll tell you what I did, I did it early and I was running out in my dressing-gown [laughs]. Well, when I think about it now – when I think I was going to go back to my bed – I was going round the back at six o'clock with this ruddy washing. Well, do you know what? The one and then the other, they never spoke to me for about a week.

Oh, I'll tell you the next thing. I didn't have box irons, I couldn't use them because I once got a bad burn with one. And we wouldn't have any electric in the houses these days, and I put it on a paraffin stove – you know, the heavy wee iron – and this old body, a kind of cousin, come in this day. 'Ach!' she says, 'that's no way to iron,' she

said, 'I've brought you my box iron.' 'Well,' I said, 'it's very kind of
you but–' She says, 'You'll just have it!' You can't argue with these
kind of people. You put these pieces of steel... you caught them on the
hook on the fire and popped them into the fire and built your fire
and they got red hot, you pulled them out, opened this little door
and popped them in and you started to iron with them. That's what
they call the box iron. So that was another displeasure. I took them,
but I didn't use them. Bits of dirt used to fly out of them anyway.

I'll tell you what they used to do, these two, they used to take
clean things out of their drawers and wet them and put them out! I
didn't pay any attention to them, it didn't bother me. I mean, as I say,
I got off to a bad start with this one being a bit related – she used to
walk in no matter what I was doing, and I used to scream with fright,
you know. She'd be standing – she'd white hair, and she was a big tall
woman, she always wore brit-brats all tucked up, you know, like a
fisher wife, but she wasn't a fisher's wife – and all of a sudden you'd
stand from this back kitchen and this great thing was standing. I used
to – 'aaach!' You know, I just screamed because she was there. I had
to go to my husband and say to him, 'Look, you're to keep the door
locked.' I locked the door – and that was a fault too – so as I could
hear her coming, and then she told me one day she had more right
to be in the house than me, because they were related, you see. Well,
you'd got to take it. I won't take it now, but I was young, you know,
and I had to take it off her.

Work

'I have always worked.'

I have always worked, not out of necessity – my husband would keep
me, don't get me wrong – but I just always felt there wasn't enough
once the boys got off my hands. When they went back to school I
had to do something or I went stark staring bonkers.

Before my first son went to school I used to bike three or four
miles and deliver potatoes and bike back up the hills on the moors.

My husband was from the farm and he would give me the rough idea, but up there I had a nice neighbour too. She said to me one day, 'Tom tells me you've never had a cow or made butter. Well,' she said, 'if you want to come along, see how it's done.' But Tom had already shown me the basic and, although I say it myself, I made better butter than her. It wasn't that I made better butter, I had a better cow. You know you could get the best butter-maker in the world, but if you don't get a good cow you'll not get good butter. She had a different way of washing hers. I washed mine the way Tom showed me, and I stuck to it, it seemed to take it out clear. But there again, it's all your cow, you know. I could dress hens. I can't kill the pig – but I can cut it all up and do anything with it.

At first I didn't have a separator and I didn't have a churn either, so I had big basins, and after I milked my cow I put it through a seive with a muslin in it and let it lie all night. So the next day I had a round wooden thing with lots of wee holes in it, I skimmed off the top, put it into a dish, you see. Well, I did this until I thought I had enough. Now, as I didn't have a churn I used to sit with this jar, shake it and shake it and shake it until you saw it turn, bits of water started to come – then you're to be careful, you see. I got a churn after that, and a separator, once we got better off. I sold bits of things, and kept the money that I made from my first butter, and I saved it up and I got a churn and a separator. And then you poured it in and you cawed a handle and it separated the milk as you stood; then I got a kirn and I turned the handle. I used to make myself twelve and fourteen pounds of butter a week. And in wartime I sent it all home – not all, most of it – we were never short of anything – and loads of lard.

I have had a cow and I have had hens, and I made my own butter and also reared pigs. In these days we made more money in our hands than I've got now. Say twenty-seven to twenty-eight years ago I got a cow and I paid nine shillings for its keep. We made money then, money you could keep. Aha, I marketed my pigs and that, and I sold my hens and I milked a cow and I made butter and sold my butter, and I made all my own jam. I've fished.

When I went out to work it's mostly been farmhouses or else the likes of old people that need a help, and then I've worked for the doctor for thirteen years down here, off and on. I did all their baby-sitting and took phone calls at night, get them out or . . . they put in the phone for me . . . but if they needed I just dropped everything and went and I had a happy time. I still think a lot of these kids.

The farming community – now I am not going to say all, but the majority – as long as you're working for them they're all nice and natty, but the minute you're not – you know. I worked for one girl, not very far from here, and I don't care who hears me say it, and she's the most genuine and honest-to-God lassie ever I worked for. She came from people that were just ordinary working folk, she was a working lassie. She never refused you a wage when you asked your money, you got it; if you worked extra you didn't need to ask it, she gave it to you, and I'll always take my hat off to that lassie.

I worked for a very wealthy farmer further down the country here, and she'd had a lot of visitors and, 'Oh,' she said, 'I am feeling terrible,' etcetera etcetera. And then she said to me, 'I've got to take out all that washing when I come back.' Well I knew she hadn't been awfully right, and I thought to myself – shall I give her a ring, see if it matters if I could be late or early? But it just so happened she rang me that day, saying would I like to be a bit later coming. So it just all blended in beautifully. Unknown to her I started the washing, and I got it all washed and I got it all dried, but I hadn't time to iron it, naturally. By the time I tidied up it was an hour and a half, you know. So when I went back – I didn't go every day, two days a week, I had other jobs in between – and she said to me, 'Oh wasn't it wonderful to come in and get all that washing!' And I said, 'Yes, it took me about two hours, but,' I said, 'I managed it.' It was less – maybe a wee bit more because I had my time to travel up and back. Well, do you know, when they paid me, she didn't give me a penny! That's why I left, actually, I was so sick of it. I said to Tom, 'Well damned the lot of them,' I said, 'they're not worth working for.' I went whether I was paid or not and that's the truth. I've helped many persons and never got any money for it, home helps and any lame dog needing a hand. It never dawned on me that I was working for a car or to get money, I'll be very honest.

Children

'I never made a shindig about it.'

When Sandy started school, I hadn't moved to Hallyburton. It was too far for him to walk from where I was before and my mother said, to give him a good start, 'Let him come to Edinburgh and we'll send him to school in Edinburgh!' So Sandy started off school in Edinburgh. They had never been away from me, I didn't have baby-sitters like, you know, and if I did go home they created. They wouldn't stay with them you see, they didn't know them enough. I made the mistake of going to see him and that upset him a bit, and I said to her, 'Well I am not going to go back for a while.' Well I didn't, but it was all wrong. I had to bring the child home – he wouldn't be a year there – and my mother said, 'You're only giving in to him.' But, as I said, if he's not happy, he's our child, why shouldn't he come home? And by then he could get to a school, you see, but it was a long way for them, they had to walk. She said I shouldn't have given in, but I said I should. It's best to come home if he wanted to come home, and I missed him a lot, to be quite honest.

You see, my boys would tell me things they wouldn't tell their father. I never made a shindig about it, I used to say, 'Well let's have it.' Or if the police come to the door and there had been anything outside – Baillie used to come and say, 'You know, Mrs Fuller, they said it was your lad.' I used to say – I'll tell you what I'd say – 'We'll wait and see what he says shall we?' He said, 'Well at least you didn't turn me away.' 'What's the good?' I said, 'We'll have to find out what he says – possibly he did do it.' 'Well,' he said, 'we'll leave it.' My boys always told me if they did. Oh, they often did, they were often at the pinching of the apples and things like that.

My son had red hair ––my youngest son – and the boy Bain had red hair, and I am not trying to defend my son – he was in plenty of scrapes, he ain't no ruddy angel – but he never did things the boy Bain did, he wouldn't break big lamps and things. He used to wear a split hat, and I used to say to him, 'That ruddy hat will kill you yet.' When the big fluorescent lights were pinged with the catapult – my son was a good shot with a catapult, I knew that – and I said to Baillie,

'Well, he's got a catapult, yes, he's got a split hat and,' I said, 'he's a damn good shot. But I'll tell you you are accusing him of it without asking.' 'Well,' he said, 'it's a sure thing, because it was a red-haired lad going up the toll and he had a split hat.' 'Well,' I said, 'on all accounts it could be Michael, but you be very sure before you come in here and accuse him of doing that, I'll not stand by him until I hear him. You just take yourself away and come back.'

The terrible thing was I knew about it and I knew it wasn't Michael, but I couldn't say it was Billy Bain. I wanted Billy Bain to say it was him, which was the right thing to do. So Baillie come up and I hadn't got time to talk to Michael, you see. 'Well you better come in,' I said, 'and I'll make the police a cup of tea.' That's the laugh, that's what everybody laughed at. He's only doing his job, let's be fair, and he had got a hold of Michael first. And Michael said, 'I ken who did it but I am no telling you.' You see, the silly young critter, so I got him hanked out. 'Now,' I said, 'cut that out.' And I said, 'Don't speak like that,' I said, 'you either did it or you didn't, that's all that's asked of you.' Well the police said, 'Sorry, Mrs Fuller, but I'll have to take it the whole way, because,' he said, 'well, it's only fair, let's be fair.' So anyway I said to him, 'I'll tell you, you're going to make a right fool of yourself. Stop and think, how many red-haired laddies . . .' I'd already been to Mrs Bain and the father said to me, 'Let them find out it's him. I am not damned well saying it's him.' 'Well,' I said to Baillie, 'is Michael to take the blame? He's got the blame many's a time for him. Oh, he's an awful bad devil that wee laddie.' And so we left it like that. I said, 'You do your work thoroughly and then come back.' It shows you how the thing goes, somebody had spotted that it was Billy and no Michael, and he'd had Michael's hat – Michael had given him that hat right enough. So that was that. Michael was an awful tearaway, you know – never did anything bad, but an awful tearaway.

My oldest boy he went into the engineering, but he took dust fever and things, and dermatitis, and had to give it all up. They're both on the farm. Sandy's a maintenance man.

Girls

'They don't have a chance.'

I never got a girl so I don't know what would have happened. The way the world is they don't have a chance, unless they are very strong-willed. No matter how much bringing-up you give them. I am glad I didn't really. I said to my sons, 'Well, do you know?' I said, 'You's have lamb and sheep.' And they said, 'Now Mother, if it's sex you're on about, we know all about it!' I used to say to them, 'Well mind, if you ever put a girl in the family way, and you don't take her after spoiling her, you'll have the decency to come and tell me and I'll see she's all right.' I always said that to them, I did always and I would always, because I think it's a shame. I don't see why a girl should be left like that, I truthfully don't. It's a damned disgrace. I don't see why a boy should spoil a girl and get off scot-free, I don't honestly, and I used to say that to ours. I remember because I'd say, 'It'll come back on you, if I ever hear about it. Don't shut the door on them, for,' I said, 'it's a shame.'

I mean we lived beside people, and I remember when one mother put her daughter out – how can anybody do that? How could a mother do that? Because of the neighbours! What the heck have the neighbours got to do with it? These things bother me. They don't have a chance. Everything lays back at their door. You can't blame a girl if she falls into the family way. I say you can blame her if she goes from man to man, that's wrong. But I don't say it's wrong if you are engaged to somebody and, you know . . . Well I mean, I don't condone it, let's be fair, but on the other hand it depends. I say that a woman's made – most women – I am not, which is a great pity, and I think I fell out on this bit – they're made to be soft and loving and kind and giving. If somebody's went say with somebody for a long time, and they do that and they fall, the man can just turn his back and walk away, which as you know he often does. Supposing even they marry, that man can walk off scot-free, take what he likes and leave them again. Well I mean, that's not right! That's wrong!

I say when there is a marriage at all from the minute you marry everything's cut right through the middle. You know, there's none of the . . . the house is the man's, this is the man's. I mean, you had a job before – this is what I keep saying when my sons say something about their women. I'll say . . . Oh, I remember my son saying one time to Anne, 'Anne,' he says, 'who keeps you?' And I said, 'Who kept her before? She could keep herself before you took her, she can easily do it again. Don't get haughty.'

I also feel that you blame a girl. A man can walk away from a thing, and if a girl's not married, well, she . . . the poor bitch, she hasn't a chance – well, not nowadays, it doesn't . . . but I am talking about in our days – they were pointed out. They couldn't keep their bairns even if they wanted to, they'd nothing to keep them. Ach, no, I think a girl, from the day she was born, I think she is doomed in a way. I don't mean every way, but in a way she is. I just feel, well, a man can rise and walk away, even to this day. Even though we are supposed to be in a much higher and better society, you're no really, did you know that? You're not really. It'll maybe come, but not yet. I think it is instinct why a woman always . . . you know . . . well, I don't know, you have your abortions and all your things now. I think that spoils a woman really, I might be wrong, but I think it must. I think it will kill something, because I have a feeling that . . . well I don't know.

I find with the modern mother she doesn't have the same care of her children that we had of ours, I find this. And the more . . . maybe they think they are more self-sufficient, I think maybe that too, but truthfully and honestly I feel the modern mother is missing an awful lot – her child still needs her. I think it's wrong. A very young child, the mother stays with it – but that's the time when the child doesn't need her, because it lies and sleeps – you could go out and work. It's after that, it's when it starts to come on between . . . say about three, your child needs you, and I find that's when a lot of mothers work. If they have to do it, fair enough, but a child takes a lot of care and if you want to help it to build it up, express itself and do something it takes time.

One regret I've got, I often wish now, I'd spent a bit more time with my two, as I . . . because I spend an awful lot of hours with my grandchildren, which I didn't with my own. Aha, I don't know why that is, but somewhere or other . . . or whether it's because my boys were near each other. Sandy was a lazy child and the younger one soon caught him and they were good company. But I think the very modern mother is too much the other way – she doesn't care. I might be wrong but I think so.

Nowadays

Nowadays people get far too much, so therefore they don't appreciate what they've got. Now I don't really think there are any poor people, even with your pension, and even with your social-security things. I don't think people are all that poor. It's people that have got far too much. And also, you know, when I got married my mother gave me twenty-six shillings for an alhambra – I thought that was grand. It's what everybody used. It's a top cover for your . . . not the very top but the one you sleep with on top of your blankets. Mine was pink – you could either get them pink . . . they had fringes. They were called alhambra covers. It was twenty-six shillings. My mother gave me that. What does your mother give in this present day? A suite, doesn't she? Well a lot of mothers do. I know what I give my own family.

Who ever heard tell of getting fridges, carpets? Even tellies, some get. Look at all these electric things you get. I mean we got ours through striving for them, so therefore I am not going to change them. I am sitting with all the furniture I had from the day I was married. My sisters will come and say, 'My God, when are you getting rid of this bloody rubbish?' That's what they'll say. They've got beautiful homes, but I . . . you see, I hold no value to my house. There's not a thing in here if you did anything to it that would upset me, do you know that? Nothing. You try it and it wouldn't bother me. And yet I've got dishes and stuff stashed away I won't use in case they get broken, but if you went and broke them, my word to God, I wouldn't say anything to you – and I'll give you an instance why. Many, many years ago, when my children were small, one of my sons – I don't know which one – lifted something at my mother's and it was something that she treasured – my mother treasures lots of things, by the way. And if she had gone over very quietly and taken it from the child it might have been all right, but she roared and the boy dropped it. I come away home crying that day, and I got the train back crying about a little thing like that. That hurt me terribly.

I've had so many things done to me and I've seen so many broken hearts with these things – what are they worth? If you die tomorrow, they're not going to bung the lot in – what are you going to do with them, chuck them out the door? I mean why treasure something that much? Why not treasure your life and try and make somebody else's a wee bit nicer? You get more good out of it, you might think you want. I mean, I am not like the man in the Bible who gives everything away, I wouldn't give everything away, I'll be very honest, I wouldn't. I'd give you anything out of the house if you needed it and said you wanted it. If your need is greater than mine, I'd give it to you that way, but I wouldn't be like the man that gave his whole all – liked no money – just as he stood. I wouldn't do that, I'll be very honest – that's stupid, but everybody doesn't look at it that way. You see, you can't take it with you, and if you've given pleasure . . . Well, that's what's wrong in this country.

I can't understand why all this amount of money is laid out and yet the houses are poverty-stricken. They don't pay big wages, it's the bare essentials, or if they can get away with less . . . houses that's not been painted. Yet they give away and ask to all these things. The young laird, I think, was to be married. I just thought, well – I didn't like the way they'd come round and ask you to give something and . . . I think if you are going to give something – you didn't know him and you didn't . . . I am not a mean person, but I just don't believe in that. I think if you want to give something, you give it – and just because they decided it's to be this and that they wouldn't look at you. You know that all damned well annoys me, and as I say there's all these things spent. A lot of people can't refuse and then they as much as tell you what to give. Well this is wrong. I give two pounds, that's plenty. I mean, I think this is all wrong, and then – 'Oh see what your workers have given!' – it's putting a face on something that's not real. I am not saying that it's not right, it is right – to an extent it's right. But there is a happy medium. I feel that there is too much wasted with it, that's what I am getting at.

Without going into politics, take your unions. Now to me the unions are a marvellous thing, they first gave the working man his chance, now didn't they? But, and it's a very big 'but', they've put politics into it. It's not worth a damn, because it was never meant to be political. It was meant for working folk, and I think it did a world of good, but now they are using it to bribe the country and it's all wrong. This is what gave working man his start, was the unions – mind, they were very good – but the men that set them up would turn in their graves if they knew what they were doing with them. They are abusing them. I mean, take your miners if you like – take who you like, take the miners – I know they've got a very bad job and all the rest of it. Now this is gospel truth – they're on about they haven't money.

I had a right go at Kirkpatrick with a miner and his wife. She was going to knock my head off and I told her to use a wee bit of common sense. I said, 'You'll get nowhere doing that,' I said. 'If you leave my head on I can argue it out with you very quietly, no knocking heads off!' And she told me, before this wee bit argument got up, about the men getting paid on a Thursday, and they drank all Thursday, all Saturday, all Sunday – they were lucky if there was anything left on Monday. Now then, she had the impudence, the ruddy impudence, to tell me they weren't paid. I am not against working folk, I know I have not really come on as working folk maybe should myself – I am aware of that – but whoever heard tell of them going for all these fabulous holidays? They haven't a ruddy penny when they come back, they spend hundreds and hundreds of pounds. Well I mean, I am not saying they shouldn't spend some, but I think they're just overdoing it and come back with nothing.

I'll tell you why I think this is all wrong. Before Tom stopped, you see, now I'll tell you exactly what my husband got. I got twenty-one pounds one fortnight and twenty-six pounds the next – that's what I got just before he finished. So that's slightly more – say twenty-three pounds. Now you take the twenty-three pounds, you got a free house – I know it's tied, I am aware of that, and I am also aware of the fact for the vans that come we pay a lot more. Some have a ton of potatoes – the old workers, not the very new ones, they don't get this as much. But we had half a ton of potatoes. I've also got my garden.

I put him in the union, he never was in it until I put him. As I say, this way, the union got you where you are, stick up for them – ah, yes, I don't agree with all their methods. The miners' homes that I am talking about, they've got everything, and if they get fed up with it next week they have a new one next again. This is . . . now I could tell you where to go to see it, if you like, but this is the God's gospel truth. The majority of them, they are wasting it, because they haven't got the sense to do anything with it. This is what's getting my goat – I mean, what are they doing with it? It's the . . . you've not got the in-between bit, there should be an in-between bit. But why doesn't the working people get a good way of living without all this fighting, all this striving to . . . why don't they get it?

6.   Jean Mormont

Jean Mormont was born in North London in the 1920s into a large family of eighteen children. She went to work in a clothing factory and left home during the war to join the ATS.

She married after the War and has seven children. She became a night cleaner in order to earn extra money – because there were no nurseries for her children, she could not take a job during the day. Despite intense fatigue accumulated over the years, Jean Mormont tried to improve conditions for night cleaners by getting them to join the Transport and General Workers Union. She helped set up the Night Cleaners' Action Group, which included May Hobbs and members of the Women's Liberation Movement. The difficulties proved enormous and she emerged from several years of struggle disillusioned with her encounter with trade unions. 'I've had such a bloomin' rough time with these cleaners – I thought I'd like to join in something that would show them they're not the boss all the time – that they can't treat us like dirt and that.'

Her family have nearly all grown up now except for her young son, Darrin. She has now stopped doing night cleaning.

Childhood

'I sort of took the strictness, I was so used to it.'

My father was very strict. He was very strict, yes, because as far as I remember it was with all of us. He wouldn't let you do nothing, he used to . . . I can always remember you used to have to sit at the table and you wouldn't dare open your mouth, you wouldn't dare speak. You know he was very strict.

My mother was just the opposite, but she couldn't sort of be easy with you because of, like, my father. She would when he was away, and she'd let you do things that you couldn't do when he was there, sort of thing. There were all sorts of things – you know, you could never bring friends in or anything like that if he was in. You had to mind your p's and q's and you had to be careful what you said and, you know, he was a very strict man, I mean I could ask my mother for money, but I couldn't, I'd never dare ask my father for money. Never. [Laughs.] He was the lord and master. He used the belt and the buckle end. I think some of them [her brothers and sisters] left home because of that, yes. I can remember two or three of my bigger brothers really get to fight with him, and they were big, really big, you know. I was still small at the time.

I sort of took the strictness, I was so used to it, I didn't know any different. But I had a lot more than what they had. I had a lot more things you see. I had a better life than what they had. They had a harder life, but we never went without, you know. I mean we weren't poor and that. He was very strict, that was the main thing – even to me, because I was, what, twenty-one – before I got married and that – and I used to have to be in at ten o'clock at night then. They'd have a fit now, see my kids. [Laughs.]

But my mother never done a lot from what I can remember. I can never remember her doing a lot – maybe she did, maybe she did . . . When they was all little, she probably had to. But from what I can remember she never worked. I can always remember my mother sitting at the window. Sitting looking out the window, that's the memory I've got of my mum. When I lived there with her and I was having my second girl, like, my boy was still small, he was getting on three, I could sit him out the front – I knew he was safe because my mother was sitting by the window. I knew she would watch him, she never used to move from there. But I think I understand more now myself, because I think after having a few children like that – I mean she had a hell of a lot, and I've only had seven, but it does take all the life out of you, this is true. I mean you don't realize it till you get older. I mean I know how I feel myself sometimes. I think to myself, I used to think to myself that she was lazy, but I realize now I'm older, I realize it myself, she must have been ill in herself, she just couldn't do it. Because I know I get me good days and I get me bad days like, but I can still nip around, but it does pull you down, it's true, it does. I can never remember my mother looking young. My mother was fat, and I think maybe that makes you look older.

School

'You used to get the cane for the least little thing.'

Then, like, you went right through one school, you never went, you know, from one school – from juniors to a different school. You went in the infants and you stayed there until you left school, and I left school on the Friday before war was declared. War was declared on the Sunday, I left on the Friday. I loved school.

My mother used to make me go shopping in the morning before I went to school, and I was always late. I was always late because it was quite a way to school, we used to have to walk like, and I was late every morning. I used to have to go and get the shopping because . . . and I used to get told off, and I was too frightened to say that it was me mother making me late [laughs] because we used to get the cane. [Laughs.] You used to get the cane for the least little thing.

I loved needlework. I used to love that and writing. I loved writing, I used to do a lot of writing. I don't do it now, but I did. My father always said to me, 'You've got lovely handwriting,' but I haven't now. I know, he used to buy me these special pens that do, you know, a certain kind of writing. He used to buy me these pens. I used to be good, you know, even though I say it myself. I used to be ever so good at expressing myself, but I couldn't now, I'm getting old now, it won't come. I haven't got much time and all. Time is the thing.

Work

'To me it was great you know . . . It was my first taste of life.'

Well, I went into a factory. I was going to learn tailoring, and the money wasn't very good, and you know . . . and I did stay there for a while. Then I went into another factory and I was a machinist. I was fourteen when I left school. I got a pound a week. I used to have to take my wage packet home. I wouldn't dare open it, just take it home unopened [laughs], and then my mother gave me a few shillings. The school found you a job. It never used to be much. It was nearly all factory work and that, you know. And then, you know, you meet other girls at work, and they tell you, you know, they can do this and do that – well, then me and my mother fell out. [Laughs.] I mean I used to sometimes have to come home and do the housework at night. I was getting on, I was about seventeen, and my sister said to me, 'Why don't you join the forces, get away if you want to.' So I did. [Laughs.]

I told my mother, she went mad like. You know, she didn't see that it give you a chance to get away like, see the world. I joined the ATS. I was in there till the war ended, like. It was a jolly good life, yes. I enjoyed it, you see, because you got so much freedom in there, like that – I wasn't [laughs] used to it. To me it was great, you know. We used to have dances and all sorts, you know, and I thought, oh, this is the life! [Laughs.] I went to Guildford in Surrey for training, and then, well, they used to move you all over the place. I was in Leicester and then I was in Buckinghamshire, other places, you know, and I used to work in this office. This is all to do with writing, you know. And I was attached to the War Office, their place was in Buckinghamshire, that's where I stayed till the War ended like, and then I came out. It was only filling in forms and all sorts of things, but I used to enjoy it like, you know.

You meet all kinds of girls [laughs] – yes, I've met all sorts, you know. That's why I think it is a good life, because I'd never really been able to mix before that, and you meet people from all walks of life. I even got some shocks and all, you know, because I met some people, and you met girls I've never . . . I never knew what a lesbian was, and I met some girls in there, and it used to puzzle me, I couldn't make it out, you know, till I was told like, you know, by the other girls, what it was all about. I thought to myself, well, you're learning all the time, and I thought to myself, good job me mother don't know. [Laughs.] After the girls told me what it was all about, they used to lay on the bed there cuddling one another, and I thought to myself, that's funny, you know. [Laughs.] Yes, they do, they do. You know after a while you just don't take any notice of it. It's their way of life, and that's it. They don't interfere with you, or they don't try it on me, I didn't mind. [Laughs.]

You get girls from all walks of life there. Yes, you know, you get working-class girls and there was girls that come off of farms, their fathers had farms, and there was – we had two girls in our barrack-room, quite . . . you know, when I say 'talk posh', I don't mean to be rude, like. You know, very posh accent and that. Quite nice girls and that. All kinds. Like you had a choice during the war, you either went to work in the munitions factory – if you was single this was – or you went in the forces, or on the land, yes, that was like the forces – Women's Land Army. But you get girls coming in the ATS whose fathers had a farm and they want a change, you see. I quite enjoyed it. I thought it was very good. It was my first taste of life.

There was always dances, and you used to go out to shows and everything. They used to take you out in lorries, in the old army lorries. I was free and easy, I didn't even think about getting married. No, I wasn't really interested, you know. I don't think you could sort of make a life for yourself, because there was all the bombing going on, and I mean there was no point in anybody sort of buying a house for theirself, or trying to get a house. And you know, most of the girls, when they married men, they were in the forces, and they was away and that, so you was like a single girl, so there wasn't much point in it really. When you came home, life was so dull, you know. I came home because my father was ill, and my mother . . . I was going to go and live with my sister, and my mother wanted me to go home because my father was ill and that. I went home, he was dying like, he had cancer. I went home but you know he never died then because he was ill for a long time with it. They thought he had ulcers and they kept operating on him, and all the time it was cancer he had. I was married when he died.

Then me mother and I fell out again, and I did go and live with my sister. You see, my mother thought, you know, that she could say to me, 'Now you don't go out today at all,' – it might be Saturday or Sunday – 'I want this house cleaning from top to bottom,' – you see. Before, you used to just get on and do it. I used to go to work all day and come home and do the housework. She used to leave the housework, she'd just do what she wanted to do, like – that sort of thing. You see, I think, what it was, my sisters as they grew up they had to take it on, and she got so used to having it done that she never used to do a lot herself, you know. The boys had to chip in, do their bit – yes, sweep and that, washing up. Just the same, all the lot. I've got a brother who'd be a good housewife [laughs] – good training.

Well, I went back to machining, I was doing machining. I was also working in this tailor's. It was not a factory, he had a shop. The people brought things into the shop, and I'd do maybe a bit of pressing on the press and, you know, repairs and alterations, things like that. My brother worked there and that's how I got the job. You know, he was a good bloke, he was. A Jewish bloke. A very good bloke he was – you know, if he thought you deserved a bit more money – that was rare in them days – he would give it you. He was very good.

Marriage

'We only got married to get away from home.'

My husband had just come out of the army when I met him, and he was working on the building. They were just starting to build flats and that, you know, like after the bombing and that. I didn't know him for long and we got married. You see, we only got married to get away from home sort of thing, you know. [Laughs.] I've never been sorry, mind you, he's very good. I'm lucky. He used to come round to me, like, and that was one thing my mother wouldn't encourage, men round the door. They used to have to stand on the doorstep. She made an exception with my husband, you know, and he'd tell you if he was here. I believe she thought . . . she really loved him, she did. She loved him more than what she loved me, and that's true. She did, yes – she used to say to him, 'I don't know how you

stand her.' She did, honest. It's his nature, you know, he'd do anything for anybody, and you know she used to like a drink, the old
girl, she'd like a drop of whisky and that.

I lived in Hackney when I was first married. That's where my
husband comes from, down near the dog track. And when my father
was very ill, well, the bloke next door to my parents he promised us
the top flat in his house. But my brother came along and offered him
a bit more and got it, so [laughs] where did I end up? Back in me
mother's house. But my father was very ill, and he was dying then.
We lived upstairs.

We stayed there then, with the kids. No, I had one then and I was
having my second – 'course my father said to me, 'You're going to
have a girl,' and I did. The first baby was premature, and then they
used to keep you in until the baby's weight was five pounds. I think
now they let them out and just keep the baby. But they used to make
you stay in there because you used to have to feed them yourself.
You had no choice, you couldn't put them on the bottle if you wanted
to, you had to feed them yourself, and also you had to pay them in
the hospital. I wouldn't say it was a lot, but you used to have to pay.
He wasn't earning such a great deal, five pounds he was earning.
Mind you, five pounds went a long way then.

I was due in the February, and I – I can't stand people when they
are drunk, I hate it, especially men, and we was living at my sister-
in-law's at the time, and her husband came home and he was crawling
on the floor where he was so drunk, and I was terrified. I swear that's
what done it. Because next morning – that was Christmas Eve – on
Christmas Day I was in hospital, and I had the baby Christmas Day
and he was only four pounds two ounces. I had to stay in there. I was
there a whole month with him. Oh, I was going mad.

Although he was a very good baby, he was really a good baby. He
was ever so good. You know he was one of them babies you could
sit him in the pram and he'd sit there, no trouble. Mind you, he made
up for it later on. As he got older he was a sod, got me in no end of
trouble. It was a bit awkward because my sister-in-law had a baby an'
all. You see, it was only a small house, similar to this. She had a big
pram and I had a big pram, and of course it was very awkward, you

know, of a night – where to put the prams and all sorts, you know. But it was nice too – they used to sit out, they was near enough the same age. And they used to sit out the front together and I think maybe that's why they were so good, because they were company for each other, they would sort of amuse each other.

So I lived there until, I think, I was about six months pregnant with my second child, and then I moved down into my mother's place. I moved in with my mum because my dad was dying like, you know. She used to cry, and I used to feel sorry, you know. Anyway, we stayed there until my mother died. Oh Christ! My mother died, my father died, and my brother – they all died within eighteen months of each other. My father died, and then my brother had an accident with some iron at work, and then my mother died shortly after that.

In them days – I don't know if they still do it, but the landlord would only allow the house to be like in the husband's name. Then it could pass over to the wife's name, and then that's the finish. If he didn't want to let it to anybody, any of the rest of the family that was left in the house, well that's it, they had to go, you see. This is what he done to us. But I was living there, and my two single brothers were living there, you see, so we didn't move out. But he took us to court, you see, because we wouldn't go – he wanted to sell the house, you see. He took us to court, and the judge, he made my two single brothers get out. But as we had the children he didn't turn us out, he allowed us to stay there. We lived on – we moved down to the bottom. We made out we already had the bottom – we never you know – but we moved into the best part of the house, which annoyed him more because we had the best part, and he kept saying, 'Nobody will want to buy a house unless they can get the bottom part.' Anyway, he kept coming there threatening us with all sorts, with what he would do. We wouldn't be able to go out to the garden, only at certain times of the day and that. I said, 'I don't know how you are going to work that one out,' because we was on the bottom – it would have been whoever was upstairs wouldn't be able to go out in the garden through our kitchen. [Laughs.]

Anyway, he gave us such a dog's life, and then the coloured people was starting to come into the country, and this is what he threatened us with, that he would put a coloured family in with us. He said, 'That'll get you out,' and it really frightened me. They were just starting to use coloured people for this kind of thing, and I was getting a bit worried, because if it's yourself, you know, you don't care, but when you've got kids . . . So two or three people came and looked at the house – you know, coloured people. I asked, you know, if they were going to take the house, going to buy it. We enquired, and 'None of your business', we was told and all that. So I said, 'Well, we're going to have a dog's life,' – we could judge by that – 'he's going to tell them coloured people what he's going to do to get us out, you know. Making our lives a misery now.' Anyway, he came along with the bright idea and he said, 'Now look,' he said, 'I don't want to see you have any trouble, I don't want to put anyone in to aggravate you,' and that. He said, 'I'll tell you what, I'll pay you to get out.' So I said, 'That's no good to me,' you see, because the places were getting scarce then, you couldn't just go and get a place. 'Money's no good to me – not what you're going to give me, anyway. You're not going to give me enough to buy a house,' I said. So he said, 'But I'll give you a flat to go with it.' I said, 'All right, fair enough – let's have a look at the flat.' And he took us to Islington – God, it was under ground [laughs] – oh dear! But, you know, there was wet half-way up the wall, and your front room was literally under the pavement – people were walking over it – and this is what he was gonna give us to get us out. So I said, 'No, not with my kid. No.' Anyway, we said we weren't going to budge, and a couple of weeks later he came back and he offered us this other flat, which was quite nice, it was. It was a ground floor, but the kitchen was in the basement – just the kitchen, our bedroom and living room – two bedrooms and living room – was up in the ground floor, which was quite nice, so we took that.

My husband had gone into the timber trade then, he went into like a wood-yard. The timber-yard where he worked was only at the bottom of our road. I don't know if you know the timber-yards at all in Tottenham – there's lots of them, along the River Lea there. When we moved up to Islington it was quite a way, and by the time he paid his fares and that it wasn't worth it, so he went to work in a factory. He used to make the icecream, and that was a really good job, he used to get good money in that. We used to sort the money out between us, you know – what's got to be paid out and that – and he has his bit for spending. I've never had any worry at all, he's always been good.

Weekends we were never in. We used to go all up – maybe just up Hyde Park, Trafalgar Square and all round there, just maybe sight-seeing and – you know, just take the kids somewhere different and that, you know. Always had the kids with me, always had the kids. I used to have a friend, we used to go to the pictures, maybe once a week. I can always go out, I mean, he never tied me down. It was the same with him, I'd never tie him down, he could always go out if he wanted to. He's homely, see. I know he never used to like me going out, and, you know, he thought I should be that way, but I used to. After all, I've got to have a little break, and I used to go out at least once a week.

I never went on holiday until 1955. We went to Thorpe Bay for a week. We stayed in a caravan with the three children. It was a change. It was still sort of . . . you know, you had to cook and – yes, it wasn't what you'd call a relaxing holiday. [Laughs.] But it made a change.

I've got seven children. The youngest, he's five. I keep wondering where he came from. The others are like, you know, all grown up. I've got two married, I've got a grandson, I'm a grandma an' all. My daughter, you know, she's having a baby at Christmas. I've got one of nineteen here, one is seventeen, one sixteen. She's starting work next week. And Carol, well she'll be fifteen in October. Then Darrin, he's five. He was a shock – oh, I couldn't put it into words! Oh, I nearly died, I did really, and that's the truth. See, I started my change, you see, my periods had stopped for two or three months, that's what I thought it was. And then I started taking queer and the doctor said, 'I'll send you up to the hospital,' and I went to the hospital, St Thomas's, and they said, 'You're pregnant.' And I said, 'I'm on the change,' and he said, 'You might be but you're still pregnant.' Oh dear, well he looked at my face, I know what I looked like, but he said, 'It's not the end of the world, you know.' [Laughs.]

I wouldn't be without him now. Oh, he's lovely. He's just started school at the top here. All that running backwards and forwards, I'm getting too old for it. [Laughs.] Oh dear, I'll tell you, when I knew I was having him, you know, the older ones were quite big and I thought to myself, whatever will they think? I said to my boy, 'Here,' I said, 'I'm going to have a baby.' 'Cor, that's lovely,' he said. I was really shocked. They was more pleased than what I was. They were, yes.

The only thing my mum had ever said to me was 'Don't have a load of kids.' You know, I got annoyed really, cos I thought to myself, what, how come you're telling me not to have a load of kids? I suppose she learned the hard way, you know, and she would try to tell me, sort of thing. Well, one thing like, you know, even for a man to use family planning, you never had the money to spare to buy them, you see, this was one thing. And when family planning did come in, I'd got all mine then except Darrin [laughs] and I wish I'd gone, and you know I'd got them all and I thought to myself, I'm not likely to have any more. You know, you get cocky like, and I just didn't bother. I think, after about five years, you know, and you've no kids and you think to yourself, well, I'm not going to have any more – not after having them sort of one after the other. It just proves you never know.

I was ill all the time I was carrying him. I was in and out of hospital, I had to have blood transfusions. The thing was I had my periods all the time that I was carrying him. I was a bit worried, because I thought to myself, going all that time, you know, but it was no trouble at all, the birth, as easy as anything. Well I was only in there forty-eight hours and I came home, because I wanted to have him at home, you see, because I had five of them at home, because it was so much better, you know. When you was in hospital, then, there was only two nights a week for visiting, you know, that your husband could come in to see you, and only your husband could come anyway, and you know it was so . . . you had to do this and you had to do that. When you had them at home, if you felt like getting up you could get up, you see, but in them days they used to make you lay in bed. They don't now, I know. This was this thrombosis and that. The baby would be about three to four days old before you could get out of bed. They made me because of my age, yes.

Mothers and Daughters

Well it just wasn't done to talk to my mother about family planning – you never – my daughters they come to me about it, I couldn't talk to my mother. My mother would tell me to – well you wouldn't dare for a start, but if I said to her some of the things they come and tell me, I probably would have got a good hiding – just for saying it, you know. I suppose it was the way they were brought up and they didn't know no different, but it made me determined that I wouldn't give my kids the life that I had. I wouldn't be so hard. I know my mother couldn't help it, you know like, but I'm more stricter than what my husband is with them. Because he is very easy-going, but I have to put my foot down now and again or else there wouldn't be no discipline at all. I was determined though that they would be able to come to me, because I could never go to my mother about nothing.

As I say, they come to me about anything. I mean, they sit here and they talk about anything in front of us. I mean they don't try and hide anything, which is what I like. I'd sooner they do that than be . . . you know, go outside and do it. I let them bring their friends home, because I think to myself, I know where they are, I know who they are with, and they don't try and deceive you then. I mean, I've got a woman next door, she's got a daughter and she wouldn't let her daughter do nothing, and her daughter tells her all the lies under the sun, you see. She comes in here and the woman is talking to me over the fence and she's telling me things that I know jolly well are lies but I just keep quiet, because I think to myself, I don't want to get involved sort of thing. But it is her own making, it's the way she treats her, you see.

I'll tell you what, you sort of grew up quick during the war. Sometimes I think to myself, I can't remember being all that young. You had to grow up even though you was young because, I suppose, of the bombing and all that. You sort of never had much of a teen-ager's life, because you had to either go in the forces or work in one of the munitions factories or something like that. I think it made you more grown up. You know I think to myself sometimes, these girls, you know, for all the dressing up and doing all that, and they think they're so old, but they're so young in their ways.

My eldest girl she stayed on at school. She only stayed on for a year, but these, they can't get out of school quick enough. They don't bother in these schools, I'm shocked. You know, they're worse round this way. Where I lived in Battersea you expect it, but I didn't expect it round here – they're worse. You know, my girl hasn't been to school for months, they don't want her down there because she's leaving. She used to go down there and they used to send her home. She's been waiting to start work. They haven't got the teachers or there's nothing to do, or you sit in a room and read a book. They don't want her down there.

Work after Marriage

'The mad scramble in the morning.'

I used to go cleaning early in the morning, at half past four, to get there by five and back by half past seven before my husband left for work. I used to get two pounds ten shillings a week. It gave you a break as well. It was something different from just being in the house with the kids and that. I would have liked to do it even if I didn't need the money, but that was the main reason. I could never get out during the day when the kids were growing up, they was all different ages, and the only jobs that were going were cleaning jobs in them hours that I wanted to suit me like. It's all you could do.

When you are younger you can take it in your stride, sort of thing, and I've always been used to working hard because I used to have to work hard at home and it didn't come as no shock to me, like, when I had the kids, I just got on with it. They was there and they was all small together, and they used to play together and I used to do my washing during the day. I used to wash them, put them to bed, I used to do most of my housework of a night. My husband's very, very good, like. He cooks the dinner every night. Yes, because I go out as he's coming in. He cooks the dinner every night – I get it all ready for him, sort of thing, I come home and my dinner is ready for me, it's all washed up. He's always looked after me, done all the washing and everything, never had to have anybody in. He's very good.

That night work was really getting me down, it was getting I couldn't stand it any more. I don't know how I used to manage then really, but I did. I used to just get snatches of sleep. When my husband came in I used to jump straight into bed and perhaps get a couple of hours' kip. It was my own fault because he used to keep telling me to give it up and I used to think to myself, well, I shall be that much money short. But when I did give it up, I thought to myself that I was silly really, because if I had sat down and took notice of him I could have give it up a long time ago. I think I was afraid I wouldn't have enough for this and that, you know. I was silly really because I could have managed, because, I mean, if he thinks I've not got nothing and he's got it I don't have to ask, he'll give it to me. I'm independent like that, I wouldn't ask, I'd go without – that's me.

To have to ask for anything, even to him – because he's told me off many a time – I couldn't even ask him, I'd sooner go without. I don't know what it is. And he'd go mad if he finds out that perhaps I'd gone short, because he always give it me. He don't smoke and he likes a drink. If my son and his wife come and stay then he'll go out and have a drink with them – we could go like, but I usually don't bother. He's got a scooter that he goes to work on, other than buying his petrol and that . . . He might go a few months and I might say to him I need some money for so and so and he'd say, 'All right, I'll give you that, don't worry about that.' It's maybe what he saves out of his money what he has for the week – if he don't spend it, he'll save it. If I want it, I can have it. He's been very good. He's in the Post Office and they came out on strike – he don't believe in all this, mind, he ain't got a lot of time for the unions.

My nephew said to me, he said, 'They'd stab you in the back, them unions,' he said, 'they say one thing to your face and they do another thing behind your back,' and I laughed at him, like. And it's true, from what I've seen – I mean, I didn't see a lot, it's true – because they just couldn't give two hoots for you. It's all number one, that's all they're after, number one. They're not concerned with the workers, they don't care. It was the men's thing, wasn't it, years ago? The union. I never had any real dealings, but when I was telling my nephew – he used to have quite a bit to do with the unions in the GPO – and I said to him I was thinking of, you know, joining the union and he said, 'You don't want to dabble. I'll tell you, they'll stab you in the back.' I laughed at him and that, and then I thought quite a bit of what he told me was true, what I've seen for myself. Maybe not with every union, but with that particular union, that Transport and General Workers', and them men that we had on there – well, they're bloody useless.

We used to start night cleaning at ten and get out about a quarter to six. See, she [the supervisor] was all right in there, she was all right until that union came in there, and then they was afraid for what was going to happen. You see, I mean, she was the kind of woman that if you let her get on top of you, you see, she could take liberties with you, she would. But if you gave her as good as she gave you, that's OK – you could go in there and you wouldn't see her all night. But if she thought she could take liberties with you she'd be up on that floor and she'd be behind you all night long, or the forelady would – she'd send the forelady up to you. I remember when I first went there, – cos I was very quiet when I first went there – I'll tell you, what really made me speak up, because it's so frightening in them buildings like of a night, and it'd be so quiet, you'd perhaps look round and you'd just see somebody move back, and I thought to myself, no, I'm getting tired, I'm seeing things. Then it would happen again. It would be either her or the forelady up there spying to see and make sure you're not sleeping and that, or sitting down. That made my nerves bad, it made my nerves worse, imagining that there was somebody there and that. Anyway I heard a couple of them having a go, so I thought to myself, oh, that's what you do, is it? I'll have to try that, cos she used to swear at you like anything in there. I never heard such terrible language until I went in there, then I ended up using it, because you had to. Yes you did. I used to hear these girls, and I thought to my-self, I don't know. She used to just sit there and laugh, and I thought, oh, that's the way is it? And next time, one night I was on the floor and I just let rip up there, said a few choice words. I said, 'I know you're up there,' and all the rest of it – she never bothered me at all after that.

You see – oh, God – it was safety precautions – you weren't allowed a window, you wasn't allowed the air conditioning, the doors were locked. Because I wrote to the factory inspector, he came in there one night, but they ganged up on me. You see, there was just me, and there was three of them from the cleaning company, there was four of them from Shell, they knew the man was coming in. I didn't even know the man was coming in, he never even wrote to me. He wrote to Shell, he wrote to the cleaning company, never dropped me a line. I put my own address on it. 'Course they came up on me, all together, and you know, I told the factory inspector what the trouble was. I said, 'I'm gasping for me breath in here some nights.' He said, 'You've got enough ventilation coming up the lift shaft.' So I said, 'OK, when I feel I'm going to faint I've got to run to the lift, put me head down the shaft.' That's the tripe they used to talk to you.

The trouble was, we were contracted out, you see, we never worked for Shell, so the union couldn't get in the building. You was beaten before you started because of that. Shell was dead against it, because they never had a union, they had what they call – I used to read through their magazines in there – they used to have a staff something, and they had their say that way. There was some of them in there, they were after getting a union, because I was reading it in one of their magazines.

The man in there – somebody in Shell personnel – I never met the man and he was telling people in there that I was a Communist and this was all political. I never met the man at all, and yet when there was trouble and they bring in somebody from the cleaning company or from Shell, he said, 'Yes, but you're a Communist, aren't you? It's all political.' 'I don't know what you're bleedin' talking about,' I said. 'Where did you get that one from?' I said. He said, 'Well, so-

and-so told me.' 'Well, who's he?' I said, 'I don't even know him.' 'You know him, he's the personnel.' I said, 'I've never met the man, and the man never met me, so how he knows what me politics are and whether I'm Communist or what I don't know.' You was, you know, fighting a losing battle in there, there was so many people against you.

Women

'You should have a fair share.'

Well, then I got to know the girls that belonged to Women's Liberation and I went to a couple of meetings and that, and I thought to myself, it's a good thing for anybody who may be a bit tied down, need to know what's going on and that, but I used to enjoy going to the meetings and listening to them. I thought, yes, it's a good thing if the women are fighting for something, and there's something they especially want, and they are that dedicated. If it's something they really want, that's it, that's how it should be.

You should have a fair share. Because I mean I know I've got sisters – two of my sisters – one of them's not so bad now, but one of my sisters, she had seven children and her husband he went off and left her. Her youngest one was three months old and the oldest one was only at school – she had seven! And she brought them all up and they're all married and they're bloody good kids. But I thought to myself, maybe you would do it if you was in the same position, but I thought, God, I don't know how she done it. She could have had them kids put in a home, and she wouldn't part with them, she brought them all up. She was ill, because at the time when she had them all little he – I don't know where he went but they couldn't even trace him. He was in the army and he deserted – he was in the Royal Marines and he deserted – and they couldn't trace him and she had to live off the Assistance Board. And in them days when she was . . . especially if they knew there was no man, you know, they were just dealing with the woman, they just give you what you've got to have and that's it. You get nothing more, don't matter what state you was in. If it wasn't for one of my brothers she would have starved to death, because she used to go without to give them kids, she'd go without for days, because I remember we used to help her, you know, we all used to help her. She'd starve, go without for days to give them kids, but she wouldn't part with them. They're all married now, every single one of them, bloody good kids, but she's ill, she's down in Norfolk now, with one of her married daughters. So that's what a man done to her.

I still do a little job like, but I do it in the evening. In September I'm going to work in the school, up the top here. I'm going to pack this evening work up and I'm going to work in a school for a few hours, private school up the top here, which will suit me better. I can do it during the day and I'll be home in the evening, and any holiday they get I shall be home with him [Darrin]. If I went out to work anywhere else during the day I would have to leave him with the girl, and I don't like doing that because, as big as they are, I like to be here with him. Sometimes the older they get the worse they get – they're worse – she torments him. I think, if I'm here I know what's going on, and that's it. She can go off out if she wants. Then I'm home with him.

7.   Peggy Wood

Peggy Wood has lived most of her life abroad because of her husband's work – he is a doctor specializing in tropical medicine. They both come from Protestant Northern Irish families and now live in a peaceful suburb of London. Peggy teaches in the local further education college and her husband is due for retirement soon. Two of their children are grown up and the third, in her teens, is away at boarding school.

She spent a long time vividly describing her childhood and adolescence, the War and her early married life, and it was her decision to end her story at that point, although obviously she has led a rich and varied life all over the world.

Childhood

'My parents thought I was absolutely bloody Christmas.'

Well, to begin with, you see, I began by being an absolute rank outsider, by being born in Northern Ireland, which makes it sound much more different because everybody always thinks, oh, Ulster, violence . . . As I saw it at the time, I lived in a province, and I wanted to get to the capital city. For a long time, in my teens I suppose, it didn't seem that there was any difference in being Irish, because we were so totally British. My enclosed, safe childhood was like living in Durham, or living in somewhere less pleasant than Aberdeen, or Inverness – you know, that I lived in a province, rather like, I think, West Indians felt they were British. You know, I feel I have an understanding about this feeling. This London is my capital city so I wanted to come to it. And this is my place and I now belong. London's it. And I think theoretically London always was. So that's that.

My childhood was enclosed, and – you know, protected and happy. My parents thought I was absolutely bloody Christmas. The difficulty about that was that I have an older sister, who wasn't Christmas because she wasn't so clever as I was. I had the great currency of being clever, and therefore able to please my parents, so I cashed in on that, and I had a very happy childhood. I had agonies – and who doesn't? – but I do get on very well with my sister now, and I have a guilt feeling about her, that I did better than she did as a child, that I jumped on her shoulders, you know? She was three years older. Just the two of us. That's very significant. Because my father has said in my hearing, and it was certainly reported to me many times by my mother, 'She's far better than any boy.'

Now when I was a child I was very proud of this, and it wasn't until middle age and looking back I began to realize that this was his way of compensating for the fact that he would have liked a boy, and that he was too good and too intelligent a man to allow himself to think that. So I was . . . as good as any boy. I went to co-ed school, so I didn't have the normal hang-ups that happen, because I went to a co-ed school and I was as good as any boy, and there was no problem. I climbed trees like anything, I used to win a hundred yards sprint, you know. Not competing with the boys, because – er – I competed with them intellectually, and I wasn't really very keen on games, so therefore I regarded that as a non-intellectual pastime for stupid people.

In fact, I think my mother was perhaps – they had a very poetic relationship, my parents – and I think in a way she may have been slightly undersexed. I don't know, it's difficult to judge with your parents, but certainly we were always dressed very plainly, and I think it was part of a class thing. My mother was middle-class, my father had worked himself up from working-class, having left school at the age of eleven or something, you know. Strictly working-class, and had worked himself up partly by brain-power because he was intelligent, and he worked in insurance . . . a lot of insurance – you know, going back and forth to England and all this sort of sea travel and he was a great expert on it, and he knew which company to put what shipping with. He knew a lot about shipping and insurance, and this is how he made a meagre amount for us to live on – it wasn't very much. But anyway, they sang together, they played the piano, they took us to theatres, to local drama leagues – all this kind of thing. They were sort of intellectual in that strictly provincial way. Still, in a nineteenth-century way, created at home. Art, I mean – my mother played the piano, my father sang, they went to the amateur theatre and their friends were acting – you know, this kind of . . . I suppose it was the same as the provinces in this island, I don't know. I imagine so, so that's that.

My father wasn't in the '14–'18 War cos he had a bad heart, but he lived with a bad heart till the age of sixty-five, then he died of it. And his firm that he was in went bust in '22 so he started out on his own, as an agent in insurance, in Belfast. There was no air travel, so everything came and went by sea. Produce of Ireland went over to England. The raw materials for the factories came from England, because, let's face it, that's what was the basis of this Irish thing, that they had no raw materials by the time it gets to the twentieth century, so the coal boats came in, the iron boats came in, the ships were built, the food went across there, the clothes came back. Everything went back and forwards. We always got the local paper and we got something like the *Daily Express* or the *Daily Mail*, one English and one local paper. And while I was small I didn't really know which was which. It took me a long time to sort out that I wasn't English, you know. You know, it wasn't important.

However, there's that, so it's fairly simple to understand, this picture which I'm giving you of the parents with very little money. My mother, who had had a slightly genteel education, being bloody determined her girls were going to get a real education and not be restricted as she was. She had been brought up to be a nice girl. She'd been brought up to paint, and play the piano, and all that kind of thing, and her parents didn't like her marrying my father because he was low class. He was rather gorgeous to look at, and, er, I don't know what else, I suppose they wouldn't have liked him because he wasn't moving up in the world, although in fact by the time I was aware, they were roughly at the same level, my father had got himself there. Therefore, what they wanted was education for their daughters. So they sent us to a rather rough, tough co-ed school, and compensated for that, as my neighbours do here in exactly the same way. If they send them to the local comprehensive they'll have, you know, music lessons, and go and play the violin and all that carry-on. You know the way parents who enjoy creative art of one kind or another try to pass it on to their children if they think they're not getting it at school. OK, we had all that. And I was a roaring success you see, everything I did I did well.

I also was taught, in a negative way, to discount looks. I mean, I still see myself, although I have been told to the contrary from time to time, as plain – I never saw myself as good-looking. This is my mother, and also my father wouldn't have liked it either, because I think it's a class thing too, isn't it? – that the working-class kids are allowed to be sexy younger, whereas aspiring middle-class kids are kept – the sex is kept repressed until older. And this works out at an even higher level, public schools and so forth are meant to be sexless. You know, twinsets and pearls till they're eighteen – certainly were in my day – and then they're let loose under mama's control. So that it was a class thing too, of emerging from working-class to be lady-like, to be non-sexy. I wasn't allowed to have bows in my hats. I longed for ribbons, you know.

I accepted it because the chaps that made passes at me I despised, because they were stupid. I had what I would imagine are normal teenage fantasies that I would fall in love with Yehudi Menuhin, or the Prince of Wales, or something like this, you know. And it was all sublimated in all this bloody work, you see – playing the violin and all this carry-on. It worked as far as they were concerned. I used to think the curate was wonderful and that kind of thing. Then I had a few passes with chaps at school, but there was a funny conflict there that (a) I despised them and (b) I had the underlying conviction that I was really far more sexy than they were, and they didn't know it. And that I would enjoy sex far more than I thought they would, for they were stupid. I certainly think this is right. I think life bears me out! [Laughter.]

So there's my mother and my father from slightly different class backgrounds. No doubt there were conflicts in this because my grandparents, that's my mother's parents, lived in the house with us in my late teens, because they lived to be quite old and they got rather weak and my mother had to look after them. She worked desperately hard, cleaning the house and making afternoon tea and meals with proper puddings and things – and a great big awful kitchen which of course one never ate in. The house was geared for the generation before, when there were maids. By the late thirties we could not afford a maid if there were any anyway. We had had a maid when we were small for some reason or other. That was easy. They all came from Donegal and got £20 a year and had to be taught how to live – how to use the lavatory for example.

The south of Ireland we despised as being a sort of peasant place, whereas we lived in a civilized country – England, Northern Ireland, whatever it might be. We were civilized. And the War was in the past, and the downtroddenness of women was in the past, because we lived in the present, and history was all over because of the League of Nations. History had stopped. I suppose many children had this idea, that history had stopped, and history was foolishness, as the West Indians say, foolishness. And now we were all wise and sensible and had the League of Nations and women were, you know, free. We had education and we could do anything, but anything. There was no problem. None. Because there we were, you know. My sister did all right. She got her School Certificate because she wanted to be a nurse, which the family didn't really hold with, because they wanted her to be something a bit grander than a nurse. They didn't want her doing something sort of potentially menial – so potentially down-trodden.

They were much more pleased with me. They first of all saw me teaching music, and then the headmaster of the school, who was a very sensible man, said, 'Look, if you let that girl do a university scholarship she'll get there,' and of course new horizons opened, and she got there. You know, they couldn't have afforded that. It must have been jolly hard for them not to have me earning, because they – but I can understand it, they got enough emotional satisfaction out of this to do them a lifetime – you know, this was everything.

University and Sexuality

'The realization that I could be sexy and intelligent.'

So I left school, having had a few flirtations with this and that which were not very satisfactory, because, as I say, I despised the men who found me attractive. At that stage I was getting a bit gloomy, because I decided: I'm clever and plain. My sister and my cousins were pretty and attractive and could play tennis and other social accomplishments and will get taken to dances, and I'll have to have a career. It was still the idea, one or the other. This was latent, it wasn't conscious, it was sort of . . . assumed, by me, that by being clever and plain I therefore could not be sexually attractive, so therefore any man who wanted me, it was obvious he only wanted his satisfaction out of it, not mine, and this wasn't poetic love like I saw in my parents – 'But one man loved the pilgrim soul in her' – you know, Yeats. It worked, that marriage.

So this was rather a gloomy time and I made myself stay on at school because I had to get this bloody scholarship. And that meant I had the humiliation of having to wear a gym tunic and long black stockings, which were far from glamorous then, until the age of eighteen, and most of my schoolfriends had either left at O-level or School Certificate, which was the entry to university. People went off to do medicine and so forth, off to do teacher training or whatever, but with a scholarship you had to do an extra year, rather like you have to for Oxbridge now – only two of us in the class, and of course I was the head girl, and therefore had to perform. There I was made less sexy by wearing this sexless uniform – this gym tunic, you know, and the long stockings and the Minnie Mouse shoes, which now girls would think were terribly glamorous, but to me . . . It was a bitter price I had to pay. But it was a price I wanted to pay because I wanted to get to London and to see the world, and travel, and haven't I bloody done that! You know, so therefore whatever dissatisfactions there may be, that fantasy was fulfilled.

And so I wanted to get out, I wanted to travel, and the way I had been trained – or 'conditioned' is the word – to see this was education, and I think they were right. I got out. I wouldn't have got out if I hadn't got educated and I wouldn't have got educated if I hadn't got the scholarship. So OK, I'm what I am because they conditioned me and I did the things they wanted me to. I've got some of the things I want and that was the way I got it. I got my scholarship, not only to the Queen's University of Belfast but to Trinity College, Dublin, which was foreign and different and much more civilized element of capital city and good theatres and conversation. Dublin still has this sort of element of civilization which is 'continental', you know, lacking in other – in provincial cities in the United Kingdom.

This was in 1938 – with the War looming. I had already spent a summer in Germany, because I was doing French and German, and had a passionate but very decorous affair with a young German, which was terribly lyrical and beautiful and terribly satisfying and terribly sad, because I had to leave him for ever and go back to university. I mean it was nice, but we didn't sleep together – oh no! My God, I might have got pregnant! You have to realize that in my kind of set-up, pregnancy was not something you dared risk. I mean, I – I had in my mind that if I ever did get pregnant, suicide would be the only practical way out. You know, there was no – it just wasn't on. It was literally a fate worse than death. I mean, you couldn't. I don't think I could have faced it. I don't know what I would have done. I couldn't have borne the shame for my parents, and their disappointment, and I wouldn't have known where to go or what to do. I had too much sound common sense to take that risk, I knew more what I was after. That was just foolishness, there was plenty of literature – you know, from Faust onwards – to tell you where that led you. It wasn't worth the risk, it really wasn't. You know. There was no way of finding out about contraception. There was no way. So that you just dare not take the risk. I imagine if I had got pregnant I would have attempted suicide, and landed up in hospital, and somebody would then have dealt with me. I imagine that's what happened to girls in my kind of situation there. As far as I was concerned it was simply not possible – I mean, that was just the end. It was something you couldn't cope with.

I sometimes wonder – you know, we had just as much excitement out of sex. Well I can see that that's totally unnecessary, all that agony, and why shouldn't they all have a lovely sexy time, but – er – I wonder. Certainly our emotions were perhaps – no, I don't suppose our emotions were very different, cos it must be exactly the same. I feel it's more the same than perhaps my children realize. I think they think we were so deprived we must have been – you know, absolutely holding on to the furniture – to keep from going mad. But, it wasn't – I don't really think it was desperately different, because I think at that stage one is so emotional at the – you know, by the time you've had a bit of sex, well, you're after it again twenty-four hours later, so what the hell, you know? I don't really think that it was all that different. I mean, how can I know? The only way I can know is by imagination and art and so forth. So I don't see myself as so deprived. It was a different kind of worry. In some ways it was a simplification. I wouldn't recommend it. I mean, I don't want to go back to that. I don't want anybody to go back to that. But in my set-up chastity of a limited kind was the only possibility and the path through life was clearer.

So I grew a little bit older and had this lyrical affair. I've forgotten about him for years! But it was awfully nice, you know. It really was quite gorgeous. Lyrical and the woods and all that, because it was so poetic, the way young love always is, Keats and all that. It was totally Keats. I never got farther than chaste kisses and passionate letters and Fanny, but I *felt* it all and it didn't last. It was all going to end. So it didn't take too long to get over. I tried to keep it a lot longer in my mind, you know, and to play it up, but it didn't really because university was so exciting.

The thing about university was that – the liberation of that was the realization that I could be good-looking, attractive, womanly, sexy *and* intelligent. This was the revelation of going to Dublin and not, to me, to a provincial English university, as Queen's University was, because most of my girlfriends, you know, they were wearing flat shoes, and I tell you that was unglamorous, and they had their hair straight, and I tell you that was unglamorous, and they didn't wear make-up, and I tell you that was unglamorous. They were all busy passing exams like mad, whereas I was going to glamorous dances and having fascinating conversations through the night, and er, you

know – you know, the joys of drink and sex. But again, no bed – not
safe, not possible. Everything short of – bed; not intercourse. It's
wonderful, incredible, how one has this self-control.

My parents left books lying around the house. They told me a bit
– my mother told me about sex, but told me in a slightly mawkish
way too young, and embarrassed me very much by telling me very
early on when I was in the bath, and I felt conscious of being naked
in front of my mother. It was an odd thing, must have been before I
had the curse, because I think I had that at the age of about thirteen,
because it was theoretically supposed to be fourteen in those days –
everything went in sevens you see. You came of age when you were
twenty-one and you had the curse when you were fourteen. My
cousin was very mature, she got the curse at eleven. That was very,
very odd – she had breasts already at that age, you know – very odd.
And she in fact did marry very young. I had far too much pain and
trouble about it, and it was a kind of – well, must be sensible about it,
but, er, you know, you couldn't be expected to play games of the same
order when you had the curse. Quite the reverse from what came up
from our elder daughter when she was that age – you know, you
must play games like mad, exercise is good.

It was a limitation, and I think it was a kind of way out into mini-
invalidism, which I have been aware of at times myself happens
through life. I'm supposed to be not all that tough . . . I had scarlet
fever when I was very young and nearly died, and therefore I was
slightly miraculous – you know, the way children are who are very
dicey at the time. This added to my sort of – you know, built me up
with my parents. It must have been beastly for my sister. I mean we
can talk about that now, she and I. So that I think there was a sort of
idea that the curse was a sort of weakening, and I used to lose a hell of
a lot of blood and feel rather dreary. But with the background of the
feminists who were so masculine, you know, so – I didn't like them
either, but I admired them, because they'd fought battles which I had
the benefit of, so therefore I had respect for them. But it was a pity
they had to be so sexless. And I was lucky because, you see, I could be
sexy because of their battles.

My mother would talk about sex in a poetical way and I despised her for this when I grew up. But later on I understood more, because you cannot talk about your sex life to your child, it's difficult, and I don't want my children envisaging my sex life. I mean, we can have better sex when they're not in the house. It's a sort of limiting factor. There must be a terrible taboo somewhere, I don't know. Oh God, bloody Oedipus. The man is so . . . I get so bloody mad at Freud anyway, you know, I want to be a bit suspicious of that. But anyway that's a taboo that I must be involved in, and therefore don't find so unacceptable in my mother as I did at the time. But sex was something my father could not have spoken to – to his daughters, who were so sort of – you know, it must have been rather wonderful to him, he'd created these two marvellous characters who were way out of the life he'd lived. There they were, we could play piano and we went to church on Sundays and we wore nice clothes and we spoke nicely. And this must have been a marvellous satisfaction for him, knowing the struggle he had to raise himself in the way he did.

He was very musical and he was very good at music and he was a very happy man with lots of friends. I get the gift of the gab from him – I could talk for ever, so could he. We had family jokes about wherever he went he always knew somebody. We once went for a holiday to the Isle of Man and we walked down the street and there he met two friends. He knew everybody. But he never talked about sex, and I have this funny thing, you know, I thought he didn't know about the curse, because he never knew when I had it. And I remember thinking to myself as a child, what on earth happens when you're married? How d'you keep it a secret from your husband? Isn't that odd? I don't know whether other girls think that. But it was something I couldn't mention to him, any more than I would – I mean I could mention it less than mentioning bowel motions – you know, just something totally taboo.

So she didn't tell me enough, but she realized the limitation of it and she left sort of ooey-gooey books around and medical books around and also . . . Oh, there was one awful book about, er, I can't remember now, it was sort of vaguely religious, and it was all about the birds and the bees, but in a soupy kind of way, and then it ended up with the birth of a baby and about how this baby grew under the

mother's heart, and I thought, now, your heart's here . . . [Laughs.]
OK, maybe it was a gentle introduction to the idea. Maybe it wasn't
so silly, you know. One is so contemptuous when one does get at the
facts, and I can see now as a parent how difficult it is to get the thing
across. Because I mean after all sex is very difficult to explain, except
mathematically, and I mean I think for myself I found it easier to try
and explain it to my children mathematically before they got
teenagey. Once the emotional side comes in, then, you know, it's
acceptable, whereas I think if I had been told the actual, literal facts of
intercourse and procreation when I was about fifteen or sixteen I'd be
horrified. So I think the idea of seeing it as the result of love, er, and
a sort of natural process, involved with the whole of nature, perhaps
it was the right way to introduce the topic – to a girl such as I was,
you know. So, I think my generation tried to let them know the facts
of life before their emotions were involved, and they were interested
in how cars worked and how this and that worked, and therefore
how human bodies work, and how the whole thing fixes, and then,
when you become sexually attracted, then you can sort of . . . fit the
two ideas together, the two sets of facts.

They were unusual, my parents, among everybody else that I knew,
in that they encouraged us to read anything, but everything, there
was never any censorship of any kind. We were sort of led along to
the local library and explained to us roughly how it worked, and we
just read. And I read, and read, and read. This was my retreat. I read
because I was no good because I wasn't very attractive. OK, I was
clever. You know, it all fitted in.

University was super because I was allowed to be an attractive
woman and an intellectual. The two fused together. So university
was *the* significant liberation in my life, I think. It was only after that
that I began to realize the difficulties of being a woman. I think I
managed without too much difficulty, too much strain, shall we say?
Because again the university was different, in that Trinity College,
Dublin, is a university with about a thousand people, I suppose – no,
less than that, I can't remember. I don't know how many hundred.
But it was only one college. So though we were within our own
schools of whatever we were studying, we were all mixed up, and

we met people from the others. It was more like a red-brick in my day, in that you met everybody who was there. You weren't shut off in your own little college. Nothing like a woman's college or anything odd like that.

Because I was poor I lived in various ghastly places. I lived in fearful YWCA and Girls' Friendly Society and had rows with them because . . . the YWCA was really rather awful, it was one of these religious things – great evangelical movement. They were all quite sure that the end of the world was coming on a certain day in June and they were all singing hymns and one thing and another, and I lived there . . . because it was cheap – it was twenty-seven and six a week. I knew my father had very little money, and this was a big struggle. I was feeling injustices hanging on, in that if I'd been a man I'd have got free rooms in the college, but because I was a woman I got ten pounds a year instead, and ten pounds a year, even in 1938, didn't buy much. And I had a terrible row with them once because I had a lot of these German magazines because I was studying German, and they had lots of bosomy women and you know, Hitler's days – all very sunburned. I mean, nobody wore bikinis, *but* they were very bosomy. And these YWCA ladies who ran the place were shocked at the magazines and said I shouldn't have these things here. I told them I was studying, and these were German magazines, and they said that Hitler was bad to Christians. I said, yes, that might well be true, but that was nothing to do with the fact of my studying German literature and the German language, and we had a blazing row. [Laughs.] So then I moved off to another one, which was run by – you know what the YWCA's like – rather evangelical – the Girls' Friendly Society was Church of Ireland, which was Anglican and therefore slightly more – tolerant.

I had a room and so on of my own, which was about the size of a cupboard. This was marvellous – I had a room of my own. Though they did have prayers there nobody really bothered very much about going. It was more civilized, I thought. Eventually, I got digs; they were elderly widows. You could only go to digs you were allowed to go to, and I went to this lot. I was busy in the early stages of my affair with David, walking round the streets for hours at night and talking about life, and kissing under trees and in backyards and all over the place – you know the kind of thing. And they were fussed by this, and they went and complained to the college that I had a follower, a young man, and I had another blazing row with them. Well, I had the good sense to go raging and screaming with tears to the mother of a college friend who was also a friend of his, and she talked sense to me, and rang up the college and said this was all a lot of nonsense, and you know, this was no way, not a civilized way for the college to behave. So that still there were civilized adults that I could turn to, who got me out of this prurient kind of set-up. And got me into the Women's Residence, where I had a – what do you call – bursary. I was allowed to live there for thirty bob a week instead of eight guineas a week, which everybody else paid. I startled the entire place by saying, 'Isn't it lucky my father can't afford for me to live here, so I'm allowed here for twenty-seven shillings a week?' In fact there were six others who had the same, but nobody before had the nerve to say so! I think this is when I started my career as a maverick.

Courtship

'*We were in love and love was forever.*'

David was the first man I cared for that I met that was intelligent. He was intelligent, apart from being attractive, and it was a very sort of gentle courtship. I could talk to him, I could communicate with him in every possible way. This was what was miraculous. I mean, here was a man who knew what it was about. And who assumed all these things that I vaguely thought, and in fact was in many ways more revolutionary in those times than I was, and didn't see why it was so surprising.

You know, he's always goaded me on to doing and saying more about what I think and believe when I've lacked courage. He's always been the one from the early days who pushed me out to do a job when I felt, maybe I can't in this set-up, maybe this'll do him harm, maybe this isn't on, maybe I can't do this thing. You know, the thirties, when you feel totally submerged in babies and domestic life and husbands' careers and all. And you think, well now, it was all an illusion and it isn't any use, you sort of give up. You think, oh well, there are compensations, let's enjoy those. When you begin to see the danger in yourself of being – which of course is a big danger – of being a domineering mum, fulfilling yourself in your kids. And this is, you know, the sort of worry. Whenever I wanted to run away from an idea he used to say, 'Well for God's sake go and get a job. Do get a job. Why don't you go and do this?'

This story you will find hard to believe. We slowly fell in love and we knew we were sort of – we thought marriage was an old-fashioned thing, but I suppose we have to get married, because you know that's the way life is nowadays. We weren't really all that different from – well, I don't find it all surprising that, er, young people, anybody, doesn't want to get married now – why the hell? See, in my children's generation and some of my colleagues at work now, they get married when they're having children, not because they think it's the right thing to do, but because socially it's easier. You know, you get the pensions better, you get the this and that. It's a kind of protection. Well, we had theoretically exactly the same ideas, but we were in love and love was forever, and the idea of standing up in front of a parson swearing this, that and the other, it was neither here nor there. But this was the sort of social kind of thing you had to go through to please the parents, so, all right, you know, we'll get engaged, we'll get married. But then, blow me down, there was a war, you see. So of course he had to go and join up. Because he was a good Ulsterman and his father had been on the Somme and because the sort of, er – the code was . . .

You see, I was busy being a pacifist and a socialist, having been totally educated by Bernard Shaw – *The Intelligent Woman's Guide* was my bible. [Laughs.] Certainly my father thought Shaw was absolutely Christmas too, so that I could be a rebel and yet – under the everlasting arms of the father-figure, and all that. But David was never – he's far more sort of theoretically socialist than I am in a way. He's far more narked by theoretical inequalities, and I'm more pragmatic. Having trailed round the world and agonized about it, why should *I* live in comfort? This is why I think I withdraw a little bit from Women's Lib, because I know it's right and I know you'll have to do it and I know it'll come in good time, in somebody's time – your time. But a much greater awfulness is in the world, you know. I've lived in Muslim countries, I've lived in the Far East, I've lived in Africa. I've lived in the West Indies . . . the results of slavery are still there, you know. There are so many other much more – to me more – awful things still going on that haven't been put right. So good for you, get on with Women's Lib, but to me, something like community relations and race relations is more fundamental, is more my thing, or something I must get more involved in. Right. So that's that.

To get back. There was a war, so his kind of citizenship was, you can live off your country in time of peace, and in time of war you do something about it, unless, of course, you're a pacifist. But you can't dither in the middle. If you're not a pacifist you shoulder your musket, or you pick it up, whatever it is. So he did. And it was a terrible sacrifice which narked me.

The War

'The War wasn't heroic, it was just a bloody bore.'

He'd finished his degree, and then he had a studentship, they wanted him to do another degree and all that. But he wouldn't. This was in 1939, when the War broke out. He did his studentship for a term, and then sort of said he couldn't stand it any longer. He toyed with the idea, perhaps influenced by me with my sort of dying pacifism – because I was a pacifist – but then came to believe that this war had to be fought before we could take up life again. The War wasn't heroic, it was *war*, just a bloody bore. The War was a hell of a bore, and a dirty job which our parents' generation had not dealt with rightly and therefore we had to do all over again. It was a sickening filthy job and had to be done. And we were angry with our parents for not sorting out the political muddle; for leaving us growing up with this dirty job to be done. That was my view of the War: so let's get it over with and get back to start again – you know. I saw no avoiding it then.

He joined up, and this was a terrible thing, you see, because naturally enough he wasn't going to do any kind of thing that would get him straight to a commission, because that – you know, it had to be all fair's fair. So he joined up in the infantry. I found it awfully hard to take, him being bossed about. It was really sort of like being in a prison – you know, the total institution thing. You take off all your clothes, you have a bath, and then they give you new clothes, a uniform. They don't give you pyjamas, they don't give you a shirt. They give you a serge uniform. You're not meant ever to have clean clothes. They wash your socks once a month or something. It was very primitive, and he's a fastidious character. And I raged. I thought, now here he is and he's so clever, and so intelligent, he oughtn't to be doing this silly thing.

Then he was offered this post, and couldn't decide if he ought to take it as it was out of the army, but in fact far more dangerous, as it turned out. And with great agony of mind and soul-searching and whether it was the right thing to do or not, he decided he'd do it. This of course was stark tragedy, he was going away for two years. We comforted ourselves by announcing our engagement, and the families all embracing one another and – da da – and this was all – you know – and off he went across the sea. Now I wanted to give up university and get involved in the War then. But he didn't want me to, and my parents didn't want me to, and they both ganged up on me and said, you'd be far better to wait till you've got your degree and then you can do something more useful. So I stayed on, and they were very sort of dead and horrible years in some ways, and therefore again I buried myself in work, because, er, the south of Ireland was neutral. But Trinity had an awful lot of people involved in the War, and I was involved in the War, and I got involved in a sort of graduate lot of people who were a bit out of the undergraduate thing, and I still – I enjoyed it, but it's hard to describe being in love with somebody who's thousands of miles away and you don't have letters very often. You have to sort of keep going in your imagination and a kind of faith. So when I got my degree, then I went whizzing off and worked in the Foreign Office, on the German stuff – you know, translating things and that kind of thing.

So to cut a very long and agonized war story short, he was away for five years. Now can you imagine that? I never loved anybody else. I had a few mild and meaningless flirtations and they always were just as meaningless as they had been at school. I wasn't interested. I was aware of needing sex, but I wasn't prepared to have sex without love. Because I knew what sex was like with love. So it wasn't worth it, you know. It's hard, it's hard – I don't expect your generation to understand this kind of thing. You don't – I mean, you know about the War, but it's hard to explain to you what it was like emotionally that you kept faith for five years and it was perfectly normal. You waited for your bloke to come home. I find it hard to look at those wartime films, you know. I find it brings it all back. The deadly boredom of it. The War wasn't heroic, it was just a bloody bore. If you want my image of the War, it was from eleven o'clock till one o'clock in the morning on a station platform, waiting for a train that never came, and the waiting rooms are shut, and it's foggy, and the canteen's shut, and you have to survive and the train never comes, and you wait and you wait and it's cold and it's dark and you don't even have the excitement of the sirens . . . it was just a bore, awful.

I spent a year at Bletchley and then I got out of it to come up to London and worked in London in the Ministry of Information, which was hilarious, and I had a flat with a girlfriend, and we did nothing but work and come home. It's maybe hard for you to under-stand, but we had absolutely no sex life. So there we were in this flat, and she's still one of my dearest friends. You know, this is some-body, a real – this is a real buddy. We sat out the bombs together, and we used to have a great laugh. There's a boring country town in the north of Ireland called Cullybacky. A dreary girl we knew at the university was teaching there, and married some dreary young man who was also teaching there, so when the bombs used to rain down on us and we'd be sitting on the stairs – you know, waiting for the bombs to stop – we used to say to one another: 'It's better than teaching in Cullybacky.' It's still a sort of joke word, it's one of these things. You know – at least we're alive for the moment, and at least we're where it is – so even in the bombs London was where it is, and that's why, like the man said, London belongs to me.

I was telling the children the other night, and the telly was on, they had this thing about 1945 and when the War ended, and David was sneering at all the crowds coming round the palace and waving to the King and Queen and little princesses, and I said, 'Don't you sneer, one of those people's me.' Jonathan looked at me in amazement, and I said, 'Yes, what else could you do?' The pubs were dry, and we just wandered round the streets, and the lights were still out. It took weeks for them all to be fixed up again. But the black-outs were torn down so the lights shone into the streets for the first time. Terrific.

Marriage

'We got out by marrying men who were on the move.'

You know, he didn't even get back at the end of the War, not until the beginning of 1946. Three days later we got married, which when you look at it was a lunatic thing to do – really lunatic. We hadn't seen one another for five years! Can you think of it? I can remember thinking, maybe this is a foolish thing. And then thinking, quite logically, well, he's only got a month's leave, and I know I'll marry him in the end, and so why the hell waste that month? In the end he got three months' leave. I never met anybody else I wanted to marry. So – you know, why not? That's what happened. I was at home at the time and recovering from some kind of flu or other, and he sent a telegram saying he was coming, and so we got married.

I was enraged that the telegram came to his mother and not to me, and my sister had to calm me down and say, 'Well, look, of course it has to go to his mother, because she's his next of kin until you're married.' [Laughs.] But I was in a terrible state, I was slightly frightened of marrying him. I had gone through periods of being frightened about it during the five years, and by the time it actually ended I'd come to this conclusion, that I would marry him in the end so I might as well get on with it, almost as if it was a painful duty.

There was a sort of – I knew I was going to. It's hard to explain, it's impossible to understand unless you can think yourself into how long and how boring the War was, and how people did get killed, and how you could only live with the idea if it was part of something that was worthwhile doing, a dirty job.

But for years after the War one of the things I found most difficult was the war memorial, kind of – you know, November 11th. They used to get me in a towering rage. Because here are all these people who were killed, and everybody's saying, you know . . . gave his life for his friend, and their sacrifice. And I knew bloody well not one had wanted to sacrifice and everybody thought, well, it's not going to be me. It was just bad luck they copped it and we didn't, that was all there was to it. It was just a total waste of time and life and everything: waste of my life, waste for the world, a waste of all the things we could have been doing. Rage . . .

Off he went at the end of his leave, and I had to spend five months waiting to join him because there were no ships. But at least I was married, and I spent the time at home. My father died in the middle of this. This was, you know, a very ghastly period of time anyway, and my mother needed support. My sister was married and had a child, and her husband had gone off to Africa. And, after my father died, I again had to fall into this role of being sort of a son. I was the one who had to organize the funeral, and sell my father's business, do the business affairs – obviously my sister couldn't do it, with a two-year-old child. So I slipped into the family role of being the non-son. This was obviously the thing to do, and I sorted that out.

My mother was very unsettled. She was determined that neither of her daughters was going to stay at home and look after her, because she had been tethered to her mum . . . we hadn't got out the way she expected. We got out through marrying men who were on the move. So we were going to join our husbands, and though we both of us felt awful about leaving her there with the old woman, and not much money, I knew it would have hurt her more to tie us to look after her. Though it was a possibility that one of us would have had to stay there to look after them. That would have been still regarded as – if she had demanded it, it would have been very difficult to refuse.

Perhaps we could have refused in rebellion. I don't know. We didn't have to. She used to tell me to get on with it. So I went out to Burma. It was terrific fun, I'd never been out of Europe, and the War was over, and I found the Burmese absolutely marvellous and stimulating and terrific fun. And they'd had a hell of a time being fought over, back and forth, during the War, but they were full of hope too that everything was going to be all right and – er – they were extremely quick-witted and very sharp and bright. They were very entertaining.

My socialist thing had been watered down to being just ordinary sort of Labour, and I was anti-colonial in sort of – theory. But by the time I'd got there, British policy was – you know, we were working towards independence, we couldn't stay on ruling these people. We knew that the Burmese were going to want independence, and that they were going to have to have it, and that India was going to have to have independence, and David, from the purely military point of view, would say, look, we can't hold them unless we put in – I've forgotten – x troops, and we haven't got them, and by what right would we do it anyway? The British people wouldn't stand for it, and so forth. We were regarded as rather dangerous revolutionaries with these ideas.

So this is how that went on, and it was terribly exciting, you know, hospital social life. I had long dresses, and we drove around in a jeep, and we went all over the country, and we went dancing all the time. We'd no money at all. We shared a house with another couple. During the War David had somehow been overpaid, and then suddenly after the War they said, 'Oh well, we've made a mistake, so we'll take back all the money you were overpaid.' So one month we got minus thirty rupees (now the rupee was one and sixpence) and another month we got ten rupees, which was fifteen bob. We were sharing a house, so we just told the people, 'Well, we won't pay our share of the housekeeping for three months, is that all right?' And they said, 'Oh that's all right' – he was much senior, this chap. We had enough in the bank to pay this one servant who was David's devoted chap who stayed with us all the time we were in Burma. A very nice man. We could buy beer and cigarettes from the hospital, so we lived in total luxury with no money at all. And we had a wonderful time. I remember one Christmas in the middle of it, and I bought David a Christmas present of a fly-swat, which cost ten annas, which is worth five p. [Laughs.] I mean we literally had no money.

You can imagine sort of, what a marvellous, terrific thing this was, you know. After all the years of the War, we had a marvellous time. But the cloud was on the horizon, I couldn't have a job. And then somebody gave some money to charity and said, would they employ somebody to run a welfare organization called the Vigilance Society? They wanted somebody to train probation officers for the juvenile court, and I with a degree in modern literature took on this job.

I learnt an awful lot – sort of real down-town Rangoon – and I learnt, you know, what it was like to be poor in a way that I never had any idea before, even in Ireland. I learnt how the poor stick together and how they sustain and maintain one another. I learnt the value of the extended family, and I learnt the sort of variability of morality that you can't tell the truth if you're hungry, you know. And you can't obey orders if it's somebody – if you've got a far-out relation on whom you're depending. How nepotism and corruption are inevitable if you're hungry and you're down-trodden. I learnt with terrible shock what the police will do to people when they want to get information out of them or just because they believe them to be criminals. I mean, this was a terrible shock to me because I didn't think that any police under British organization would ever behave in this way. I was twenty-six, twenty-seven, and it was a revelation, a kind of eye-opener that stayed with me when I went to other countries later. I lost the dew off my eyes.

But I was ashamed to take this money, because I felt in some ways I ought to be doing this for charity. Yet I knew that a wealthy Lebanese businessman had given the money so that somebody would be employed to do this. I knew that even when we were paid we got barely enough to live on, because the pay was the same as pre-War – can you imagine? Nevertheless there was a conflict of my liberal do-good parents, not *noblesse oblige* so much as sort of, er, just being sort of middle-class – kind of, the undeserving poor, and the deserving. That's how I learned about the undeserving poor.

I ran a children's home which was financed by this nineteenth-century do-good thing, er, and this was not only for the waifs and strays, but for juveniles in need of care and protection of the court, we had kids on probation. In the total chaos of post-War Rangoon, many of the children were prostitutes at the age of about eleven, with venereal diseases of various kinds. They were in sort of robbery things. If the police got hold of somebody and there were child witnesses, they had to be sent to our place and kept safe until they could appear in court – all this kind of thing. So we had all these children here, and we also had four probation officers being trained for work in the juvenile courts. Because one of the lovely British things that was going to be left was probation service. And I trained the probation officers by the simple device of finding a psychologist, a lawyer, a doctor, a this, a that and the other, who would give them lectures. And then they helped administer this home, and look after these kids, and take them back and forth to the court and so forth.

Big drama when the matron got pregnant by one of the probation officers. [Laughs.] It's all very well, but it was also a rather awful background. There had been a home there before the war, which all the nice ladies had looked after, and collected money in silver bowls at tea parties. And in 1942, when all the British had cleared out, the matron had been given the money to take the children up-country to get them away from the horrid Japanese, and she led them on foot farther and farther and farther up in the hills of Burma. And then they were never heard of again. After the war she turned up in Rangoon. She said she left them with various homes, you know, with various people in the villages up there. People said she sold them – children were always being sold into kind of chattel slavery to do housework and that kind of thing. Other people said they'd all died of typhus, and the woman that I took on this from, a very stout-hearted woman, who I admired very, very much – you know she's dead now, but she was the one graduate I could talk to – she believed in this matron, and believed that they were wicked stories. So of course this matron, at the advanced age of about thirty-two, got pregnant by this Indian who was about twenty. Well, everybody said, 'She always was immoral. No doubt she had all those children murdered.'

I knew the people and the conversations, and so therefore it was a terrific eye-opener to me. I was a hell of an intellectual snob. You know – my liberation had been through the intellect and through the university, and I didn't expect to get on with women who weren't intelligent. So therefore I got on with all the Burmese men, because they were educated at one of the universities and so forth. I got on with the Burmese women who were educated.

I taught in a Buddhist school, I taught Burmese history. There were no books, it was mad. That was another great education. This woman I was very pally with went off to be the Burmese delegate to the Unesco conference in Paris. And she said, 'You'd better teach in my school, founded by my mother who was a devout Buddhist.' I said, 'Well I don't know the history.' She said, 'Well never mind, you know more than they do, and they haven't had any schooling for four years.' So I said all right. I went there, and I found they had no books. The Port wasn't opened by then, they were still bringing everything by small sampans from the big ships out in the middle of the harbour. Somebody had a book of Burmese history written by some Englishman in 1900. I brought this book, and I would say, 'Now, this is what happened.' I'd make them write on the board, and if somebody put up his hand, he'd say, 'But that's not what happened at all. My father told me that this happened. And my *penge*' – that's the priest – 'something else had happened.' There were possible factual things, but always a lot of supernatural came in about armies of black ghosts on dragons and things like this, you know. I would get all these things and write them on the board. We'd put them all in a row and then discuss it, and I'd say, 'Which do you think's most likely? Mr Burns the historian says this.' Then we'd discuss which was the most likely. They would never agree. So I'd say, 'All right, one of you is going to grow up and learn history and write your own history, but meantime that's the only one we've got, OK?' And we'd go again. [Laughs.]

So I found this fascinating, but it cut me off from all Brits, all the whites – yes, it was very odd. Everybody kept telling me how marvellous Burma had been before the War, and I couldn't possibly know, could I? You know, how they played bridge in the morning, and then they had gin, and then they all played tennis for the afternoon, and the Burmese were so good then, it's all changed now. I wasn't strong enough to reject this totally, you know. We were the youngest and it was fine, and all that, and they all took us out and they all fed us because we had no money, and they all had us out to dinner and took us to the club, which we couldn't belong to because we couldn't afford to . . . I didn't want to sort of – things were bad enough without me introducing a private rebellion. It wouldn't have occurred to me.

I began to feel that I would never be any good as his wife. I couldn't fit in, and, you know – the cloud, as I say. I was able to do less and less in the children's home because law and order was gradually breaking down. There were more and more riots. I couldn't, without causing trouble, go into that part of the town, because – well, David's view of it was, and I had to go by what he said, what else could I do? – if I and my jeep ran over a dog, there'd be a riot. Because I was white they would attack me, and even if they didn't it would immediately be in the bazaar that a white woman had killed a child, and there'd be a riot. The most tactful thing I could do was keep my nose out of it. It was horribly true. If I'd been there long enough and been there in my own right, to be accepted, you know, as white or black or whatever, or yellow or cream or pink, which people can be if they are accepted as people, and not as symbols of their pigmentation. . . Very often, until things get really difficult, they can maintain their position, but the one that's not known is the cause of the rumour that starts the riot. So therefore all I could do was retreat into the wifely position and I wasn't very happy about that aspect of it. We could see the thing from the Burmese point of view, and we were very happy about Independence.

I would have been satisfied with life then if I'd had a child, but David was determined we weren't going to have any until we came home, because he's very fussed about medicine and hygiene and he was afraid that I might die in some filthy Burmese hospital, you know. It was quite possible. I had a hell of a trouble with the curse. When you think back it must have been psychological perhaps, the way they say everything is now. Horrible. I did go in and have some kind of curette, which I'm sure I didn't need, and I found the whole process appalling, ghastly. I think it was an almost sexy experience, and therefore totally appalling. And after this I thought, well OK, I'm not going to have a baby in this place.

So then, we were there for their lovely Independence bonanza. And it was lovely, it really was terrific fun. January '48 was Independence. We came home a fortnight after Independence. We came home on an ordinary cruiser.

Children

'They were right when they said it was either a career or a family – you can't have both.'

We wanted to go to countries where we could bring up a family, because we were already against the idea of boarding school. So, we had Jonathan in the next year. I thought, having a baby is going to be absolute hell. You know – childbirth is going to be agony, and I will just have to go through with this process. And David kept saying to me, 'Why don't you read something about it, so that you know what you're in for? Why will you . . . ?' And I'd say, 'I just don't want to know anything about what happens, and I'll put up with it, and then it'll be over. Whatever it is, I'll go through with it, because I must have a baby and that's final. But I don't want to think about it.' Mercifully my elder sister, who is three years older than me, had her first child in unnecessary agony, so learnt about Grantly Dick-Read and had her next child popping out like . . . So she wrote to me in great excitement and sent me the book, and I read the book from cover to cover, and since then I've had three children that have popped out like peas out of a pod, with much less agony than I've had with tummy upsets . . . no problem.

So I go and have this most gorgeous of all babies. And he really was, you know, quite startlingly beautiful. I mean, that's maternal of course, but he really was a very good-looking baby, and he was, you know, a rewarding baby, so I just wallowed in maternity. I fed him for eight months, you know, and it was very, very satisfying. You know me, all or nothing, and when I went in for maternity in a big,

big way. . . . It is a very emotionally fulfilling thing, and feeding a baby is a very physically satisfying thing. I don't say it's the same as sex, but it's the only way I can describe it. I don't mean it's exciting and pleasurable in that way, but it's satisfying, it's a really physically satisfying activity. Not ecstasy but calm joy. I really felt fulfilled in feeding this miraculous infant. He was such a rewarding child, and he adored it, and there was no problem, and . . . I can see how – I can see how it can be a very fulfilling thing and can take up a lot of your life, and I can see how, you know, if you were likely, say a hundred years ago, to die at forty after twelve children or so, that it could be quite enough and you could have quite a fulfilling life. Not me of course, but at the time – you know. I suppose it's the same as, you know, the dissatisfactions of surreptitious sex at school. That total sex is gorgeous, and total maternity was parallel, if not equally gorgeous you know. It didn't last so long, but it was a very fulfilling thing, and the only thing I wanted to do was to have more and yet more babies.

So I got pregnant again. And then this was the beginning of a very bad time, because off we went to New Zealand. I was monstrously pregnant and felt grotesque, you know, on board ship, with everybody dancing foxtrots and things, and Jonathan was sickly sickly sickly all the way. And I felt, you know – well I do get immense in pregnancy, I don't know quite why, but I was just seven stone when I came back from Burma, and I was eleven and a half before Jonathan was born, with the result that I've never had any tummy muscles since. It was after the War that he was born, and there was still rationing. You must get all the food you can and stuff it in you, and eat for two, you know. Nobody ever said don't eat carbohydrates. I was so healthy, and so marvellously fit and all that. Isn't it awful? I was so grotesque. It didn't matter living in Hampstead, but being on board ship . . .

And then Jonathan had whooping cough. We had a terrible experience in Sydney. We were stuck there. We were in a hotel full of fleas, and I was like a great big bun – you know, one of those currant buns – covered with flea-bites. They had awful shortages there because they'd had floods in the Hunter river, and there was no butter, and there was no milk. And I couldn't get anything to feed this child on. I didn't know what was wrong with him, and some relation said, 'Oh, he's got whooping cough.' And then when they said this – these people were to take us on a ship to New Zealand – said that they wouldn't have a child with whooping cough on the ship. I'd have to stay in Sydney. Then our friends in Sydney said they couldn't get me into a maternity hospital. The baby was due in seven weeks. David sent a telegram to New Zealand and they said, 'Well, you'll have to leave your wife behind in Sydney and come on.' And I was going to be left behind in Sydney – this was what they suggested – with no maternity hospital, a child with whooping cough, and nowhere to live – flea-bitten. It really was – you know, I got sort of hysterical about this, and ashamed I got hysterical.

We finally, er, smuggled the baby on board, feeding him chocolate all the time. Every time he started to whoop I gave him a bit of chocolate. We had very good friends there and we smuggled this child on board at the very last moment, straight down to the cabin. The captain of the ship had actually said that if he discovered a child with an infectious disease, er – he would put the mother and child off the ship in a lighter – anywhere inside the three-mile limit. Now once you get three miles outside Sydney Heads, you're in the big Sea of Tasman, and the very idea . . . ! I must have to a certain extent believed him, but of course I know now he couldn't have. We must have believed it to a certain extent, and I was terrified. We got this child on board the ship, then the ship sailed. I kept feeding him chocolate all the way out, through the Heads, and the ship began to tip up and down and we got about three miles out, and he was sick all over the place, you see – oh, dreadfully sick. And the matron, the stewardess, came in and she said, 'I hate to tell you, dear, when you're just expecting another one, I hate to tell you, but I really think that child's got whooping cough.' I said, 'Oh, oh no!'

And when we got to New Zealand they had no house for us, and they wanted us to live in a house six miles out, and we had no car. And the hospital director was lately married, aged about fifty, and I had to explain that I couldn't live six miles out with no phone and no car because I was going to have a baby and I couldn't be alone.

Nobody came near us. Nobody brought us even sheets. We found a house for ourselves, and we got a shop which was still open at seven o'clock at night. We slept on the mattresses with our coats over us. Nobody came near us. Extraordinary. It would be far better really if the husband came first and got the home set up and then the wife would follow. But you know, we wouldn't have had the money to do that anyway, even if we'd considered it. So it really was rather awful.

And the doctor wouldn't give me an appointment for eight weeks – he had a receptionist, you know, and all this kind of carry-on – so I had to, you know, scream down the phone and say that I was going to have this baby, and that I'd written to the doctor and he'd said he'd have me. It was all a terrible time, feeling sick all the time. By the time the baby was safely born – I had no trouble with the birth as usual – I was covered with a nervous rash from head to foot, and it was awful – you know – it really was terrible. We had to move house when she was three weeks old. So that the beginning in New Zealand . . .

And immediately cocktail parties – before she was born I had to go to a cocktail party to welcome us. These cocktail parties . . . in rooms about half the size of this, everybody smoking, and the noise, and the exhaustion – you know, standing for hours. And I would get all dressed up – you know, even to my face made up and hat on – and then I would feed the baby and then I would button up my dress and rush off to the cocktail party.

I think that I began to realize that it was all a bit of a cheat. I didn't formulate it, but I just knew that it wasn't like what they told me, you know. I knew that. I then said, all right, it's not on. If you're going to be a wife, you can't – I mean they were right when they said it was either a career or a family – you can't have both. And I wanted a husband and I wanted a family, and this is what I've got to pay for it. So therefore I was bad-tempered and I was – nervy and not easy. There must be something wrong with a woman – you know, it must be me it was wrong with. I must be neurotic, because otherwise why would I be so bad-tempered, why would I be so nervy? And David could always introduce the argument that for wives of chaps in business it was far worse. Their lives were far more intruded upon about who they could entertain and who they couldn't, and at least we met interesting people. And it was all true. So in fact I was lucky, don't you see? And I believed him. You see, I was lucky I was married to him, not married to someone in Shell.

I had a group of women friends, er, who all did pottery and painted, and they used to sustain one another in a kind of pre-Women's Lib scene – one or two of them had unhappy marriages, and one or two of them had blissful marriages. And they were very intelligent and creative and it was like a sort of, er – rather a secret sect – I mean I was asked would I like to join them when they met. And they used to give one another lunches and we went in for rather exotic food. They were all a good deal older than I was. They had made their compromises. They were like a little religious sect sustaining one another in an alien hostile world, quite secret, you know. People didn't know that they met. Two of them sort of had studios at the bottom of their garden, and their husbands, who were civilized guys, thought it was lovely that their wives had this nice thing to do, you know. It was a pity they weren't too keen on actual gardening, but they were all good housewives too, and they were all creative cooks, too. They didn't just endlessly have roast beef and two veg.

There were intellectual outlets in a way, now and again, but secret. Because the way to get on with people was not letting them know, because if they knew that you were a clever woman they would be hostile to you. And I had to get on with them. I mean, we've got another family joke about this, about a dairy farmer from Taranan who only had one eye and slapped me hard at the cocktail party and said, 'Aren't you glad you're not one of those clever women?' And to me this was a terrific compliment, you see, and I accepted it as a compliment, because then I could have my quiet laugh at him – that I was a clever woman and that he didn't know. Can you see the secret society?

It was a very bad time. I had always been comforted by my confidence in myself as the intellectual clever girl. I never let *anybody* in New Zealand know I'd ever been to a university. It was the only way I could get equal with them and beat them at their own game. OK, I made all my kids' clothes. OK, I did all the cooking to vast parties as well as the family. OK, I learned to whip up sponges and make meringues. Anything they could do I could do better. But it wasn't very restful for anybody. So that was a bad time.

If that was the life, if that was the way it had to be, then OK. You know, the Protestant ethic. All right, if that's what has to be done, I'll bloody do it. I'll give the cocktail parties. And in fact, you know, a lot of it was fun. You see there was the scenery, and it was gorgeous. The New Zealanders were so nice. It was a lovely place to have small kids. Life was geared for small kids. And, you know, one gets a certain kick out of 'Anything you can do I can do better'. In fact, I didn't do it better, but some things I at least could do. You know, the 'Look, no hands!' syndrome.

8.   Norah Kirk

Norah Kirk was born in 1926 in Nottingham, where she has lived all her life. Her father was a miner and a soldier and then worked as a time-keeper in a hosiery factory, but during the thirties became unemployed. He left the family when the three children were young and her mother had to struggle to support them. William, her brother, was killed in the Second World War and Vera, her sister, died of pneumonia at thirteen.

Norah Kirk worked as a sewing-machine embroiderer, in a laundry and in offices until she met her husband, an electrical engineer. They have three grown-up sons and she now helps her husband in his engineering business.

Childhood

'There was no money coming in.'

The thing that stood out was fighting. My mother and father fighting because he was a bit of a drunkard. He used to say he'd be in at a certain time and he'd come in drunk, and of course dinner would be ready on the hob – it was called a hob then. Like then the fireplaces were the old black – it wasn't a range really, it had an oven on one side and a boiler on the other, with hot water in, and you used to have to have a ladle to get the water out to have a wash, and cook in the oven. This was black-leaded every week with blacking. There was a brass fender and brass coal tongs and a poker by the hearth. All terraced houses had the same kind of hob. When I was about six years old, he'd come in and they'd get fighting over the dinner, and she'd throw it on the back of the fireplace in a temper because she never drank, you see.

During the Depression a lot of the workmen got the sack, and especially them that was disabled during that time. Of course he was. There was no money coming in. He was in the army actually, and then during the First World War he got wounded and lost the use of his right arm, my mother told me. Then after that he was what you call a time-keeper at the hosiery where they used to make all this, the Nottingham lace and that. I think it was the army life, with having three children, although he thought a hell of a lot of us, you know, thought we was wonderful, and my mother said he used to take us out quite a lot, in prams and looking after us. But he used to go on what you call perhaps a week of drinking, a spasm sort of thing, and then of course all hell was let loose then, and of course he was a bit fond of the women as well, from what I could gather. I don't think my mother was jealous of him, I think that it was just that it made her life a misery, with her not going out drinking. She didn't think it was the right thing to do, especially when money was tight. He had a pension that kept money coming in a little bit, with him being wounded during the 1914–18 War. He was a reservist, called up at the outbreak of war. He would be in the army for quite some years. He'd previously served in South Africa and India. When I was seven he left us and of course she had him up then for maintenance, and of course he very rarely paid, and then she'd have to go to the courts to tell them that he hadn't paid, you know, and all the time she was trying to keep all three of us going on barely nothing. Then she took in washing. We didn't really have what you call a very pleasant childhood.

She had been married before, and her first husband had died – an accident. He'd been in the – it was called the lunatic asylum in those days – they call it mental homes now. He was in there for seven years till the day he died. And you see she met my father and that, he was out of the army when she met him. He'd lodged with her, and they lived together as man and wife. Mother had Bill in 1922, and then Vera was born in 1924, then I was born two years later, and of course he was a married man, but she didn't know this at the time. He kept putting her off about getting married. She knew that something was wrong, and she found out herself that he was married. He'd left his wife and had no children, so obviously he wasn't paying any main- tenance to his wife. According to my mother he only had his army pension. We were never told until my brother and I were in our teens.

He just left her, but of course she could get maintenance for us, up till we were sixteen. Once or twice she had him put in prison for not maintaining us, because she couldn't get what you call Relief in those days – like the Social Security is now, it was called Relief. She couldn't get it, because my father was supposed to be maintaining us, but more often than not she didn't get it, so she had to apply for the Relief money. It was a big room, I remember myself as I got older I had to go and collect it. I used to have to have a note from home saying she wasn't well, and you'd be all sitting in this room with forms, and in turn people stood before a bench of men and women. You used to have to go up to this bench with all these like JPs behind the bench, and they'd ask you all sorts of questions, even if a child went for the money with a written consent from the mother or the father. They'd try to trap the children by asking different things.

Because my father left her and that, from time to time when she couldn't get the Relief money she had to take in washing. With it being a terraced house, washing had to be done in a copper which was in the scullery. Mother lit the fire about five o'clock in the morn- ing, and she didn't finish until about four o'clock in the afternoon. One of my jobs was to scrub the scullery floor after school. The old sinks, they used to be rather big – big sinks, where you would put your rinsing water, then you'd have a bath of blue – you know, to dip your white clothes in – and a bath of starch, and you went from one thing to the other. If the Relief knew that she took in washing they would have stopped it – which they did when my father sent maintenance.

My mother, she didn't neighbour an awful lot, because she was too busy all the time, making ends meet. I mean you've either got to make your own jam, make your own bread and that sort of thing. She was very handy in that, and doing all the things for us. She used

to make us ginger pop and keep this in a hut in the back yard so
that we wouldn't buy lemonade, it would be cheaper. Times were
hard, very hard. William had a paper round when he was about ten
years old to earn extra money and even that was reported to the
Relief by a neighbour. The houses was that close in a row on both
sides of the street that everybody was watching everybody else, if
you know what I mean. Any amount whatsoever that was coming
into the house it was definitely looked into. She only had a few payments from my father up to the time I was fourteen.

The houses were built in a row on both sides. They had one living-
room and scullery and the living-room door opened into the street.
There was a toilet across the yard facing your neighbour's toilet.
There was two bedrooms – the front bedroom was rather biggish,
the back bedroom was very small – and then you had the attic which
came over the two rooms which was very big. I slept with my sister
in the back room, my brother slept up in the attic. With him being
on his own, he used to shout down the next flight of stairs to me and
my sister, keeping us awake half the night, shouting down little
jokes, children's jokes.

I would be about fourteen and my father came and saw my
mother, came back to see my mam – 'course she didn't really know
where he was living even then. He was paying maintenance more
often by then. When he came to see her this first time I'd be about
fourteen, and of course he wanted her to take him back. And she said
no. She said, 'You can come and see your daughter and come and see
me whenever you like, but I'm not going to leave this little home
and go with you.' He wanted her to go to Doncaster. He had this
council bungalow that belonged to his wife. He went back to his
wife when he left my mother, to live with her, and she died.

I can remember my mother sending me upstairs and I asked her if
I could have the money to go to the pictures when me dad came to
see her. She sent me upstairs and she wouldn't let me go, and I felt so
depressed that I was going to jump out the bedroom window,
probably because I couldn't get my own way, for one thing, and
probably because I wasn't in the conversation of seeing my dad, you
know, and all the time behind my mind I was hoping that my dad

would come back. Because he was very good to us when he was at home. Even though he used to get drunk and knock her about, he wouldn't knock us about, and if he had any money in his pocket, or a penny or something like that, he would give it to us when he used to come home sort of drunk. I can remember him waking us up, Vera and I in the back bedroom, and bought us the biggest bunch of bananas, and he said, 'Don't eat them now, or you'll have tummy-ache, put them under your pillow.' [Laughs.] If he saw anything that we might want he used to bring it, and my mam used to think he was more or less trying to bribe us in a way. I don't think so really, he knew that we were his children, he never denied that, and he thought a lot of us in his own way. Yet on the other hand if you look at it in a light of him leaving her when we were all young, he couldn't have thought that much of us to have left her with the children – whether he liked her or not.

She told me afterwards that the thing was that he would have liked to have come back to her and she told him he couldn't. And I said to my mam I said, 'Why did you say that?' – because I would have loved them to have been together. So she said, 'No,' she said, 'I'll never trust another man.' She said she'd had enough. She had no interest in men at all. She never went out. The only time when she went out was to take me to Skegness for a day, a trip. Sunday used to be a cheap trip and she used to go out then. She had what you call ulcerated legs in any case, from the kick that my father had gave her during the fighting, and there was big ulcers on the front of the shins of the legs. Of course she was under the doctor with these. They used to put these plasters on that they ripped off, cos it used to run right through, and it smelt horrible. People still have them now, and they do take I believe some getting better, because once they get into the blood it sends all the blood bad round it and the leg goes black. So of course she had got these ulcerated legs, and then she had what you call rheumatism, all in her hand it was, it was beginning to be all deformed – and she said that she had gone through the worst part of her life, without my father coming back again now things had got easier.

She knew very well she hadn't had a good life. Nothing ever

seemed to go right with her. She was embittered with life. If I had done anything wrong or turned round and said to her – you know, cheeked her back or gave her what you call a 'slurky smile' – and she used to say, 'Well, you can wipe that off your face,' and something would be thrown at me. You know, her temper used to come up very very quickly and she used to really belt at me, really go at me in these tempers, till I was sort of black and blue. But then when the temper died down she'd get hold of you and love you and cry and say to you and that, 'Well you're so antagonizing to me.' And of course the neighbours – you could hear anything going on, any rows or anything like that, you was that close – the neighbours used to think that she was so cruel to me and used to feel sorry for me when I was a child, and I used to cry an awful lot. A tremendous amount of crying.

School

'The teacher used to get on to me so.'

Some subjects I was clever in, but not others. But my mother was so keen for me to go to school, she wouldn't let me have a day off school. By the time I'd come home at four o'clock on a washday, I used to have to scrub the floor through after she'd done her washing, it was my job. I used to come home at dinnertime and chop wood, and fetch coal in for the next day in buckets. The happiest moments really were at lunchtime when you used to have to come home for your dinner, because she always had a good dinner for me, all these suet, fruit puddings – she used to make sure that I had a good dinner at dinnertime. But you used to have home-made cake and bread and butter for tea, or bread and jam – nothing much for tea. School itself . . . I rather liked to be at school, because I was out of it, all the work and trouble at home. I didn't mix an awful lot with children in the street or anything like that. As I say my mother never kept me off school at all.

The history and the English teacher wasn't very nice to me because I was so backward in it. But I came nothing under sixth in the class at mathematics – 'course it was called arithmetic in those days. I used to love to do what you call gym – gymnasium – in those days. But I can't really recall anything particularly. The uniform we had was a serge tunic and a red jumper during the winter, and a white blouse during the summer with the tie and the collar, just a strip showing the colours of the school, and then you had a black blazer with the badge on. More often than not I never got the blazer because I couldn't afford one really. You had to buy your own things. I always remember the tunic, the serge tunic, and I used to have to press it myself, and my mother used to make me a pinafore for when I got home, to put over it so it was kept clean. I never changed into other clothes, only on a Saturday. I had to have this pinny on, you know, doing chores in the house, to keep it clean.

School itself I used to like. As I say, with being a bit backward on the English and the history, the teachers used to get on to me so. I would be about seven or eight years old. We had this new man teacher and his son was in the same class at primary school. His name was Nicholson – it's something I'll never forget. I am left-handed and he was trying to make me write right-handed. He used to hit my knuckles with a ruler, I used to have to change hands, and it got you rather backward, because I just couldn't write with my right hand. Until my mother went up and explained to him that she didn't want me to be knocked about and to leave me as I was, so he never tried any more and he said that she'll always be backward because she's using the wrong hand. In those days they thought and that, that you was . . . well it's alright for boys when they are using tools, and they are right-handed tools in the industry, but I mean not where a girl was concerned, it shouldn't affect her in any way. Whether they thought about machining in those days – most of them did go as machinists at fourteen, learning a trade. Whether he thought that would make you not able to do the jobs that was available at the time of leaving school I don't know.

I was thirteen and a half when the War started in the September, so I was still at school when they started the evacuation for the school-children and they came round to the schools. They came round and asked if you would like to be evacuated, and of course my mother wouldn't let me go. I was the only one at home with her, she knew very well I should be starting work in six months, so there would be no point in evacuating me. We was issued with gas masks straight away and that was pretty well about a month after the War started. You had to apply to the schools then because they started in the evening opening up the schools to recruit men. We were issued with identification cards, gas masks and ration books, for all your sweets and food and that sort of thing. The roads were all blacked out, no lights, houses had to have thick curtains.

Work

'My mother wanted me to go in a trade.'

I left school in 1940 at fourteen, and then of course my mother wanted me to go in a trade. She sent me to a garment factory about one mile away. It was quite a little step, you know, I walked it. There was a Number 8 bus which only run in the morning, at lunchtime, and in the evening to bring people back, because it was just beginning an industrial estate. This factory made dresses and on these dresses there was this embroidery. Not hand embroidery, machine embroidery, what you called Singer and Connellying. You'd got to start at fourteen – they'd put you on one of these machines. But for a whole year all you were doing was knowing where the silks were and how to thread the machines, sweeping up, doing tea, and all this sort of odd jobs. They put you on the machine for perhaps half an hour from time to time, showed you where the shuttlers went and how to handle the machines. I wouldn't say it was a tremendously big place. Charles Butler had his own shops in Nottingham. I do believe he had another factory near London somewhere at that time. Anyway, my mother put me on to embroidery – Singer embroidery. I was sweeping up and I earned twelve and sixpence a week. My mother had the ten shillings, which was a lot in those days, and I had the two and six for spending money a week. Out of that of course I used to have to take my own bus fare if I did want to go on the bus, and that were to take me to the pictures a couple of times a week.

We had somebody that we knew, that I used to have the left-offs – she was one of my mother's friends with some daughters – and that's how I got most of my clothes, or my mother used to perhaps go somewhere where you could buy second-handed things.

I was doing this embroidery and then at about fifteen and a half they put me on my own time doing this Singer embroidery, and I come out with five pounds a week in those days, because the girls that was professional, had been on it for years, was earning a tremendous amount of money on their own time, on this embroidery. And it used to be embroidery on the front of dresses doing what you call eyelet holes. You put a different plate on the machine, it's like the slide plates that you had, because the main one had a great big slit through it where the needle would bob up and down to catch the silk, so that you'd use this knee thing, it's like a lever, that would open up the stitch and make the patterns. You put different coloured silks on the machine to bring these patterns up, and then they did eyelet holes which you put another plate thing on with a hole in – they'd already be punched in the material. Your patterns were marked with chalk on the material, but you only had what you call a facing of the material which was machined up to make the dress. You didn't have the whole dress, you just had what you call a panel, you see, on your machine, and you used to have these piled up in about two dozen at a time. Some was good work, some was bad work. I earned five pounds.

This went on for about six months and of course we were really rich, as you might say. 'Course mother always used to say, 'I'll put a bit away for a rainy day.' She did save a little bit at a time, and then I got a part-time job on a Saturday at the cricket ground, where they played the Test. It was only on for the season. You used to get packed solid and I got a job doing sandwiches and tea at the tea kiosk. They paid me ten bob on a Saturday for all day from about seven a.m. in the morning, and they finished about eight o'clock at night. Ten bob – well of course it helped and that.

I only had a certain amount – I mean she wasn't greedy, when I was earning good money she'd give me perhaps a pound of it for spending money, and anyway things were going great. The War was still on, and all of a sudden all the silks went off the market – couldn't get them at all – so there was no embroidery done on dresses, the War had put a clamp-down on it. They asked me if I would go on a machine, ordinary sewing machine, and I said no. I didn't like sewing machines – the embroidery, yes, but sewing machines . . . whether that has got anything to do with being left-handed I don't know. I never sort of took to it at all. When you were on these machines you had to be careful the needle didn't go through your finger. There was no guard against it like on ordinary sewing machines, and they were a lot bigger needles. So I said I would leave. They had an awful lot of work in, because then they was doing what you call denims and underpants for the army. They had to just stop doing all the dresses – you used to get odd suits, ladies' suits, in from time to time, it depended upon if they could get hold of the material at that time. So I left there.

I would be about sixteen, or sixteen and a half, because when I left there, you used to have to then go to the Labour Exchange and get a green card. Everybody had to register to show you were eligible to do war work. I asked them if I could go into one of the munition factories. The work was hard but they was earning a tremendous amount of money and that at munitions. I was too young; girls had to be seventeen and a half. The Labour Exchange sent me to telephone components – Erickson's, the telephone people. Of course telephones was a war effort. Telephones for the army, walkie-talkies and radio sets and that sort of thing. They put me on these spring sets, that went in between the telephones. When you put the receiver down you can hear a click – it was like a big spring set that goes across those two knobs. I don't think it was knobs in those days, it was a bar on the telephone, you pressed these down on these springs. The girls sat on a row of benches on high stools and you had two screws sticking up in this bench and they used to put a piece of wood – they had all been specially cut out, at Erickson's themselves, sort of mass-produced – pieces of wood with holes in, and then came a certain spring, then you had what you call a screwdriver. When you had put all these things on, you had like a little pattern at the side of you telling you all the different little springs that you put on. It come into a kind of a thick one, half sort of plywood and half springs, and you'd screw it down, and of course you was doing this all day long, throwing them into boxes.

The basic wages was very small. You got a bonus on a certain amount that you did, but you only got your bonus once every six months. I didn't like the job, and I had to catch a train to get to this place from the Midland Station – I had to leave the house about six o'clock in the morning. Quite a lot of Nottingham people worked at Erickson's and the train was absolutely packed solid in the mornings, because it would be perhaps half an hour between each train and it would probably make you late by the time you caught the next one, so you'd got to be on time.

Anyway this went on for about six months and I was ill with the shingles. My mother took me to the doctor – this was the old family doctor, he had been the family doctor ever since we'd been little. He was Dr Bell. He said, 'Oh she's got the shingles. It's most unusual for a girl of her age to have it.' He asked me what job I were doing. He thought it was really monotonous. He knew a lot about the family, my mother and background and that, and he knew I was more or less working hard to keep things going.

At the Labour Exchange they said that I was old enough to be a bus conductress, because they had all the young girls, taking the fares on the buses. So of course I goes home and tells me mam, and me mam said, 'You're not going on no buses, not if I can help it.' You had to go on shifts, you see. You was on until twelve, the buses were running. You got quite a lot of nasty people, a few drunks, and there was the army coming home on leave, and you'd got all sorts of people, and we'd heard quite a lot of things going on on these buses. Anyway, she was a bit upset about this.

I went to see the transport doctor for a medical. I was very, very thin in those days. I just looked as though I might have wanted a good pudding, which I'd had, but no matter what I ate it didn't make any difference. I was about eight stone four pounds. I was all more or less bone. When I was thirteen and a half I had a pair of roller skates through these tea coupons – you used to save your tea packets, cut them out – and I'd had this accident with them, split my knee open, and I'd had to go to the hospital and have some nine stitches across my knee. The transport doctor looked at my knee and he said, 'Does that bother you?' 'Well,' I said, 'it does sometimes. I get a little fluid round it, which the doctor just told me to bandage up until it went again.' He said, 'There's something out, the kneecap's been put out. You ought to go to the hospital and have this seen to.' And he said, 'It would bother you to run up and down stairs to collect these fares.' So I thought to myself, goody goody, that got me out of that. [Laughs.]

So I went back to the Labour Exchange again, and I was still trying to get to one of these munitions factories, but I was still not quite old enough. They sent me first to Boot's pharmacological department, but I got ill again doing fire watching two nights a week. So they sent me to the laundry. The laundry, in those days they used to be so busy, they used to have to do all the army uniforms. There was a lot of Americans stationed here as well and they used to take those in, and of course they thought it was a real worthwhile job. So I went into this laundry and I was behind a calendar where the laundry came through all starched, you'd have to take it off and fold it on these tables, and it wasn't long – I must have been in there about three month – before one of the office supervisors came to me and asked me if I would like to work in the office, which I did, I went in the office.

Of course there was Americans everywhere. All the office girls were going after the Americans, marrying them – you know, the G.I. brides. While in the laundry I joined up with the Women's Air Force Cadets. It wasn't really recognized at that time. We didn't have a uniform but we did have the authority from the air force to have hats made, like little slit hats, and you had a tie with the Royal Air Force shirt. Well of course I'd bought all these myself, and I'd joined it, because I knew my brother was in the air force, and of course I don't know whether that would influence me or not. 'Course the Royal Air Force, during the War, were called the 'Brylcreem Boys' and they seemed as though they had the best of everything, more than the army or the navy. I said to my mother that I would like to join the air force when I was seventeen and a half, and she said,

'Oh, no you don't.' She said, 'One's enough.' She said, 'If I lose you I've lost everything, I haven't got nobody.' I mean I could understand that, I were her only bit of company she had got. She'd got no relations on her side at all.

Courtship and Marriage

'We didn't have no honeymoon.'

I was at the laundry when I first met my husband. It was one night we went out to – we had a fair, a little fair in Nottingham, not the Goose Fair, but it was what you call like a Nottingham Wakes – it stayed in Nottingham, if you know what I mean – and I met my husband going walking round there, wandering round there. He was an apprenticed electrician, and he got about twelve and sixpence a week. He was about nineteen then, he was about eighteen months older than me, and of course he was earning a bit more money than I was in any case. 'Course this office money wasn't too bad actually.

Anyway I met him and that, and that started the romance, and of course I took him home and my mother thought he was a grand lad, she was quite happy. At the beginning of the War apprentices were exempted until they became tradesmen. He went on what you called 'improvers' pay'. You get a bit more money than you do being an apprentice – what they call an 'improver'. His mother used to give him half of his money back, so he paid half of his clothes. She had the rest of it for her board, and he had the rest of it for his spending money, so he got a little bit more than I did. He was exempt until he was twenty-one because he was an apprentice electrician. At least they thought he would be, but he was twenty when he went – had to join up because they were wanting them so bad. He joined the navy, went to Portsmouth for nine months' training and then was posted to Scotland for quite some time – Scapa Flow, I believe it was.

I got engaged at eighteen and a half. Early in 1945 he was being posted abroad. We had got this fortnight embarkation leave and we decided to get married – if it was all right with his mother and father, which it wasn't really. They thought he was too young. My mother was all right about it because she thought such a lot of him, and she knew that I'd be settled. I think this is the thing where she was concerned. I think she was so ill in her own way that she wanted me to be settled and it didn't matter any more then. It got to that stage, because she used to say, 'What'll happen to you if anything happened to me? You're so young and under twenty-one.' I think it's one of the worries at the back of her mind. That was in the May. I thought such a lot of him, he was the only real boyfriend I'd ever gone with – and he felt the same way, of course it's not like it is now, houses were bombed and you had nowhere to live really, there weren't flats like there are nowadays. So we decided to live with my mother in any case, because I didn't want to leave her on her own. So we got engaged a week before his leave, and his father suddenly died with TB. Of course, TB in those days, it was a killer. It was called consumption years ago. His father died, so of course it put that off. He put his embarkation leave back, because he'd wrote to his officer and told him that he wanted to stay over for his father's funeral. The ship had gone. He had his leave extended, they did allow it under those circumstances during the War. Then he had to go back to Scapa Flow, waiting for another ship. We didn't get married; besides, things were a little bit upsetting with his father, so of course it just put that back.

By Christmas 1945 my husband got another posting, he'd got another fortnight leave to go abroad. He didn't know where he was going to be sent – they were still sending them, Japanese War was still on, so you never knew – they were still fighting on the Pacific waters. We were still rather frightened and worried about his going. Anyway we decided to get married then. I was still working in the laundry office. We'd got such a nice lot of girls working with me at that time – they was egging me on to get married.

We had a fortnight to do it in. We went to see the parson at St Nicholas's Church. George's mother's side were all members of this church, a very old one in Nottingham. In those days you'd still got to put your banns in for three Sundays unless you was married by a special licence, which was two guineas. George's mother wasn't very pleased about it, being her only son. She thought that I wasn't good enough. She was the type of a woman – not that I want to call her anything – but she was like my mother's neighbours. She went into my background by talking to neighbours, to get to know everything about my mam and me, and the family. With having not a very good background she thought I wasn't good enough for her son, so it caused quite a bit of trouble. But George was twenty-one then and he could please hisself what he did.

We had a fortnight. We went to see the vicar and we had a special licence and we got married – he came home on the Saturday and we got married on the following Saturday. Of course we didn't have no honeymoon or anything, because we wanted to be in Nottingham because his mam was upset. We hadn't got the money anyway to go away. He came out of the navy with ten pounds for us to get married on; I think I'd got about five pounds. My mother gave me two pounds, because she'd only got a little bit of money saved. I thought that was an awful lot of money in those days. My next-door neighbour at Sutton Street, she'd not been long, about seven years married, and she said I could borrow her wedding gown. You got coupons then, you hadn't got the money. You'd got to make do with the clothes you had got or borrow from one or the other. She said, 'And my sister will lend you her veil.' One of the girls at the office lent me a white prayer book. One gave me a ribbon to put in the Bible which had artificial orange blossom down it, it looked very, very pretty. You couldn't afford a bouquet of flowers. Another girl in the office, she wanted to be the bridesmaid, she said, 'I've got a bridesmaid dress myself.' So she became my bridesmaid in it. Well of course George got married in his uniform. The only difference in the uniform was a piece of white ribbon hanging from the collar, you usually have a black one. So we got married and then he went away to Australia, and he was supposed to be going for about three years – no one knew for sure when the War would be over in Japan. Well, it would be about six months.

I was still very thin and I kept having bronchitis, not just certain times of the year, but, you know, continual bronchitis. They found out that I'd had TB. They said it was an old scar, they worked it out that I must have been eleven years old when I had TB. I should think it would be with all this worrying, at eleven, you see, when my sister died. They said it was quite a big scar and it had healed up on its own. Anyway they was very worried about it. So they gave me extra rations, I had double bacon, and it was really a laugh because my mother said, 'Oh good, goody goody!' Everybody was managing on nothing, we had about two ounces of lard and two ounces of butter and four ounces of margarine – well of course I got quite a lot, I don't know whether it was double or treble, because they thought that I really needed it, and I got free milk, free orange juice. So of course everything went really rosy. I did gain weight. I was watched every week, I used to have to go to this place called Forest Dean every week to be weighed, X-rayed and that, and I was under them like that for five years.

I'd never left my mother, because we stopped for the week with my mother when we got married, in the little back bedroom. I was still working, then I had my army pay, which I never touched any of that at all, it was all saved for furniture for when he come back, for anything that he wanted. Cos we'd got no home or anything of our own at all. It was July 1946 before George got demobbed. Tradesmen were demobbed first but lost some of their gratuity pay, I longed for him terribly really. He came out under the 'B' scheme. because he wanted to get home. When you've not been married long, I suppose everybody wanted to get to their wives.

So he came out and I was at the pictures, my mum was listening to the Saturday-night play on the wireless. Whenever I was courting while George was at home before he went in the navy, even mostly Saturday nights, I'd sit with him and mother and listen to Saturday Night Theatre, and thoroughly enjoy it, all in the dark with the glow of the fire. This particular Saturday night I went to the pictures, but I always left a message with my mam where I'd gone in case he came home. On this big screen, they took the picture off and put written on the big screen, they must have put up kind of a card in front of the camera which came big on the screen, and I was sitting there looking at this picture, lovely, and it said – I'll never forget it – it said, 'WILL MRS KIRK PLEASE GO TO THE FOYER'. 'Course I went dashing out – I'd got him on my mind – and there he stood, brown as a berry from Australia, they'd had a marvellous time there. He said something about, 'I've brought a great big kitbag full of stuff for you,' and he'd brought me all tinned fruit from Australia, coconuts, all the things that we couldn't get, and glassware, and half of them had broken.

We made our home with my mother. My mother was getting worse in her mind over what life was doing to her, just tearing her to pieces bit by bit. She used to do some funny things. Most of the housework I used to do for her; it got so she used to just sit in a chair and she used to be looking blank at things, you know. Her temper was still there, whether she was in pain or what. Then she'd sit down and cry. She would sit in the chair and be a bit, what you call, bewildered. It got on George's nerves so, and he didn't seem to like her cooking. I mean I was used to it because I'd had it all my life. She'd more or less tell you to go in a temper, although she didn't want to be left. We went to live then with his mother. I was going down every day from the laundry at dinnertime for my dinner at my mam's to see her. I'd be taking her stuff because she hadn't got like no money coming in again, so I would be taking her stuff for her to eat, and helping her out. I've always had a conscience. I couldn't possibly do it to a human being. I mean she just wanted somebody and she was my mother when all's said and done, wasn't she? But on the other hand I can't say I loved her an awful lot, because she wasn't one of them sort of women where . . . I think it was probably her temper that made me dislike her so. Even when I was married to George she slapped me right across the face in front of him, because I'd said something back to her, even when I was married.

We took the front room. It was a lot bigger house than my mother's. It wasn't a terraced house, it was what you call a double house with front room, and I think that had . . . she only had three bedrooms, but there was no attic. It had a cellar, and it had a kitchen and what you call a good living-room and a front room, so we took the front room and one of the back bedrooms. 'Course we paid her like for it and that. I had a few bits that my brother had sent me from

India, because he knew George and I had got married so he sent me a parcel from there. You couldn't get linen, so he sent me some table-cloths from India, and a big – it was like velvet background with all gold gilted on it of the Taj Mahal and it had 'To Sister' on the bottom of it, and very proud I was to have it. She said how untidy it looked – well, she was interfering with our little life, if you know what I mean.

Anyway, this particular Saturday morning I'd been shopping early because we were on rations, and I'd come back and she said something about, 'Go and get that brush and get that front done,' or something, 'you haven't done it.' Well I said, 'I'm going to do it now I've come back,' and she was ever so nasty with me, she hit me on top of the head with the brush. She'd got a nasty, very nasty violent temper. I know my mother used to cry and say she was sorry afterwards, but George's mother was – ooh, she was violent! I can't say she had a good life either, thinking about good lives and that. She's one of them sort that used bad language. I couldn't stand that, because my mother never swore. I said to my husband I said, 'I can't do it, I can't stay here. You'll either have to stay here yourself and I'll go back to my mam.' We only lived at George's mother's for a fortnight.

He came back to live with me like and my mother. I must have upset her during the fortnight I was away, because this condition of hers was getting worse. There was no washing being done at all. From the time I'd been away, she hadn't done anything. So I had to do her washing as well. And of course my husband got a bit annoyed about this, and he said, 'Well, something's got to be done, you can't keep going out to work and doing all this work as well.' So anyway, I said to my mam, I said, 'We'll have to get a bit more severe with you mam, you'll have to do things.' So she said, 'I will, I will.' I fetched her potty down this particular morning – you've got to do it every morning, you've got to empty them you see. I said to her, 'Now go and take that across the yard yourself to the toilet and empty it, and I'll wash it when you come back. A little walk across the yard will do you good.' And she went and fell, the potty in her hand, she broke her thigh.

I laid her on the settee – well of course we didn't know at the time that it was broken. I went to Dr Bell's and asked him if he would come and see her, and he'd got so used to coming to see her, he used to come sometimes – because it was rheumatism and there was nothing he could do, and it was partly that she was getting into a sort of a rut of her own, that no doctor can help. They go into a – I can't quite explain it to you, you find this an awful lot when people's had enough of life and they don't want to be pushed to live any longer – they are giving way to it, they kind of go into a trance. Anyway, I sent for Dr Bell. I went to see him, early in the morning – I should have been going to work – so he said, 'I'll come and see her.' So I said, 'Now mam, you'll be all right.' I put her on the couch, I put her some water at the side, I said, 'I'll have to go to work, because they'll be wondering what's happened to me.' I'd had an awful lot of time off with her from time to time, weeks off. She was almost crying, telling me not to go to work, she wanted me to be there. She just wanted somebody to be there, didn't matter whether she was nagging at you or not, or shouting at you or rowing with you, so long as you was there. 'He said he would come as soon as surgery had done,' I said. 'Well, I've left the door open.' 'Course he knew I'd got to go to work. They were telling me off at work with having so much time off.

I came home at dinnertime and he still hadn't been. So I had to go round there and see him again, so he said, 'Well I've been so busy with my calls.' He thought things weren't so serious as they were. I told him that she'd had a fall, and he thought she was sort of having me on a little bit, because she'd had the doctor on quite a lot, how ill she said that she felt. Really, he said, she'd got to get out of it herself, no medicine wouldn't help her, yet she was complaining to the doctor that she'd got something wrong with her – you know, more than rheumatism and that sort of thing. Anyway and that, he hadn't come, so I had the afternoon off. It must have been around about teatime before he came, because I was getting quite cross, because she was looking really ill, she was saying how her leg hurt her. Anyway he came and he said that she had broke her thigh. He said, 'We'll have to get her straight up to the hospital.' I mean she had been left all that time, all day really – and if he'd come in the morning – anyway they got her into hospital. I stayed with her because it was the evening and we got her settled in.

They didn't take any X-rays or anything like that when she first went in, just what they did was to wash her to settle her down for a while. Next day she'd got a cage for her leg. Anyway I said to her, 'How do you feel?' So she said, 'All right.' She said, 'Did you bring me those things, that I told you to bring?' 'Course I had collected up a few things because she had to go to hospital, what she wanted and that, and it appears that I'd forgotten the towel – in those days you took your own towel to the hospital. She said, 'Did you bring those things?' And of course I'd brought her an old towel. My mother used to save new towels, sheets and blankets for an emergency. The old one had got to be worn out completely. I took her up this old towel when I went up to see her and she threw this towel at me while she was in the hospital, with her temper, she was sitting there – '*That* weren't the bloomin' thing I wanted!' She said, the new ones are in such and such a drawer, and I thought to myself, oh mum, not in here. It didn't matter how old she felt, she never lost this nastiness from time to time.

I kept going every night to see her – I couldn't go through the day because I was working. About a week went by and she began to deteriorate. At the same time I was still under Forest Dean, they were still getting agitated about me. I told them that my mother were ill in hospital and they gave me a paper through my doctor and put me off sick for two months. I'd got to have two months' rest. This was just at the peak of the time when she was deteriorating at the hospital. Dr Bell was in touch with Forest Dean and he knew that I was getting all worked up because I was always crying, always crying. The least little thing and it'd upset me, even when I got married. If George shouted at me I'd be crying. Even if the doctor was a bit nasty with me it would bring tears right down to my eyes, and I would sob, really sob my heart out. Anyway, just at this time and that, they said, 'You've got to have complete rest,' you see, so they put me on sick. Well of course the firm didn't like it very much, it was either that or packing up my job. So I packed up my job.

My mother deteriorated. You could see that she was slowly going into a coma. I had visited her in the evening, the telegram came about eight o'clock and she had died in the night, so her leg never did get mended. She just let go, absolutely let go. She kept saying to me, 'Well, I know you're all right,' while I was in the hospital. She'd say, 'I know you're all right.' She said, 'I've nothing else to live for now.' Just completely let herself go. She was sixty-three.

Childbirth

'It's a wonderful time, birth is.'

While I'd been saving I bought a bedroom suite which was in George's mother's sister's, so what happened was I just took out my mother's furniture, put it in the back place and put our own in. So we was all right, and he got good money then as an electrician and over twenty-one, he was on good money.

I was twenty-three before I had Paul, the first one. Of course we wanted one, we'd been trying for two years, because we'd got mother's house then, although as I say it was rented, we'd got somewhere to live, and we'd made it our little home. Paul was born March 1949 and it was just becoming the end of the rationing, and I was still under Forest Dean. When I was carrying Paul, I went to work up to about six months. I was working for Boots and they put me on part-time because I was having quite a bit of blood pressure carrying him, and of course they used to give me a medical in there – they had like a small office with a nurse and everything, and I used to go in there and have a check-up or a rest. They was very, very good to me.

Of course I had to go regular to the doctor's and the clinic. I had quite a bit of trouble carrying him really. 'Course I had to go in about twenty days before I had him, I'd put on such a lot of weight. I was twelve stone then, about twelve stone four pounds – I was tremendous, I couldn't sort of carry the weight. They said he would be a very big baby. 'Course, they had to force him. He was born on the twentieth of March and on the day that he were due I had no pains or anything, they just broke the water, they just forced him – forced

me to be in labour – and of course I was in labour then for two days
before he was born. It was what you call a dry labour in those days.
I had to stop in about another three weeks, about another twenty-one
days after I'd had him, because they thought it might start the TB up,
with carrying him. Paul weighed nine pounds three ounces – but as
I say I was quite all right.

I was in labour with Andrew about fifteen hours, but he got his
shoulder stuck – he'd got very wide shoulders. I was bleeding very
badly, they thought I might have to be stitched and they laid me on a
kind of a cot in the delivery room for twelve hours and never moved
me at all. Just put swabs on me to stop the bleeding. They thought
that Andrew would have to have a blood transfusion because I was
Rhesus negative blood group. However they took tests of his
blood and it appeared it would be all right. I was in hospital
again. They was more worried about this TB starting, you see,
than anything else. Andrew was the tiniest, he was eight pounds
four ounces.

My doctor told me not to have any more children, not because
there was anything wrong with me particularly, because he thought
I'd had enough with the two, he thought, and what with all the
trouble with my mother and that, and I was still a bit nervy. I found
I had enough to do all day long, and I was still under him more or
less, keeping a check on me all the time. Once or twice he had to
give me, you know, tablets or something – tonic and that – with
having the two youngsters; because I mean George were working
hard, so I mean I never had any help from him as he was too busy,
and we could not afford a holiday then at all. Anyway, in December
1952 I became pregnant again. I was so upset about it, because as I
say I didn't particularly want another child, I thought two was
enough. I went to see my doctor, Dr Bell, again, and he examined
me and said, 'I am afraid you are.' I was so upset at the surgery that
they had to calm me down before I was allowed to leave the place.
Because I didn't want any more, I found that very difficult to take,
for some reason. I'd just got it on my mind and that, just to have two
children, I think. However through the months I got used to it, I
didn't mind after a while. Three, you see, before they all went to

school, really is quite a lot. You're just getting rid of one lot of nappies when you are starting another really.

They're toddling around and you've got to keep your eye on them all the time, because you know they're either wandering out the back yard or taking things off shelves – you know, you've got to be careful, kitchens with saucepans and fires, and you've got to watch them all the time. 'Course, when Paul was little he was a devil for the fire, he'd chuck anything on the fire and that, chucked cushions on the fire he would off the settee if you didn't watch him. It was a big range that stuck to the side of the wall each side of the fireplace, where you could put your clothes on it, but it used to go over the top of the range, anything on the fire, and he used to think that it was lovely to watch it burn, you know. So I mean, really two was enough for us.

Anyway I decided and that, that I wasn't going to have Mark away in hospital, and they said it would be all right and I had him at home, and he weighed nine pounds twelve ounces, and he was the easiest birth I'd had. I was in labour at about five in the morning with him, and I'd got to go to the hospital that day – they sent for me because he were three weeks overdue. Anyway it started at five o'clock, but I'd got all my hairpins in. I'd got my hair all frizzy to go in the hospital. It was ever so funny. By the time the midwife came – it would be about two o'clock in the afternoon – she came and she said, 'Where do you think you're going to?' I said, 'I was going to the hospital today.' So she said, 'Well you can take all your pins out now,' she said, 'because you'll be going to bed.' Anyway he was born by three o'clock, and one of my neighbours came in to help me. She was marvellous, absolutely marvellous, and of course they brought the gas and air in those days, the midwife brought it, and you breathe through this like – gas-mask affair. It's like a small oxygen tube, and she kept taking it away in between the pains of the baby when you are contracting – they take it away from you so that you are sort of pushing down in between, so it wasn't so bad really.

As I say, this lady came in. Actually she lived facing me, we had been friends for years, since I had been a little girl she was living there, and she'd had children the same age as mine. She didn't get married until she was late in life, and they played with one another, you see. I think you feel more comfortable if you've got someone like that over the first one, because you know when you've had your first one, you know exactly what's happening to you, but I think and that, a friend or – not a midwife really or a nurse, because you really don't know them well enough – to be there with you, you know, talk to you and hold your hand. I think you feel a lot more comfortable and time seems to go past very quickly during it. She knows exactly and that . . . I wouldn't have wanted a man there or anything – you know, my husband or anything like that – but when you've got a neighbour or a dear friend, just to hold your hand, I think . . .

I suppose George must have been worried really. I never asked him, to be honest with you – well you don't, do you? I think you're so much concerned about yourself just at that time. You know, no men like being on their own, do they really? Looking after themselves, and of course he were running up and down to the hospital every night to see me. I wouldn't want anyone there myself, but I think it might put him a bit off sex, really. I think it is a thing and that, women – well you know, men doctors are used to it, I know that – but I think that it's something private of your own. I mean a woman borns the baby, she has the baby, and I don't think that men ought to interfere with that. It's been there for years and years since the world began, and I don't think that men can do any good standing over there watching you – it would embarrass me really, I think. Because you do a lot of 'oh-ing' and you know what I mean and pushing, and – it depends on the person, women and that do get away with it without any chore, but I mean very few – so you do a little 'Oh!' now and again. I wouldn't want to think that my husband could hear me being mardy – it isn't being mardy really, that's the way I look at it anyway. Besides and that, it's a wonderful thing birth is, there's no doubt about it. But I always seem to think that it would put men off a bit really, to think that you can have a baby where you had the sex, sort of thing – there's such a lot of love there during the sex time. I think it just might put something in the back of the mind or a man's mind or think about it – 'Oh God, what she's gone through, I wouldn't like to see that again!' – and they probably wouldn't have any more children, some men perhaps, when they've seen it. You never know what it does to the mind sometimes. But on the other hand it might do a lot of men good to realize what women have to go through. But I am not one of them sort, I don't want my husband to be there, they can't do anything for them until the baby's born anyway. I mean the responsibility is there, it's been born and it's a man's place then to take the responsibility, once a child is born. I don't see that he can do anything about it while she is in labour, unless, as I say, some women probably like them there because it soothes them, they feel and that a bit more contented probably. It depends really how you look at it.

I think when people – a lot of people in pain – doesn't matter whether they're having babies or what, they want to be on their own, you know, they don't want a lot of fuss and bother. I am one of them sort of people. The more people fuss over me the more I get upset, I do. I don't want any sympathy at all really. I want people to care, it's not that, it's just that – 'Oh dear, oh dear, you are in some pain, oh you poor thing' – you know, and all tears start coming, because you realize yourself that people feel sorry for you, and I think that people need their own sympathy sometimes, don't you? You know what I mean? People suffer, and some people they say nothing at all. I am very good at being sympathetic, and I feel very sorry for people and that, that's poorly, and I'd do anything for them. It's not that. I feel the opposite when people give it to me. I feel sorry for them in a way, because they think that you need it, and it's them people that really need it themselves.

Children

'I didn't quite know how to hold mine.'

I didn't know much about having children. My mother talked to me and that, but we never spoke much about having children, because she said, 'If I was you I would never have any.' Well of course, with all her worry and trouble over the three. I love children anyway. I knew it right from the beginning, I sort of felt it with dolls and that sort of thing. We always understood that we'd never like to go through our life without having any children. I love children I do, I like watching them growing up. I think it's the most marvellous thing, it's like putting a plant in the garden and watching it flower. Oh yes, I love children. I don't think I shall ever lose it really, but I haven't got as much patience of course. But even now you see the young people and that they bring up the children entirely different from what we did. Not in feeding them and that sort of thing, but they let them sit up too late instead of having a certain time for putting them to bed – the habits of training them at meals and that sort of thing. Of course they don't feed babies now until they are hungry. They used to make sure that they got the food at a certain time, they sat down to regular meals, like my mother brought us up.

I didn't quite know how to hold mine when I first brought Paul from the hospital. You find that. Well that's only natural for every mother that is, definitely. Especially when it's washing its hair, when you are holding it, you are terrified you are going to let the head go and it drops underneath the water or something. You've got to handle it so carefully at the back of the neck, and be careful of its eyes – you know, you get soap in its eyes. It's only a natural thing that is. That'll never change with the times, will it? There are a lot of incidents really through life that'll never change.

When they were all tiny you used to have to bath them in front of the fire in a tin bath, one after the other in the same water, because by the time you filled up your copper for hot water, you emptied it and put perhaps half as much in again, and while that was getting hot to empty into the bath to hot it up, you more or less had to use the same water as you washed them. I used to have to do that every Saturday night, they had a bath every Saturday night. I used to have one in the kitchen afterwards, about half past nine.

I had all three and I never went to work until Mark went to school, until he was five, and then I went on part time in the mornings because he was only at the London Road School – all of them were, they all used to take each other to school. Everyone in the street went together, so they'd only got kind of a little field to cross, and there was a warden on the road to take them across to school. I used to see them off to school and I used to work part-time till lunchtime, until one o'clock, then I used to see them at dinnertime and then they used to have their meal at night – they used to have a little snack in the afternoon. So it worked out very well until they were all old enough and I could go on full time – office work, clerk more or less, accounts in one way or another.

Moving House

'I don't think we would have moved if it weren't for my nagging.'

I used to put all my money away, you see, what I earned, in the bank. George saved quite a bit of money himself and found the deposit – 'course we were a year looking for a house, before we found this one. Well I mean it was in quite a mess, and we bought it because it was so cheap. And of course we did quite a lot of the alterations on our own, gradually, because it was six months before we came in it, because it was in such a mess – we'd to get things straightened up and things done. We didn't mind as long as we'd got it, it's just a matter of knowing that you are going to move. I am afraid I was awfully naggy – you know, with the children and George. I don't think we would have moved if it weren't for my nagging so much. I couldn't make him understand how I felt about the house, although I was out at work, but as soon as I walked into it at night I just felt that dread about it, I felt I'd just had enough of the walls, and everything being the same. I detested the house, absolutely dreaded it.

They were very bad memories, although I was happy, you know. I've always been happy with George, I wouldn't change him for all the world, and the children, but I'd got this behind me all the time. He used to say, well, if we moved anywhere else it would just be the same. I felt as though it didn't matter where I went, I was going to get out of the district altogether. It wasn't the people, the neighbours, they were very, very good – mind you, apart from the fact that they knew all the history of the family, because you lived that close to everything that went on, everybody knew about it. If one neighbour got to know, the rest got to know. You couldn't keep anything a secret, you lived too close. They were very, very nice neighbours, although they was more or less living on top of you, popping in and out, but if ever you were ill, they'd look after you, do things for you. But here you hardly see them at all, to say good morning to, so you're living in an entirely different world in a way. I felt different in myself and I was leading a different life. When you've got memories of the same place a lot of things have happened, you find that your life completely changes, the environment anyway, that you move out of.

So you see, coming into a place like this, where you've got a bath and an indoor toilet, it's bound to – the boys were that chuffed when they first came in that they had to have a bath every night, one after one another, because they couldn't quite believe that you'd got hot running water. [Laughs.] Mind you it soon died down, they got fed up with that. They was all going to the same school, London Road School, then Paul went on to Mundella and then as Andrew got eleven he went to the school in between a grammar school and the secondary school. He was in a kind of grammar stream, what you call a grammar stream, but not quite clever enough to have gone to the grammar school, so he had to go three miles to his school. I had to buy a bike for him to get to school every day.

I think they liked it more in the old place because they lost all their friends when they moved, really. Yet when their friends came down to here, they would have liked to live here. Strange isn't it? It's the environment again. You'd got more room, and a garden and everything. You can tell they've changed. Their opinion changes from year to year on various things. Every youngster is the same. We never argued with them at all, regarding our opinions – you know, how it differs from them – but we've had discussions. Especially George's opinion on politics and one thing and another, of course. I mean their hair is not very tidy, not that you want it short nowadays because we know it's not in fashion, but at least it wants to be tidy, to get anywhere, and clean clothes more regular. And of course it hurts, it hurts every mother, because you see, you bring up your children and that – well I've always brought mine up to be clean and tidy, put things away, look after their clothes and themselves as well

– and then you see them deteriorating under your very nose, and you can't say anything to them because they are living their own lives.

I've gone from one extreme to the other, but I am quite happy and content, although I was very lonely when I stopped going to work, but I am not now – I've got plenty to do all day.

9.   Fiona McFarlane

Fiona McFarlane has lived all her life in the Glasgow area of Scotland. She is now in her late forties, is divorced and lives with her son, Dick, a university student. She comes from a working-class family – her parents worked in various hotels. They had five children. Her grandfather, father and husband all drank heavily, which has deeply affected her attitudes towards men.

She left school early to help out her mother, but in her twenties she decided to continue her education by attending evening classes and sitting for her Highers (the Scottish equivalent to the GCE). She was successful and attended teacher training college. Her main interests now are connected with her work as a Labour local councillor. Because of her divorce, she says she would like to move away from the area she now lives in and find a new life in Canada.

Childhood and Family

'It's a wonder any of us grew up normal.'

I was born in the Royal Maternity Hospital in Glasgow in Rotten Row, and the reason I was born there was because my mother couldn't afford to get the doctor in, and up there they could take her in for ten days for a pound. I was the fourth of five children and my father had a reasonable job in India Tyres, but he was a typical Scot, thought his money was his own, and he would only give my mother literally the pocket money whilst he drank the rest. The first two boys were twins. My mother and father had both been in the hotel line. They were very snobbish about it, they only worked in hydros, they only worked at the very best. Marvellous tips in the hydro. We went there for a season at a time.

My mother only married my father because she was getting on. She'd been well warned off men, she was afraid of them, and she was thinking it was maybe time to get settled down. She was twenty-five, twenty-six, she thought she was getting a bit past it – she had never gone with a boy. She had been so frightened off them, made frightened of them by her father and her brother. But she wouldn't go out with any of them, she used to spend her time when she was off duty in her hotel in her room sleeping. Just to pass the time, and she was always tired, you know. She still is always tired. When I was a girl she used to always have a nap in the afternoon – take us to bed with her while she had a nap.

She'd not had any education at all. Her father had been a terrible drunk and her mother had died when she was quite young and they had all been brought up in homes, all in individual homes. You know how they split up the families. They took her family of four and they put them all in separate orphanages and they did not see each other again until they left the orphanages when they were adults, about sixteen or seventeen. She had a brother who was a baker. They had quite a big family, I think their mother had a baby every year. My grandfather really was a wild drunken man, and my uncles and my aunt can tell her. My mother thought the world of her father, she thought there was nobody like her daddy, but none of the family even ever associated with him – she was the only one, she took him in when he was an old man – because they could remember their mother lying on a mattress on the floor delivering her baby, and him coming in drunk and taking her by the hair, you know, and giving her a beating up because his food wasn't ready. Anyway she died of blood poisoning about two weeks after the last child was born, and his very respectable – he only had one sister – very respectable sister came. She had a boarding house and took the baby away and gave her a very good education. My mother and her younger sister Jenny were put in homes.

When my mother was a young girl she had nowhere to go and she had no home and she used to spend her Saturdays and Sundays going round all the halls in the 'twenties in Glasgow, and listening to all the speakers of the time – John McLean, Harry McShane, Jimmy Maxton, the lot, she heard them – that was her political education. And of course although my father was a drunk, her brother who had been a baker, he was very active in socialist politics. He was by this time working for the Co-operative and was actually in charge of the bakery section – he had started school in Glasgow and had come through from Edinburgh to Glasgow, and he was an ILPer. He was a JP, and of course he would tell her that the evils of society were caused by the system, this sort of thing, and she used to tell us about all these speakers and what they had said – and again about the atheists, that there was no such thing as a God.

She got married intending to start a boarding house of her own. As my mother says, they got the boarding house, but non-paying guests – five children and my father – as it turned out. I think my mother's sexual attitude might have been to blame a wee bit too, because she was so afraid of it that she wouldn't have any sex, and I think any time she did have, she became pregnant, you know. She didn't know anything about birth control and she says that if in those days she had gone to the doctor they'd have chased her – because she didn't have enough money. The working classes weren't supposed to know anything about birth control or abortion and how to prevent these.

In my family there were two boys, twins, and then my sister fourteen months later, and then three years later my younger sister. And they agreed between them that that would be the last. Well I think there was never any sexual relations from the time that my sister was born, my mother will tell you this. I never knew my mother and father to even sleep in the same bedroom. They just never slept together.

It's like when I had my periods. I had no idea what this was. I woke up one morning and blood was streaming from me – and I was screaming through to my mother in the kitchen. Nothing was sore, I felt nothing, but I thought there must be something wrong with all this blood about. All my mother said was, 'Stop that nonsense, that's you coming a woman now,' and that was it. I never associated anything I heard with *me*. You know it was quite a frightening experience. I stayed off school. I think that was the only time I ever stayed off school. And then she didn't bother explaining that this would happen regularly, and this happened later. I couldn't understand it. I thought there must be something wrong with me and I didn't tell her. I managed somehow by, you know, washing all underwear. I was thirteen, washing my own underwear. I managed to keep it going. I don't know how I managed – I must have used rags or something to ward it off. About a year later she took me to the doctor. She didn't say what it was until I was in – and I was so embarrassed – and I sat down and she said I had had a period on my thirteenth birthday and I had nothing since, you know – and all this time I had been hiding it from her, so afraid in case there was something wrong with me.

Through reading women's magazines – they never did mention it in those days, this would be 1946 to 1947, it just wasn't mentioned – I gradually worked out that these periods must happen regularly, because look at all the advertisements for sanitary towels there were, and if it only happened once in a lifetime you wouldn't need this massive advertising campaign, and it was then I realized that this must happen regularly. I think it must have been books in the library, I don't know how I found out that this happened every twenty-eight days and it went on for several days. I still have a hangover of terrible embarrassment. If I go into a chemist and it's a man, I would never dream of buying anything; it's a self-service place I do go to, that's it. And I always take it to a woman and only in passing.

It's ridiculous, isn't it, that we should be ashamed of something that's perfectly natural and normal, and we should be sort of shouting about there's nothing wrong with it, it's a perfectly normal function. It was like pubic hair. I thought there was something wrong with me yet again. My mother's very hairless and I hadn't seen my sisters' and I don't know, I just didn't seem to notice anything, you were too involved in what we were doing – I was a bit of a tomboy. I went to the art galleries and looked at the great paintings of nudes, just to see did they have this too, and of course they didn't – they didn't. So I was quite convinced that it was me – you know, I was terribly frightened of anyone ever finding out that I had this hair. It was just ridiculous.

We weren't close at all, we weren't a very close-knit family. In our house there was never any affection shown. She used to tell us none of us were wanted. We were all unwanted and because of that she made a martyr of herself. She wouldn't allow us to do a thing to help, it had to be carried on, this great martyr herself – she did without so we would get, and this drunken sot of a husband coming in. He was pitiful, coming in on Saturday night, falling in the front door drunk with our frozen fish supper. And he was so mean – he wouldn't give you money. You know what Scots are like – all their money is for themselves. Now he has changed a bit, but I feel very bitter. I could never forget what he had done.

Oh, my father was just a – he didn't exist. He was just a figure in the background that sort of embarrassed you with his drunkenness. It was quite a good thing on a Friday night when he really got drunk, he used to come in and good-naturedly empty out his pockets – all his money, all in silver – I think he must have kept changing notes. And he would tell us to count it, and of course I used to and my sisters used to count it, and we would slip the odd two-shilling pieces out and hide them and slip them to my mother. This would give her extra money – she quite liked this.

My father was also a gambler, you know, he used to have a flutter on the horses, and you used to often find under the linoleum near his bed his hoard of pound notes and ten-shilling notes – and of course you would take a couple. We did show my mother where the plank was. She would take two, or you would take one, give it to her, and that was a great relief for her to get some money for a change. She used to sit totalling her debts every week, for weeks ahead, and she used to tell my older brothers all her trouble, and how was she going to get the money to pay for all this? She had an account with the warehouse which she paid weekly, and it must have cost her a lot – well, how much would ten pounds buy before the War and during the War?

My father was a drunk – but I think we were a highly respected family in the neighbourhood. Of course my mother with her Edinburgh upbringing was an utter snob and she mixed with no one, she wouldn't speak to the neighbours, they were beneath her. Of course we were always first in the class – if there was a McFarlane in the class they used to say, 'Your kids have no chance of getting a prize that year.' We were examined for going out, if everything wasn't right, you know. Everything had to be right: you had to make sure your clean handkerchief was in your pocket, and put on your white gloves or your chamois gloves, and white socks, and the three girls were all dressed alike, and we weren't allowed out without our hats, they were panama hats. We were the best-dressed kids in the neighbourhood.

She was determined that because there was a big family of us, and she always used to say – we were not allowed to get into trouble, we hadn't to mix with the other ones, we had to have the best of everything so that nobody could ever look down their noses at us, you know. She used to paint the outside steps white, and the window sills, and the curtains were always hung with the pattern out so that people passing would see the pattern – I thought this was the right way. We always had to learn proper table manners, and the table – maybe we hadn't much to put on it – she always had a big pot of soup – but we had to hold our knives and forks in the correct way and we had to use napkins. You know, even now I am disgusted by the way people hold their knives and forks, and I get furious at people not correcting their children, or if they don't leave it properly when they have finished eating. But some of it clings – you know, your underwear had to be perfect just in case you were knocked down – because she couldn't possibly be ashamed to go up to the hospital to claim you. She was quite lucky, all her family were very clever, they were always top in school.

My mother used to bath us all, we would be in our night clothes, and naturally my father was never ever there, and she would gather us round her at the front of the fire, and as we ate our toasted cheese sandwiches which were made in a shovel pushed under the fire – it was great – and we had our hot milk, she would read to us things like most of A. J. Cronin's work, she was very fond of them. She would borrow them from other people or maybe even got them from the library, although she seldom went out except to do shopping; and we got all these tales told to us. They were really tremendous stories, a chapter or so each night. And if there was ever any romantic scene there was always silence for that while she scanned it swiftly – and we'd realize after a while there was a pause, and we'd say, you know, 'What's next?' And she'd say, 'Just a load of rubbish – just a minute till I get to the right bit.' And she would wait until the romantic scene was over, you know, and then she would start again at the point where it became respectable again.

I think this is why we all read without apparent effort so young – was that my mother always was reading and she read these marvellous stories to us at night that we were desperate to get our hands on books and start reading too at that time. There weren't all that many books in the house. There was a set of encyclopaedias, *General Knowledge*, and we had one or two books, but we had built up quite a library through prizes and through joining all the Sunday-schools round about Christmas time, and the Guides, so that I would get a book at Christmas. All the *What Katy Did* books, and as I said I got – the teacher gave me, you know – she must have been quite a good teacher, she realized that my reading ability was more than just picture-book type – when at eight I got *Uncle Tom's Cabin* by Harriet Beecher Stowe, and I enjoyed that immensely, and I think that was about the first full-length book that I had read.

Then I joined the library and I was able to get a book every three days, which wasn't enough because I could read a book in a night – so I joined in my sister's name and in my mother's and got three books. So I would come back at the end of the three days with these books and take them in. I used to take them into school and read them in an afternoon under the desk if it was something boring and take it back in the – I would have it on my knee. I would have read anything that was in print. I don't think any of us ever were taught, we all went to school reading, and she used to get *Forward* – Francis Williams I think was the editor of that, if I remember rightly – and she used to read us extracts from this and when we were old enough we used to read it ourselves, and of course we got the *Sunday Post*, which was a deplorable paper, but she got it for 'Oor Wullie' and 'The Broons'.

Now she's become a queer mixture of reaction and radicalism that – you know, she thinks that they get away with murder today, we get things too easy, and she'll read this muck in the *Sunday Post* and the *Daily Express* and she'll say, 'That's quite right, that's quite right, they should bring back flogging and hanging,' and all this sort of thing – 'Far too many crimes and criminals'. Although she is violently opposed to capital punishment, she still thinks, you know, they are getting it too easy and maybe they should. They go through this period when they see great injustices and they want the injustices put right, and when they see the injustices largely getting not put right but slightly improved they then, I think – they don't like the consequences. They would like us all – I think they think it is good for us to have a struggle. My mother was very puritanical of course, and I think all of us are tainted with it. So it's a wonder any of us grew up normal, but I think we are all inclined to be tainted with it.

Courting and Marriage

'I was afraid to do without.'

I often think that, you know, that girls in Scotland are easy game because they are so starved of affection – their mothers seem to shove it all on to the boys, all their affection, and forget they have got daughters. Girls don't seem to need it, and they do desperately, so that they are easily conned.

I was about thirteen when I first had boyfriends – well, they were not boyfriends in the way that you would speak about it now. It was just sort of meeting them after school. I didn't know how babies were born. I thought it was by kissing. I remember going with my husband when I was fifteen, sixteen, and him kissing me in the pictures – you know, one of those tonguey kisses – and holding my breath afraid to swallow, and rushing away to the toilet to wash out my mouth in case I would have a baby. It was really ridiculous.

I left school when I was fifteen. I was one of the top pupils in the year, I think I was actually third, and when they heard I was leaving – this was 1948 – they sent for my mother and my father, but only my mother went up, and they pleaded with her to keep me on and she said, 'It's not worthwhile, she's only a girl, she'll only get married. What's the point in educating a girl?' You see, both my brothers were learning apprenticeships and there was no money, and I started as a junior shorthand typist with a civil engineering firm.

It was very good training because it was a tiny office – they were building a power station and the contract was to last ten years. It was a tiny office with very few staff, so you learned to do everything – you know, you learned to operate the switchboard, you learned all about pricing and costing and invoicing, and everything that was to be done in an office, you knew how to do it. I was there fourteen months. That was where I met my husband, he was working there and he showed me how to operate the switchboard, he showed me all the system. After fourteen months he went into the army to do his National Service, and I left the firm and started in another firm as a shorthand typist.

I met another boy while my husband was in the army and I stopped writing to him. It was really, you know, seeing the world through rose-tinted glasses, it was a marvellous feeling – I have never experienced it since. This other lad, Sandy, was what, seven or eight years older than me, but it didn't seem much of a difference. I remember the night I met him I was at the dancing and he danced with me. We had coffee together and he saw me round to the bus, and I told him I had a boyfriend and he was in the army, and he said, 'I am going to make you see so much of me that you'll forget the other boyfriend,' and I thought, big-head, but he did – he phoned me up there four times a day, he called into the office to see me, he sent me presents. He wrote to me practically every day, and you know, within a couple of weeks I had forgotten that the other one existed.

Sandy was killed in a motor-cycling accident and I was in hospital, just before I was eighteen. My arm was still in plaster, I had a broken arm and compound fractures – and I don't know, it is one of these things – I missed the lad so much, I kept looking for him, you know, I couldn't believe he was dead. When my future husband came out it was nice to have someone else again and we got married – which is the greatest mistake of my life, just sort of rushing into it. Actually I think it was after Sandy was killed I was afraid to be without.

I was only seventeen. I mean it was absolutely ridiculous. He was twenty-one. We just got married in a Registry Office and sent telegrams saying we were married to both the sets of parents, because both of them were opposed to it. They didn't believe that we were going to get married, and I don't know why we did to be quite honest, I really don't know – we did nothing but fight and quarrel.

My husband's mother is a very domineering woman – she's always right, a very selfish woman – in fact her son is very, very like her. Everything was for her. I got on with her reasonably well at first until she tried to sort of take over my house, coming in and re-arranging furniture, changing curtains, replacing ornaments – telling me how she wanted things done – and without saying a word I just stopped being about, you know, I stopped being there. He said he had seen his father losing his self-respect at an early age and he vowed that he would never allow any woman to do that to him. So he was the opposite, he became a domineering tyrant with me. When his father died, I always got the impression that he was trying to show his father, 'Look how I am treating this woman to make up for the way . . .' He was getting at his mother – it was his mother he was trying to punish, just for being – for what she had done to his father – instead of me.

He was very hard brought up. He left school at seventeen, but it was just a matter of sheer luck. How he got through I don't know because I didn't think he was particularly bright. He had a good head for figures but his English was bad, his spelling was atrocious and his writing was almost indecipherable. He sat his Highers in 1948 and failed miserably and left school. So he has always had this chip on his shoulder, and he used to always say to me that if he cared to sit exams he would get through with no bother, and I used to say, 'Well why don't you?' But I knew that if he had sat the exams, and failed, he could never have faced – you know, the humiliation of failing. He used to say things like, 'I know you're clever,' he used to say, 'but I have an original mind,' you know, himself.

His money was for him, what he earned was his alone, and I think that I had too much pride to ask him for money and I used my own wages to keep us. I was totally bewildered, I couldn't understand how he could change so much just by the simple act of getting married. We had fought a lot, we had parted a few times and had always come together again – you know, parting in a fight one night and a couple of nights later he would turn up at my house to take me out and again we would go out. I was literally afraid to give up my job because I didn't know what I would do without money. When I gave it up that time and he said to me, 'Well, I think four pounds is enough,' which was less than I was earning at that time and that was 1952. . . 'Four pounds is enough to keep us' – and I had just to manage on that. You did not get one penny more from him; you never got one penny less – but you never got any more.

And there was one time – he used to keep a wad of notes in his pocket, and one time – he used to count it you know, he used to count it a couple of times a week. . . One time a ten-shilling note was missing and he came into – I think this was the bedroom and I was in the kitchen – and he came into the kitchen where I was sitting, and he threw it down and he cursed and swore and called me an effing cow and a thief and all this sort of thing – I had taken ten shillings of his money, and he said there should have been – maybe there was ninety-two pounds there and there was only ninety-one pounds ten shillings, and I was crying because I hadn't taken his money. It is the last thing that I would have done – take any of his money. And I picked it up – I had tears streaming down my face – and as I picked it up I was counting it, and he had two ten-shilling notes wedged like one. And I was so angry I picked it up – now I wouldn't do it – rolled it up and took it back and threw it at him where he was sitting on the bed, and I said, 'You should count it properly before you make accusations,' and threw it at him, and of course he came through all apologetic – it was great, I think – he was great at making up.

I think that it could never have lasted, our marriage, as long as it did if it hadn't been that he was so – he put on such an act – after he had, you know, gone mad for a time – of repentance that you just had to forgive him – and you thought, well he won't do it again, until the next time, and a couple of weeks later he'd be off again. There was no need for it, my husband at that time must have been earning about twenty pounds a week, but it was his money. He worked at the factory, it was my father that got him in there.

Married Life

'He wanted me totally dependent on him . . .'

My parents wouldn't even acknowledge that I was married. I was embarrassed when I was given presents of double bed-sheets – you know, it was dirty, my mother – they didn't sleep together – it was dirty.

When I was pregnant, I didn't dare tell my mother, because this would have meant that I was having sexual relations with a member of the opposite sex. By that time my husband had shown his colours. I mean he used to go off when I was pregnant Saturday morning about ten – he would make some excuse and go – maybe he was going for cigarettes – out into the country, and I wouldn't see him until the early hours of the morning, and he didn't want to be seen with me because I was pregnant, because I was fat and ugly, as he said – oh no, I would never have dreamed of it. And of course, as I have said, he wouldn't hand over any money. The money I had earned had made such a difference naturally. I used to be sort of grey-haired wondering how I was going to get through the week. I was really distraught with worry, wondering where I was going to get enough money to feed us for the rest of the week – the pittance my husband gave me more or less went on the weekend shopping. A ladder in my nylons was a major tragedy. Of course we were brought up that appearance mattered, what you wore mattered, you didn't go out with ladders in your stockings, you didn't go out with shoes needing repairs. It was a tremendous effort to try and keep it up.

I didn't know anything about contraceptives. But when I had Dick I was only eighteen and it was a particularly bad birth, you know. I went in on the Wednesday, and it was induced. It wasn't born until the Saturday morning and in all that time I never had less than five minutes between pains, you know. They didn't give me – because it was induced, they didn't give me any pain-relieving gases or anything. Towards the end they had to give me oxygen because I was so far – I had just absolutely nothing left, and it was a breech birth, and it had to be turned two or three times, you know, and I had to have stitches. Anyway the doctor got hold of my husband and he said, if I had been twenty-one I wouldn't have been able to have a live child, and he would strongly advise against having any more.

It was after that he appeared with a contraceptive, a French letter, this thing, but you know after that, just through mistakes, with withdrawal and this sort of thing, I have actually had four abortions. We were just lucky that we knew somebody. It was through my husband's mother. I mean he was only about three or four months when I discovered I was pregnant again and I couldn't do anything but cry. All I wanted to do was to commit suicide, and it was my husband who went to his mother and said that I was pregnant. She immediately rushed me off to this woman who had given abortions to her daughter and various other members of the family. She lived quite a distance away. I remember travelling through to get my abortion.

It was after that he appeared with a contraceptive, a French letter, and she used a douche and soapy water and a wee sort of powder stuff which I never found out what it was. She gave me her address and said, after the second one, instead of coming through my mother to write to her direct. So I used to write to her directly, she would come down immediately. It was about twelve pounds she used to take – I don't really know how much she really took because any time she came I'd give her any money. I had a couple of pounds – and I must have been quite difficult to get rid of, because she used to have to come five or six times, and the last time I ended up in hospital. The final time it was just not coming away, it was – there were clots coming away now and again, and I had to go to the doctor and I said to him, I thought I was having a miscarriage, and he gave me pills and I lied so that I could go up to the hospital, and up I came and they asked me to come in the following day, and that night it all came away, and I went up and I think they did a D and C, and I discharged myself a couple of days after that because it was the holiday time, you see. My husband was complaining bitterly about missing his holiday because I was in hospital, so I discharged myself.

I've never ever been at a family planning clinic. In 1962 or thereabouts I heard of the pill. In conversations with other women I discovered that quite a few of them were on the pill, and I went along to the doctor one night and asked him – and said to him that I didn't want to have any more children, and he immediately said, 'Oh well the pill's the thing for you.' He said, 'If you are going to have any children, have them now, or else you will be too old.' And I said, 'I don't intend to have any more.' He said, 'Right, the pill, we'll get you on to that for a couple of years.' And I've been on the pill ever since. I am still taking them, fourteen years and no side-effects as far as I can make out, and no ups or downs.

We lived in a top flat house and I was unused to this, and I used to feel actually like a bird in a cage. I feel very sorry for animals in a cage at the zoo. It shouldn't be allowed. If they feel anything like we feel. So when Dick was a baby, I used to make him a couple of bottles and I would put any odd bits and pieces of food into the pram, and I would wheel him out and I'd go down to the park and walk all around the estates and the woods in the area, just for the sake of getting out, because I felt so trapped in that house. I was never without visitors. My mother-in-law used to come and see me every day with her husband and her daughter and a friend, and I used to do an awful lot of baking because I knew that every night I would have a house full of relatives just for the baby. They all would come to see him when he was bathed. Well, I used to have to bake every day, and I made scones and pancakes and fruit tarts – just so that when they all came there was something in the house for them to eat – and if I couldn't afford to do that, sometimes as it happened it would be toast and butter. But I enjoyed it because I felt so cooped up, so starved, I was glad of any human company.

My child possibly had a deprived upbringing. I made every mistake. I used to sit with my knitting – I couldn't afford to buy him clothes and I had to knit them for myself – my knitting and a book, and my husband would be maybe at the other side, and the baby would be playing with his toys on the carpet quietly, and there wouldn't be a word spoken the entire night. And during the day – I used to rise early because I was always afraid of anyone coming to the house and finding anything out of place. I wasn't actually house-proud, I was just afraid of being caught out as a poor housewife. So I would be up at six o'clock or half past and started getting the linoleum polished – we couldn't afford carpets – to try and get a shine on this expensive floor, which was difficult. I used to polish it out of sheer boredom three times a day.

I first went back to work when my son was in hospital. We were in the kitchen and I was boiling nappies in a pail, and he was walking very early, he was walking at six months, and he came rushing towards me as I carried this pail from the cooker to the sink and caught me by the knees, and the water spilled over and down his back and he was in hospital for quite some time. Once he had been in about four or five weeks and they said he wouldn't be out for a good long while, so I took a job, and stopped it when they said that he was getting out, so he was in round about ten months to a year. But it was just shortly after that – when Dick was about a year and a half – that I worked for that telephonist in a local firm for six weeks.

When I went for the interview there were quite a few people at it, and the letter came in telling me to start on the Monday, and of course I showed it to my husband and he said, 'You're not taking it, you can just write back and tell them that you are not taking it.' He wanted me totally dependent upon him, he didn't want me out working at all. He liked the situation as it was, with me having no money and being totally dependent.

Well I took this job, and when I finished he was quite annoyed because he got used to the money. But the first day I started, I was up at six o'clock and I had the house all cleaned and the washing all done, so that he couldn't say that I was leaving anything undone. And when I came home at lunchtime – my mother had been up to collect Dick because my husband used to start work at three o'clock, he was on a shift – and I rushed and made the dinner and I put it out, and he was angry, he was sitting all – you know, he had been shouting at me when I came in, I was a wee bit afraid and I was rushing to get the food ready – and I put it down to him, and he picked up his plate of food and he threw it across the room at the wall, you know, it all fell down. And I just rushed and put my coat and bag on and ran out of the house and away, I was afraid to stay in it. But he did things like that, he had a terrible temper, he would just lift the first thing. Well, he had to go to work at three o'clock anyway. He wasn't in until eleven o'clock that night, and by the time he came in he had calmed down a bit, and then, as I say, after six or seven weeks he got used to the little extra luxuries that my money was bringing in, and when the job ran out he was quite annoyed about it, and I had to get myself another job, which I did.

I landed very lucky the next time, I got myself a job with a carpet manufacturer's that was just opening in Paisley. There were about forty of us there for an interview, and to my astonishment I got the plum job. I was starting in charge of the office, they gave you a wee sort of ability test – you know, IQ-type things as well as additions, subtractions and multiplications. I would have been twenty-one – twenty or twenty-one – and then I got the word to start and I went along and there was nobody else there, and they took me through to their main firm and they took me all over it, showed me it, and they gave me about a week showing me all round the departments, and then it suddenly began to dawn on me, that this wasn't just the ordinary clerkess, and actually I ended up in charge of the office.

There were fourteen girls and we had a great time, because I believe in making your workers as comfortable as possible, and we were sort of hard worked – you know how they do work women harder than men, and pay them smaller wages. I was getting a very good wage for that time, I used to get ten pounds, but a man doing the job – I was doing stock controller for the entire Scottish Region – would be getting maybe at that time twenty pounds.

I was there two and a half years and then I went to the Education Authority. I was working as a secretary in the schools and I was appalled by the standard of teaching. The teachers were virtually coming in and putting their feet up, and it seemed to me that you were lucky if your child got one good teacher in three years. You know, it was those ones that were carrying all the rest. They complained bitterly about their working conditions and their wages, which were considerably higher than mine, and I thought when I saw some of their qualifications, I thought, this is ridiculous – Higher English and embroidery, and for teaching! So I got hold of some old Higher papers and looked them over and thought, I could do that, so I sat it. I must have been twenty-seven or twenty-eight. I sat Higher geography, Higher history and Higher English and I passed them all. So the next year I did biology, and you had to do arithmetic.

I went to classes in biology – I went to two classes in English and it became embarrassing, because it was as though I was showing off. We were doing *Hamlet* – and this was marvellous, this was like opening a new life. I had been a deprived child, you know, and here I was at last getting into it. The rest of them sat around, and either they couldn't answer or they wouldn't answer the questions, and it was me that was answering them and I thought, this is terrible, they'll think I am a right big-head. And the teacher in charge said to me, 'Oh were you at the grammar school?' – as if all the clever children went to the grammar school–'Have you done this before?'–and of course I hadn't – so I didn't go back, I put my name down for the exams and I sat them. Biology I did go to because you had to do experiments, and then I did art, and what else? Modern studies, and economics, and I got them all.

I went to classes in economics, but the modern studies, the paper just looked to me like common sense, I could have done it without any study. If you were aware of the political situation, if you read the newspapers, you could sit modern studies exam. It was ordinary level, and when I heard they made it Higher, I took a day off college one day and I went down to the Town Hall, and they were so used to seeing me that they said, 'Oh there must have been a mistake, they haven't put your name down on the paper.' So they wrote it down and they let me sit the Higher exam and I got an A-level pass. I was quite pleased I was able to do it. I knew I would have – you know, I knew they would let me sit it, because it was the same examiners that turned up at the Town Hall every time – not the examiners, the invigilators. I sat the exams and I got nine Highers and went to college.

When I went up for the interview they had all my qualifications before them but not one of them suggested to me that I could go to university rather than college, and it wasn't until I had done a full year at college that I discovered that I could have gone to university quite easily. I did four years at college, because I wanted to get the best qualification I could. I carried this chip on my shoulder that I'd been sacrificed for my brothers – who incidentally are both in very good positions now. My parents then couldn't afford for me to go on, and they said, besides, if they couldn't afford to send their sons to university it would look bad to send their daughter. The daughter didn't matter. When I was going to college when I was thirty and they told me I was accepted, my father said to me. 'If you are short of cash, if you need any money, don't forget to come to me.' And I was so angry I said, 'Where were you when I was fifteen?' He didn't seem to see it that way, you know, and he was quite convinced that my husband would stop me going if he could, which he did try to do, you know – he was very nasty.

My husband also had an eye for the ladies too, and he had a violent temper, which my father had had, and he was a moody man. I stuck it for years because I thought I had nowhere to go. I remember sitting my final exam, it was history and I had to be at the college by half past one, and I couldn't drive, and – I had taken driving lessons, but each time I went to sit my test my husband would put the car in for a major overhaul or to be checked, so that I was never ever able to pass my test, even though I bought the car, it was my money I had to save up because I unfortunately – the pattern repeated itself and I married a drunken no-use. That's my husband, my father and my grandfather were all drunks. My grandfather really was. When he was fifty-five the doctor told him that he wouldn't last six months if he didn't give up drink, and he never drank another drop for the rest of his life, and he died when he was ninety-one.

The only way I could stop my husband getting his hands on my money was to put it into jewellery, because he used to threaten that he could claim me for half of what I saved, because he could say it came out of the housekeeping, though how anyone could save out of seven pounds. . . So I said, right, well, if it's not in the bank he can't get it, let's see him fighting about jewellery, the only thing I could think to put my money into. So I – when I was in Gorbals I was working near a pawnshop, and I used to go in, I got to know the lady, and I could pay up maybe a diamond ring, a hundred and fifty to a hundred and ninety-five pounds. It started off about thirty pounds or thereabouts, and I gradually traded in the cheaper stuff to get really good stuff, so that I have got some really beautiful jewellery, and of course I'd been around years before this to other shops picking up very nice pieces of jewellery, and the only reason I wear so much now is that I've got so much, it seems a pity to have it lying about in boxes.

About four years ago I went for a cancer smear, and the doctor told me that she had found something, and I got such a fright, and I – you know, I had been brought up to think jewellery's vulgar, you don't wear it, you wear a little brooch, a small discreet brooch, or you would wear one ring, but you don't wear a lot. And I believed this until then. Of course I don't know about you, but I was brought up that you changed out of your good clothes the minute you got home and you kept the clothes only for good occasions, so you ended up with a wardrobe of stuff that was so dated that you can't wear it and it was too good to throw out. Well I decided there and then, look at that – all those clothes I've got, they've never been worn because I have been keeping them for special occasions, and look at all that jewellery not being worn, so I decided there and then that I was going to get pleasure out of the jewellery and out of my clothes now. I'd just go into my wardrobe and take anything and put it on. Even though I am wearing it to work, I still can go out somewhere special with it on. Sometimes I fall by the wayside, you know, and really do keep it for a good occasion, then find maybe a year later that it's just a wee bit out – and of course you end up giving bagfuls of stuff, good stuff that you have never really had any use out of, to jumble sales. What's the point of buying this stuff for jumble sales? So now I wear it all. That's me.

I have a friend – it was when I started getting interested in the

Women's Lib, and I went on various marches and demonstrations and we got involved in quite a lot of things – and my hair, I always used to wear it very short, about an inch all over, because it suited me and it was handy to have, and no one could say that I looked mannish by any stretch of the imagination, and yet my husband would start telling me I was dykey, I must have lesbian tendencies – 'dykey' is lesbian, another name for lesbian – and he would speak of me and my lesbian friends. And yet he loved going to Women's Lib parties because he said it was the only time he met intelligent, good-looking women who could hold their conversation with him, he loved it. If you ask any of the older members they'll tell you, 'Oh, Jim's a fun person.' He was only a 'fun person' when he was having a drink – you know, he had to have a drink before he could even go and mix with people. And that's why I started to grow my hair long, and it was very, very long. Then I just got awful fed up with it and I thought, this is ridiculous, and I cut it.

You know, you felt that – people associate long hair with female-ness, with femininity, which is a word I loathe – because I think if you are a female, if you are a woman, you don't need to stress it, you're either a woman or you're not. It's like masculinity – you're either a man or you're not. There should be none of this terrible stress that's put on us with advertising and social mores. It's ridiculous the way it is all sort of emphasized, if you don't wear this you're – you must be queer. So I grew my hair very long, and I cut it off. So that's it, that's why I am back to short hair again.

Labour Politics

'I was very dissatisfied with the state of women in politics.'

When I was sixteen I remember going up to the school, there was a political meeting advertised and it was a local MP, and at that time for the first time ever it was a Labour man. I can't even remember his name now – I think he is long since dead – and I went over to the school to see him, and they were forming a local Labour Party in the area, and I formally joined it and paid my subscription and took on the job of addressing envelopes so that we could send out some literature to everybody, and that was my first start in it. When my father heard what I was doing he was very angry and he said he didn't want any Jenny Lees here, and that my mother wasn't to encourage me and I wasn't to go out – I had to have a normal, sensible upbringing rather than this.

My husband was a Tory – naturally from his attitude he is a fascist. It was after he left the army, he had worked in an office and he didn't want to go back into an office, and my father got him a job in a factory and he was earning big money on the production line, and it was a couple of years after that when I got the vote for the first time. He used to go down to vote – he hadn't voted, he never bothered to go – he used to go, and – he'd say – to 'cancel out my vote', by voting Tory. He was the producer, and he saw the different people within the factory and he saw the different standards of work – living, one could call it – within the system. And from being violently Tory he became violently opposed to it, but he pooh-poohs the Labour Party – 'You'll never get anything done through the Labour Party.' He has called himself an anarchist, he calls himself a Marxist–Leninist, but he has never – he hasn't got sufficient intelligence to be associated with any group, the people would find him out if he was associated with any group. He has never lifted up a book on politics in his life and read it, he has never studied it.

I was very dissatisfied with the state of women in politics. I felt we had made absolutely no progress, absolutely no advances, since we got the vote. It's shocking when you look at how few women there are. And when you look at the laws and see how they are framed by men for men, and how unfair things are. A simple thing going in to get some hire purchase for about twenty or thirty pounds, and you have to take a man along with you to sign the form because you're not considered a competent human being. It's degrading and it's disgusting. There were so many occasions when – like even your child which you go into labour for and which you carry, you've all the fuss and trouble and the discomfort and the pain bringing them into the world, and yet you are not even the legal guardian, or you weren't up until the Tories got in a couple of years ago. I mean, all that took

– it didn't take any great legislative powers. The Labour Party could have done that years ago, there's no earthly reason why they couldn't do it. But I felt they needed more women. Women had to see other women in positions that were normally held by men.

When I got on to the Council they were all happy and delighted. This was great – 'A touch of glamour on the Council. Oh it's nice, I'll be able to sit opposite and look at something nice for a change.' They were all lovely to me until they discovered I wasn't going to go in there as a yesman or a yeswoman. I was in there for some principles, and I was going to see that if I could I would change it to suit the woman. That's why we have that social clause in the tenancies; that's why we have joint tenancies. You know they all think that maybe I am a wee bit weird because I push this. You know – they'll say, 'Oh you can't say that because Fiona's there,' and 'Don't get up on your Women's Lib platform!' – this sort of thing. But to me jt's not a Women's Lib platform, it's just sheer justice, it's human justice, it's common sense. That was the main reason why I went in, other women have to see women, and if women think they are capable of doing it. . .

They've been at me for years to go in, you know, but you know it takes a lot to do it, because you are losing your anonymity, and you know that there is a lot of ill-feeling because you are declaring yourself with a particular party. You know that you will have a lot of snide comments and you've got to think of your family. I said to my son, 'Would you like me to become a councillor?' And he said, 'Oh no, mother,' and my husband said, 'Suit yourself.' He never lifted a finger to help, he sat on his backside.

People would come up and they would help me campaign, and I was in a marginal, I was only in that seat because it was a marginal, and they said things to me like, 'You're a woman so you can't hope to win. We'll get in by maybe nineteen votes or we'll lose by about nineteen votes, but don't take it to heart, because a woman for the first time – I mean they are just not used to it. They won't vote for you.' And I got in by over three hundred votes, so it proved that people are perfectly willing to vote for a woman if they think she is competent. However, it's very annoying the red tape that everything is tied up with and the time it takes to get things through and being the only one continually fighting the same battles.

A couple of years ago when I was on the Council we had functions where people were invited – the police, they regularly come along, and the firemen, people like that – I think maybe this was the Town Council officials and ourselves, so it was more intimate – and you're all expected to entertain, and of course they said to me, 'Come on, Fiona, we've never had anything from you. Come on, give us a song.' So I got up, and although years ago I used to sing, I haven't sung in years, I hadn't opened my mouth in years, you know – too miserable. I knew a song. My mother said her father taught it, and I remember singing it at school when we were all asked to do something and the teacher being horrified by it, and I couldn't understand why and I still don't understand why, because it was a perfectly normal – you know, 'If I were a member of the Council of the Town, the man who wore the crown, I would turn him upside down. I'd keep the poor from starving and let the world go round, if I were a member of the Council of the Town.' So I got up and I sang this, and there was a sort of a shocked silence and I said, 'Now everybody clap.' So they had all to clap – the Tories included: 'Where did you learn that?' And I said, 'At my mother's knee, where we learned most.'

Separation and Divorce

'I am very wary of men, very wary.'

It was last August that I put him out. He wanted to court me, he still wants to come back, even though he has got his girlfriend and now is seen openly, you know, going about the streets with her. He lives with his mother for respectability, he's got the same streak of respectability as I have too. And she's – her husband left her to live with another woman, she has got two young kids, one under school age and one of school age – about six or seven – and he's now seen openly going around holding hands and with the two kids.

When my husband left he used to come round to the house, and if Dick wasn't in it was very difficult to get out of having sex with him.

Even at Christmas he came round, he turned up at a Labour Party dance, he said he would create a scene if I didn't let him come home with me and stay the night – in the dance in the Town Hall – so I – 'All right, keep quiet.' Well he said, 'We'll no fight, you promised, I am coming home with you,' and he came home. In January it was the same. He would come round to take me out and he would phone up – 'I am waiting here at the corner.' And he came to me after the elections, round about March, and he said, 'Well your man got in, you worked very hard.' And I said, 'Yes.' This was a Thursday or a Friday and he said, 'You're coming out with me on Saturday night.' And I says, 'Look, we have absolutely nothing in common and we have nothing to speak about now as far as I am concerned – it's finished. I just don't want anything to do with you – I don't want to see you again.' And he's never come back, because after that he said, 'If you don't have me back,' he said, 'I'll go to her.' I mean, imagine any man saying that to you, have you no pride? And you're not supposed to – you say, 'Oh well, come back to me rather than go to her.' I said, 'Do what you like,' and he went to – well his mother said, 'Well, there's no one else.' She can't understand why I put him out, because he is a model son! She's deliberately closing her eyes, how could she? People meet me and tell me, you know, with jokes like, 'You have got two additions to your family.'

But my husband hadn't spoken to his mother for over ten years until I put him out, and then he had to go to his mother, he had nowhere else to go, because he wouldn't pay the money that people were wanting for lodgings – he used to give seven pounds a week towards the housekeeping, that was his total contribution, he thought that covered everything. And of course when I told him that he had to leave the house – otherwise I had reached the point where I was – I had to keep myself from getting a carving knife and stabbing him – it's a council house and it was in his name. But with me knowing the rules that houses are given to families and not to individuals, and if the social behaviour of one is such that it makes it impossible for the members of the family to live in it, then the person who is the cause of it is asked to leave, and in this case it is the husband.

But you know he's reached the stage now when I honestly believe that the kindest thing I can say about him is that he is terribly in need of psychiatric treatment. My mother was saying about six or seven months ago that I have punished him long enough, you know. I had put him out, and even though she knew that I was getting a divorce, she said I have punished him long enough – there are worse men than he – it could have been me with a drunken sort of husband and no money and a squad of kids – and she said he wasn't the worst, and at least we only had one child. She said, 'You could always go out and work,' she said, 'so take him back.' And my son, he was standing listening to this, and he turned round in a rage and he said, 'Grandmother, you have no idea what you are talking about.' He said, 'If my father came back my mother and I would end up in a lunatic asylum,' he said. 'You have no idea what it was like living in that house with him.'

My son used to take the most dreadful migraine attacks and he would come out in a bad rash and spots, and he hasn't had an attack of migraine since I put my husband out last August, and his face has cleared up, you know, his skin trouble has gone. He is very quiet, and he always says, 'Men like my father should be brought up some close on a dark night and really given an awful doing for the unhappiness they cause to so many people through sheer selfishness.'

After my husband and I separated I was actually afraid to go out, and he would meet people and say to them, 'You tell her if I ever find out that she's got a boyfriend or going out with another man I am going to do her in.' A couple of friends one night were up at my house and they said, 'This is ridiculous, you sitting in, you've got to get out. You're still a young woman, and you've got most of your life ahead of you, get out.' And they took me to meet various people and I have been going out. These friends came to me – we had been parted about six months, it was after the May elections, it was about June – and they said to me, 'Look, it's really silly you sitting at home now.'

Men had asked me out – in fact I was afraid to go out, because after the experiences I had had with my husband, I am very wary of men, very wary. I wouldn't believe anything a man told me – in fact, you know, we were having a discussion about this a couple of weeks ago. . .

Anyway, I started to be very selective and choosing men that I would
go out with, and it's only ones with money, it's only ones in a good
position, and they've got to be married because I don't want to get
involved and it's in their interests that they don't get involved either.
We only go to the best places and I take great pleasure in seeing them
pay the bill, they pay it with such delight. I mean fifteen pounds – I
wish to goodness they would hand me fifteen pounds. For a dinner
and drinks, and they pay this with no bother at all, and you know
you think to yourself – what's his wife doing when he's out with me?

Anyway, I have met this bachelor who is eight years younger than
me. I have shown him my son, he must be able to calculate the ages,
but he keeps saying, 'Age isn't important.' Now nothing can ever
come of it because eight years is too big a difference when it is on the
wrong side for me, and you think to yourself, well, as I get older, you
– when he says how beautiful I am, which I don't believe in the first
place, you feel another wrinkle appearing and another line. He was
saying – we were out with another couple, and we were having a
discussion on this, about my attitudes – saying that I will never marry
again and don't believe what a man tells me – I am wary of all of them
as far as I am concerned – I'll go out, I'll have a good time, but I'll
never take any of them seriously. I'd never put myself in that position
again of a man thinking that he owned me and could do and say
exactly as he pleased, just because of a marriage certificate. And this
lad is pointing out to me that because of this attitude I may sometimes let slip through my fingers a really sincere person, but it's too
big a risk to take, I think. How do I know they are sincere? I don't
believe anything they say.

My sister loves ballroom dancing – she's a widow, her husband
died very suddenly last year – we went to the dancing on Saturday
afternoon and it was a case of – you'd think that there must be a book
that they all learn up on because they all give you the same line. You
know, you go over to her and you say, 'Do you know that I am the
most beautiful girl in this hall?' And she says, 'You can't be, I am
the most beautiful girl in this hall.' You know, all this rubbish, all
giving you the same old line. It gets monotonous. A lot of men ask
you out – I think a lot of them think, 'Separated, oh . . .' And of

course there was a smear campaign started against me when I was standing as a District candidate. I wasn't going to stand and they persuaded me to stand, and I was sorry I had done after, you know, I had heard all this ridiculous scandal: 'She's put her man out – who's she got ready to take in?' and 'Oh, she's entertaining men all the time.' Well, I lived in a goldfish bowl.

My son was a tower of strength at that time, and the barrister said to me when all this was breaking around me and I was bewildered and I thought – what have I done? He's the transgressor and I am getting all the blame. And he said to me, 'It's like this, Mrs McFarlane, you look so young that your son walking beside you – it is like a boy-friend.' And of course sometimes we would be joined by maybe one or two of his student pals, and this must have looked terrible, me with all these young men. 'Entertaining in my home' – they were coming to see my son. Well, 'Would you vote for a woman who put a man out and is living with a long-haired student?' Now the 'long-haired student' is my son.

It was when this campaign started you know, that I was a Communist, sort of going under the Labour Party ticket – this was one of the things that the Orange Lodge were saying. A vote for me was a vote for the Communist Party. And also, 'Would you vote for a woman who put her man out and was living with a long-haired student?' Another of them was I had gone soft on the Catholics because I was having an affair with one, and this is why I was pro-Catholic, which was ridiculous, I was neither pro-Catholic nor pro-Protestant. I think that religion is there to split the working classes. So I had all these sort of smear campaigns going round about the time of the election, and what had been a three hundred odd majority dropped to a one hundred and twenty loss – I lost that seat. They didn't vote. The voting dropped by about eight per cent or nine per cent. They just didn't turn out. It was the strife within.

It's horrible. That's why I want to get away from the area. In fact I am changing my name. I asked the lawyer. I am reverting to my own name – he said I can do it, but it's got problems. You have to inform the bank, you have to inform the Inland Revenue, on my passport I've got that – I need to send them a pound and a declaration. I am sending in my forms to Canada and America in my maiden name, Quinn, and really, you know, the difficulties involved just because of all these years. But I am *not* Mrs McFarlane and I refuse to be known as Mrs McFarlane, and he's an embarrassment and a humiliation to me and has been for years and all I want is – anything that he touched, I want to be rid of it, you know. I don't want to be tainted with him at all. I want a complete break from him because he was really rotten – he was a reptile. I should have been in a lunatic asylum for putting up with him.

I have taken out papers for Canada and I have sent away for America, because when this divorce comes through I want to have everything completed so that I can either go to Canada or America and see if I can start a new life for myself. As it is, I feel that I have wasted twenty years – how do I ever get back those twenty years? I am not joking now – twenty years utterly down the drain because I kept thinking he would change sometime, because of the way I was brought up. It wasn't nice to be divorced, you had to stick it out and stay married to him no matter how bad it was – you know, 'you've made your bed' attitude, you had to lie on it.

10. Barbara Marsh

Barbara Marsh was born in Kingston, Jamaica, in 1941 and was brought up by her granny until she was thirteen. She barely remembers her father, whose business went bankrupt when he took to the bottle and was sent to prison. She returned to her own family reluctantly when her grandmother became too old to look after her. Her real love remained with her granny, where there was more closeness and freedom than with her own mother, who was often too harrassed to show her much interest or affection.

After having her first child, Audrey, by her boyfriend, Lloyd, Barbara Marsh came to England in 1962, where she met Lenny, also from Jamaica. They married and have four children and live in Hackney, London, where there is a large West Indian community.

Apart from the difficulties she has experienced in finding somewhere to live, she has watched racial feelings harden over the years she has lived in Britain. She has worked in factories and as an office cleaner, all her jobs being badly paid and boring. She longs to go back to Jamaica but feels it would be impossible now that she has lost all her roots there and her children have been brought up here.

Childhood

'My mother never like me and I never like her.'

When I was a little baby my granny fell in love with me, so I went to live with her when I was nine months and I stayed until I was thirteen. I would visit my mother sometimes, but I didn't really like her, because when I was at my granny's I could do as I liked. Well not . . . do as you like in a certain sense – you know that kind of freedom you have with your grandmother, you are the only one, then, and any-thing you want you can get.

When I was with my grandmother we used to sleep together, and my grandmother was not fat, not big fat – but she was fat like, you know, medium-sized, and she had all those veins standing up because she was old, and I used to love feeling them and I would sleep and hug her and those things. Everybody was jealous of me with my grand-mother because I was her darling.

My mother never like me and I never like her. You know that way. Let me tell you, I didn't love her because I – she didn't know how to show love to me, then I was cold towards her and she was cold to-wards me. Even a few years back, parents wasn't really communica-tive to their children. They would just give them anything they needed, but not the type of lovey-dovey. For instance, if I was at home and they tell you to go away, if you didn't go, they would slap you. They are a bit strict, children were seen and not heard, if they said, 'Don't mess about,' they meant it. My mother used to work in a restaurant. When I went back to live with her she used to work shift work, so sometimes we would be on our own and she would come home in the night – well she didn't come home until after ten. Now I realize how difficult it was for her with four children to bring up and if she was strict with us it was for our own good, but after I come home, back to my mother now, I didn't really like it.

I went to the cinema every Saturday from about – I leave home at about say twelve o'clock and walk, a long journey; walk to the library – I used to read a lot, maybe that's where I used to derive my migraines from. I would ignore eating just so as I could keep up with reading. I wouldn't bother to eat up; you know if my dinner is even ready I would ignore it just so that I could finish that story, so I used to read three or four books a week. Going to the cinema now, was something which was akin to the bargain. Some children would say, 'Well I've been somewhere,' when they didn't go. Like they would leave for school but they didn't go to school, they went somewhere else. Well I didn't do that, I said, 'I'm going to the library,' and I did go, but when I go to my uncle I didn't stay long because I'd been away too long already, spending two hours in the cinema for film, come out, take the bus because it was over a mile from where the cinema was to my uncle. Get up there, spend an hour, jump on the bus back, come down back – and then come home, but I did go. Every Saturday I used to go and visit my granny until she died – I was really upset when she died.

I used to like plenty reading. I used to have a little pocket money every week or every month. There was a *True Story* I used to buy, *True Story*; I used to buy *My Weekly* and all those little picture love-story books. I used to buy them, any love thing I used to buy because I was a fanatic reader. I used to . . . I tell you, if my father was different I would be well away, because I was bright. There wasn't any real free education, because you get scholarship, but only about two children can get a chance for the free scholarship, and even if I could afford . . . say if my mother was working, I could pay then, we could afford to go to Technical, but even to find – say she could find the five pounds a year for me to get in a Technical, you still have to be able to afford the books.

But the whole family was different, all thinking of theirself alone, and we could – they weren't a family who would help each other. They only think of themself. They would give us things but not money, we could get any old clothes – when I say old clothes I mean clothes in good condition, things that don't look shabby. Because at home, people got lots of clothes owing to the fact that you haven't got to have four-season clothes, you have one-season clothes, really – night-time it get a little chilly and then you'd have a shawl or a cape. You'd have a lovely shawl, and a stole and those things. If they give you clothes they don't look old at all or anything. And they really smell nice because they've got money to buy expensive perfume, and even when you wash it . . . sometimes they give us some crêpe de chine slip, in those days it was crêpe de chine – anything you have got in this country now, we had it the same time or we even had it before you.

I wanted to be a doctor when I was a small girl, but afterwards I had to forget the idea because there was no money to send me to high school and you have to have money. As I tell you, if my mother was working at a better-paying job, if she was getting the right pay for the job, then she would be able to send all of us to high school and then you would be able to pick the sort of training you want. Now things has changed back home a little, where you are getting free education, but there is still people who can't afford for it because they have to buy their own books still – you can get into the school but you still need things. We didn't go to school looking shabby, yes, but there was basic things we needed we didn't get. For instance, there is one thing I blame my mother for, she didn't push me because I was bright; she would pay for private school lesson, but she didn't really realize that she should ask me to do those things, but she didn't. Mark you she was also in for herself, she didn't really think those things.

I remember before I was thirteen I found that in one of those books I borrowed, it must have been a biology book, that babies were no bigger than a pin-head, yes, but when I became older – I had my period at fourteen – my mother didn't tell me anything, she never said nothing until this day. I was at school, it was a February Monday, it was February and it was a Monday. I went to school, I always wear uniform and this day I didn't wear it, I wore a white dress; and when I got up – it was sewing day – and one of the girls said, 'Barbara, your dress is dirty.' I got up and I walked up the class, I didn't say nothing, and I walked straight home in the rain to make sure I wash out the dress and make sure the rain soaked me, so that it wouldn't show that the dress was wet. It was raining heavily that Monday, I didn't really take any shelter, I just continued walking in the rain and got soaked. I went home and I did the same thing, I put on two panties, and then the next morning she never said nothing. Well I didn't go back to school for the rest of that week. So when I went back nobody didn't really seem to remember. They are not the sort of girls who would take the mickey out of you, you know. They weren't that sort, and my friends they were ladylike. I wouldn't keep friends with those rough ones who fight.

We didn't get any biology lesson. I wasn't frightened owing to the fact that I used to read those grown-up books. They mention periods – they call it 'menstruation', they didn't say 'period'. I didn't realize it was biology thing about it – but at the same time I know it

wasn't anything dangerous, but I didn't understand. I knew, I read it,
because I remember once reading that magazine and the book – I was
littler then – and this boy and girl kiss and gave me a thrill, but I
didn't know why it gave me this thrill [laughs], and I didn't understand it. But I really read those, lots of magazines. Basically it was
educating me to be aware of things but it still didn't register, so I
wasn't really scared when I had the period. The only thing that
worried me, true, was, as I said, my mother wasn't very friendly. I
didn't know how to go and tell her: 'Well, it's started.' For instance
people was so silly, if you start having breasts, they start telling you
off, as if it's something wrong you done, and it's nothing wrong, it's
not your fault, it's something natural, but they didn't treat you as if it
was natural.

And then in this place where we were living, in the yard, there
were three bungalows, there was a little fellow over the other side, I
used to talk – I liked him but I wasn't thinking of him in the sense of a
boyfriend, I was only thinking of him as a little friend because he was
the quietest of all the boys around. I don't like noisy boys, I like quiet
ones. Neville, I didn't love him, I just like him, because I didn't know
anything about love. Well I used to like talking with him because he
was quiet and he didn't make noise like the other boys; and he was
with his aunt, and his father and mother used to live in the country,
and he went home and he wrote me a love letter. My brother knew
I had these magazines and he wanted to borrow it and I refused to let
him, so he said to me, 'If you don't lend me this magazine, I am
going to show your mother this letter that came, Neville sent you.'
Because I didn't know what was in the letter, I said 'Sure.' Then I
was being cheeky, and oh, she made a fuss about that letter, that I was
so ashamed that if I could hide I would hide. She went round the
front garden and showed his parents – well it wasn't really his parents,
it was his aunt – you know, this letter – show mother the letter, ring
a ding! When Neville came I used to hide and talk to him – so my
mother catch me round the corner talking, and she made a big fuss
again.

It never dawned on me in those days – nothing to do with whether
I was a boy or not, because I could do anything just like a boy. I

could climb, I could swim, the only thing I never learned to do was to ride a bicycle. It's not because I didn't have the opportunity, I just wasn't that mechanically minded to learn to ride, I was a coward, I don't like getting hurt. I blame her just for that one thing, not seeing to it that I pay more attention to my lessons.

The only thing I didn't do that boys do was to skate down the street. They used to make this skate and they used to skate down the street, and I didn't do it. I didn't fancy it. I didn't fancy being a boy. I didn't mind being a girl, because the truth is most of my friends was girls and I used to be in a girls' circle – well one of my friends had three brothers and we didn't play with them like. When I started to be aware of boys I like them, but I didn't mind being a girl because I didn't know any other way, cos I had two sisters. I just stick to girls and I didn't know anything about wanting to be different. For instance, my uncle had four children, it was one boy and three girls, most of my cousins have mostly girls, so I didn't really have that opportunity to say, 'Well because I am a girl I am treated this way.' There wasn't anything like that because, boys climb trees, I tell you, I climb tree! I used to swim, I spend all day down at the seaside.

The only thing I used to say . . . well there was once I was really aware there was a little difference. Well there was a woman named Edna and she used to be a fisherwoman. She alone used to go out fishing. Well it's only men who used to do that, and she used to dress like a man, and act like a man, you know. She wear pants and the way she wear the pants, she didn't just wear them occasionally, you hardly ever see Edna in a dress. She didn't just wear slacks, for slacks' sake, she was permanently in men garments then, but she was the only one I realized then there was a little bit funny. I only wanted to be a girl at the time. Even now I don't mind being a woman; it's only when life is hard I say, 'Well it would be nice to be a man,' but still if life is easier I don't mind being a woman.

Because my life was hard when I look back sometimes. Some things which you didn't realize which was right, sometimes you say, those food used to be nice what you'd see, but you didn't realize because you were poor, you don't realize it . . . if you were poor you would have – as they would say in England – you have just bread and dripping, and it tastes delicious because – well, you are hungry, and it's the only thing you have got. When we were little, Sundays we always have a nice dinner though, Sundays especially, if we didn't have a good dinner during the week. You would have meats or fish – chicken we didn't have every day because chicken wasn't so plentiful – but you could have beef or pork or fish. Sometimes my mother would buy fish, especially when she pays rent. You see we would have the cheapest fish because we couldn't afford the expensive one. Mark you, when you look at the price now compared with us, it wasn't expensive, but it was expensive if you didn't have the money.

But when we started working, us girls, things begin to get plenty better, the minute we started working, because we started pooling our resources – we weren't girls who just took all our money for ourselves, because it would help pay the rent and help to buy food and pay any bill. For instance, when I was there they didn't care about me, then it was after I left they write and tell me – oh, they miss me – yes they did, because she write and tell me. It's just a bad habit I have, maybe it's good and it's bad at the same time – I love to see plenty food about the place, and even as a teenager if I have money I would go and buy plenty groceries because I love it. I like to know the place is well stocked, I cannot bear poverty – no, I wouldn't like to be really poor because I couldn't stand it.

As a child I didn't understand . . . it's very bad when you see this rich system and the poor system operating, you know. I used to go down to the Yacht Club at Christmas time, and we little poor children standing by the side of the fence looking in. Well it was all white people over there, no black faces wasn't over there, except who was working. I didn't know anything about racialist things at the time. They had a big Christmas party and the children would get big presents from Santa, you know. They were all white-skinned. Well I didn't really want it because I wasn't that hungry. But at the same time it was really like a dream, just to see how the better-off lived. Like when I went to my cousin's house, you really feel big going there because they have a nice luxury house, because also my mother was the poorest one in their family. Over the other side was a Chinese man. He had a big place down town, he used to live over there, and we had a storm in '51 when a hurricane – in 1951, a real bad one – and that morning now, everything blow away coconut tree. We climbed the fence and went over the fence and were picking up the coconuts, and the man took out his gun. Well, mark you he wouldn't shoot us, but at the same time he still threatened us. He still threatened us.

Adolescence and Boyfriends

'Isn't love silly?'

I left school in 1956. I was fifteen in 1956 and then I started working the Christmas. I used to work where my mother worked during the holiday, because I used to go down there and help on Saturdays, they were very busy. I was serving my apprenticeship, so I started out in the underwear department, then I went to help in other departments. Then I left the small shop and went to work in a big store. I was in the shoe department. I was a trainee buyer. I worked there for six years until I come to Britain.

When I get older and start working, then I used to go to the cinema on Saturdays, now I start going on Wednesday afternoon when I leave work half day, or I'd go to the beach. Whenever church have a dance at month end I used to go to the dance. I used to go to the dance over there, and we were supposed to come home by twelve, you see, or eleven o'clock, and I would come home a little after one. Then my younger sister went with me. My mother was very miserable, but she was only paying attention to our welfare. When we would get in there, on the radio she could hear it was one o'clock, she'd say to us, 'What time is it?' I would say to her, 'I don't know,' that was the best lie. But my sister would say to her, 'Oh, it's ten o'clock,' and that would send her wild, because she knew it was after one, because the dance was over at one o'clock and we had to stay until it was finished.

We are Catholic you see, Roman Catholic, and then we'd go to church every Sunday, and every time it was – I used to go to church, and in the church I was a Godalist. I really was a church fanatic –

you know, everything. Catholic Church is different from the other
religions because you could dress up and wear lipstick and all those
things, and they didn't criticize whoever wanted to drink or smoke.
They didn't interfere. Well this dance was held once a month down
at this school, so we used to go with my younger sister. Then when
we started work we had a little more freedom because we were
working. We would say we are little woman now so she can't
dictate to us – you know, cut us off. But I was still afraid of her. If we
were going out and she started quarrelling, I wouldn't go, but my
other sister didn't care, she would dress up and go the same night –
I was peaceful then.

Well we had our little boyfriends, but it was not at the dancing I
met them. My first boyfriend was when I went up to the girl I used
to buy those comics from, Pam. Because of those comics I got this
boyfriend. I was fifteen then, I went up there this night and this
fellow come to the gate and he said, 'Pam, can I see your friend?'
She said, 'That boy wants to talk,' and I said, 'I don't want to talk to
him,' and she shouted at him to go away from the gate, but he didn't
go. He waited until I came out and talked to me. I was so shy, even
when I was his friend now, if he come along and he didn't say 'Hello
Barbara', I'd be there for the rest of the night, and I would never have
said a word to him until when he left, and I remember one night he
caught me looking at him and he said, 'Pam, Barbara is getting
bright, she is looking at me.' I was really ashamed, you know, I
really liked him, really loved him.

He was studying for his Senior Cambridge and he couldn't come
out every night to see us, you see, so if he didn't come, I would take
a walk up past his house. I felt good even just passing his house, and
if I didn't see him, or if I was having a headache and I see him I felt
better. Isn't love silly? I remember one night, it was Christmas, and
Pam and myself were returning from work, we were really having a
good old giggle and we were coming – there is a place named Chest
Clinic at home, you know, it has a long wall around it, so if we are
walking along here you won't be able to see who is around the other
side. Well he come around the wall – mark you, it's not ladylike
back home to make noise on the street, like they do here. So when

I come around and we were laughing real loud, just the two of us, all of a sudden I went, 'Pam!' – she didn't realize what had happened to me all along, she said, 'What happened to you, Barbara?' I say 'Barry'. She said, 'Barbara, why didn't you tell me, and let me get to see him?' I went all weak.

He was a 'face man', as they would call it, he'd plenty of girl-friends. He was tall and dark and handsome, as they would say. If I saw him come along and he still didn't speak to me first, I never speak to him, all because when I was a teenager, girls were jealous of me and him and they used to say I forced on him, and because I didn't want it to be said that I was trying to force my friendship on him, I never speak to him unless he speaks. Maybe because of that I treat him bad, but he could get any girlfriend he can. He had several girlfriends I know, I knew them – he was friendly with that girl round that road and he was friendly with that one down there. But he still used to talk to me, but I was shy.

I had another boyfriend, Lloyd. He was my niece's father's cousin. So it was a little family relationship, that's how I met him, and I used to talk to him a lot, and he used to come and visit me. I didn't even realize he had other girls. And he used to visit me twice a day Sundays – that beast! That wolf! I didn't realize he had another girl. He was a mechanic, engineer. He worked at that motor place. I like him but I didn't adore him, because he was wild. I like him because I was going with him.

For instance, look now, our system back home is different from here. Honestly, but it is a silly system over here and a selfish and mean system. They cut off all communication, and then – you see, that's the English system where you are taught to suppress everything. Hide things like a skeleton in the cupboard. That's not necessary. I wouldn't tell anybody about Audrey – I will tell our own people, but I wouldn't go round and tell English people because they wouldn't understand. Because the first time I do anything with Audrey's daddy I got pregnant. But my friend always said to me, 'Barbara,' – that's the woman who I came to Britain with – she always said, 'Barbara, if you ever do anything you got to use everything in the book.' We used to laugh, because I didn't want to do anything.

That night when I got pregnant he had a pessary with him, but truly we were brought up to believe that if he used those things, it's only prostitutes do it. You're cheap and common, that it's usually cheap common people that use them things you see, knocking about. And I didn't want to do – I didn't want to do nothing, but because he insist – because if he didn't capture me in a corner where I couldn't escape I wouldn't have done it. I used to wear these shorts, I had plenty shorts, so at night time when I came home from work I put on my shorts, and me midriff – show off my pretty legs. [Laughs.] The next thing, you know, he used say I am ever so sweet, because I could get the Revlon and things at discount. Back home it is different, you can shower every minute. So when I come home from work I shower and put my hair up. Mark you, maybe it was my fault, still, because that night when I got Audrey I was all dolled up to go out, and I think he was going to take me to the place that I wanted to go. And I could have had somebody that would have taken me, but he didn't want to go. He promised, he said he would go to the drive-in cinema. Then he took my sister down to the city. By the time he come back it would be too late to go to the drive-in cinema, because if we were going to the second showing it would be eight o'clock or nine o'clock. I was really upset. I went home, I go into the fridge, take out an apple and come outside and sit in the car.

When I got Audrey I nearly died. Mark you, I could have lost Audrey. Isn't it funny? Over here, when you get pregnant, you go to the doctor. But I got pregnant . . . I'm going to tell you I got pregnant tonight and the next morning I was really tired. I was dead beat. My mother said, 'She's pregnant.' And it was like my world dropped out. You know, I was afraid. And I said to Lloyd that night, 'You know my mother said I am pregnant.' And the Monday morning I couldn't face my breakfast to go to work. I went to the doctor the next Monday. One week after. And the doctor tell me I was pregnant. He gave me some blue tablets to take, and the Friday night I saw a little tip of blood in my panties, and I never take those tablets again. Because I said, 'I don't want to lose my baby.' I didn't. I love Audrey from I got her until when I leave her.

When I found out about his other girls I didn't want anything to do with him – Lloyd. Well you know he drinks a lot. But I was young, I didn't think. I thought I would have got married, but he never venture anything about getting married. I love Audrey and I was proud of her. I used to dress her in the very best, make she look nice. And I went back to work and my sister look after her, because she had a baby the same time. So she looked after my baby and I worked. I haven't forgiven him for Audrey. I love Audrey as my baby, but not him any more.

Very few men take interest in their children, even if they are married to you. Remember that if they can have you to knock a little piece off of you now and again you may find them coming round and giving you money. I was ashamed, because I used to go to church a lot and everything, and I kept away from church. If the Father see me . . . I didn't want . . . then after a while everybody start to ask me, am I getting married? And I couldn't face it. The humiliation nearly killed me. And then he [Lloyd] wasn't behaving right. He never ventured to say we'd get married. But if he did venture, I had money saved up, I could have got married, because I had over a hundred pounds saved up from my pay. So I could afford to get married. I used to see him still, but I wasn't friends with him any more, I wouldn't have any sex with him, and use them things, even when I was pregnant. It used to annoy him. One night he pushed me over and said I treat him like a stranger. I didn't want to share with anybody, I didn't want to be with anybody else's property.

I had another boyfriend who liked me – not liked me, loved me. He wanted us to get married, and say, 'Keep the baby.' But I never liked him. I like Lyn but I would never love him. If I had loved him I would have married him, but I couldn't kiss him. We used to go out a lot and Lyn didn't know about the set-up, he used to think, well, I was expecting his baby. But I wasn't. And he used to take me out a lot. And at Christmas I cried until I could have died. Lloyd never come near, Lloyd never even buy me one little Christmas present. And the shame of it nearly killed me. Christmas he never come near me, and I could see him down – I see his car down there and know he's down there, and he never come near me, and Lyn did buy me a big Christmas present. He bought me an iron for Christmas, and some costume jewellery. Plenty of times I go out with Lyn and I say, when I come back I will kiss him. I come back home to the gate and I run inside and I say, 'Goodnight.' I never kissed that fellow. And he know I like hot dog, and every morning at ten o'clock he used to send me two hot dogs, every morning – I used to give my friend one. Every morning he used to send me one.

Because it was complicated I just made up my mind and I say, 'Oh I'll come,' and I am sorry I didn't have plenty money to go back at the same time. I wasn't really looking for a boyfriend and a husband, I come here to get away from such problems. It's the boyfriend problem what has me up in the air in this prison, what hang me up in this prison, boyfriends – just a gathering of all the complications that I was getting into. I used to have quite a few boyfriends and it was getting too complicated. I couldn't stand too much pressure so I was running away from it and I end up here. But it would have been good to spend six months . . . If I went back six months after I left, then I could get back into my old groove – I can't get back ever again. All that is finished. I am old now. I am old now . . . because all that teenage friendship, that circle – and you've lost all of them, you would have to start from scratch again. I didn't come here to get a boyfriend – I come here to get away from a boyfriend, not to get a boyfriend.

Coming to Britain

I landed at Southampton in 1962, 26th May, and I come to Waterloo, and then I went to Highbury to live. When I came to Southampton the place looked funny. Well I said, 'OK, when I get to London it will look different.' I saw all those little two rooms with those little chimneys on top, and I say, 'Well the houses in London must be different.' But here everywhere you go it's the same – it doesn't look no different. You see, owing to the fact that I go to the cinema a lot, seeing the films about the place – cold and dark and dreary – it wasn't strange, it was only to experience it. Because I always read about chilblains, I didn't know what chilblain was until I got chilblain, then I know how lovely chilblain can be, because I came here on 26th

May and I got chilblain, when I came to Southampton. The parts
coming up from Southampton to Waterloo, it didn't look no
different. Coming up Clapham and all those places – the same little
two rooms. When I get to Hamilton Place it didn't look too bad, but
when I went in they had paraffin heater, and I was looking for the big
log fire, that I usually see in the films, and I couldn't get warm.

Lenny was living there. I didn't want any boyfriend, I didn't come
here to get a boyfriend. I did like him but at the same time I wasn't
really interested, I wasn't looking for that friendship, but eventually
I got in with him. Oh I've had him twelve years now, it's a long time,
ain't it? He does electrical work and because of it he moved. . . I went
down to Walsall with him, and then when I left Walsall with him I
came back to London to live, and then when I came back to London
I was in the Archway, and eventually I went back to Coventry to
him, then I come back from Coventry – I come back to London. I
went to Coventry to him and by the time I get there he was off back
to London to work, so I was on my own down there again, but when
I eventually got Sarah I came to London, and I never go and move up
and down with him again.

I was there for a long time until I got Sarah, then I came back to
London, and when Sarah was over a year I went to work down at
Willing's doing electrical work again. After that, I left that place and
went to a surgical instrument place. He travels but now he comes
home. Before I had Caroline, he was working at the Isle of Wight
and he stopped over there. But he doesn't do that kind of staying out
since he has got this family commitment. He stay at home now, he
comes home every night even if he goes long distance, but first time
now, he would stop away. Even when Sarah was a baby I used to be
on my own – he used to work in the country up in Leeds, and I was
down here on my own.

The first job I got I didn't even stay, I was there four days. I got a
job doing finishing and I only did a few days, then I went to Coventry
to live with Lenny. I came back to London to live and then I went to
do some machining, and when I went back to Coventry with him
now I mucked about until I finally got a job, because it was very hard
to get jobs. Then I got a job at GEC and I worked there for a long

time until I came back to London to live. Then I had a full-time job, that's my last full-time job, was working in London Transport, and then I got Rosie and I haven't been back to work since full time, and then I had to do this little part-time job. I did other little jobs just for economy reasons but nothing else – office-cleaning.

It's surprising, office people, they haven't got no manners and they have very dirty habits. They are not very tidy and they are the type that would come in the office and see you and never say 'Good morning' to you because you are the cleaner, and the bigger boss he will come in and see you and say 'Good morning' to you. Not because you are coloured, this hasn't got anything to do with colour now, it's just that they think they are nice and you are only the cleaner.

When I first came, and went out to look for work, they keep on telling you about experience, and nobody realizes that you must start somewhere to get experience. I didn't know anything about coloured then, because I did just know that I was me. Now if I go I must always remember that I am different, where back home, you go for something, you go on your own merits, never got anything to do with you being coloured. Even to get a cleaning job sometimes they don't like coloured ones getting it, but if it's hard they will take you. It's no good they telling you it doesn't exist – it exists.

Now I have settled. It's no good going back now when I ain't got no money to buy a house. If I haven't got enough money to spend I get miserable. I am happiest when I have money to spend, that's why I am willing to go and do the little cleaning work. I am happy just doing it so that I can go at the end and spend and don't have to hesitate, or even say, well . . . If I ask Lenny for some money and he say he hasn't got it I don't ask him again. Some other people's husbands . . . Lenny is mean that way, he is mean . . . you don't realize he is mean until when somebody else tell you what their husband does, and then you realize that he is mean. He is a 'Dr Jekyll and Mr Hyde' – he pretends that he is very generous but he is mean, he live in a land of pretence. I am different, I am more . . . For instance the other day he had the cheek to come and tell me that I am a miser. It really annoyed me, because if I am a miser it's his fault, because it's the money what he gives me turn me into a miser, because what he feel that . . . if he give me – say he give me twenty pounds today, I don't go away and spend it all – he feel that I am a miser then, but it's not because I am being miser, I am being wise. For instance, sometimes I say to myself, why should I? – he come and borrow money from me.

When I worked at the surgical instrument place I met two lesbians, Lizzie and Janet. Lizzie said Janet won't wear pants and look like a man – she's a butch but she doesn't want her daughter to lose that sort of motherly respect for her, but she's the man in the relationship. They found my sex life distasteful and I found their sex life distasteful. I didn't mind them as people, it was only because they kept instigating that what I am doing is nasty and I know what they are doing is dirty too. And they was so silly, if any of the men speak to Janet . . . for instance, that bloke behind me used to like Janet and he would give Janet any money. He had money. Janet and he were friendly until when Janet and Lizzie got in together.

Lizzie told me that she slept with Janet's husband just to get Janet, and Janet's husband didn't want to lose her so he was willing to share her with Lizzie. Well Lizzie only went with Janet's husband just to get Janet, because she mash up that marriage. And while she took on Janet, she had another friend named Sue, and Sue left her for another woman who could buy her car, and that woman had money, so she gave that Sue everything she wanted, and Lizzie can't even afford a car. So Sue have everything now – luxury life to what she had with Lizzie. And Lizzie and Janet used to bicker about the simplest things, whereas when Janet was with her husband she had a more comfortable life, she didn't have to pick her pennies; then Lizzie start bickering at her if she used too much sugar, because Lizzie complain to me about it – eventually I would be hearing one story from Janet and one story from Lizzie. And then I didn't know they were like that till one of the men said – that same fellow, I forget his name – said to me, 'Somebody caught Janet and Lizzie kissing,' and then one other time Lizzie said to me that they were like that. But I still didn't behave shocked, I was only amazed. I was only amazed, you know.

Coming over here, the only thing I don't like over here is it's much harder. Look how much I have to do, when back home you would get somebody to help you – you know, you are willing to pay somebody to help you out, but that's not possible here unless you have lots of money. The grandmother over here don't want to be like the grandmother in Jamaica, they won't help. There's no time to help here, that sort of thing is not available. Mark you, if we had more room, I would have more wardrobe and such things. For instance, Lenny doesn't realize there are so many people's clothes, you know. He feel I've got too much clothes, but it's not enough – he doesn't understand, he never do.

For instance, when I am having migraine, you know, I have to force myself to get up, but he doesn't realize this. It's really a great struggle to really pull myself together to get up, because I am just dying to lay down, and he ignore me completely when I am having my migraine, he'll disappear. The other day when I had migraine, not this last time, I said to him, 'But Lenny, how is it you didn't even come and ask me how I was?' He say he came and saw me and I was asleep. But I know he never came. If he saw me asleep and he know that if he speak to me and I am asleep and I'll get cross and say I don't like him to wake me up when I am sleeping. But that's not true, I don't really like to be disturbed when I am sleeping, because if I am really having a migraine and I want to sleep, the more I want to sleep the more I keep awake. But he don't understand that. I hate being sick, because if I am sick it keep me back, I can't ever seem to get on with my work. Actually every month I am prostrate for a week nearly, and I think it is to do with my period. I have irregular periods, and the doctor say nothing is wrong with me, it is just that – it has to do with my emotions, and maybe I take things to heart too much, and then I don't get my period. It's my emotion, I am too emotional. It's stress and strain, but they don't think of that, they try to lay all the blame on women.

For instance, with Lenny you can't have a quarrel with him and settle it, you know, because the minute you are ready to quarrel with him and really get it out of your system, he sulks, so you find that if you're willing to really go at him, that's where the tension comes from, because you can't really tell him what you think. So if there is something bothering you he just shuts up and don't say anything, because he try to make you believe that you are the one that make all the trouble.

He believe that I am really troublesome and I make all the trouble. For instance, he come to tell me about the mice coming up here now, he will tell me it's because I don't keep the floor tidy and this. I say, 'Yes, I call the mice outside,' – I really get cross you know – I say, 'Yes, I send out the garden to tell the mice to come upstairs, there's plenty things on the floor in here.' I do, because it's not my fault the mice are in here, in these rotten old houses. He don't like cats – because if I mention to him somebody is getting a cat, he says, 'If you would clean up the floor, and keep the floor tidy, the mice wouldn't get in.' What are the mice doing in the wardrobe, tell me? They are infested! They are in the cooker, they are in everywhere, and they gets on my nerves. You are always doing one work three or four times. You can't finish your work in this house with the ruddy mice. You can't finish, you never finish, because the mice are there. Back home if we got a cat in the house – there is a cat in the basement, and the mice are still in here – if we have a cat in the house the mice know that the cat is there, so they disappear. They are highly educated – they pass the mousetrap, the food is in there and they don't pay it any mind. They won't go near the trap, they won't bite, and they see the poison and they look at it and say something to themself. They must watch Tom and Jerry, they do.

Mice crawling all over the floor! You wouldn't have that at home. It's not because I am so terrible at housekeeping, but these situations get you down, you know. Even if you have got money in this town they tell you about housing shortage, and you have to still think twice before you get it, because they are not going to give you because of – you know? If you go after a nice place – say I move from here and I go to a nice neighbourhood – well, the minute they see me there's going to be some toffee-nosed neighbour who is not going to want us to live there. My friend had a flat, she had a maisonette in Clapham – you know one of those places in Clapham – and when she went there first, the people didn't want her to live there. I meet her sister and she said to me that she is ever so lonely. Mark you, she don't want much friendship, but the coldness make her lonely. I don't mean the coldness of the weather, I mean the coldness of the people. They don't want her there, so our people say they can't do that, they can't come to our black country if they don't want us in their house.

Contraception and Pregnancy

'Maybe the poor women are just not so cold and calculating as the rich ones.'

Lenny and I were together for four years nearly before I got Sarah, they just didn't come. I wasn't using any family planning. I didn't think I was going to get pregnant and then I got pregnant. The first time I had this . . . I started irregular period, I thought I was pregnant. I went to the doctor and he said I was, and afterwards he said I wasn't. I begin to get fatter from I start having irregular period. But when I didn't get Rosie I didn't use nothing. I just was relaxing and never get no baby. A little before Sarah was four I got Rosie, and then Fiona. Fiona and Caroline is the two quickest ones.

Caroline was a bit of a surprise and a shock. True. I was having irregular period and I went to the family planning clinic – and I said, 'I missed period the month before and I want to put in this coil.' So she said, 'Mrs Marsh . . .' – she saw me look a bit vague and I said, 'Well don't put it in, let me have a test first.' I went back, and when I went back she say, 'Mrs Marsh, I am afraid . . .' I said, 'OK, don't worry, if I am pregnant I don't want an abortion because I don't believe in it, but I will have this baby and I will have it – I will do something.' I don't believe in abortion. Reading the paper this morning they said that the poor women have more children – maybe the poor women are just not so cold and calculating as the richer ones. You see the richer ones are usually cold and calculating – they are! They haven't got no feeling towards putting down anything – because now I have Caroline I really love her. When she first came out and I saw her I say – 'Well how could I kill you?' – and see her looking at me – no, I wouldn't like to know I am responsible for that.

You know what put me off getting the coil the first time? Silly thing about husband must sign paper. My doctor know Lenny, and he know me quite well. I hesitate, and then I went next time and I signed the paper myself; I told him about it and I say, 'You'll have to sign the paper,' and he said, 'All right.' So then I didn't bother to go back to him again, and I signed it myself, and tell him. He knows that I put it in, but I didn't bother to go back to him about it again.

It's nothing to do with them. Well you see, I tell you the truth, why they do it, some of these women put in these things and use things just to be wild, and because of those women, those who wouldn't do it have to pay the price. It derives from that. Because I know someone, since she go on those things she's gone wild – that's why some of the husbands refuse to sign those papers, because they are afraid that you are going to go astray, because you won't get pregnant so there is nothing to prove that you are not running around.

This shows you how society and everything was built against women, when you look over it. For instance, if a girl get pregnant everybody look down their nose at them, no one ever remember that there is a boy who helped to put her in that position. If the girl get pregnant and she go to the boy's mother and tell – I wouldn't like nobody's mother to say that about my daughter, because I'd go round there and tell her what I think – she turn to you and say, 'Well, it's not his own.' How can she say, 'It's not his own'? When he was begging you, she wasn't there! And the boy is very wicked when he turn and say it is not his own either, because if he never go there she couldn't say it is his. It doesn't take nothing to get you pregnant.

I am willing to tell my daughters, I want them to know about it. I don't want them to get pregnant unnecessarily. Mark you, one time when I got pregnant, it's just because of my stupidity – it's not stupidity, it's just a thing must happen, because you could still use something and still get pregnant – but even before I done it and my friend said to me, if I do anything I am going to have to use everything under the book, because I was taking all these sort of tonics to build me up. I don't mind them using family planning thing – the only thing I don't want them to do is knocking about with different boys, because you get a bad name – mark you, not even getting a bad name, looking at it – all those different-sized things attacking you things is wrecking you. It's going to be stretched out, not all elastic in it.

Look at those women who are prostitutes, after a while they lose all their – all their little gumption, you know. They do! They need a plumber to plumb them up after a while. They do! That's why some of the time . . . None of the men will marry prostitutes, they will have them for the side but never the . . . you know? Because after a while not even the prostitute want, because they aren't satisfied, or they just cannot be. What I mean is – if a woman is a prostitute or if a woman keep knocking about with different thing, after a while she can't be a . . . because if she go, for instance, if she go with a little thing, it's different, but if she goes with the bigger thing it's going to stretch it out – it does!

Say you are using French letter – I don't like it, it doesn't give me no thrill, so if I am to use it I may as well don't bother. I have tried it. Back home the prostitutes use it because – well, they are not doing it for pleasure, it's only for business, so they don't really care whether the man get any kicks or not. That's why I wouldn't use it, because I don't like it, I don't get no thrill.

But everybody who I know who have the coil find fault with it. It's like my friend, I don't know what happened, but she said to me when she had the thing first, everyone going to say, 'Well you can't stand this thing with so much bleeding all the time.' 'Course she has so much periods now she's never dry, and she had to take it out. Why is it we don't stop like back home, everybody just stop without using anything? Well some of my relations just . . . they are not . . . they don't breed a lot then. The most they ever had is four. They never seem to get any more again. I've got so much hormones. I have got so much motherly hormones in me.

I love babies but I don't like these feelings. I don't want to have to feel that again. For instance I haven't got long, difficult labours – quick – and hot, you know – finish quick, not a long-drawn-out thing, but at the same time, even though it was a short time, it seems an eternity. Just to go through that pain it seems an eternity, sometimes I wonder just that one time to say, well if God is good, how do they make you that you can stretch to that dimension? And when the baby come out, no matter, nothing can really stretch it that much as before. You would have to get definitely those medical equipment to really get it stretching that way. Well the only thing is if you over-stretch yourself you can get a tear. I did get stitches before, but this time I didn't get none. But I have quick labour – it's quick, short and hot!

I had two before ambulance come, because by the time I turned round they're out! I was hoping that Fiona wouldn't come out before the ambulance, because by the time I decide to call the ambulance I had to run to the bed and, you know, I went to the potty and I felt it – and I say, 'Oh no, not again!' Because I knew she was going to come out. Well, this time because of that they had an excuse to give me induced labour. I had a good experience with she and the induced labour – the only thing I can say is a good experience – I have never heard none of the babies' hearts beat, and this time I heard the baby's heart beat, and it was good to hear it beating, because you know with all my babies I never hear none of them hearts beat, and I heard her heart beat and it going 'thump, tum tum, thump', like a tom-tom. It was good you know, it was a good experience just to experience hearing it. But when she came out I didn't even want the nurse to tell me, 'No, it's not a boy,' I ask her first, 'Is it a girl?' She say 'Yes' and I just satisfy myself. Nature must know why I get all girls, no boys.

It's funny, when I am expecting a baby I am always drawn towards girl things and sometimes I can't see it, that is a girl I am going to have, because somebody is trying to convince me not to buy what I want to buy because I may have a boy. That is not to say I don't love girls – I love them, I always do. There are women who prefer boys to girls, but I do like my daughters. I only hope they don't go and get pregnant, and then have problems with the fellow, you know. I don't want that, because some of these boys can be very unkind; they get you pregnant and take off, leaving you to face the music.

You see, I don't like the pain but there is no escape. Why did God have to make women have pain? Why should we suffer? I wouldn't like to go through that thing again.

11. Pat Garland

Pat Garland is in her mid thirties and lives in a northern industrial town with her husband, Stuart, and their three children, Sally, Kate and Kevin. She started sociology at university and married soon afterwards. When her youngest child was three she decided to go back to work part time as a social worker, and she now works full time in a local hospital. She has been active in various campaigns on women's issues, including the National Abortion Campaign.

Childhood

'I suppose I was regarded by people as a tomboy.'

I was born in 1942. My mother lived in London, my father was away in the RAF at the time, and we lived in a flat in London. I can just remember the War. I can remember some instances of the bombs. The house next door to us was bombed – well, a bomb fell into the garden and we had to leave our flat that night. I can also remember the day my father came home. I was three. Obviously my mother had talked about my father, I am not quite certain what I knew about him, but he was a person in my life. I used to look at his photograph, and then suddenly he was there in the flesh. I can remember these things quite clearly, and then my memory is quite hazy after that until we moved up to Birmingham, which must have been when I was four. I suppose it was just after the War. I can't really remember anything; also my mother had another child by then, but I can't remember anything about the birth of this other sister.

I was the eldest, so I didn't see my father until I was three. It's quite interesting when I talk to my mother about what it was like during the War, and how she had to manage. Obviously I suppose she found it quite difficult having a baby and without her husband being around. Also the facilities then just weren't very good, she did go to a private nursing home, but there was no doctor to deliver her. I think there was just a nurse there.

She had been a secretary, in fact she was working during the War, and she had quite an exciting life. She got involved as a secretary in one of the Secret Services. She didn't realize what the organization was when she applied for the job, but it turned out that it was MI6, and there were plans to ship them all to Canada if the Germans invaded. She had been an ambulance driver as well, but after she got pregnant she had to finish this work. In fact she didn't work again after that.

My father was in the air force all through the War. But he had worked in a furniture firm, and afterwards he got a job selling, as a representative of a furniture firm, selling furniture. You know, going round to shops and selling furniture. He felt that he could improve himself by moving away from London and going to the Midlands, he had an offer of a job and he took it. The funny thing about my father is that he is in a sense the stock Commercial Traveller, he does have a load of jokes and things. He gets on well, he enjoys it, I think. I should hate to have to do it, but he doesn't have to push it – really he goes around and just takes new orders. It's not that he is plugging something that nobody wants to buy, they do, and he's just the – well, he is the representative for the firm. I think he enjoys the freedom that it gives him, as well.

I suppose I didn't really know him and he didn't know me. It was a bit difficult for him to establish a relationship with me. I can't really remember much about it – whether I was sort of happy, or pleased, or not. I was curious the day he was coming home. I can actually still remember opening the door and seeing him in the room in his uniform, but I can't really remember what sort of relationship I had with him at that time. I think it was a fairly normal one, once I went to school – you know, I looked forward to seeing him when he came home at night from work and so on. He was not a strict father or anything.

My father is somewhat younger than my mother. In a sense they had quite a love affair, I think. He was working as a young office boy at his firm and she was the personal secretary to the boss. She was in her thirties, I suppose, and he was only twenty. They still haven't really told me, I suppose I feel too embarrassed to talk to them about it. I think there was lots of opposition from my mother's family especially, because they were quite correct sort of people, so it was really quite a romantic thing. Then of course they got married. I think they got married in 1939, after the War had started, and then he went away for three years. So I think on the whole they did get on, but the age difference I think eventually had meant that there have been slight clashes, and my mother has always been a fairly anxious person, and now that she is sixty-seven, and my father is still sort of in his early fifties, I suppose . . . there are some problems now. They've always been fairly happy. I can only remember a few actual rows that they had where my mother was really upset, and when I think of rows that we have now it's really awful. I was really very upset when my mother cried at all, it really hurt me; but I cry in front of my kids – I suppose they've got used to it or something, it doesn't seem to bother them very much.

It was rather tragic in a sense when my parents moved to the Midlands. They had me and this new baby, and she got ill when she was about fourteen months, and the doctor didn't really know what was the matter, he thought she had some sort of a virus. By the time she had gone to hospital they diagnosed meningitis, but by then it was too late to do anything about it. I think there was penicillin, they were just using it, but it was only in the early stages, so the baby died. And I think this probably did have quite an effect on all of us, particularly on my parents, obviously, and on my father. I mean, he hadn't seen my development, and then this baby died. I think possibly my parents didn't realize how much I was affected as well by it. I think they were so caught up in their own grief about it that they rather neglected me. I didn't go to the funeral; I can actually remember the day of the funeral, going to a neighbour's and having poached egg on toast for my dinner. Also, I can remember that the people in the street had collected money for a wreath, and my parents hadn't been there for very long, and they were really touched by this – you know, that the people were so concerned about it, and had done this.

So in a sense I feel that my early upbringing was more like that of an only child, since I was almost seven by the time my other sister was born. So in a sense I lived a fairly solitary life, and I used to read quite a lot and have lots of imaginary stories going on in my head. I had friends to play with, but there were lots of times when I was on my own. So I didn't perhaps get involved too much with the sort of games that girls play. There were two boys around in the street. I suppose I was regarded by people as a tomboy. I enjoyed climbing trees, and even fighting. Unfortunately my nose bled quite easily and I was always getting bloody noses. Once I got involved in a fight coming home from school. It was outside a British Restaurant, and these women took pity on me and brought me inside and mopped me up and were very nice to me.

My sister was always too young really for me to actually see her as a sister. I didn't mind her, you know, I was always wanting her to grow – I wanted her to walk and talk, rather like one does with one's own children. But I mean, now we do get on very well, now that the gap doesn't seem so wide.

Adolescence

'It was just I was unhappy because of growing up.'

I think I found adolescence quite difficult because I was tall. That was a real handicap, I felt ungainly and tended to be much taller than most of my girlfriends, and a lot of the boys at the youth club. It was agony going to dances, because you'd sort of sit there and somebody would come up to ask you to dance. Then you'd stand up and find that your head was above theirs and they were sort of looking at your shoulder rather than the other way round. That was a horrible period. I went to girls' grammar school. I mean, this was what my mother wanted me to do, and I did it. There wasn't much contact with boys. I sang in the church choir, so I met some that way, and there was a church youth club, but I always felt that I couldn't really get involved in the groups that were there. I wasn't able to flirt, I wasn't able to sort of – in a sense, have fun, I think. I was too serious, and I just found it very difficult.

It was rather funny, because at that time my parents were having quite a social life of their own – they got involved in some sort of social club which was connected with the church. They were always going out, in fact I had to baby-sit a lot, and I didn't really have much of a social life at all apart from occasionally going to some of their dances. That was all there was in those days, dances. Although as I got older . . . I think the turning point came when I was sixteen, because some people at the youth club started a jazz band and we used to go along. It was held in Lichfield and we used to go along on Friday night, and this was really a high spot, going to this jazz club and jiving. That was really terrific, and I met lots of people there, and that was nice. They weren't the people I had known, they were a different group of people, and they didn't know me of old, they hadn't sort of watched me grow up, it was better.

I don't think I had any real clashes with my parents. I was unhappy, but it wasn't really because of them, it was just I was unhappy because of growing up, I suppose. And I always felt that the ideal thing was to have a boyfriend, a steady boyfriend, which was awful really. I think that girls seem to feel this, that they are incomplete without a boyfriend, and I couldn't really get into things enough, into other things, which probably would have been just as interesting. I was always sort of on the look-out for a boyfriend, in a sense, and I think this is a handicap which I don't think boys to the same extent share. They've got their own mates and they can gain just as much from being in a crowd of boys and going off somewhere, whereas girls can't. Well, I think perhaps it's different now, but in those days if one was spending an evening with a friend from school it was because there was nothing better to do.

We were – I suppose you would call it middle-class. It was fairly prosperous Midlands people, living in their own houses, but not at all intellectual. In fact my parents actually had some friends whom I wished I'd got to know better, who were Labour Party activists and

Catholics, and they were really quite nice, but of course they lost touch with them. It was just a fairly prosperous middle-class area where we lived. We had moved, when we first went to the Midlands, into this working-class area where my parents bought a house. It adjoined a big housing estate, so that the first school I went to, the primary school, was a very working-class school. But then I went to this rather posh girls' grammar school, so I had the two contrasts, and in both places I didn't feel really at ease. In the one I felt I was considered to be a snob because I talked funny, because I came from the South, and in the other I felt that there were people there who were really very wealthy. Although you all wore a uniform, there were certain ways of distinguishing the very wealthy . . . although I quite enjoyed it, I had a group of friends at the grammar school, but I hated all the petty restrictions.

I used to have a pony-tail and then I suddenly thought it was, you know, a bit too young-looking, and I had it cut, I had it cut quite short. But there was that terrible agonizing bit between fourteen and sixteen. Well I didn't really have a boyfriend like some of the other girls did, and I really wanted that, although I had a boyfriend when I was on holiday, a sort of holiday romance in Wales. And he was four years older than me, but it was only – I only saw him at holiday times. I got a bit embarrassed in a sense, because he was quite keen on me. I only wanted the surface, I didn't want the real involvement or anything. And certainly I am quite amazed that now there is all this sort of very young sex, with these young girls. Because I certainly couldn't have contemplated it.

I think it's rather sad in some ways that girls don't go through this period now – well some of them don't – of just necking and that sort of thing. They seem to plunge right in straight away. Possibly they are more mature, and socially and psychologically more mature as well. I am not giving moral judgement or anything, I just think it's rather sad really that this seems to be the norm, the sort of thing one does, whereas in *my* day the question was whether you allowed them to kiss you or not the first time you went out with them, and you were thought – considered – to be fast if you did. We had this elaborate system, we didn't actually talk about these things, but we had this code of one to ten – one was holding hands and ten was the real thing, and then you could tell people what happened by saying, 'Oh, well we went up to number six,' or something – you know, you didn't actually have to talk about it even to your friends.

School

'I can remember just being bored.'

I was interested certainly at first. I was very keen because I wanted to beat all these girls that had been to private schools and knew French and appeared to be more knowledgeable than me. I think in the first and second forms we really worked hard, then there was this gradual sort of decline in the third form. I remember the headmistress when she used to come round and she used to say: 'You know you have slipped down this year, and once you get on that sort of slope it's very difficult to come back.' And there was a period in the fourth and fifth years when we hated most of the teachers, and what they were teaching us. But O-levels seemed to be a kind of way of getting back at the school, saying, 'You see, you thought we couldn't do it but we did it.' So I was quite keen to do O-levels, I was quite keen to succeed academically, but somehow I didn't agree with all that was going on at school, especially because of the English teacher and the sort of things we used to do in English. I was quite interested in science as well. We had a very inspiring science teacher. She'd apparently been very good at ballet and had had to choose between ballet or science, and she had chosen science, so she really sort of dinned it into us, you know, and was very keen for us to do science, and I did in fact decide to do science in the sixth form, really because of her and because I didn't like the English teacher.

I think in a sense I was more interested in English and history, but you know there was this terrible split when I could only do one or the other, and there was nothing like – you didn't have any other things, any arts subjects, if you did science, your timetable was very full. But then I wasn't really good enough at maths to really cope with the physics and even the chemistry. I think I just had a fairly good memory – I could work out equations, that was about it really. Biology was all right. So I got disillusioned with it, and that was why I decided I'd like to perhaps study psychology or sociology. I was rather put off by the headmistress, and she actually said to my mother: 'I don't think psychology is a very nice subject for girls to study.' So in the end I decided to do sociology.

The English teacher was drippy and she – well there was a good English teacher, but we got this bad one, and she didn't seem to have any soul, she wasn't really interested. She was very analytical but didn't really bring out the feelings in the stuff, and it was so awful hearing her read poetry, and then we'd have to go over it line by line. We just weren't taught any kind of cultural perspective in anything that we did. It was all not linked to what was going on, there was no linking up at all of history and English or anything. They were all separate discrete subjects and that was – we had to study the most appalling things; our novels, they were shocking, and the poetry was nothing modern at all. Well, for O-levels I think I read *Kipps*, which was about the most modern – you know, H. G. Wells, which I enjoyed in fact, but nowadays when you see the A-level syllabus . . . I don't want to sound so sort of griping all the time, like how appalling it was and how marvellous it is now, and these kids of today they don't know how nice and how good it is, but it does seem to be different.

It wasn't a hard slog at school, it was really so boring. I can remember just being bored, constantly – thinking, day-dreaming, doodling, looking out of the window. I always chose a desk down that row by the window so I could look out, because, oh, it was just so boring. But at least I stayed. I suppose I did decide that – I mean my parents wanted me to, if they hadn't I am sure I would have left. A friend of mine did leave at sixteen and got a job in a library, and we really envied her so much. We used to go and see her after school and she had a boyfriend then and was going to get engaged, and it really seemed, you know, so much nicer than our life. There was the awful school uniform business as well. I mean, we had atrocious gymslips – well, we could wear skirts when we were in the sixth form – but macs, these horrible raincoats!

University

'I lost my virginity in a little flat off High Holborn.

Well my parents wanted me to go. I'd really chosen the wrong subjects for A-levels and I had to decide on something else, and how I got to LSE was really a question of elimination. I wanted to do sociology, I wanted to go to London, and I didn't want to go to Bedford College, because that was all women. There was LSE offering sociology, and saying that you could have any A-level. I didn't know anything about it, as a place, apart from the aura that it had of being a sort of home of Bolshevism, I suppose. I got the prospectus about the courses and about LSE and it seemed so fantastic! I just was terribly keen to go. I went for my interview, which was disastrous because I told them I didn't want to do science because it was far too finicky and you had to be so sort of meticulous and they said, 'Oh well, sociology is scientific too.' And that just shattered me. Actually I had such a bad interview and they sort of said, 'Oh well we have a very high standard, and if you're doing science and you don't even like it, you probably won't get high enough marks'. And they said, 'Where else have you tried?' I said Liverpool and Leeds, and they implied that I'd probably stand more chance there.

Anyway I suppose that, looking back, that period of time when I left school and went to LSE was one of the most exciting in my life; that sense of real – what's the word? – just real pleasure at leaving school, I was really so pleased that day to leave. My parents have moved away from there now so I haven't really been able to sort of wander back and see the old place. But the other month we drove through it and I just went to see that school and it's still there, and it looks just the same, you know, and I have the same feelings about it, just negative feelings, I suppose, in a sense.

So I left school that summer and I got a job working in a tea factory. I'd had lots of holiday jobs – because that was another thing, I didn't get much pocket money. I certainly didn't get enough money to buy clothes and things, and I always did work in the holiday, mostly catering jobs. So I'd had lots of odd jobs in that respect, but

I'd not really worked solidly, and I got a job working in a tea factory. This was my first taste of a completely different life.

I had to get up quite early and get this early bus which contained workers on it and go to the factory, and the work was very, very boring. Also, not only was it boring, but it was back-breaking work. You had to load up the finished tea packets, they were wrapped in – a very complicated process on the machine – wrapped in paper into big bundles and we had to stack them on a trolley and it was very exhausting. The time just seemed to drag so much, and the noise . . . when you first go there – I think it's the same in most factories – when you first go, the noise seems absolutely deafening, and the smell of the tea . . . but you just do get used to it. The money was quite good for me. It was a nice feeling anyway to be going out and earning your money and not to have to think about essays that you'd got to write and work that you'd got to do and exams you'd got to prepare for, so I enjoyed that. I started reading *The Social Psychology of Industry*, I remember I used to read it on the bus every morning, and that was quite a sort of revelation in a sense as well.

Then my friend and I went to Paris that summer, it was the first – well I had been on a school trip to Rome, but that didn't really count in a sense because we weren't given much freedom, so it was my first time to go abroad on my own and that was really marvellous, we just enjoyed it so much, being in Paris. Suddenly my life changed from being rather restricted, it was sort of opening out a bit, which was really nice. When I went to L S E I sort of felt very much – well, I mean, there were lots of people there who obviously came from a background of books and there were people whose parents were actually university lecturers, and I did feel quite out of it in a sense, I suppose. I joined the Drama Society. I think you had to join some sort of a group in a sense to feel you have some niche there.

Then in the summer we went to Israel, which was another revelation. Of course now I wish that . . . we stayed on – we took a play, *Midsummer Night's Dream*, to Israel and we stayed on quite a few *kibbutzim*. We asked them a few questions, but we obviously didn't know quite the sort of questions to ask. I certainly didn't go and visit any of the various age groups, the nurseries and the schoolchildren, and talk to the children and that. We just talked to some of the parents, mostly English people that had gone out there, and we were a bit sceptical about it, we thought it didn't sound a very nice thing that the children didn't sleep with their parents, the children were in separate dormitories. The parents told us that in fact they felt that they spent more time with their children, because once they had finished work at four p.m. the children came to them until it was bedtime, they weren't sort of – they didn't have to be getting the meals and things. I think they probably did, they probably do spend more time with them.

By now I'd got on to the next problem of whether or not one sleeps with anybody, and I'd still got it in my mind not only did I want a boyfriend then, I wanted to get married and then have this fantastic wedding night!! I wouldn't sleep with anybody at first, but I had this bloke, who was really very dominating, and I was very dependent on him. He was in the Drama Society and he singled me out because he thought I was innocent and nice and sweet. I wouldn't sleep with him, I still thought, oh, no. Then of course he finished with me and I was terribly heartbroken about it. I think it was really more that I didn't really trust him or feel that he was genuine enough, and really we were totally unsuited, he was quite upper-class and, you know, I just felt very unable to say much to him at all.

Then I met an American, he was about twenty, he was over here for a year, and he was so different and we got on very well together, and when the sort of same conflict came up with him it didn't – I didn't seem to – well there didn't seem to be a conflict any more, you know. The only problem was that I was living in digs, I had a landlady, but she didn't mind if I went out to parties. So I lost my virginity in a little flat off High Holborn and I really felt great afterwards. I mean, the experience itself wasn't all that marvellous, but I felt so terrific the next day, and I swaggered down Holborn and looked at everybody and thought – one gets this terrible sort of curious feeling that one's the only person in the world that's actually doing it, you know. It was really terrific. It was actually at the time I was just about to go to Israel with the Drama Society and I had to go off. Unfortunately we didn't have a lovely kind of morning, because I had to go off to rehearsals. So had I this really nice romantic first love, and Peter went back to the States and then I could write him long letters and he'd write to me and we'd plan about me going out there, and it was all rather pleasant. So in a sense I suppose I was quite lucky.

He just used a sheath when we slept together, although he had had fairly sophisticated girlfriends in New York who had caps. There was a way in London at that time if you went to – not the FPA but somewhere else – and you said you were getting married, then you could get one. Or you'd have to have an engagement ring or something, you couldn't just *say* you were getting married, and a friend of mine actually went to a private doctor and got a cap, but for some reason I didn't want to go – I think it was the guilt. It was the guilt of it; I did feel guilty about it, and somehow going and getting a cap made it worse. I mean, I think it is probably why some girls don't go on the pill, because then it makes it much more explicit really, if you are taking the pill, that you intend to embark on a sexual relationship, whereas if it just happens then you can say, 'Well I didn't really mean it to happen, it just happened.'

Well, I went to America, but by that time I had met Stuart, so there was a sort of difficulty. I met him at LSE, but we hadn't actually slept with each other. I was being loyal to my first love, you see, it was all very sort of prim and proper. But, you know, we'd been going round together, I suppose in a sense we were going out together. It had been all sort of nice and perfect, this first love. It was so silly and romantic – I still felt I needed to see him, which was probably a very cruel thing to do. So I planned to go out there, so I did go out there, that summer in 1962. I got off the plane and I felt awful, I just felt that I shouldn't have come. Peter was living in an apartment, and he had an awful job where he worked till ten o'clock at night, so I was on my own and I felt really awful, because it was in New York, and although I love the place, I didn't quite feel I was at home there. And I felt terribly bad about Peter because he didn't really react – you know, he didn't show that much emotion, and I think it really did affect him in a sense, the fact that we were kind of split up. You know, I had to tell him about Stuart and then I said I didn't think it would work out, and I kept sort of leaving him and then coming back.

But I wanted to get a job and I wanted to be sort of away from him. Also there was this terrible sort of dishonesty – my parents thought I was staying at his father's flat, and they were sending my letters there, and I had to go there, and they didn't know I was living with him. They had wanted me to get a job anyway, because they didn't want me to kind of stay with his father all that time – his parents were divorced. So I felt guilty about that.

I did get a job actually as a mother's helper, sort of au pair girl job, which turned out to be quite interesting. The husband, the father of the children, turned out to be a psychoanalyst. So I had this incredible time with them – it's very odd, because they were just amazed that an English girl should want to look after their children, because in the States, at that time anyway, all the mother's helpers were black, and so they just thought there must be something very odd about me. He immediately said to me when he came to fetch me from the station – you're supposed to have a blood test, all the kind of advertisements say, you know, blood tests, medicals – and to see that you haven't got syphilis and things, and he said – I mean it was his way of finding out things – 'You didn't have a blood test?' I said, 'No.' I said, 'What's this about a blood test?' 'Oh, if you have been – you might sort of possibly have VD. Have you been having intercourse with anybody?' I sort of confessed, it was a real confession, I sort of confessed all to him so he knew all about it, and he wanted to know all about it.

When I applied for the job I felt so low that I wanted in a sense to punish myself, and I thought, well I'll probably get in with this family which is really awful, with awful spoilt children, and it would be my fault and I really jolly well deserve it. They turned out to be a really lovely family. His wife had been to college but of course left before she finished her degree, and he was a psychologist and he had then done psychoanalysis. He was a non-medical analyst, I think they are called. They lived in Forest Hills, which is a suburb of New York, and they had these three lovely children, one was eight, one was six and one was three, and they were all girls and they were really sweet kids. And we went on holiday to this sort of summer place, and I used to have long discussions with him – the bloke – about various things, and of course the inevitable happened, he sort of made a pass at me.

It actually happened when we were swimming, this rather odd thing; it was sort of the classic thing, and I reminded him of his wife ten years ago – she was about thirty by then. She was idealistic when he met her and I was like her. If I was analysed it would all go, it was only a neurosis, being idealistic and so on. I was sort of quite flattered and I quite liked him, but I certainly didn't – I wasn't that madly sort of struck by him that I really wanted to sleep with him, and he was anyway very guilty about it, and I think, I should imagine, that if it came to it, he probably wouldn't. In fact I really did like his wife very much, she was a really nice person. I think in a sense I wanted to remain loyal to her. I felt a bit awful about it really – I mean we just had a few snogging sessions together when she wasn't there. But it was a nice sort of thing, it was just a sort of little event, I suppose.

Reading Betty Friedan's book was a revelation. I could realize that that was what was going on in that family. It was so much like what was happening, and in fact, you know, it was really a well-run household, and you know the children were very well looked-after, and their mother was totally involved with them, and they don't start school there until they're six – there is a sort of kindergarten thing they can go to, but it's only half-day – so really she had really dedicated her whole life.

The terrible thing was, you see, they were my model. I was unhappy, and here was this happily married couple with these children and they were sort of models for me and I wanted that life. I couldn't see anything wrong in it, it seemed a good life. I really was taken in by it, that somehow being a home-maker as such was quite a good thing to be, and to be interested in cooking and – because I hadn't really been very interested in cooking at that point – and children, and these were delightful children in a sense, really rather nice things. I didn't know young children like that, I hadn't really had much experience of them. And so I came back thinking that marriage and the family were something which I wanted. And also I wanted some sort of stability, I think, I wanted this. I did really think that having a man and having children would stop me feeling depressed. I think when I was an adolescent and when I was at university I did used to get depressed and I sort of saw it in terms of because I was lonely, and I wanted to share my life with somebody, and then if you did then it would be all right.

So then my third year was spent at LSE with Stuart and we sort of finally made it. He was older, you see, than I was, he was a mature student, and he also felt this need to get married and have children, because his friends were married and had children, and he sort of wanted this I think. So I suppose that's how we got married quite soon – well, a year after I had left university, and because I knew he wanted to have children, and I sort of felt somehow incomplete, not really very sure of my identity, although I had been to university and got a degree, I still felt I didn't know what I wanted to do . . . the sort of pressures . . . certain friends went on to PhDs and I didn't really want to do that. Well, I did know what I wanted to do, I wanted to be a social worker, but I felt, you have to be sort of mature to be a social worker, and there was a stress in those days on not just going into it straight from university. So I thought, well you know, get married and start a family, do it that way really.

I think this came out once at one of our women's meetings, when we were talking about why we got married and everybody was sort of saying, 'Oh, well, I didn't want my grandmother to have a heart attack.' But I actually know that I got married because I wanted to, it was one way of breaking away from my parents. You know, although I had physically broken away from them, I still felt that they influenced me in a sense, and getting married, they wouldn't and that. By then my political views were quite different from theirs.

Work

'I suppose the getting married bit was just to escape the job.'

I felt quite depressed after I'd finished university. Partly just leaving LSE, looking back now I realize I just didn't want to leave. Stuart was still there, because he was a year behind me. I had applied as a temporary probation officer in the summer, and I was turned down, and this upset me quite a bit, then I got a job working at a Family Service Unit summer camp, which was quite nice, just for a while. They deal with – well they see the so-called 'problem families', and they see them over a long time and do a lot of intensive work. After the summer I saw an advertisement for a job in a girls' approved school in London, in Streatham, so I applied and I got the job. Unfortunately I told the headmistress that I was interested in criminology, and that was one of the reasons I applied for the job; and she told the staff that she had got this criminologist coming – and all the staff, they were already all ready to down me, and I had a terrible time. I was a housemistress, or whatever you call it. It had been a home for sort of fallen girls in Victorian times and now it was this girls' approved school. They are still 'fallen girls' in a sense, because one of their kind of 'crimes' was that they had indulged in sex. You would say, 'What are you in for?' And they would say, 'Sex under age.' They were fourteen- and fifteen-year-olds, and in several cases some of their boyfriends in fact had been prosecuted and sent to prison. It was pretty horrible all round.

It was a classifying school, the girls came there first and they were classified and they were sent on to the appropriate training school or approved school. There were a lot of women there who were divorced, the staff, and they were obviously quite jealous I think, in a certain way, although they would never have admitted it, about these girls – that they, you know, had had this sexual experience in a sense, and I think they really were. And they were quite punitive towards them as well because of this. The fact that their own lives obviously hadn't worked out . . . I just think that they were the wrong sort of people, and it was the wrong sort of place for girls to go, because they weren't even criminals. A few of them had charges of some sort of violence, but most of them had just done petty thieving or had literally just stayed out at night and run away from home and that sort of thing. It was a fairly – it wasn't a very – well it was a very dehumanizing place for them and for the staff.

So I stayed there for about four months and then I got a job teaching as a – well I applied to do supply teaching, but I was given this school to teach history in Tottenham, a girls' school. At first this seemed OK, and it was so much nicer than the approved school where one had to be in in the evenings, we didn't have much time off. But there again it was the problem that one had these ideas and ideals of what one could do as a teacher, and then when it came down to it you couldn't. I particularly had discipline problems. I didn't prepare my classes very well, but I gather that a lot of people do, you know, when they first go to a school. It's just the fact that kids get pissed off with so many changes of staff.

I had a flat by then. Stuart lived at his mother's. [Laughs.] I saw him, and our relationship had its ups and downs, I think. Particularly when I was at the approved school. He was in his final year and he felt that I should be around. His mother wasn't there then. She had gone to America. And you know, he felt I should – in a sense be around to, not exactly look after him, but certainly . . . I've got a letter, I found a letter of his, and it's very funny because he's complaining about me and he says – he talks about this other girl that he rather fancied and 'at least she was going off to see this bloke of hers every weekend', and he implied that she was going off cooking him meals and really kind of looking after him. It's such an awful letter. He was quite amazed when I read it out to him, he said, 'Did I really write that?' – you know. I felt he was being a little bit unreasonable when I got the approved school thing, because, you know, I had to get a job some-where, and in a sense it solved the accommodation problem as well. And I did see him on my days off.

Anyway, the only nice thing about this school was the people there, some of the women teachers. At LSE I had not really made any close friends, no women friends at all. Partly because of having a boyfriend at last, sort of thing. We went round as a couple and I just didn't sort of develop any relationships with the women that were there. I also had a friend who came from school with me to London. So I didn't need in a sense to develop. I mean I had some-body to go to the pictures with if I wanted to, and I could sort of see her. And of course I see a few people that I knew that were there that had sort of stayed around in the same sort of political groupings.

But apart from that, I didn't have anybody. But at this school I met people who I liked. Quite a lot of the staff were very sort of boring. They would just talk about their husbands. The funny thing was, I found these women boring and they were all married, newly married, and they'd be talking about domestic matters. I found it boring and yet I still wanted to get married myself.

And it was really – in a sense I suppose the getting married bit was just to escape the job. Because Stuart got a job outside London, and I could start a new life and do something. I mean I did have doubts about it, and I got wild fantasies of all the money I had saved up from my well-paid teaching job, and sort of going off to America. It did cross my mind, but then all the arrangements for the wedding had been made and everything. We didn't have a church wedding – you know, I didn't really want to hurt my parent's feelings, but Stuart sort of insisted that he didn't want a church wedding. My mother said 'Well,' you know, 'I wanted you to have a church wedding because I wasn't able to have one.' You know, it was wartime and you had to go to a Registry Office. She was a bit -- she was disappointed, but luckily my sister had a church wedding, so that was OK. And they quite liked Stuart. I think they thought he was fairly reasonable.

Marriage

'For the first time, I was aware of being discriminated against.'

I left this school and got married. We came up North and then I think, for the first time, I was made aware of what – sort of being discriminated against. I think – up to then I had never really been discriminated against. It had always been my fault that I had not really known what I wanted to do after university. Not sort of pushed to do research, and dithered around. But I applied at the university for an MA. They had got a project going on and they had some money for four MAs, and I went to the interview and they said to me, 'This is a very important project, you wouldn't have many holidays. We see that you are married, we are a bit worried that you might get pregnant or something and . . .' You know, they really implied that they thought I was a bad risk as I was a married woman. I wasn't – I didn't – I just sort of said, 'Well yes, I would – you know I realize the importance of it, and I'd work hard and wouldn't expect long holidays.' But they – you know, that was it, I didn't get the – I didn't get offered one of these. I was very depressed about it. I think in a sense then I saw having children as a way out of that dilemma too. I still didn't know what I wanted to do. I got a job teaching liberal studies, but it wasn't even a full-time job. You know, it sort of made up about three days. And – so there it was, I became a sort of housewife, I suppose, already, before having the children.

It was inevitable, I think. I didn't even *think* about the decision to have a baby, it was just – *when* to have it – it wasn't a decision about having one. I just wanted to, and I thought I might as well have it sooner than later. In fact I was quite disappointed when after the first month I didn't get pregnant. But I did get pregnant after three tries. I was really extremely happy. I can remember, you know, all my kind of moments of happiness; I can actually remember where I was walking, the places where I was walking along, and I can remember going down the road, walking down a particular street, and feeling tremendously happy. You know, when I go down that road I can still remember that feeling. And I did enjoy being pregnant. I didn't get too many bad things happening to me, and I really felt my status rose within the people we knew. Well, I felt it – I don't suppose it did, I am sure it kind of fell, but I felt much easier. [Laughs.] I am sure I bored people stiff. I didn't know anybody with babies – although Stuart's sister was pregnant about the same time as well. And she'd had a daughter. I think that was another influence, his sister got married and had a baby, and the family was so kind of caught up in this baby, you know. I suppose I felt very much – very insecure within this family, because it is quite a big family network.

Stuart's got two sisters and a brother, and there's a very, very close kind of family thing going on, and I felt very much that I'd kind of – I didn't have anything to offer in a sense in that setting. There was me, absolutely nothing, you know. Sort of just a mere student from LSE. And I did feel ever so insecure, you know. They used to have lots of big family lunches and I just couldn't say anything. I just didn't say a word. I think reading Margaret Drabble's book, *Jerusalem the Golden*, I identified with it. It's about a girl who goes to London and gets caught up with a family who she really likes, and they are so different from her family. I think I experienced that same thing with Stuart, and all his friends as well. Something totally different to my background really. They just talked about different things for a start. They were interested in politics, but from a different sort of angle. just generally, much more sort of sophisticated, I suppose. You know, the whole thing about foreign cooking, using garlic and red peppers and green peppers. I really felt very insecure about that. I just felt that I was very – I was pretty bourgeois, I suppose. I was easily shocked about everything. It was a nice kind of atmosphere, but I did feel insecure. I mean now I really enjoy it. Meeting up with some of his family and that. I no longer feel insecure, but it's taken a long time for me to develop that feeling of being safe in my own identity. I really did have to go through that process of having children before I could feel that.

Children

'In a sense it was almost a sort of vying with one's mother, wanting something different.'

Anyway, Sally was born and, it was a very – you know, all the things that were said about childbirth were true, that it was a good experience, for me. I suppose perhaps if it had been a bad experience, it might have been different. I really kept thinking about the birth. One day when the nurse – this was when I was still in hospital – the nurse that had actually been there to deliver me, and had washed me afterwards and washed the baby, walked past and she didn't recognize me, you know, she didn't notice me, I was one of the hundreds that she delivered, and I felt terribly hurt, that there had been this fantastic experience that we had shared together and yet she hadn't even . . . she just walked past and that was it – oh gosh! Anyway she was quite a sweet baby and all the family responded, all the relatives. Oh, it was near Christmas time and we went down to London and Stuart's mother had a party for us, and, you know, showed off the baby. This was Christmas, and as the winter wore on I think I got a bit depressed about being at home all the time. But she was still quite fascinating, although I was very cut off because Stuart's colleagues, the wives were mostly older and they had jobs and things or they were younger people who didn't have kids, so I was in that kind of limbo of not knowing anyone. There was nothing around, you know, like women's groups.

Then we met a couple who were in a similar situation and it was really terrific meeting them. They also had a baby about the same age, a little bit older than Sally, and that was really nice. That was a sort of turning point for me, I didn't mind being in the North so much. And I was very sad when politics got in the way of our friendship in a sense, and I always blamed Stuart for this. And it really hurt me a lot when we hardly spoke to each other. I was just in that very vulnerable period at that time, I needed to have people round me, and for people to sort of practically – what's the word? – shun us. . . You know in that way it was really horrible, and I really sort of hated the politics that Stuart was involved in then, because – because of this it seemed that the political differences led to personal differences.

Then disaster sort of struck. Actually Sally was six months old, everything was fine, I had breast-fed her and, you know, the whole thing, it was really terrific, and then I got pregnant again. It wasn't that I'd thought that by breast-feeding I needn't sort of bother about contraception. I had actually been and got myself fitted with another cap and everything. But something happened, I think we – I didn't like the cap and in fact I really hated using it, and I tended to use any excuse, thinking that it was the safe period all the time. I am sure that this is what a lot of failed contraception is really. People not actually using it rather than any proper accident. I am sure the cap is probably safe but it's just that people tend not to want to use it all the time. So I got pregnant and I really did feel awful about it. This time – you know, we couldn't sort of tell people about it. We felt awful and we didn't want to tell our parents or anything. And they were shocked, you know. And Sally was, you know, quite a handful, I felt tired; and it was just that she was a delightful child and I didn't want to have to split my time, I think, between her and the new baby. I didn't like the baby at all, and just before she was born they discovered that she was in the breech position, and they couldn't move her because I was too far on. So this seemed to be another omen in a sense. It meant also that I couldn't have her at home, but I'd got to go into hospital.

Her birth was fairly eventful. We'd been to – there was a Polaris demonstration, and she was due in a fortnight's time, so we decided to go. We took Sally and she was on my lap all the way and I felt a bit funny when I got up, and I thought it was just that – a bit achey, because she had been sitting on my lap. Then I started getting these feelings every so often and I suddenly realized that I was actually – that they were contractions, and I was really panicky that she'd suddenly arrive. I think once the birth is actually happening it's an exciting time. Anyway, we felt quite sort of pleased that it was actually happening – but we managed to get back home. In fact it wasn't born until the next day. I did have to go into hospital because my waters broke and somebody told me that if you have a breech and the waters break you should be in hospital in case one of the limbs comes – an arm or a leg can come out quite easily.

So it was a much more difficult birth and I had to have an episiotomy and it was very painful and very tiring and I had to have my legs in stirrups as well, which I think rather degrading. You just feel that you're there as a victim on this slab, you know. Also a breech is quite dangerous, if it takes a long time for the head to come out after the body's come out, the body has to hang down to gradually bring the head out. Luckily I didn't need a Caesarean or anything, I didn't even need forceps, I think the doctor sort of assisted the head out, but I felt so totally exhausted after it that I couldn't respond to her at all.

I can quite understand how people don't respond to their babies afterwards and feel unable to sort of make relationships with them. I really felt like that I think. Because I was exhausted and tired and I was worried about Sally, how she was getting on. Anyway I came home after forty-eight hours – I was very sore from the episiotomy and the baby cried a lot. It wasn't really her fault, I am sure it was me, I sort of wanted to feed her again, I thought I ought to breast-feed her. She did get this awful colic at night, she only got it late at night after the ten o'clock feed. She seemed to sleep quite well in the day-time. I think it was because of all the tension that had built up. So this was a kind of different experience I suppose.

After Sally was born I had thought about going back to my job at the College, because Stuart didn't teach every day, he could have looked after her. But because I was breast-feeding her, I somehow felt that it would be so difficult to organize it, so I didn't – I didn't feel that urge to leave her. But obviously after Kate was born things were more hectic because I had two young children. It didn't occur to me that I could perhaps plan my life so that somebody came to look after them and I went out to work. I felt I'd got to kind of – it was my lot. You know – that I had to look after them. I am sure I didn't do it very well. I used to sit in the playroom – they had a sort of bedroom-playroom with toys in it – and I just used to sit with them and let them get on with it, I didn't really play constructively with them very much. It was quite a difficult time. I mean Stuart did help quite a lot, and he was able to come home at lunchtime and – I think he did probably more than most people. Yet I still got quite depressed really most of the time.

Things got a bit better in 1968 when Kate was about a year old. Sally started to go to play-group, and I met somebody there who had two children about the same age as mine whom I was able to have as a friend and whom I could visit and the children could get to know her, and then she introduced me to somebody else, and I started to find a sort of network of people that had young children. They were actually university people, but they were in the Psychology Depart-ment. They weren't political at all, you know. I am still friendly with one of them, because we went through an awful lot together, although perhaps politically we are not on the same wavelength. I like her very much. I am quite close to her, I think. And she certainly has helped me out an awful lot when I was doing a course last year. So I suppose that was a – once I had got to know a few more women, at least I wasn't so isolated, and felt that life was worth living again I suppose. Then we moved to this house as well. Which meant there was more – there was a garden for the children to play in, they didn't have a garden in the other house, and so that was quite nice.

I did do some disastrous teaching actually at the College. I was doing a kind of liberal studies course, but I think they only had me for a term, and then they pretty well sacked me. I've seen an essay I wrote from that period; it's all very academic and not connected with me, about the changing family, etcetera. There was a gradual sort of – equality was gradually coming, you know, with equality of opportunity and the Welfare State and all that. So I did do a little bit of teaching when I had the two children.

Then comes the big crunch. I got pregnant again. And I really – here again I was on the pill – by that time I had already managed to have a cap and a coil and the pill and I'd not enjoyed any of them. The coil had – I'd had very heavy periods. And also I was terribly worried, there was all this talk that it could actually give you an infection and you'd become sterile. And I didn't want that, I mean I really didn't . . . and it was partly because I had had such a rough time last time, I in a sense wanted a good time – you know, to have – to go through it and for it to be OK again. But partly also I had wanted – I had always seen in my mind that I would have three children. I come from a family of two and I think, in a sense, it's almost a sort of vying with one's mother, wanting something different.

I think at one point there was this emphasis on just two children. Then it became very trendy for middle-class intellectuals to have bigger families and unfortunately I . . . I have been talking to a friend of mine about this – we were just at the end of that, we just caught it unfortunately. Now the trend is completely the other way – I mean to have no children or perhaps to have one. You know, I was on this sort of trend, because all our – well Stuart's friends in London had all got three children. Though I notice up here that most of the people I knew whose oldest children are Sally's age, they've – most of them have got three children. There seems to be a university thing. And also I suppose because we've got two girls as well – I think if you have one of each sex then perhaps you decide that's enough.

So I got pregnant again. I had been on the pill and there was a conscious decision not to take the next month's supply. So I mean, in part it was just a sort of laziness. If I hadn't conceived that month, I think I would have gone back on to the pill again. It was just a month you know. And I can remember actually saying to Jean, 'I think I am pregnant, and if I am not I'll definitely go back on the pill again.' It is a bit silly, you know. By then it was too late, you see. Also one of these friends of mine who I'd met, I was sort of influenced by them a little bit. She was also pregnant at the time, so in a sense I had got people around me. So I was pregnant again, but it was better this time. The children were – Sally was still going to play-group and Kate was – well she was eighteen months I suppose when I got pregnant. But I had organized my life a little bit better. Somebody came to look after the children once a week and I went to an extra-mural English class, which was really nice, it was so different from the sort of English that we had done at school and I enjoyed it very much. So that was a day off in the week. But I did need that time off, it was very necessary.

Women's Liberation

'I think at the beginning the stripping-away process of layers of half-truth is very painful.'

And then comes this period of when – there were vague things happening. I can remember Jean showing me something from America called *Notes from the First Year*, I think, or something like that; it was a brown-covered thing, which seemed a bit odd, these people talking about their orgasms and things. We read it, and we both said it looked a bit – they seemed a bit sort of – oh, a bit odd, typical American! Sort of worried about themselves. And just about this time Juliet Mitchell came to talk at the University. She was saying things like, the family had to go, and of course I was absolutely appalled you know, and I questioned her on this. I saw the alternative as being a huge institution. You know, I couldn't see any other alternatives. And also that children needed love, which I think they do – you know, they need love, they need a loving relationship, they need security. But obviously the sort of security they get in the family, they can have in a different way elsewhere, but I was really quite appalled at the idea of doing away with the family completely. Although some of the things she said made sense, the whole business about children in the family, I didn't really go along with her. I was more thinking about it in terms of disturbed children. That you get a lot of children that actually are really disturbed and you find that it's always because of broken homes and things, and I think I was thinking more in that way, because I mentioned this thing about disturbed children and she sort of implied that there was a lot of disturbed children around because of the family. Which of course is true.

Just after that I must have read Betty Friedan's book. Now the funny thing about that is, it was on my mother-in-law's shelf, *The Feminine Mystique*, it was a Penguin. And I saw it and I picked it up and I thought – oh, and I thought it was going to be something about sex, and women – you know, women and sex – and I picked it up just to read and give it an idle look, really. I didn't look at it then, I just took it back – brought it back here and I started reading it, and I was absolutely – she just described my life, you know. It was horrible.

First of all I started reading it and I was very against it, because she kept implying that having children and being at home was terribly unsatisfying, and that all these sort of neurotic American women, who felt that – you know, that their lives – well I saw them as being neurotic . . . I think gradually it dawned on me that she was saying an awful lot of good things, although I think then I was still fairly hostile to what she was saying, but reading it again I think it is a very good book. It describes, you know, what happens to middle-class women who don't *have* to work, whose husbands can earn enough so that they can stay at home. I mean obviously this is a privilege and it's not the condition of a lot of women, and also I think in America there's much more kind of a status about the sort of house you have and the type of dinner parties you give. I don't think I was ever kind of into that sort of scene. Well, I didn't worry so much about housework. I can always remember in that bit that talks about two women who plan to go off one day to a movie or something, and they say, 'Oh well we can get everything prepared the day before,' and they even think that they can make beds, and then they realize that they can't – that they can't prepare everything the day before. Their whole lives are so caught up in this 'getting things done', you know, doing the housework and so on. They are just so caught up in it they can't just live their life each day.

Then I think that about this time, a girl in the University was very interested in setting up some sort of women's discussion group. So we had meetings and I went along and I felt very defensive because I was pregnant and I had two children as well. I think in those days there was much more a feeling that – that somehow having children was a sort of – you know, something that one didn't have to have and anybody that did, in a sense it was their fault; and they were more interested in looking at – well looking at their own lives and how they were just oppressed by their boyfriends or something. So I felt a bit defensive about it. Well Jean had a child as well but there weren't many of us. They were mostly people who were – most of them were married but they hadn't got children. And in fact now I see that the people that were in that early group have got children, and they actually want to talk about completely different things. It's rather funny.

This is the horrible thing, I think, that in a sense one thinks, well – just you wait until you have children! You know, there is this horrible feeling of non-solidarity – actually wanting somebody to – you know, to have a difficult time, because you'd suffered, and I think a lot of the older women perhaps, who are very antagonistic towards Women's Liberation – the fact that they had actually managed to cope with it, and therefore, you know – why should these young women be making all this fuss? When they'd even got better consumer goods – you know, domestic help in a sense, with washing machines and things like that.

When some friends of ours came with their two young children the other weekend to stay, it really came back to me then. That they were just involved with those two children all the time – one is about four months and the other is about twenty months. I remembered then all the awful things. You do gloss over them. I suppose this is why women can continue to go on having babies. [Laughs.] I mean you do forget even the sort of awful things of the birth. I mean that pain just goes, you can't imagine it – you can't, you know.

Actually, when I had Kevin it did work out quite well. I had him at home, which was really nice. After I had had him, I really felt – well this is the last. I didn't mind, and I think that if I hadn't had him then I probably would have hungered after another baby. You know, I might have even had one much later on perhaps, because I think this is what happens to some women, they, you know, have another child when the youngest goes to school or something. So I didn't mind having him. Although obviously having three children is far worse than – in a sense – than having two, you can't really park them on in-laws. Two is all right, but three – it is difficult. I did decide as well that I wanted to do some work, not just mess around, and that I would leave him with somebody, you know. In fact he was a year before I actually got a job. That first year I think was fairly difficult in different sorts of ways though. Sally wasn't at school. She used to go to nursery class in the afternoon.

But it was a much more crucial time for me discovering myself and finding all sorts of awful things about myself in a way. Really hating myself for being the sort of person I was. Learning . . . this sort of conscious-raising thing where one looks at one's past in a completely different way and really feels, oh God, what did I do? All the terrible decisions and choices that one made. And just sort of hating yourself in a sense. Also I felt very isolated. I really got rather paranoid about people and thought they didn't like me and oh, if they came round, they usually came round just to see Stuart, you see. I hated that, people coming round and wanting Stuart or wanting something, and then not actually saying anything to me, not even talking to me, you know. I can remember people coming and saying, 'Oh, Stuart promised to lend me a book,' and I'd go up and get it and they'd thank me and that was it. And you know, I was on my own and I needed people to talk to. I am going to burst into tears in a minute. I really did, you know.

I can remember also somebody came round and didn't look at the baby. This was just after he was born, they came to talk about something, and I was ever so upset about it, he didn't actually say, 'Let's see the baby.' I mean it's really awful that you should feel that one's got to, but at that time you are very vulnerable. Very in need of people around you, I think, to respond to you, and I did feel very sort of without anything. Yes. But it was partly my kind of feeling a bit stripped of myself by going to these women's meetings – you know, you have a stripping-down and you've got to build up gradually. I think that at the beginning the stripping-away process of the layers of humiliated half-truths in a sense is very painful. I am continually finding new things about myself and learning, but – I felt very exposed, exposed to everybody in a sense. I felt people were unsympathetic because I had a baby, and yet I wanted to get involved but I didn't quite know how.

Andrew

'I'm sure having an affair is more interesting than losing one's virginity.'

I think it was about this time that I met this bloke Andrew, who was a student. He was one of these people that actually is fairly sympathetic and does talk to you. And he'd come round and talk. He lived round the corner. Stuart had known him politically before, and he used to baby-sit for us. I got this terrible sort of fantasy about him. Going to these Women's Lib meetings I suddenly thought as well, that not only was I – I'd got all these children but I'd only – my sexual experience was so limited, you know. I'd only slept with two people, and being near the University, one also – I mean by then everybody was on the pill. We had one student living with us and he slept with his girlfriend, and various girlfriends used to come and sleep. And it seemed a whole new scene and I'd kind of missed it. I really felt that our marriage was pretty shaky. I mean Stuart was very kind of threatened by my going to Women's Lib meetings. He always used to ask me, 'How many people went?' – really wanting to know whether or not it was a viable thing.

Well Andrew is this – sort of fantasy. I actually read a book once – I always seem to have to relate my experiences to books – where a woman – it's a very nice story about this American woman actually, who had got a thing about a young boy that she was tutoring and she used to follow him around, and eventually it ends in them kissing or something, you know, that's all. Well anyway, I sort of felt that I was – I got very attached to him, and he had a girlfriend who used to come over you know, and I was friendly with both of them, but I felt this desperate urge to tell him about my feelings.

He left in the summer to go abroad for a year. I felt I wanted to say something to him, or give him something when he left or – I don't know; and he came round to say goodbye to us – came round in the evening, and I was just putting Kevin to bed and I was holding him and Andrew came, and instead of even being able to just kind of give him a little hug, I'd got Kevin, I was held back by these children. So he said 'Cheerio' and I said 'Cheerio' and I was in that terrible state, which I think only women get in – perhaps men do – where you feel you've got to do something, you have some sort of plan and you're desperate, and so I decided I would give him a book. It was too late to buy one so I had got to give him one of my books. I gave him Simone de Beauvoir's *The Mandarins*, which I later found out he thought rather boring. I saw him in the street, and I gave it to him – I think he was a bit touched. Anyway something rather odd happened, he left his jacket, and he phoned up and said he'd left his jacket in the house – could I send it to him? So I did, and of course I wrote him a letter, which was disastrous. Oh, the number of disastrous letters I have written to people is so awful. I said a few things in it which were quite embarrassing really.

By then he was abroad, but he had gone for the summer, and then he came back and he came and stayed with his girlfriend here, I don't know why, because he could have stayed round the corner. I think his girlfriend wanted to stay here. So there was this awful tense kind of situation with him and his girlfriend staying here, and me eating my heart out. We were quite friendly. The upshot of it is that eventually I did sleep with him, and in a sense it was far worse then, because at least before I had been friendly with him and he'd written letters to me, and it was all right, but after I slept with him I think he was a bit embarrassed about Stuart and everything, and it changed. He just wasn't so friendly, you know, and I felt very much that it had not really worked out. I felt he just didn't know the extent of my feelings. I have never been able to talk to him about it, and there have been periods when I have seen him in London and if he just says, 'Oh, why don't you stay the night?' and I say 'OK', that's been fine, but if I've had to ask him, if I've had to phone up and say, 'Oh look, I am in London,' and he says, 'Oh well do you want to come round?' and been very non-committal, it's been disastrous. I went to a party with him once and it was so awful because obviously he didn't really want to drag me along there, he had obviously planned something, and he'd got to drag me around.

I think in fact I've got over that. I really went through this period of – I mean after I slept with him I really wanted to go off with him. I know I just couldn't do that at all. But in a sense I am sure that this whole incident with Andrew was because I'd not really suffered in love, everything had been smooth; in a sense I wanted to go through that, it was a kind of adolescent thing. I had not experienced it and there was me experiencing it at the age of twenty-eight. I hoped that I suppose we could somehow just be friends – but it didn't really work out. I did write one or two disastrous letters to him, he only wrote back if I wrote to him. He was a bit – I don't know what he wanted. I think in a sense I was exploited by him, he wanted a good screw then he went down to London.

I felt so awful doing it, Stuart knew about it. The thing was – he was almost – he felt for me, I think, when I was upset about it. I don't think he felt threatened by Andrew at all, so he didn't mind if I was away. He didn't like it if I went off and he didn't know where I was, but if I'd go away for the weekend I don't think he minded, and he also had had an affair with somebody, so there was sort of a bit of a scoring thing going on. The last time I saw Andrew I felt more in control of the situation in a sense and I knew that I wasn't going to get hurt by it, and it was OK then.

I am sure having an affair is much more interesting than losing one's virginity. It's much more – I mean when that happens it's not usually very good the first time, but having an affair is a slightly different thing, and I did feel very much more secure in myself after that. I felt that I wasn't just somebody that was married and leading a boring life – it is a substitute really, when one's life is not very active. I don't think it is a particularly good substitute. I am very mixed up about this whole thing about monogamy really, or, you know, relationships – whether one can manage more than one relationship at a time. It seems to be a bit unfair on the other person – you know, they have to put up with you, all your moods, and yet you are having jam on it in a sense. Maybe it's my puritanical attitude. I still can't work this one out at all; I think intellectually it is a great idea, and then when it comes down to it for me personally it always is very complicated.

I think Stuart doesn't seek alternatives, doesn't feel the need for them as much as I do. I felt this was the only way I could actually have a separate existence, whereas he had his work and his political life so he didn't need to, he felt secure in himself. It's the old story of living life through men; even to see them with other people is using men for your own inadequacy.

Now I want to actually have relationships with people that are just not defined by sex. I think it's more interesting; I mean you can actually have friendships with people that are quite exciting and nice and I suppose eventually it would be nice to sleep with them as well. Particularly where other women are involved that you know – the other woman doesn't mind. I think this idea of just wife-swapping is a bit too ridiculous. I suppose this is what probably happens amongst married people where they have close friends, you often get that two of them want and the other two reluctantly agree.

I think I have changed some of my ideas in the period of time I have been involved with Women's Liberation. I suppose at the beginning it seemed, there was all this talk of whether one had to adopt the feminist perspective or a socialist one, and now it's not as clear-cut as that I don't think. Obviously capitalism damages any relationships, but that doesn't mean you can't really do anything about it. I don't accept the other feminist thing that *all* the problems are caused by relationships with men and women, that men oppress women, that we should practically have nothing to do with them. It seems to be that certain things can be done, and I think there have

been changes in our society already, which have been influenced by
the Women's Liberation, particularly issues involving contraception.
I know that there is all this emphasis on population control, and so
it's timing quite well with that, but I think that the Women's Movement can put a different point of view, because in all these population
things they emphasize the desirability of limiting one's family
because of the needs of the nation, not because of the needs of the
mother – that never comes into it at all. In fact bearing children is a
fairly arduous process, and tiring, and therefore . . . It's the same with
the nursery education thing, it's connected with education, that
educationally it's good for a child to go to a nursery school, but not
so much that it's socially good for him or that it's good for the
mother for the child to go away.

We went to this club to talk about Women's Liberation. This one
woman – I always remember this – said, 'Well, I *like* being at home,
I have enjoyed my time bringing up my children.' This is what you
always get, I think, when you talk to an older group. Then afterwards we were talking and she came up to us and she said, 'Actually,
it's not quite true. I am now doing this psychology degree.' And you
always seemed to get this, people at these meetings would talk and
disagree with you, but afterwards they would come up and really
tell you how pissed off they were.

We went to another Young Wives' Group. It's really quite painful
because I feel very much in a sense that middle-class women are
oppressed; they are psychologically oppressed. I know they are not as
oppressed as working-class women are, but they do have a fairly
rough time looking after young children, being isolated on the
housing estates. I found it a bit difficult really to talk to them, because
they were women about our age but they were slightly different
socially. We talked to them and it was the same sort of thing – that
they enjoyed it – then they would start thinking of the difficulties in
their lives. We talked about how children were brought up differently. They would then talk about things that happened to their
children, school and things, and realize what was happening, particularly to their girls.

I think the nice thing about Women's Lib is the idea that you can, instead of being envious of other women and seeing them as rivals, as somebody that you envy and fear as well, that you can share in all the problems and triumphs as well, you know; you don't feel envious any more. I don't mind talking to those groups. I don't feel contemptuous – I think that some of the people perhaps in the Women's Group do – of women that have chosen that kind of life, it's quite difficult for them to alter it, I think. I think a lot of women are going back into doing things, once their children are a little older.

12.   Christine Buchan

Christine Buchan was born in 1939 in Glasgow. Her family moved to Aberdeen when she was nine. As a small child she was a cripple and unable to walk. She has one brother.

She comes from a working-class background; her father was a trade-union official and her mother comes from a fishing community in the north-east of Scotland.

She did science at school and attended university, where she became active in the Campaign for Nuclear Disarmament and the New Left movement. She met her husband there and they now have two children. She works as a laboratory technician and is active in the Labour Party and the Women's Movement.

Childhood
'I always thought there was something odd about me.'

I was born in Govan in Glasgow. My parents came from Aberdeen. There wasn't a lot of work and my father got a job down in Glasgow and we stayed until I was nine. Then I went back up to Aberdeen when I was nine. I can remember quite a lot about Glasgow. We were born in a nursing home on the banks of the Clyde. My brother was born just during one of the blitzes and I can remember that, because I had to shelter under the stairs. I think I remember because my aunt was looking after me, she wasn't very used to children and I was a bit upset because my mother wasn't there. I remember feeling all stroppy.

I was born with a dislocated hip, so when I was eighteen months I was put in splints and not allowed to walk till I was four. When I was four I was taken into hospital for a longish period of time, I used to have cages in front of me. So I always thought there was something odd about me. I felt very definitely from a very early age that there was something unusual about me. Well you know, I was a cripple – in that sense unusual. I used to sit in the pram and people used to speak to me and used to give me presents because they were sorry for me because I couldn't walk. And I used to look at other girls that were my age and it was a funny sensation, I thought maybe there was something wrong with them. I thought there was something wrong with me, but really only boys could run about and girls that were doing it were misbehaving themselves really, they should all be sitting in prams like me. It must have been a way of trying to keep – to keep my spirits up or something.

I remember as well when they said I could walk, the doctor said that to my mother, and he said, 'She needs a lot of encouragement, because,' he said, 'she hasn't walked for years.' And my mother got me home and went through to the kitchen to make a cup of tea, and when she came back I was throwing myself from one chair to the other and falling on to the floor and everything, and in fact it was the other way round, I couldn't wait to walk, and I didn't know how to walk – I just sort of threw myself across gaps, and then what I got was terrible cramp, because my muscles weren't ready for it.

My mother taught me to knit when I was three on a pair of nails, long nails, with odd bits of wool. I didn't read until I went to school, because my mother didn't try to teach me to read. You were told that you shouldn't teach children to read before a certain age. I could do jigsaws. I had lots of books, but I didn't read them – you know, with pictures. I was in hospital and people up and down the street made a lovely doll's cot with a doll in it and sent that to me, and they all sent in books and I got lots of dolls. Mainly it was knitting, you know, because I could use my hands, I couldn't move my legs.

As there wasn't television, there was very little for me to see. My mother used to sit me out on a stool in the front garden and I could watch the people going by and they would speak to me. And I had this foolish way I worked out how to manipulate the stool, I used to sort of dig my heels in and pull it. Apparently I shouldn't have done it, it destroyed the hip quite a lot. I had X-rays about six years ago with my hip and there's no socket there. I mean it's just impossible asking a child to – at one point they wanted me to lie flat on my back all the time. They were feeding me through . . . it was a thing like a teapot. In all respects, apart from the leg, I was an active little child – you know, I wasn't ill. And they tied me in, I had these things on – they used to tie me to the bed to keep me down – called re-strainers. They do that to the people in the lunatic asylums as well, you know. Of course it was during the War.

Once or twice I remember waking up and fearfully hurt children lying quite close to you, they were putting them in anywhere, and I remember once looking across the ward at night, and the other kids told me . . . he had screens round the bed and there was a light inside and we could see shadows of people inside round the bed, the kid's parents, and he had died. I remember this child lying in this bed right next to me, completely covered in bandages, you couldn't see his face at all, and the bandages were over the top and bottom half of its mouth, and it could open its mouth a bit and it was crying for its mother over and over again. I thought it was crying for its mother because the bandages were getting inside its mouth and hurting it. I think it must have been very badly burned. Children in those days, you only got to see your mother for half an hour a week, and that child, you know, was really ill and screaming for its mother, and they weren't doing anything about it at all.

I was taken in, in and out with splints, until I was four; I was in for a year, maybe six months to a year. It's a wonder I didn't end up in a loony bin. There are some things I did . . . I got asthma, I developed asthma then. I also had hallucinations that my mother was standing at the end of the ward. I had it over and over again. I thought I could see her outside, I thought she was outside the window, when I was four. I was scared of the dark after that, I had to have a light on when I got home. I think partly also we had a light in the ward, and I sort of thought the pool of light – I thought my mother was standing at the other side of the lamp, just in the darkness, I thought I could see a vague outline.

Some of it wasn't bad. We had a birthday party for the whole ward – we pushed all the beds round, we had a cake and cut it and everything; and we all got jaundice, an attack of jaundice, the whole ward, which was great – everybody went this horrible colour, and your parents couldn't get in, you had to look through the doors in the ward, but by that time you see, you had lost interest in your mother by then, you were more interested in the nurses, you know, because they were the ones that looked after you. I didn't really care whether my mother came or not, I had rejected her by then.

A boat had arrived in the Clyde – it was during the War, you see – with a lot of oranges, and because it was jaundice, we all had oranges in great piles all over the ward on all these lockers. And we had dates as well, so dates were brought in, and you always knew during the War what boat had come in with something that was relatively scarce, because it always landed up in our ward.

Parents

'It must have been pretty hellish.'

My mother left school at fourteen, in fact she completed two years in the top class at school. When she got to the top class she wasn't allowed to leave, so she did her final year in top class again. My father was a bit younger than my mother, and by that time children that had some promise after fourteen, they went for a year or two to a kind of senior secondary. My father did that. Then my mother was too young to work in the factory, so for a year she went into service and worked for a headmaster in a country school, but I think he must have been a socialist because he gave her a lot of books to read. She was only allowed to work for a certain amount of time during the day, and before they ate – she used to eat in the kitchen and the family used to eat in the front room – but before they ate the wife would come through and give her her share before anybody else got theirs. My mother always thought that was a rather nice thing to do. Even if there was people in for afternoon tea, if there was a cake, my mother got the first cut of the cake. She said the cake went through

and wasn't whole; my mother thought that was a super thing for her
to do. But she got off one afternoon a month to go back and see her
mother, and I can't remember what her wages were. I think she was
very homesick.

She said as well, she had been brought up in a slum in Aberdeen,
with an outside toilet, and water outside – I think it was on the
stairs, they had one of those flat sinks on the stairs – and she went to
be a maid in this house, and they had a lot of vegetables in the
garden and it was the first time that she realized how peas grew. She
had never realized, you know, she had seen it in shops, but she had
seen no photographs – and how turnips, carrots and things like that
grew, and they kept bees and she learned all about that, and hens,
they kept hens. It was a country school.

Well when she was fifteen she was old enough to go into a factory.
She got more money in a factory, and she worked from when she
was fifteen until she was twenty-nine at the same machine in the same
factory, and over that period of time they cut her wages. She was on
piece-work and they cut the rate drastically. I mean as she got more
skilled, in fact, she was earning the same wage. It was 1923 when she
went into the factory. Sometimes if they were slack, she said, they
were laid off. She didn't get involved in politics until quite later on,
it's surprising. Once or twice she said they would obviously feel that
they would lose their job, but often – of the family of five children
and a mother and father, she would be the only one that was working.
I think her employment was more secure.

It must have been in the mid twenties she got involved in the
Union. They had scholarships through the Union to send people to
Ruskin – it involved writing an essay, and maybe some other things,
and then you went to London for an interview. She did that, she
wrote this essay, she said she always remembers it was called 'Half a
Loaf is Better than No Bread'. So she wrote this and she went to
London for an interview and got a scholarship for two years.

She's not all that political, you know – with her and my father,
they had a fantastic fear of Communists. I was brought up to believe
that they ate babies. Not only were they utterly wicked, but they
were clever as well – you know, you had to keep your eyes open or

they would get you, and their aim in life apparently was to smash any well-organized movement, they would come and take over and smash it. When I speak to my father now, it's amazing how it's just all personalities. He went to Ruskin for two years. They were also trained to think that middle-class conscience was the best. And my mother knew a lot of songs that her father taught her you know, she comes from a fishing family background. We used to have to get her drunk so that she'd sing songs, because she thought they were not very nice, and my father used to buy the most boring records by Brahms and he tried to listen to them. He thought you know, that this was culture. It's awful sad.

My father is a trade-union organizer. He's very involved in politics and very bitter because he tried several times to – he's been a candidate at General Elections, but always in seats where there wasn't a hope. He tried for about five years to get a safe seat. He never did get one, and he thought there were Communists organizing against him. The thing is that he is not a very good public speaker, he's not all that articulate, you know, and I think he wouldn't be a good MP, but anyway. . .

My grandfather was a great freethinker and he was also a great trade-union man. He drank like a fish as well. He was particularly bad to his family. When my father was born my grandfather went to America for three years because he couldn't get work in Aberdeen. He came back when my father was three. In fact when I was small I remember if I asked my father for a drink of water his hand used to shake so much holding the glass up that you couldn't drink the water, and I used to think that was very strange, but he must have had a pretty shitty sort of childhood. He's a lot better now, his hand doesn't shake very much, a bit sort of calmer. It must have been pretty hellish. They didn't like my grandfather, his children, I think he was pretty violent to them. Their mother couldn't stand up to the father, she got very ill about him. There is a story about she had a ruptured appendix and they didn't get her into hospital until it was quite late on, so she got a kind of blood poisoning, and she was an invalid for the rest of her life and lay in bed all the time. One of my aunts tells me the story about my grandfather coming back drunk and going into the room, looking at her on the bed and saying something about, 'High time you were dead.'

School

'I remember my brother and I standing back to back and taking it all in.'

My father always fancied – it's part of his right-wing thing – having a house of his own. So he bought a house in Glasgow. He couldn't really afford it. We lived out in a suburb which isn't as posh a suburb as some of them further to the south, I think. But it was quite posh. Five rooms, kitchen and bathroom – a semi-detached house – and just a wee garden. So we went to this school, it was a state school. It must have been during the War, they were moving people out of the centre of Glasgow at that time and we had some really tough kids coming in. And then, after we moved to Aberdeen, we went to the wee country school and these kids said to us, 'Oh those people from Glasgow, they're running around and slashing people!' And I remember my brother and I standing back to back and taking it all in.

But that was good up in Aberdeen at the country schools. The atmosphere was super, the teachers knew everybody, and their parents and their grandparents, you know. I didn't like it to start with because the methods of teaching were very old-fashioned, learning by heart in fact. The first teacher I got wasn't very satisfactory, but the second one I got was super. She was interested in absolutely everything, and we had a very mixed school, you know, with doctors' kids and farm labourers' kids all in the same class. There was this fantastic mixture and I became bilingual. I had to speak Aberdeenshire – very broad Aberdeenshire – in the playground so that the other kids could understand me. I remember writing this story and I said that this girl 'cried another one to come over', and the teacher said you couldn't use 'cry' like that, it wasn't the correct word, it was 'call', that was the correct term. And I couldn't understand this at all, because I thought 'cry' and 'call' were the same; because if – in Aberdeenshire, if you call a baby a name you 'cry' it that, that's what they call it. I mean she understood as well, she was

from the same area, but I had this business of where she carefully
eradicated the words with an eraser so that you understood correct
English. There were other things. You need to get held up for saying,
'What like is it?' You know, we had to say, 'What is it like?'

I went up to Aberdeenshire and that school when I was nine, I
left when I was twelve. And then I went to a school in Aberdeen, an
all-girls school. Like a grammar school. There wasn't a senior
secondary, there was a junior secondary, but they had two sections in
it. A top section which was supposed to be similar to a grammar
school, but it stopped at fifteen. So I did the eleven-plus for that, but
my parents they wanted me to stay on at school till I was eighteen if
possible. The county just didn't provide a place in the secondary
education at all. The Education Act had been passed saying that they
had to provide secondary education, but they didn't do it. They
thought that people who were good enough to go to senior secon-
daries, their parents would pay the fees for them to go to the fee-
paying ones in the town. The only other class of person in the country
were the farm labourers, and of course they were too stupid ever to
need senior secondary education, so they don't provide it. That's true.

There were a few fee-paying schools in the town that you could
go to, but my parents could never afford that, so I went to – and that
was a terrible experience, I remember being really emotionally upset
when I first went to this girls' school, because I never came across this
business of – women, you know, just all one sex and the teachers all
women. And the girls all had the same clothes, and it was a huge
school as well, I had never been exposed to – just the size of it, and
the organization! And then very quickly you got all these myths
about boys and men in that set-up. To begin with it amused me, but
gradually I suppose I succumbed to it as much as anyone else.

I got quite friendly with a girl called Norma, and she didn't do so
well in her exams as I did when we were about fourteen–fifteen, so
she was placed down the scale into another class, the same year but
down. I think they had five classes in a year, in a stream. We were
both very upset about that and we met at intervals in the playground,
and we always used to have school dinners, so we used to meet and
have school dinners – and some of the teachers must have noticed,

and God, our parents were called and they said we had an unusual relationship – you know! As far as I can remember it wasn't – well, we were very close, but that was it. I remember because there had been a thing with two girls who had a lesbian relationship in a school. I think it was one girl's grandmother in Australia, and she found the kid's diary, and that had been published in all the Sunday papers round about that time, and I think there was a sort of feeling of a girls' school wasn't all that natural and they'd keep their eye open for anything unnatural. I had this feeling about the girls in the older classes. I looked up to them. I thought they were gorgeous, and terribly calm and able to cope in all kinds of situations, and the young teachers as well. We used to sit and talk about them.

The terrible thing was my brother went to a grammar school which was a boys' school, and he's now thirty-two and he's never had a girlfriend. I mean he was – I think I can understand, because my parents never showed any affection towards one another at all in public. I never saw them together. When somebody told me about sex I just couldn't believe it, I just couldn't believe that my parents could get together in that way. It wasn't disgust, it was just, you know, it was an unbelievable thing for them to do. They never showed any affection. A boy told me about sex when I was seven, when I was on holiday. I am a very gullible person. I don't know how, but I had kind of suspected as well, that it must be something like that, but I think that that's one of the reasons why my brother has never been able to have any kind of relationships with girls. I used to think maybe he does and we don't know, but speaking to him recently, I know he hasn't. On the other hand he seems reasonably happy, he's had a sort of very interesting life, so. . . My parents go on at him now – why doesn't he get married and have children? It's not natural.

When he was eleven he went to an all-boys school, he went until he was eighteen. My father because of the trade union was never at home, so there was just my mother and me, and he got involved with the Scouts as well. I think that because my parents were so unemotional towards us . . . you see there was all this stuff about my father disliking my grandfather, loathing and hating him. He was a pretty brutal bloke and my mother once said to me that my father knew when they were having sex because he could hear it, because – I think it was thin walls – and I think he must have thought often that my grandfather was hurting his mother. I think he vowed that his kids would never know, you know, they would never have to worry about things like that; but it went completely the other way, I never saw them kiss one another. My mother only ever kissed me if I was so ill, so I knew I was really ill and they were going to get the doctor; because I would get a kiss I knew, I thought, God, I am really ill now! But my father never – I remember once or twice when I was very young, thinking that I didn't like it as much as when my mother kissed me because he had – you could feel the bristles and I didn't like the feel of that.

I did maths and science at school. English and art I really liked, but I never kept up with them. Art you had to drop in your fourth year if you were going on with science, because you couldn't cope with the timetable. I remember the art teacher saying I should stick with art, and my mother saying, 'Well you don't really get good jobs just on art. If you take science you'll get a good job and well paid, you know – stick with science.' It was unusual for girls to quite like science, they encouraged me a great deal. When I got to university, I realized that half the stuff I had been told was rubbish. I had to re-learn fantastic bits, and obviously the boys were really widely read, and had a much better understanding in the topics before they had ever been to university. They ran through stuff very quickly and I knew there must be a huge backlog to learn that I hadn't got. But maths, we had a good maths department and one or two really good maths teachers, so I managed maths reasonably well.

I had no real idea what I was aiming for, I knew I didn't want to teach. I hadn't liked school, and the teachers seemed to be so divorced from reality. In this girls' school most of the teachers were from – an awful lot of them, their families had been ministers of religion, and this was the first – well most of the women seemed quite old. There were one or two not so old, and the Latin teacher was quite nice. This was the first generation of women being allowed out to work, and the respectable thing to do was to teach. Even now, I know there's girls that went to school with me, went to university and then went straight back to the school to teach, and they are still doing it. It really is quite horrifying.

Adolescence

'Judy's influence meant that I managed to socialize with boys.'

I had a very sexy cousin, she matured very early from a very working-class background. Her father was a painter, they got married – her parents got married very young and they were very poor, and Judy was a mistake. She was born later on, she always knew that she was a mistake. She liked boys, she was about ten. She had red hair, I thought she was good-looking, she had bright red hair and freckles and a very forceful personality, and we used to do all these awful things like reading books about beauty and tips about deportment. When she was fifteen she got a summer job and she went out and bought a book called *How to Attract Men*, and you know, a working-class Aberdeen background, her father had a fit! He was climbing up the wall and screaming at her, and he was terribly embarrassed about having such a stupid daughter that would buy rubbish like that – all this stuff about raising your eyelashes up and down. You can get an implement for curling your eyelashes, a sort of pair of tongs. Well she used to buy – I mean, she always had a nice complexion and good-looking and all that – she used to buy all these fantastic creams that are really meant for old women, she used to, you know, do summer jobs and save up and buy all these night creams and all sorts. She also put on mudpacks, but by that time I was beginning to lose her, you know.

I mean this is sort of typical, she had her period when she was eleven, I think, and she was pregnant by the time she was sixteen. About sixteen or seventeen she got married to this bloke who had just left his school and his parents wanted him to be a musician. So he was sent to London to the Royal School of Music in London, but he wasn't very good – you know, he was adequate, but not good enough to be a great musician.

And I think that Judy's influence meant that I managed to socialize with boys in a way that I wouldn't have – my mother thought that that was all utter rubbish. She had been brought up like a boy, it's this fishing background thing. Again, she had no emotions, utterly hard. There is a lot of one-parent families in the fishing community, and real poverty. There was three boys and then there was my mother, and she always wanted to be a boy, and she went around with boots and a pair of trousers. There was this sort of masculine thing as well, she is very unfeminine, my mother. I think she's smashing now, but she used to embarrass me like hell, she really used to. There was another woman that was eccentric and I remember meeting her daughter, after she left home. She had exactly the same thing as my mother, I always wondered what she was going to do next. She always outdid your wildest expectations, you know. Ken, my husband, likes my mother because he's never gone through an adolescent stage where you felt that your mother was something that you would be, you know, ashamed of if she didn't do things properly. I think that is how I sort of – I had boyfriends and things, I don't think my mother ever did. She met my father through politics.

I felt very resentful towards my mother's attitudes to my father when I was an adolescent – she used to serve him first at meals with the biggest helping, that's very common in the fishing communities, and I think in other communities. And I used to get furious with it, I used to have rows about it. I don't know what I wanted her to do – serve the women first, I don't know. I just found that ridiculous, you know. Not only that, she used to eat in the kitchen; she used to serve us all with our food, she'd be running in and out serving, doing bits and pieces in the kitchen, she never sat down.

University

'There was never any idea in my mind that I wouldn't go on.'

I thought I wouldn't have the capacity to cope with it, I was frightened when I first went. I thought I wouldn't have the ability, and the first day in chemistry, my first chemistry lecture, there was this sod of a lecturer, very much a showman, a bit like Bronowski. He ripped through Einstein's Theory of Relativity in the first bloody lecture, and I thought, I'll never be able to manage this – he just rattled through stuff that I had only vaguely heard of. But by the end of the year . . . I did quite well in my first year. I got ill sometimes; I got pneumonia because I got a cold and I was scared to miss any lectures in case I fell behind. My mother got tranquillizers from the doctor to give me. You see there was also this thing about – you haven't to work too hard or you'll hurt yourself, sort of feeling; and 'Don't be unhappy,' – you know, this is a girl – 'Don't overstrain yourself, you don't really need to do it, do you really want to? If you are worried why don't you give it up,' you know, and 'You've done very well so far.' Despite the fact that both my parents were very ambitious for us as well. There was never any idea in my mind that I wouldn't go on. It would be terribly shaming to have taken on something and not see it through to fruition.

Then in the second year I got involved in politics. In fact in my second year CND began to get moving, and people in the Humanist Society, which I had never joined, were also in CND. And we went to see the film about nuclear war, *On the Beach* – it's actually a terrible film but I saw it recently on television and some of it still stands up. I had seen posters up, I had been interested . . . I was brought up – well my parents were atheists, I didn't find that out until quite late, but I had come from a home that didn't have any religious training at all. We had a kind of ethical – they taught you, you know, honesty, truth, this sort of thing. So I had been interested in the Humanist Society in Aberdeen and it had been going quite well then, and they were giving these lectures which caused fantastic controversy. It could only be in Aberdeen, because they thought very strongly about religion in the middle fifties you know. So I had been into that and I had listened – I had gone to a lecture about Divorce Law Reform, which I thought was very interesting. I was quite reactionary about it. The lecturer said there should be sex education at schools and I said – I think I was about seventeen – something very stupid, like, 'Girls in my school think far too much about sex anyway,' you know.

That was in 1959. But I decided for some reason before that to go to Aldermaston. I remember a bloke I knew, and he picked me up at a dance really. I didn't like him very much, he was sort of 'Let's get into bed quick!' I decided he wasn't for me, and then I saw him in a coffee bar a few weeks after and he said, 'Ah, I am going to an Anti-Apartheid Demonstration tomorrow morning, are you coming?' And I said, 'Oh fair enough! I'll go.' And I went on that. There was only three of us, it was ridiculous. This demonstration in Aberdeen, that's another story, and I met other people involved, mostly Anti-Apartheid and CND, and somebody said they were going to Aldermaston. What I wanted to do, that Easter I was going to Russia, they were running a subsidized trip to Russia for thirty pounds. My mother was against it, and I couldn't raise the money, and the alternative was Aldermaston. I thought, well I'll go to Aldermaston, and my mother didn't put up any objections, she thought that the march was at least in this country.

We went down in cars, we got lost a few times, and it was a fantastic experience – I was very politically underdeveloped, I had heard of Marx and people like that – and you all started off in this place, I can't really remember, but I remember walking along this country road, and in contingents, and each contingent had its name up, and we'd got Aberdeen and there was only about six of us. And not far in front of us there was this trumpet player playing 'The Saints', and you know, it was really a super warm weekend, you know, and the grass was all growing and there were flowers. That was the big take-off – that was the Aldermaston that really got huge; and it got bigger and bigger, all the time it was getting bigger, and of course the media took it up and kept reporting.

It was incredibly pseudo – all these banners and flags that we had, and we used to dress in black as well. I was dressed in black – I still have a sort of tendency yet – and people did it as well, dressed in black and started looking at old clothes – you know, not caring too much about your appearance. And Randolph Churchill said, 'There wasn't a good-looking girl on the march' – do you remember that? The *Daily Worker*, they took photographs of umpteen women and plastered it all over the front page and said, 'Where were you looking Randolph?' Or something awful like that.

I think Women's Lib is very – there is an awful lot of similar emotions to CND. CND was a middle-class background movement. It encompassed a fantastic number of different groups of people of different beliefs. Lots of different kinds of Christians, and Quakers, humanists and atheists and sociologists and psychiatrists – they all had a wee banner that they walked behind. There wasn't a women's section – well, not in Aberdeen, it was so small.

We were in the Young Socialists in Aberdeen, and people from the Communist Party used to come to our meetings, and after they left an anarchist group started up. We were so small we knew everybody else, so we all took our positions, you know that kind of thing. I think the numbers must have been fairly evenly divided, there was I think as many men as there were women. It wasn't biased towards women.

I started to learn after that. You see, I could never put a label like 'Marxist' on myself. I mean I think I come under Marx's influence. I mean, once a theory becomes understood people accept it. Do you see what I mean? It becomes part of the accepted tradition of thought. I am not a Freudian, right, but I accept the stuff he first wrote about infantile sexuality, some of it – I think everybody would – but I certainly don't accept a lot of his ideas. Everybody uses a lot of Freudian stuff as a kind of shorthand, and Marxist stuff as shorthand, so you're supposed to know where you are getting to in the discussion. And it's the same with things like the Theory of Evolution – it's really well understood and people accept it, and it's used kind of in a shorthand sense. You refer to it when you are in a discussion.

Well, I read *The Mandarins* by Simone de Beauvoir, and I met Ken at the CND, after I came back from Aldermaston. I joined this Socialist Society, because I had been talking to some people involved in it. I remember I went to a YS meeting in the town, it was the start of the new Young Socialists and now they were starting in the University, and I went along, not long after it started, and met some students from the University, like myself, but they were involved in the Socialist Society, and – that's right, the first time I ever saw Ken was at a New Left meeting. He had been drinking and he was going to be sick and I saw this bloke across the way who really looked ill, and he rushed out, and I think that's how I noticed him because he looked so ill.

The New Left had just been founded in Aberdeen, I had heard about it at the Young Socialists and gone there, and I met Ken and some other students there, and I joined the Socialist Society and we were involved in the CND. But you know, it's amazing, it must have all taken place very quickly, within a few weeks. I can't remember the chronological order for it now. It all seemed to happen together, and the next time I saw him he was at the Aldermaston March, and I went on with the Socialist Society and he put me on the Executive.

They insisted I go on to the Executive, and I knew I was taking on too much. This was the summer term and I said I didn't want to be on the Executive because I could maybe cope with CND but I couldn't cope with anything more at that time. I had never been involved in organized politics before. That's really how I got to know him, and he pushed me forward because they knew that my father was a trade-union organizer; they didn't know what kind, but they thought that that must mean that I was politically OK and able to cope with things like that.

I took a long time to develop a relationship with Ken. It's funny, I don't think he ever had many girlfriends, so he had this fantastic aura of sort of being an intellectual at university. He was a bit older than me and he was doing a PhD, which he never finished or got, and he was older than the other students and he read strange books. He'd written an article which he'd got from Simone de Beauvoir – reading that Simone de Beauvoir thing, 'Why Crucify de Sade?', or something, where she describes, you know, how it was only after he had spent an incredible amount of time in prison that his sexual aberrations started to develop. And Ken wrote an article in one of the University Reviews about de Sade being not altogether a bad guy. He went around with a sticker on his arm and everybody thought he was a kind of sadist. And also because he had been able to see some films – he's crackers on films – and taken up this stupid Wajda trilogy and wore sunglasses. You see they were unusual at Aberdeen University – I mean most of the girls wore twinsets and imitation pearls.

They had no experience of the theatre or – very little cinema, apart from Hollywood films. We were unusual.

You see, for a long period when I went to university I went round with working-class blokes, which was very worrying for their parents, and for them, they couldn't quite cope with it either, but it was the only men that I could relate to, I couldn't relate to the men at the University in my year, or any of the others I came across, because they had this thing about getting away from political talk. They thought that a good night out was a night out with the boys where you got so drunk you had to be carried home, and if you spewed all over the place that was even better. And we used to go to dances – I was going to dances since I was about fifteen, with other kids in the school – and we used to sort of – you know, these men used to come over and ask us to dance and we would carry them round the room until the dance stopped and then you sort of carried them back to their seats, they were so drunk.

I stopped doing it after our first few weeks in the first year. I went back to ballrooms, the working-class folks went there – the Beach, the big Beach Ballroom in Aberdeen – and then you had quite a lot of blokes there that were apprentices in engineering works and things like that and I went round with them quite a lot, they were – you know, they were nice. I was always treated very carefully by them. I mean at night you could go to films with them and you could go dancing. They were never very keen to share expenses, I remember always – I quite insisted on it, but never doing it when their friends were there. You know, making sure I contributed to pay for tickets, I paid half. But I knew I'd have to do it when I got involved in the Socialist Society, because then I met men who had quite a different attitude to booze and women. When first they got me involved in it, it was just like all the rest, very alcoholic, and their attitude to women was really horrifying. I remember once condemning men and that to Ken, and he saying, 'Well – you shouldn't condemn them, because how are they going to get any sexual experience other than just trying their hand all the time, with any woman they come across?' Because men are pushed in the same way to play roles as women are – I don't know if they are now.

I got more and more involved in politics and less and less interested in university and I failed second-year maths – I got it in the re-sits. But I failed my third-year degree completely, and yet in the second year the Chemistry Professor had asked me if I wanted to do honours. What was in fact fear that I couldn't do it in my first year developed into sheer boredom, you know. It took quite a lot of work to understand, you know, physics and chemistry, just to understand and to remember all the sort of theory, and I wasn't interested and I thought it got to be more and more irrelevant, you know, and I got more involved in politics, and I failed the third-year chemistry. Sociology, politics or economics, something like that, I could have connected up, but I couldn't with chemistry. I think now I could see connections, I mean the work I have done since I have always found interesting in all sorts of ways.

I think I was very impatient as well then, I was impatient with politics, I remember sort of being impatient with people whose views were different to mine. I should have just sat and listened, I shouldn't have been writing everybody off if they weren't just so. It was a kind of sectarian attitude, I suppose. But I didn't really do anything like enough work so I failed the exam, and I passed it in the re-sits in the autumn. Ken and I were going to get married in the summer, so we put it off until I had done the re-sits. The Professor knew I was in politics, because I was involved very much with the CND and demonstrations in the University, up and down Aberdeen in the street, and we rushed off to the various places.

Work

'It was cancer research and it was really very interesting.'

I was born in 1939. I was twenty-one when I got married, and Ken tried for a job in Aberdeen as assistant lecturer in psychology. He didn't get it, so he tried for one in St Andrews and he got it, so we just went there. I got a job first of all teaching. It was very unsuccessful, they didn't want me to teach because I had no training in teaching, so they moved me very quickly. Also I had no discipline with the kids, you see, and I didn't go to the religious assembly. After six weeks the headmaster said the Education Authority would offer me primary education; as I hadn't any training maybe primary education would suit me better. I never fell out with anybody or the kids – I mean it came out of the blue, there was never any explanation, why I should be moved, except you know, I wasn't keeping a class quiet – I mean they made a lot of noise. I wasn't allowed to teach any chemistry, it was all maths and it was simple arithmetic which I hadn't done since I was at school, and I decided that I didn't want to do primary. I thought that would be even more difficult than secondary teaching – I had absolutely no training for secondary – and I had a good idea I just wouldn't be able to do that.

I had only got on to teaching because I couldn't think of anything else to do and I needed money. So Ken heard from somebody in his department that a friend of this guy's was a doctor and he needed a technician and I went along, and he said, 'I can't use a pipette, can you use a pipette?' And I said, 'Yes,' and he said, 'Are you sure?' And I said, 'Yes, do you want me to show you?' He said, 'No no, that's all right, you've got the job.' It was a ridiculous thing – 'Start on Monday.' I got paid quite well. It was cancer research and it was really very interesting. It involved taking cervical smears in women and trying to relate the results you got from smears with their condition.

The chap that I worked for was very good, I mean he trained me up to take them very quickly. Partly I think because he didn't really fancy taking them himself, but I didn't like it very much either, because the women were all so terrified, they hated it. And I had to take sample smears from women who had cancer or thought they had cancer, and they would ask me and I couldn't tell them because I didn't know anything about it. They were desperate for information and they were saying things like, 'Have I got the same as that woman further down the ward?' – because maybe I knew what she had – or, 'I think that woman over there is a lot worse than me, isn't she?' – you know, they were trying to get information.

And I took smears in the out-patients department in the Dundee

Royal Infirmary. It was an old hospital. One of the doctors I worked for was sympathetic but the other one was very unsympathetic. We used to have students in the ward and in the out-patients department. When you examined the women they would have students and they would talk to them about her, and there was only one really good doctor, and when a woman asked to be sterilized he would always say, 'Well, if she's asked for it, that's what she should get.' I remember the students always would say, 'Oh but she is too young, she might change her mind after.' I mean some women had four or more children, and they never gave the woman the benefit of the fact that if she had got to the position of deciding and coming all the way to that and asking and arguing for it, she should get it. There was all this, sort of, it was their decision not hers.

Dundee is still a depressed area; nearly all the women work, and there's not so many jobs for men. Well, I noticed an awful lot of women were called Mrs so and so, and you had their case history, and when you were looking back they said, 'Oh, I have been married, my name is something else,' so you had to change it. But often – I worked there for – oh, it was nine months, and in nine months quite a few of the women had changed their names three times. Now even with divorce law reform, well, the way the divorce laws worked, they could never have got two divorces and two marriages in nine months, and I think it must have been they were staying with different men. As one man had to move away after work they were on their own for a while, and then they started living with another man. I remember a stupid woman who was a social worker, she came up from England and she said, 'Some of these children, they've all got different fathers. And I went into a house' – a lot of the women worked in rope work and you get fleas from rope work – and she said, 'I went into this house and I said to this woman, "Do you know that you've got fleas?" – I could see them – and do you know what this woman said? She said, "After a while you just get used to it."' And she thought that was shocking.

None of the women liked having an internal examination. You knew right away that they had great difficulty relaxing and they used to sort of grip the sides of the bed. I remember this woman who was a tinker – well they call themselves travelling people, not tinkers. She lay down on the bed, and she had some sort of gynaecological history so she was having smears done regularly, and she put her feet up against the bar at the end of the bed and grabbed the top, the head of the bed, with her two hands and drew up the top of her into the bed, and her spine was right off the bed – you know, there was sort of air between her and the bed. She was sort of holding herself absolutely rigid like a board, wedged up against the top and the bottom of the bed. She never made a sound, she had her teeth gripped together just waiting for it, just bearing it until it would be over. I was standing there with a speculum saying, 'Just relax.'

Now they have plastic ones which is slightly better, but they were always chrome steel and they are very cold, and they look as though they are going to hurt. They look like a duck's bill and you look at that great bloody thing and you think, God, are they going to stick that inside me? – it is going to hurt. And they've got a lamp that they focus right down between your legs. When I was taking a smear I used to have to look to see where I was going, I always got my head between the lamp and what I was trying to look at, it's quite a difficult process. The worst thing I really hate was old women who had never been married and had never had any men and were elderly, because they were more embarrassed than anybody.

We were very involved in politics, in the CND, for the three years we were in Dundee. It was becoming a very big thing then. We weren't at all involved in the Labour Party at that time, partly because Dundee is so corrupt. I had come from Aberdeen, which is relatively uncorrupt, and I couldn't take the stories; either I had to disbelieve them or if I accepted them I couldn't go along with being involved in the Labour Party. The Communist Party in Dundee were very Stalinist, which you'd expect from that kind of – it's an industrial town, and there's not much else to it. The women in Dundee are very interesting, they've always gone out to work because of the kind of industry there is in Dundee. So that there are more nursery schools in Dundee than there are in Aberdeen or in various other places, and the women are more involved in the Union. You see, because I had opted out of the Labour Party, etcetera, I never really got involved in that kind of politics, it was all CND. We used to have almost every night something going.

Children

'A kind of possessive feeling really . . .'

Then we came to Glasgow and I went through quite a bad period, because Luke was born, I had to give up work and we were quite hard up. When I came to Glasgow I lost contacts that I had had, and all the other people I had known from Aberdeen who had come here by various means were all having kids as well. So I really dropped out of politics a great deal. It was easier for Ken to go to Labour Party meetings, as it involved me getting a baby-sitter and I didn't know quite how to do that. My mother never went out when we were kids, she always stayed at home all the time, I can't remember her ever going out. So I just accepted that. I found it very difficult to ask people to baby-sit.

Then when Luke was not quite three, I got him into a nursery and that was great. It was three years of horror. And then in the third year when he was three he got into a nursery and I got a job again – I had a full-time job in the Dental Hospital, in the Biochemistry Department, because I had done biochemistry before. This time it was somebody we had met in the Labour Party; no interview again, I just got the job – I mean this job I've got now I never had an interview, somebody said, 'Oh I know there's a job going in so and so, would you like it?' And I said yes and I got this letter, '. . . after your interview we have decided to offer you the job.' I sometimes wonder if I'd be any good at interviews.

Anyway after the three years and he went to nursery I went into this job and I worked at it for five years, and I got fed up because I got involved in research and nobody knew what I was talking about. I wasn't properly supervised, they kept changing the supervisor. I quite fancied having another child, so I deliberately got pregnant and worked through my pregnancy, and I even read a paper in Cardiff when I was seven months pregnant. All the dentists had a fit, because their wives sit at home and have kids and sit through nine months of their pregnancy and hardly move in case they miscarry, and I went down to Cardiff on this train, juggling about all the time, and gave this paper and came back again. They were going to fly me but I didn't fancy flying. They thought that would be healthier for me.

And then I was going to have Sally and go straight back to work. That had not happened the first time because I was so upset about getting pregnant – that I didn't want to get pregnant the first time, The second time I quite deliberately wanted to get pregnant, and when I had Sally I had this terribly strong bond with her, I really enjoyed it, I enjoyed looking after her. Yet I had been wanting to go back to work. Before I gave it up I found myself bursting into tears when I was standing in a bus. I would be going into work and telling the technicians what to do and saying, you know, 'I'll be coming back full time in a week's time,' and coming home and seeing Sally and thinking, I can't possibly leave her to somebody else, you know. I get far too much enjoyment out of her myself. You know. A kind of possessive feeling really, a feeling that I just didn't want to leave her. So I eventually decided, and I resigned and I didn't work again until she went to school.

Sexuality

'I really thought that the top of my head was blown off.'

I never had an orgasm until I was two years married. Yet I had a very enjoyable sexual relationship with my husband – well I mean we lived together for six months before we got married. We got married because his mother kept having heart attacks at the idea that we were living together. It was a stupid thing to do, looking back on it, it was utterly ridiculous, but at that time it was the easy way out, you know. I was very dubious about it, but both my mother and Ken's mother thought that if I was dubious about it, it meant that I didn't really like him, which wasn't true at all, I was just dubious about the act of getting married and making a legal sort of – ah, it doesn't matter one way or the other. But I remember six months after Luke was born, so I had been married two years, it just happened once, an orgasm, and I thought that – I really thought that I had hurt the top of – that the top of my head was blown off, and – in a lot of ways I am very lucky to have a relationship with somebody like Ken. I got this terrible roaring in my ears and I knew – after that, that if I got this, there was a good chance that I was going to have an orgasm. It says in Masters and Johnson that in fact your blood pressure goes up fantastically. But I had no idea about clitoris and vagina – I mean we just happened on it by chance actually.

It's obviously very much better, but I mean I still don't have an orgasm every time. Some women have said to me, 'Oh, I have an orgasm every time!' I then wonder if they ever have one at all, you know, because – you become skilled in it, it's not that easy to achieve, I think – it's still enjoyable you know, even if you don't. Anyway Masters and Johnson is a smashing book to read, I think.

Work

I am a technician now. I print very fine circuits using dyes, light-sensitive dyes, and they're printed in very clean conditions, because obviously a bit of dust on top of a very fine circuit would short-circuit right across the different leads. The air is filtered and we have to wear overalls and hats and things, and I got that job. I was really looking for a sort of biochemistry job, like I had done before, and I had great difficulty, because nobody would take anybody on part time, and I wanted to do part-time work, because I felt if I worked full time I would have to get somebody in to look after the kids and someone to do the house and I would have to deal with those extra relationships as well as working. And I spoke to the wife of a chap – well they are both in the Labour Party and they are both lecturers at the University – really about did they know anybody in the bio-chemistry field that needed somebody part time. The husband phoned up that night and said there was a technician's job and he thought they would be willing to take me on part time.

After they had agreed to take me he said, 'Now it's a bit of a problem in this lab because it's all men; we did have a woman and she got sweet on one of the other senior technicians or a lecturer and started to buy his kids presents.' So I said, 'Well, I promise I won't do that, but there are dirty old men in a lot of labs, that's not a problem, I don't really understand why having a woman and that she might fancy someone should be a problem.' However, I started the job and they were all very, very nice and very helpful and willing to show you what to do, more so than men used to be in jobs. They really were super and they explained it all very carefully.

The first day I went there it was explained that all the technicians had their tea down in the basement. Technically I was a technician, but I was a woman, so they thought it would be better if I had my tea with the secretaries, and with these girl computer programmers, because he said, 'The air gets very blue down there and we have quite violent discussions.' And I asked him if they hit one another, and he said it was political discussions that were violent and I wouldn't be happy in a place like that, so I acquiesced and went upstairs with the other women. And for a whole month everybody was fantastically nice and careful and very willing to show me things, and if things went wrong they would discuss it with me in great length. But if I made a simple mistake they wouldn't tell me. I made a mistake with some machine – I wasn't getting a proper reading on it. They obviously must have known why right away, but I think it was not to hurt my feelings, they didn't like to say, and halfway through describing this and me saying, 'I don't know what the hell's happened,' I suddenly said, '. . . I surely never zeroed that properly?' And they all went, 'I think that's probably what happened.'

You know, anyway . . . also the other thing, nobody swore ever, nobody swore at all. There was this great feeling of tension, and I thought it must have been because of this other woman and they were all being very careful. And then one day I was working in the cleaning room and a graduate student came in, and the place where you put your dyes down has to be kept very clean, and somebody had walked away and left it all covered in splashes of dye, and this bloke – you see I was dressed the same as them and I had my hair covered, and I had got overshoes, so you couldn't really tell if it was a man or a woman, unless you looked at me, you know, then you would recognize me, if you looked at my face – he said, 'This place is like a fucking shaghouse!' And there was this sort of fantastic silence, and I just carried on working, you know, and there was this pause and everybody started to talk again.

And then for the next three weeks they swore every single time; if they tripped up they swore, if they dropped anything they swore, if they just did something very slight, you know – great long reams of curses and swearing and – I mean even chart paper going into chart machines, they would say, 'Chuck over the lav paper!' – instead of chart paper, you know it was – it was hell of a funny, you know. I began to really feel . . . every time a head came round a door they would start swearing – they never swore at me, it was always just incidental swears . . . and I began to feel quite conscious of it, I was very conscious of it, I just sort of felt I'll have to just ride this out, you know, and gradually it dropped away, and now they swear occasionally. And another thing, because to start with nobody else swore, I didn't swear at all; and I began to swear a bit – you know, just sort of damn or hell or shit or something – if something was a mess or I had made a mistake, and I think that relieved it a bit, and now they swear occasionally but not by any great length.

Individually, they really are all very nice, and one is a great fisherman and he tells me all fishing stories. He tells me about his – he has two girls who are seven and are twins – and that's right, I found out there was this chap who never spoke to me and it took me two months to realize he was my boss. He was a lecturer in fact, but he had been a technician who – he was called a 'senior research' – oh, I can't remember the name, but technically he was on the university staff rather than being a technician, so he's head of the whole lab. And this is the guy that this woman had fancied, you see – she was about forty. And he's white-haired, you know, and very odd behaviour, and just recently I said to the chap that got me the job, 'Ron was very peculiar for a long time but he's great now, him and I sort of scrub out the floor and that, and he's no bother.' And he said, 'Ah, well it was Ron that that woman fancied, and poor soul he was in a terrible mess over it, and he didn't know what to do and he was losing sleep, and he really had a terrible time.' But think of all the times, though, when men set women in corners and things. It was the other way round.

Politics

'There are so many things I have to do in the Labour Party that I hate myself for doing.'

There was a New Left Club in Dundee and Ken became Chairman and it collapsed, and I used to think that he had this special gift of becoming Chairman of things. It was collapsing all over the country. We couldn't get speakers; there was this sort of rota of speakers and once we had got through them all nobody else seemed to be appearing, and all the speakers seemed to be saying the same thing. And we were supposed to have committees for people in the nationalized industries or the Health Service or something, and that was all theory. In fact nothing ever happened, there was never enough people to man it, and CND was more important, and then CND just died a death. There was this fight about the Labour Party, the Labour Party wasn't big enough to take in CND. I think that was the death of the Labour Party as well, you know, that was the real slide down-hill for the Labour Party, and you know there was an incredible number of people involved in the CND that must have just gone out of politics altogether at that time.

And I had a kid, and I wasn't all that happy about not being involved and I gradually got back into politics, because first of all I got out more, because there was this baby-sitting group. That was just when Sally was born, so Luke was at a nursery, I was working full time, and I used to do the house and that at night, so I wasn't all that involved in politics even then. I was in my union and went to union meetings and I was on a strike once, but I was really involved in the Labour Party. Technically I was a member but I hardly ever went to meetings. Then after Sally was born I got into this baby-sitting group and we got out more together to see films and go to meetings. I didn't like the baby-sitting group, it was full of nasty middle-class women who talked about blacks and things like that.

There was one or two of us that were socialists and we formed a Labour Party baby-sitting group which was better; at least you don't get people going on about the Pakis, not keeping themselves or their house clean or something. And it was another woman who got me back into politics in the Labour Party. There wasn't a Labour Party ward here at all, and everybody said you wouldn't be able to produce one. I was the Secretary and we ran this ward, and now, it's better – it's still only the five of us, but it's better – and we started turning up at constituency meetings. Partly I got back into Labour Party and politics from being here, partly that Ken decided that he wasn't going back into the Labour Party when we moved, he was going to join the International Socialists, and I was having terrible arguments with him about that. You see I wasn't all that clear about the Labour Party then, I am much more critical about it now than I was even then. I was critical then, but it was in an apathetic way, whereas now I can see exactly all the things that are wrong with the Labour Party. The only reason I am still in it is because I can't find anywhere else to go, and yet because I am involved in the Women's Movement I can get some of the things done. I don't get that much done, but the women in Women's Liberation can't because they are not so involved in institutionalized politics. I mean, they are involved in politics but not the sort of institutions.

There's so many things I have to do in the Labour Party that I hate myself for doing. I have to support the candidate at the General Election who's a – you know, a fool. I have never heard him saying anything that wasn't the official policy of the Labour Party. He's a young bloke, about my age, and it's pathetic that I've got to go and shove stuff through letter-boxes about him, written in stupid adjectives about what a great guy he is. I have to do that because otherwise I couldn't get the things I want done, done, you know. I mean all the time you are balancing up the 'fors' and 'againsts', and I mean the 'againsts' are so bloody colossal, for the few 'fors' that you get. I mean Ken always said this about the Labour Party when he joined and he's in the same position again in the International Socialists. The amount of work he has to do in order to alter attitudes – he achieves very little.

It's always the same, I think. Everybody involved in politics has got this terrible problem that once you have got this idealized idea of what you would like a political organization to be – and at the other extreme you've got actual organizations that are very far from perfect, but you've got to either work to them or become uninvolved in politics, I think.

Well, when I met Ken he was interested in feminism – and I had read *The Mandarins*, so I talked to him about that and he gave me her first book, *The Second Sex*, and I didn't think it was all that smashing. I was a bit worried about it at first, you know – women are taught propaganda really: you could get as much just by being a woman – all this fluttering your eyelids up and down – as you could by demanding your rights. In *The Second Sex* de Beauvoir tends to – it's her way of dealing with the problems of women, and I understand it better now, but she talks about figures in literature, and I wanted hard solid facts. I didn't want figures in literature, I wanted . . . women oppressed. I've still got this argument, I think there are fantastic bits of solid evidence around that you can show anybody, and women in Women's Lib just refuse to use it. But I can see the other argument for it now, that this was all part of the culture about the way women saw themselves and the way men wrote about women and the way women wrote about themselves. I can understand that, but at the time I thought it was a rather dubious argument – it wasn't a proveable argument, I felt, if you did it in this sort of subjective way about figures as you saw them in Dickens or French literature. But I liked *The Mandarins*, and then I didn't read her second book – the second half of *The Second Sex* – until we were married and I liked that a lot better, because that's much more dealing with the present-day French society, and I thought that was really excellent, and women's attitudes to their children and working-class women's attitudes, and it was very much an eye-opener. But on the other hand I've always felt suspicious of all women as I grew up, I think Jean was one of the few that I didn't.

We used to be called the 'de Beauvoirites' because we had all read the books. I felt very close to them and affectionate towards them. I think that was the start of it, and now when I am back in Women's Lib . . . I came back in through being involved in the Labour Party. A girl wrote an article about Women's Lib and she came up one night and she gave me the address, where they meet, and I went. I always felt in spirit that I would. Of course I supported Women's Lib. I knew an awful lot of what it was saying was interesting and important. I think I first got committed after reading *The Mandarins* and *The Second Sex* and I have always been committed ever since that, and I think I wandered in and out of left-wing politics always feeling very disappointed with it.

I don't get that feeling of disappointment in Women's Lib, I get a feeling of annoyance, you know – and fear that a lot of it is going the wrong way, and also fear that it could all collapse overnight, because there is no structure. Nobody knows of a place to write to in London where you would get information about Women's Lib, there's all these wee groups, and it took me ages to work out that that's how it is operated. All I could see was that they seemed to have a huge number of conferences, and I never realized that that was the only way they could keep anything like that in harmony, and keep contacts with one another – it's the only way of doing it. They do shy very much away from structure, and I mean I can see why, you know, if you look at the Labour Party – my God! One of the reasons they are so corrupt is because of the structure and because of the bureaucracy. People take a long time to understand it, and get fed up and leave.

13.   Irene McIntosh

Irene McIntosh is in her early thirties and comes from Fife in Scotland, where her father was a shipwright and her mother a nurse. She was the eldest of two girls and did well at school, despite the teachers, who were sceptical about her because of her working-class background. She went on to teacher training college, where she met her husband, also now a teacher. They live with their two children in a pleasant modern block of flats near the centre of a large Scottish city. Irene McIntosh taught in schools for maladjusted children, and after having her own two went back to teaching, which she loves.

Childhood

'My father would have liked a boy very much.'

Well I was born 1941 in a working-class town, grew up around the naval dockyard. My father was a shipwright . . . so he was really working-class. And he'd been in the Merchant Navy before that, and he left the sea to get married and settle down, and I think he's resented that a bit, you know, he's always wanted to go back into the Admiralty, he was a shore man, and that's it. And my mother came from farming people in Aberdeenshire, and they lost all their money in the slump and ended up in Botany Bay in the middle of Aberdeen, sort of really working-class. And so the whole background's like that. And she took a job nursing when I was I think about five or six – I was very young anyway, and my sister was still quite young – well she'd be about two. Just two of us.

My sister was born about three and a half years after me, and she was a difficult baby, it was a difficult birth, and left my mother phlebitis.

I was sent away while my mother had the baby, to relations and when I came back there was a baby, and my mother in bed not well because of this baby. So that it wasn't a very good start. I remember coming in, and being really overwhelmed at seeing my mother – sort of threw myself on to the bed, and her yelling, 'Ouch, get off my bed!' And she didn't mean to be unkind, she's really quite a sympathetic person, but it was just a very bad beginning, and I've never got on well with my sister, and I don't know how much that's got to do with it. We've been completely different types of people all our lives. I'm quite fond of her, and I wouldn't see her stuck – I mean, if things went wrong for her, I would want to help her. But I'm not interested in cultivating a friendship with her, because we're just too different.

I resented having to take on – I think every older child resents having to take the younger one. But unfortunately she was deaf – this was not discovered until quite late on in her school, until she was about nine, that she had a perforated eardrum. And my mother did actually go on at doctors about this. . . She had an unfortunate childhood because everything was stacked against her. And so she was slow at school, and she wasn't a good playmate, because of her – she wasn't hearing properly. She was an introverted sort of child, and right from the beginning, you know, I was the sort of extrovert, she was the introvert. I was the bright one, she was the dull one. I was always considered a bit better-looking than her. And I don't know why I resent her when I had everything going for me, but I just did. I suppose because my parents always felt sorry for her, so they built this big wall of protection around her, you know, sort of – special – must be careful about Ann.

When my mother was out working, at the beginning it was all night duty. I can remember about the age of ten being expected to get up and have the fire cleaned out and ready for her to light, and a cup of tea ready for her. I was always expected to do that. My sister never was, even when we grew up. It was always if the things weren't done it was my fault. And it was just because I was the older. And it's not because my mother was particularly hard. I mean, she was a working woman, and she came in exhausted after a night of night duty, but if she couldn't put her feet up and have a cup of tea she felt a bit miffed. But I don't remember being particularly unhappy about her being out to work. Sometimes we missed her, you know, in the evening, when it was just my father and my sister and I. Sometimes I felt it would be nicer if we had my mother there too. My father resented it an awful lot, but then, we needed the money. But he had this thing, if he got invited anywhere, or he wanted to do something, and she was out, then he got annoyed and used to have rows with her. But they never really rowed a lot in front of us, they'd try to keep it to themselves. But if you live in a small council house, you just know what's going on.

My mother worked, so she had an interest, and we heard about her job, and her union. And she'd come home and talk about these poor miners' wives – she'd see them have child after child. She'd be maybe talking to the neighbour, but you were there and you picked it up. And she said, 'It was dreadful, and he wouldn't let her be sterilized, and I think it's bloody awful men have this say over women,' and we got this, you see, as well. I suppose that helped make me a bit different.

My granny, she was – my mother's mother – I think she was one of the original Women's Libbers, because when they had this farm out in the wilds of Aberdeenshire . . . she'd come from a town family, and she hated the country, and she hated the way women were treated by the men in the country. And I remember my mother telling me that she went down to help some woman who was in labour, and all the way down to the farm she berated the husband about the fact that this woman shouldn't be having this child, and he was just an animal the way he treated his wife, and it was high time he did something about it, and if he couldn't do anything about it he should leave her alone! In her own way, she had quite modern ideas for her time. I remember one of her great stories was when she asked my grandfather for more money, and he said, 'What the hell have you done with the money I gave you?' So she said, 'I just sat down and wrote where every penny went.' And she said: 'There you are, that's what I did with it, so you'll just have to give me more!' You know, she wasn't the sort that kowtowed.

My mother was quite proud in her own way, too. And I think that's why she stuck out the job when my father was against her, and quite a lot of her friends were too. They said, 'What're you doing, leaving these children?' And she just said, 'Well it's my life and I'm going to do it. If I haven't got the money I'll jolly well go and get it.' She's still nursing. You see, she never . . . she says the thing she regrets most now is that she never sat any exams.

She went to nursing when they lost the farm, and they lost all their money. They moved back into this tiny flat, it was just two rooms, and a shared toilet on the stairs. And the two boys, the older boys, they went into the army, and the two older girls went nursing, and my mother was at home for about a year, and then, she said, living in this tiny flat with her parents – and occasionally the girls would come home in the evening, and there'd be four or five of them, and there was only two rooms. . . She got so claustrophobic she decided to get a job nursing too, because she knew she could live in a hostel and have a bit of privacy. So when she was sixteen she went and applied for a job in a mental hospital – never mind about her age – and they took her on. And she started nursing when she was sixteen. But she finished her training as a general nurse, and then, after she was married, she took up nursing in a maternity hospital, but she didn't do anything about getting her midwifery or anything. So she's just stayed a plain nurse. Because she'd been part time as well. She hasn't been promoted. She's never really worked full time, or not – I mean she works what I consider a full-time week a lot of the time – I mean it's eight in the morning till two in the afternoon, and then sometimes on again from four to six or something to fill in for somebody else, which really is quite a full working day. But then she's considered part-time, because she doesn't do as many hours.

She said everything was against her. She did think about going and taking exams, but she said, 'You were so small,' and she said, 'Your father wasn't keen about it.' She suggested doing this, and he said, 'Oh yes, you're going to make a bloody trade of it, you don't want to be my wife and bring up my children.' She said, 'It would have caused too much fuss, I just didn't do it.' And now she's nursed for over thirty years in the same hospital, and she's just in the same position she was when she went in. She does get given more responsibility than other nurses, because the doctors know her – I mean, some of the doctors have been there as long as she has. If they've got a difficult patient – a woman with depression or anything, it's inevitably my mother who is sent in to nurse her, because she's got so much experience with these sort of people. She's got a good way with them. But then she doesn't get much money or . . . recognition. So she's been exploited all her life, I suppose.

She was quite a warm person, but I mean she wasn't the sort of mother who sat down and made us dolls' clothes and so on. She'd read us stories, but then she was – as I say, she was working, you see, three nights a week, and her time was limited. I remember most of the things that we did were good fun in a way were more done with my father than my mother. And she tended to be very much the domestic figure who fed and cooked and cleaned and all the rest of it, you know – read you stories and tucked you up. She worked night duty when we were small, so that we weren't unattended. It was supposed to be three nights, but quite often with a short staff she was working four nights and even five nights a week. I think that's partly why she hadn't anything left to give except just to make sure that we had a good home and were well fed. This seemed to be her big priority, that her children, because she worked – and I suppose at that time she was a bit unusual – that other women round about were at home all the time, and she was criticized for it, but she always used to say, 'Well my children are as well fed and as clean as anybody else's in the street.' And that was her sort of criteria as being a success. And I suppose it's carried over to me in some ways, my attitudes about having a job and bringing up children too.

Well, my father would have liked a boy very much, and he used to encourage me to be sort of wild and rough when I was little. And my mother would chastise him for that, and say, 'You shouldn't make her do that.' And he was – I mean, my father was a good father, he used to take an interest in us, even though we were girls and he would probably have liked a boy. He used to take us out for walks every Sunday I remember. We'd go for a long walk with father. I suppose that was his way of helping my mother, too, by taking us off her hands and everything. And also he enjoyed it. And we went for family holidays. I remember having a super holiday in Shetland when I was about nine, I think. And my father took me fishing, on boats, and you know, he did all sorts of things with us. And he was always very keen on us doing well at school. I think that was because he had had very muddled schooling. He came from Shetland to Aberdeen, and he was in about seven schools the whole of his school life, which was only till he was thirteen. So he was changing about once a year, more or less. And he was keen that we should do well at school. He was good at drawing. He used to draw us quite often when we were little, and he was quite a talent, but then it never got developed in any way. But it came out in the fact that he was good at working with wood, and you know, he enjoyed it. He made toys for us, and – wooden toys, you know, and this sort of thing. We had quite a good relationship with my father.

I think my father helped me a lot, because I remember when I was at school, we used to have great rows. Well not so much rows, but discussions about politics, and I remember – this was one of the good things about my parents, that they did talk a lot about things. My father was a union man. And he would come home, and he would discuss union matters, and if you asked him a question he would explain to you. And I suppose that made me different from a lot of girls round about me. Because a lot of the girls didn't even know what their father's job was!

School

'This was my big ambition, to be a teacher.'

We went to the local primary school, and did fairly well. I don't remember anything outstanding about school, except I found it difficult when I was quite young to make friends. Mother said I was a sensitive child. I think that's exaggerating it a bit. But I was a bit sort of introverted. At school, doing fairly well . . . and I got over this sort of shyness and things after about the age of eight, and made quite good friends at school. And then went on to the local secondary school, and went into the second top stream. But most of my friends who came from my own locality with me went into lower streams.

At secondary school, well, most of my friends went into a lower stream, so after the first year I deliberately did badly in exams to get put down a few classes to be with them, and, because I found the girls I mixed with in the upper streams were not the sort of girls I had been used to mixing with – sort of Town Clerk's daughter, and businessmen's daughters, and girls who generally had had a far more materially better background that I had come from, in lots of ways – and I found them difficult. We didn't have much in common, you know, and I preferred to be with the girls that I knew. So I got put down a few streams, and I mucked about in the second year, and it came to the end of the third year, and my mother got such a bad report she said, 'You come away from school, you're going to get a job. There's no point in wasting time.' And then at fifteen I realized that there wasn't anything I wanted to do except – I'd always said I was going to be a teacher; this was my big ambition, to be a teacher. I think it was partly because I had two very good teachers when I was at primary school, and they were people that I really admired, and they were . . . they just seemed to be so good to me – you know, that was the sort of person I wanted to end up being. And since they were teachers I thought that was how you got to be like them.

I said, 'Well I don't want to leave school, I don't want to work in an office, and I don't want to work in a shop.' By this time, I had started working (I was fourteen) part-time Saturday jobs in Woolworth's and things like this, to get a bit of pocket money, and nearly all the girls in our area did that. It was the only way you could get any extra money. And at about fourteen you started going out with boys and smoking, and trying to be more grown-up. And to do all these things you had to have money, and your parents wouldn't give it to you, so you got a job. I said that I would work to keep myself at school. And she said, 'All right . . . but you've got to prove that it's worth it to us.' So I did, I got on quite well after that at school.

But then I had lost so much time mucking about with my friends, who didn't care, they were going to leave school anyway. I mean it was quite determined by their parents that they weren't keeping a girl at school, because all she was going to do was going to get married. There was no point in educating her any further than that. There were only two girls from our street and me, and it was quite a big street and there were quite a lot of children about the same age, and there were only three of us who stayed on, and all the other girls were taken away and put to jobs. Of the two that stayed on with me, one left at sixteen to be a bank clerk, and the other wanted to go into nursing, the only Higher she got was nursing. And so, I mean, it didn't pay her parents to keep her on at school. They were absolutely furious at having her spend all this time at school. In the end she didn't go into nursing because she didn't have enough O-levels. So I was the only one out of that bunch that actually got enough to go on to college and further education.

At school, it tended to be very much the working-class kids in one sort of group, and middle-class children from the sort of business section in town, in another. In some ways the Rector was to blame. Of course it was understandable in a way, although it was wrong, that it was the middle-class children who made the scholarships, who got places in university, who it was sure would go on and give the school a good name. And so everything from about fourteen onwards was geared for the children who came from that sort of home. And don't think we imagined it, because a whole lot of us felt that we were done out of things, and courses in the school, which we should have had a chance at, and we just didn't get it, because he knew we were from working-class homes, and he knew the chances of success for us were slimmer, because we just didn't have the background or environment which encouraged you to go on and think about going to university. So I think things were kind of weighted at that point against me. But I managed to get through.

In fact, one boy who came from a working-class home – it was an even poorer home than mine, and mine wasn't all that good – but his parents really struggled, and he was very clever, and he won a scholarship to Cambridge. I remember in the sixth year his final gesture before he left was to write this long letter to the local newspaper, and he listed several injustices he thought had taken place during the last three years at school. And he wrote a very good letter, and the paper published it, and the headmaster was absolutely furious, and said that if he found out who was the culprit – and he knew who the culprit was really – but he said if he did find out, he would make sure that person did not get any further in their career, for slighting the school. He did get to Cambridge, and I think he was quite successful. I heard he got as far as second year anyway, and I think he probably got a good Honours. But he was one of the few, and most of all the working-class boys, even if they were kept to sixth year, there were very few of them went on to university. There was only about a handful that I can think of, and of that about three, I would say, dropped out.

Once I got to college, I found it was a walkover, and I thought, well, why didn't I think about going to university? And I've regretted it ever since. I mean, I don't know that I would have got a degree, but I would have liked to have had the chance, but you just – you weren't encouraged to think that that was within your class. The fact that I got to be a teacher . . . I mean, my parents were tremendously proud of me.

Boyfriends

'I didn't even know what he was doing.'

I had a boyfriend when I was fourteen. I had one or two very tentative affairs, sort of meeting on the street corner, chatting, and then, you know, walking home . . . hands in the pockets, and we weren't sure what they wanted, and they weren't sure what we wanted, so nothing happened, you know. And then, there was all sorts of other escapades. We used to go to a local youth club, which was considered a pretty wild place. This was in the next town, actually. And this town was considered very rough, because during the War there had been a lot of brothels there, and it had got a bad reputation, and it stayed that way. And it was quite a rough town. It was a poorer sort of town in a way than the one I lived in. There weren't so many amenities. And they did tend to have, you know, poorer housing and this sort of thing. But there was an awful lot of nice-looking boys went to this youth club, so a crowd of the girls went along, and one night there was quite a fight started with some of the boys, and the police were called in. There was an upstairs window, you could get out and on to the roof and away, so we went out this way, away from the police and home. Then we were terrified to go home in case the police had got lists of names and addresses and were knocking on all the doors to find out who'd been there . . . and this kind of thing.

I mean, that was the extent of the sort of trouble we got into. Nothing, you know . . . I can't really remember any upset with boys and girls that I went around with at that time, doing anything. I mean, we didn't do anything like vandalizing property, we didn't do anything like – these things that happen at football games, with bottles, and fights, and everything. I don't remember *anything* like that. In fact, I went to football matches a lot when I was young, and went out with footballers. It was quite safe at that time to go, just two or three girls to go to a football match, quite safe. So I suppose things were very much different then.

The first sort of real boyfriend, who lasted about two years, he was in the sixth year at school and I was in the third year. And he was a prefect, and was on duty at the third-year dance, and he asked to take me home. So we went home, and we went out together, and he was quite good fun, but he had a father who was a lay preacher, a Baptist lay preacher, and he kept on and on of course at his family. The older brother, who was at university, he wouldn't have anything to do with it. But the boy I went out with, I don't know what happened, but he got the bug, and he became converted, and nothing would do but I was converted, and I said, 'No, I'm not that convinced.' We continued to go out, but what we did was completely different. I wasn't supposed to wear makeup, and I wasn't supposed to get my hair cut, and we just went for walks. I mean he seduced me and everything, when I was about fifteen, and that was all right – we kept that side going!

I mean, I didn't even know what he was doing, really. I kept going back to my friends and saying, 'Well he stuck his finger in, is that it?' 'No,' they said. [Laughs.] So eventually, you know, it dawned on me what had happened. And, I don't really remember even being worried about having a baby. I do remember once my period was late and I said to him, and he got in a most terrible sweat, and it dawned on me, then, just how awful it would be. Because, really, he wouldn't want me if I was pregnant. And then I began to get more careful, and then I began to say, 'Well, look, you think you're so bloody moral and all the rest of it. Why are you still using me like that?'

And I remember it came to a great head after one religious meeting. Actually, we hadn't seen each other for some time, he was at university by this time. And we arranged to meet, and I remember it was a nasty phone call. I phoned him at his digs, and I think perhaps he had a girl there or something. Anyway, he wasn't very nice on the phone. And I asked him what he'd been doing, and he said, 'What've you been doing?' I said, 'This and that, and I went to see a Jerry Lewis film last night, and it was a scream.' And he said, 'Oh, you've found your level, have you?' And I thought, ooh, you sod! I agreed to meet him the next night – 'But I'm not going to any prayer meetings or anything, so you can take me to the pictures or something.' Oh yes, he promised he would do something. So when I met him he was handing out religious tracts in the High Street. Of course, half my friends were walking up and down, so I just walked straight past him, and waited in a doorway up the street till he'd finished handing out his tracts, and I said, 'Where are we going?' And he said, 'Actually, my father's got this big service on, and there's this convict coming, and he's been converted, and I do want to go.' So I went along and I suffered all this, and I thought, this is the end. So we came out and went for a walk and I said, 'It's all over, I just can't put up with any more of this.'

And, I mean, he did use me in lots of ways . . . the fact that I was much younger than him, and the fact that he was quite a catch for a young girl like me to be going out with a university student like him, and him so clever, and he'd been 'dux' in school, and all this sort of thing. And I did things that were really stupid, just to keep in favour. Well, he went by the board, and my mother was so pleased she gave me ten pounds just to go out and buy clothes and do what I wanted. And she hated him because he used to come to the house and say things to my father like, 'If there's anything about the Bible you don't understand . . . I would be happy to explain to you.' And my father used to say, 'What the hell d'you think I want explained to me, what I don't know I don't need you to tell me,' sort of thing, and there used to be terrific rows, you see. And I'd say, 'Well if you're going to talk to him like that I'm leaving, and I'll go and live with him.' And then they'd say, 'Well, you wouldn't last long.'

So anyway, that packed in, and then – oh yes, I started going to dances with my friends, and in the fourth year there was this American boy came to the school, and his sister, and you know, they were the big attraction because they had American accents and they were very good-looking – American clean-cut kids, you know? And they used words like 'mortified', which just slew us. [Laughs.] You just don't hear people say things like that where I come from. And he came one evening to the dancehall and took me to coffee and things and asked to take me home! Great! So that lasted about nine months, and I was considered, oh, quite the belle of the school – you know, I'd got him. And after him came a succession of other boys about the same age as me, and, you know, sort of very casual. More friendships, in some ways, than, you know, love or anything like that.

College

I got into training college. I was one Lower short of a group for training college, so they gave me an interview and then said, 'We'll accept you because you seem to be quite keen to be a teacher.' And as I say, you know, twelve of us went, and I was the only one in the group who went in with an interview, the rest all had the group of Highers needed. So I worked very hard the first year, and I got through without any re-sits, and I got a nasty letter saying, 'Don't think that because you got through the first year that's it. We're going to watch you next year, and if you don't pass your exams next year you'll be out on your neck.' And I thought, right, what a nasty thing to do. So I worked hard the next year. I followed all the rules and regulations and everything, and I got through second year without any re-sits. Then another letter which said: 'Oh, that's all very fine, but just remember, you're only here because you got in on an interview, and you won't graduate unless you do very well in the third year.'

By this time I was sick of them, so I started skipping classes, and I got into trouble. I told them what I thought of them and their system, and by this time . . . they hadn't anything on me, definitely – I mean, once they said I'd skipped a few classes, and they asked me why. I said, 'Cos I thought they were bloody silly anyway.' It was modern dance or something. I said, 'If you're going to have classes like that,' I said, 'why do all the married women sit out and all the single girls have to do it?' I mean some of the married women that sat out were only about thirty, and they could easily have got up. They didn't have to do it. It was considered undignified for a married woman! Yes! You have no idea what it was like! 1961 – I mean, it's not that long ago! The gym instructor said it is undignified if you are married and things to be . . . It was modern dance, you know, it was 'Imagine you're a tree,' . . . 'waterfall' and 'You be the tree,' and things. Well this was to teach you to teach children, you see. But there was this little group of married ladies, about twenty-eight upwards, who, because they were married and over twenty-five, didn't want to do it. Nobody ever asked questions. It was just assumed that because they were more mature they didn't have to do it.

At that time I travelled from home. In the last year, I said, 'There's no point in me being a student if I'm never out and enjoying myself.' So there was a great 'Oh, what's wrong with your home? What's wrong with us?' 'Nothing wrong with you, I just want to be independent.' So, after the ups and downs I went to a bedsit with another girl. But then I was called in to the lady adviser and asked why we were going into a bedsit and not a hostel. 'Do your parents know? And do they realize the things that young girls can get up to, you know, living in bedsits? And why are your skirts above your knees, while we're at it?' And all the rest of it. By this time you're twenty, and they still go on as if you are a schoolgirl. So we told her we didn't want to stay in a hostel because you'd to be in at half past ten. And anyway the hostels cost three times as much as bedsits, and the food wasn't as good as what you could cook yourself. So we just laid it on the line . . . and she couldn't stop us.

It was quite quite incredible. I mean, you were just treated like you were at school. You were given no sense of responsibility, or the fact that you were maturing and you were about to go out and do a very responsible job. There was none of, that discussed – at all. It was all to do with, you know, 'Have you written this essay? Have you got this done up to date? And you missed that lecture, and don't forget your signing-in this time, girls, and everybody at that lecture...' I mean, I look at students now and I see the freedom they've got... If any of us had turned up in trousers you'd have been *expelled* without question! You wouldn't even have been given a chance to change into a skirt, you would be out – you know, 'We just don't have people like that.' It's incredible.

This girl Beth that I teemed up with. She and I – well, we really went wild, we went to men and drink and smoking and turning up late for lectures, and what the hell. We began to realize just how little they could do to you, if you kept within, just within the law. And you knew which lecturers were on your side, although they didn't dare speak out, and which ones would shop you, you got all that sorted out. So you would be able to sort of live it up a bit. And I enjoyed the third year finally, and then, eventually, I graduated. And I remember graduation day, when we all turned up – the group that had come from school with me, all twelve of us sitting. And I said, 'Right, you sods, you all got in here, and you've all got through,' and I said, 'I'm the only one that's never had a re-sit.' I was quite pleased about that.

And then, towards the end of – oh, it was after I left school, I'd been at college for six months, I got invited back for the Former Pupils' Dance at school. So a crowd of us got together and we said, right, we'd go back, in teeny-bopper skirts – if you went to the school dance you went in a long skirt, you know, very sedate. So we bought a bottle of whisky and got absolutely paralysed, and we all went along in our deep V-necked sweaters and short skirts, and big shoes and things, and made an absolute cod of the whole thing. And I ended up going home with a chap who'd been in the same year, but I'd never paid much attention to him – Lenny. And I started going out with him. It was one of these things that just sort of grew and grew, and I was very keen on him, and his parents got to know my parents, and it went on for about two years, and it was assumed that we were going to get married.

Then I met Andy, and by this time I knew that I wasn't going to marry Lenny, because he kept wanting me to be different from what I was, and used to say, 'Oh, you're wearing too much make-up; I don't like those clothes. And why d'you have to drink so much? We can't pass a pub but you want to go in.' And I kept thinking, well, if we're at this stage now, what the hell would it be like to be married? And I remember a friend not long ago asking me what I thought the difference was, how you knew somebody that you really wanted to marry, and I said, 'Well, it's a funny thing, it's a sort of negative. You go along with people that you like and you think, yes, this could be.' And I said, 'Then you try to visualize the future, and you can't, and you think, well, if I cannot visualize it – you know, being happy or anything like that – what's the point?' And I said, 'When it came to Andy,' I said, 'I just didn't want the future without him, that was the difference. I could have got along fine without Lenny or any of the others, it wouldn't have worried me that much when they'd gone. I would have cried and been broken-hearted for a week, and then have bought a new frock and gone off with somebody else. But with Andy I really felt if I could never see him again I'd just die, you know . . .'

Well I always said, I maintained solidly all the way through college – school and college – that I wasn't getting married, and I wasn't settling down, and I would never get married before I was twenty-five, and I was going to South America. I don't know what I'm going to do there, but one place I wanted to get to was South America. Because I'd learned a lot about it and I'd done a big project at school on the Incas. And I got really involved in that. It was out of the things I did really well at school. I had this big thing about what South America would be like and it would be a place that I'd like. So this was to be my big ambition. So of course I met Andy and never got to South America!

I was a bit naïve about sexual behaviour. I mean I thought you went to bed, you did it, and then you stopped at that, you know. And

I mean the fact that there were other things that you did besides that, I was completely naïve about. The first time I was put in a position of being asked to do something else besides that, I said, 'I don't want to do *that*.' And the bloke was most hurt, and that was the end of that, you know. But he was a medical student and he knew everything, you see. Well you see, I never had an orgasm till I was married four years – I didn't know what it was. I mean, I never just went to bed with anybody because they wanted me to go to bed with them, or anything. If I didn't like people, I just didn't, and if I did, and I really liked them, that was fine. And I enjoyed it, and I tried to participate as best I knew how, which wasn't very good in those days, I'm quite sure.

And ... and then I met Andy and it was – we met at this party, and he'd brought this girl who'd been a real bitch and he was wanting to get away from her. And I turned up late, and the booze was finished and as far as I could see all the men were taken, so I just sat in a corner with my own little carry-out and got sloshed. He found me sitting in this cupboard telling somebody I was a witch, so he asked, 'Can I take you home?' I said all right, so we got into the back of this psychology lecturer's Bedford van and started, right away, you see – I couldn't tear myself away. When we went to my digs, we went in and finished the job. I woke up the next morning and I thought, my God, I don't even know his name! I'd never been in that situation. So I spent the whole day thinking, oh crikey, I don't even know his name, what shall I do? He probably won't even speak to me. I went into college ... he was waiting, you know ... it was a big mad passion, see?

And then of course, and then, sort of after three weeks it began to ... he said, you see, 'I'm not really the kind that is meant to settle down, and getting married.' So I said, 'Oh, I don't want to settle down and get married, it doesn't matter to me.' And then it sort of began to dawn on me that he was trying to tell me that he didn't want to get involved in a big long serious thing, and I thought, that's fine, let's enjoy it the way it is and when it's finished it's finished. And then, when we were going off on holiday ... and I thought, well this is it. This is obvious that ... he's not keen – he goes off on

holiday and he just doesn't get in touch again. So we sort of had a
sort of farewell dinner, you know – 'Goodbye, and I hope you have a
nice holiday.' And he said, 'I'll get in touch when I get back. . .'
Anyway he did. He had a miserable time on his holiday. He came
back and said, you know, 'This is it, you know, we've got to get
married.'

Work and Marriage

After I came out of college I was very keen to work in a large mental
hospital, where I had done some teacher-training practice, and this
was a children's psychiatric ward. I don't know why I was attracted
to it, but in the second year they allowed two students, who were just
two names out of a hat, out of all the people who were interested,
got sent down on teaching practice. And it was just to give some of
the students on the course an insight to working with disturbed and
handicapped children. I tried to get on it and I wasn't successful. So
in the third year I went to the head of the Psychology Department
and said, you know, 'I'm very keen to go and see this place, can you
wangle it so I get teaching practice there this year?' So he said he'd
do his best, and he did. And I absolutely loved it. You know, the
work and the set-up. I thought, this is great, this is what I really want
to do.

And so I was very lucky. The girl that was the teacher in one of
the – that was three sort of little units, and the one that dealt with
children aged five to ten . . . were a mixture of behaviour problems,
psychotic children and children with – autistic children, this sort of
thing, you know – all sorts of combinations of problems . . . she was
leaving to get married and the job came up. So again I was told by
the training college that if I did a job like that I wouldn't be considered a proper teacher, and I wouldn't get my parchment, which in
those days, after you taught two years in Scotland, you were given
this piece of paper which said you were a fully qualified teacher, you
had done your teacher training, and you'd done your two years –
they really are very strict about it. So I went; the head of the Psy-

chology Department got two directors of education from different counties to say that was a lot of rubbish, and that if I wanted the job I should just take it, so I did. But then, you see, I had Andy, so I was sort of torn between the job . . .

I went back home and lived for six months, which was just sheer hell, you know. Because by that time I'd lived away from home for nearly two years, and the fact of going back, and my mother, you know, expecting me to be the same girl that left home. I'd been home quite intermittently, you know, but it wasn't the same living there. We both got on each other's nerves. And then also, at that time my mother wasn't well, she had an overactive thyroid, and so that made for friction as well. So it wasn't a particularly happy time, that, before I got married. They were very upset at me chucking over this chap, you know, that I'd been going around with for two years. They knew his parents and things, and that was a bit of a blow.

There was one girl in particular when we were at school . . . Marilyn and I, very good friends, and even right up to going through college – she was the one that wanted to be a nurse, failed and went into the Civil Service – and I felt I'd changed an awful lot away from her, and she stayed the same as I would have . . . I would have been like her if I hadn't gone through this process of going to college and things. I would have accepted the same sort of standards as her. Whereas my standards changed, my aims became different. And she just eventually got married and settled down and completely dominated her husband, and they have two children, and got fat, and you know, she's just what an awful lot of girls round here become. And even the ones who went through college with me – a few of them are teaching, but it's very much a sort of bringing in an extra bit of money. They don't consider it a career, and their husbands wouldn't want them to, and they're all home-orientated, husband first. And I'd say, out of the whole lot, I'm probably the only one who's gone on and had some sort of a career, and done some different things, and ended up higher up the scale than just in the classroom.

Andy had left art college the year before, and he didn't know whether he wanted to be a teacher or not. No art student does when they come out. But we knew we wanted to get married and settle down together. And he had come out of college and decided that he would teach. You see, he came out of art college and he did a year's teaching, uncertificated at that time. But he was still undecided at training college, and then eventually, when he met me, he had the same problem – that if we were going to get married, and do anything about it, we would both have to have jobs, and so he would have to get a teaching job. I travelled back and forward most weekends to see him.

Of course neither of us had any money, and you know, we couldn't afford to buy a house or anything like that. So, Andy's mother kind of took over that situation, and found us a furnished flat, which was quite nice – we liked it. Then, we got married, and we were absolutely clueless about money. We got our pay cheques at the beginning of the month, and we just spent it, and at the end of the month gasping on your next pay cheque and then went out and spent that. We never got into debt, and we weren't the least bit acquisitive. I mean, we didn't spend any of it on furniture. I don't really remember what we spent it on – except we had huge parties with lots of drink and food and lots of people, and we became the central figures of a group of people. Simply because I think at that time we were the only two that were married, so people could come back to our flat and sit and drink till two o'clock in the morning! It wasn't our furniture, so it didn't matter if it got beer spilt on it or anything like that, so it was a very sort of free and easy atmosphere. And we had a great time.

So, then, we drifted on like this for eighteen months. And I remember then very much wanting to have a baby, and this was, I think, influence, because all my friends had got married – at home, not the people I knew in the city, that I met through Andy or independently at college. But all the girls from home were married with babies, so I thought, well I'm married now, next step's a baby. You know, I still thought in that direction. And Andy said, 'Don't be ridiculous, how could we have a baby? We can't even keep ourselves, how are we going to keep a baby?' That was a very logical reason. Also I was quite sure he just didn't want us to have a baby. It would be too tying and, you know, a big drag and things. So that was about the only thing we really bickered about. I mean, we had the normal fights that people getting used to living with each other have. You know, you rub up against one another and you think that's bloody annoying. I wouldn't think things would be like that – you know, silly little arguments about nothing. I mean I packed my cases about three times. I never left.

And, then Andy's parents decided – they're sort of middle-middle-class – his father was a director of one of the big shops in the city and they lived in a big house, and his sister was at university, and they were really about three steps up the ladder from us. And my parents never felt very at ease with his parents, you know. I got on fine with them, his parents were nothing but the soul of kindness to me. I mean, they're red-hot Tories and the rest of it – that side of it I can't agree with – but just as people to meet they've been really super. So they decided to buy us a house. So we trailed round looking at everywhere, and eventually we got this little flat. They paid the deposit, paid the lawyer and everything, and we were left with the mortgage. And we got in there, and it was nice – I liked it, to begin with, anyway.

And I thought, right, here we are, got a little house and everything, you know, people giving us odd bits of furniture and everything. It wasn't a swell house by any manner of means, our furniture was nearly all broken-down and second-hand and things, but perfectly all right. And we actually got round to buying curtains and a bed and a cooker, and the basic sort of things, and I thought, this is when we *do* have a baby. And Andy still didn't want to. And I started getting sort of really restless, and this friend of mine, Beth – we'd been at college together – she'd been living with an art student for two years, and she was getting fed up with that arrangement, and she started hankering after London. 'Would you like to come?' So I thought, yes I would. So I thought, you know, I'm really getting a bit bored with this. You know, you get a house, you put things in it, and that's all right, and you go dragging on at your job – and he won't have a baby, and he obviously doesn't want to settle down, I might as well. So I started thinking about it and getting restless.

And then I started a stupid affair with Andy's best friend – you know, typical thing. He initiated it, and I thought, let's do this as a bit of a sideline for a bit of a laugh, it's better than what's going on at the moment at home. I really flaunted it in front of Andy, and Andy just ignored it. And I mean, at parties I'd go around kissing this bloke; I made assignations and I'd go to friends' flats and all the rest of it, and all sorts of things, and everybody knew, and Andy still wouldn't see it.

I did everything I could to make him look at me in a different way, because I thought he'd got to a point where he just accepted me, the same way he just accepted the house, and his job, and all the rest of it. And I didn't want it to be like that. I felt that something had just gone flat about the whole thing. And I was trying to stir it up. And I succeeded. Because eventually, of course, somebody at a party said to him, 'When are you going to do something about that lot?' And he said, 'What lot?' And they said, 'Well, Irene,' and he said, 'What d'you mean?' And he said, 'Oh for God's sake, we're not going to spell it out.' Of course he knew, but just wanted somebody – or at least I don't know really if he did at least, but anyway, it all came to a head and there was a great big row and he said, 'Right,' he said, 'you either stop seeing him, or the whole thing's finished.' Now, presumably he didn't want the marriage to break up, when it was put like that. So I said, 'All right, I won't see him again,' but I went to see him and I said, 'You know, if you really wanted me to leave Andy, I would.' And he said, 'I don't.' [Laughs.] He said, 'No, I don't want to get mixed up.' And I felt quite – I felt really used in a way, and it was my own fault. I mean, I had laid myself wide open in that situation to being used like that.

Well, they were very gentlemanly about it. I mean, he did come and see us after that. Things were a wee bit strained, and . . . then he gradually drifted off with another crowd of people who weren't married, and all the rest of it. He wasn't married. Actually our sex life and everything took a great big 'oomph' up from there, you know! It was about a year after that that I conceived our first child.

By that time we thought things were better financially, and we had been married for four years – if we don't have a family we're going to get to the point where you've been so long free that you don't want to get tied down – and neither of us really wanted to put ourselves in that position either, so we decided we better do something about it now. And I think that also helped our sex life, because we weren't having to think about contraception. And then, I had our baby.

I've always enjoyed my pregnancies. And I mean I've not had a big Mother Earth thing, but I've never felt sickly or ill, annoyed about being pregnant, and Andy always has been really nice when I've been pregnant. So the pregnancy went fine, and then I had the baby. I suppose it was just like everybody else who has a first baby. I mean, you're nervous about it, and, you know, you're unsure of what you're expected to do. I had this funny feeling when I came home from hospital. This was lovely and there was my baby and wasn't she nice, and all this. But I had this feeling, somehow or other, that I wasn't totally responsible for her. That somewhere somebody would come along and say, 'It's all right, dear, I'll see to that. Don't you worry about that, just you go off out with your husband.'

It dawned on me gradually. I mean, we went through feeding difficulties, and things began to go wrong, and it wasn't all just nice and clean. She was crying, and I couldn't stop her, and I got frustrated, and I felt it was all my fault. And Andy said, 'Christ, will she not shut up?' And then I would feel it was my fault she was crying, and you know, things were really sort of tense and horrible for a while. And then it dawned on me that there she was and that was it. And things would have to change, and Andy would have to start going out in the evening and I would have to try and develop myself in another way. My first sort of thing was to be domestic, and I can remember getting some material and a pattern and hand-sewing a dress – you know, a quite complicated dress – and when he went out I would get it out and this would be my little thing, you know. And I completed it, and I thought, so what?

And I remember one night some people phoned up, and it was about festival time, and I couldn't get out. We just didn't have a baby-sitter. And we were quite fortunate for baby-sitters really, because we used to get the kids from school to come along and do it, but on this occasion there was just nobody, and he said, 'Oh, well,

I'll go and meet them for a drink, and then we'll come back and have coffee here, and at least you'll see them and have a chat.' And I said all right. So while he was out I made coffee and sandwiches and things and sat there. And then when he came back he said, 'They're going on to a party, they're terribly sorry they can't come.' And I said, 'What d'you mean you're going on to a party?' And I said, 'I've got coffee and sandwiches.' 'They're all wanting to go to a party . . . and I want to go too.' And I said, 'I think that's fucking rotten,' I said, 'I'm sitting here all night and you're gonna . . . [scream] – you're not going.' And he said, 'I am going, don't try and tell me what to do.' This was the first confrontation like this we'd ever had . . . horrible. And it ended up with somebody from the group downstairs coming up and saying, 'Are you coming, Andy?' And I yelled, 'Don't dare open that fucking door – I'll kill you!' And he said, 'I'm going down the stairs.' And I went out and shouted down the stairs, 'You fucking bastard!' You see, I didn't care what the neighbours thought. I came in and sobbed myself to sleep.

He came back and there were big rows. And then, I don't know if he did have a good time at the party. All I thought was he was away. And what made it worse in a way was the group he'd gone with was his ex-mistress from art college and her husband and some people that he'd known at art college, and they weren't people that I was really familiar with, and I sort of envisaged it as being the old in-crowd and him with this girl. I mean he'd written to her, and he'd kept in touch with her and – she was somebody I didn't know an awful lot about, and I was a wee bit wary of her. And she was quite glamorous at that time. She'd just lived in Sweden and she'd just come back. She'd long blond hair and things, and you know, there was me still a bit overweight from having a baby and not able to get out, and I'd done these coffee and sandwiches and . . . [grr].

Things got better, and then, you know, the baby got over the difficult stage, and it began to be a sort of routine day: you got up and fed the baby, you went out shopping, came back, you had your coffee, read the paper . . . you went out in the afternoon to the park, you came back, you got your library book out and you had a read or . . . I was trying to do screen-printing. I hadn't enough money to buy the right materials, and that was a disaster. And then, I got to the point where I'd be sitting at the door waiting for Andy to come home from school, and I'd say, 'What happened? Who did you see? Did you see Jeannette today?' – she's the gym teacher, a friend of mine – 'How's Roy? . . .' And he'd say, 'Oh God, I'm so tired, I just want to have a kip.' I'd just about go crawling up the wall! I thought, this won't do. And where we lived, I never seemed to meet anybody, that I got friendly with. There were people I said hello to – the only girl near me that had been at college and I knew, but I couldn't stand. I avoided going to her house, and when she came to mine, you know, I made coffee and talked about things that didn't interest me in the least, now I come to think about it. And then the house began to get on my nerves, and I thought, I never wanted this place, it was his mother that bought it for us – there's no garden, and it's noisy . . . It began to get me down.

So then, friends of ours . . . there was this girl, that was his ex-mistress as well. She and her husband moved out to a New Town. Her husband was an architect. And they had this . . . what seemed to me a very nice house with a garden. We had money troubles at that time too, because we were down to one salary, and the mortgage was going up and the gas was going up and the electricity was increasing, the price of food was increasing, and things were getting really difficult. And we got an overdraft and couldn't pay it off. I started scheming about – if we got to the New Town we could get a three-bedroomed house there and we could get an au pair and I could get a job. So Andy, from the money angle, thought that was sensible, because if we sold the house we'd have some money – if we moved to a council house we wouldn't be spending the money buying another house, and this would solve all our problems. So I went ahead and organized it all. I got myself a job, got myself an au pair, made the move and the au pair walked out on us.

We went through a disastrous six months. Andy hated the New Town and he hated driving in and out. The money that we sold the house we bought a car with. I wasn't out of the house except to go to work and come back again – for six whole weeks. I didn't see any of my friends or anything. And I felt desperate. And then, I found somebody who could look after the baby, a woman along the street. I felt terrible, I felt guilty about this – you know, leaving her with somebody that I really didn't know, although obviously the woman was clean and kind and everything you could want. Andy's parents didn't approve of this whole thing. And oh, it was horrible. Anyway we survived that.

Andy never liked living in the New Town and I can see why. It didn't bother me so much, because coming from the background where you live in a council house and a whole lot of council houses that look the same, it didn't particularly annoy me. There were things I didn't like about it, I remember. There was a lot of Glasgow overflow people there, and I remember once we had a row about something and I said, 'You call yourself a socialist,' and I said, 'you hate living amongst the things that you really should be trying to do something about.' And he said, 'Well, I suppose you're right. You know, I never thought of it like that.' But he said, 'I just hate these people, and I hate living with them.' And you see, it didn't bother me so much, because I'd been brought up with people like that, and I'd known them. I knew how they thought, and I could accept it, and it didn't bother me. But it bothered him because he'd never had it before he had always lived in a big house with a big garden, he'd never been – living right with people. It's just that he wasn't very happy.

So we were there for three years, and by that time the baby was about three, coming up for three, and I wanted to have another baby, and I had problems. I think it was to do with the fact that I'd been on the pill, and I miscarried about three times, and you know, we had a rotten doctor there and he wasn't much help to me.

And then it was about Christmas time, and Andy came home from school one day and it was heavy snow, and he had an accident with the car. Now, without the car, it meant that he couldn't get in and out of town easily, the bus service was terrible. And he was hating the place anyway, and I had stopped working anyway, because the doctor had said, 'It might help if you can just relax – not work – try and get a spell off from working and see if you can try and conceive when you're more relaxed.' And he said, 'It might also help you carry them more if you're not dashing about teaching.' And being at home again, I was beginning to think, this isn't the ideal place. I was beginning to feel that it had served its purpose in a way, and we wanted to move on. And then we had heard about these houses, and we didn't think we'd a hope in hell, and we thought, this is the answer, we won't need a car. And you know, we don't have to buy it, we can rent it. And we didn't think we'd a hope of getting one. We put our names down, and we did. And I remember the week we heard, the insurance company came up with the money to pay for the car, and we got the house, and I was pregnant again – it was marvellous!

So we moved back into town, and then really things have gone just super since then. You know, I had Jenny, it was a smashing pregnancy. I got in touch with a whole lot of people that I hadn't seen for a long time because we were out of town, and Andy really liked living here, and we got our oldest child into the school round the corner, which turned out to be a really good school. This was another thing which worried us about the New Town – the schools were not good. They had a big turnover of teachers, and they weren't well equipped; although they were new schools, they hadn't spent the money on the basic things like pencils and paint and all that. They had beautiful furniture and all the rest of it, but none of the things kids need to get educated with. And so that had solved itself. I went back to work. The baby was about eleven months old, and again, it was the fact the rents were high here. I mean, we could always have scraped by, but there was always the fact that I can teach, and I like teaching, you know. I want to go out to work, so it was easier just to solve our problems by me getting a job. So I went back to teach again.

I taught a whole lot of different things by this time. I had worked, as I say, in that hospital to start with, then I'd done real teaching, then I came into town and I got a job in a unit for disturbed children – maladjusted children. And I was a sort of arty teacher – I mean I wasn't an art teacher, but I did the sort of arty-crafty things. Most of the ideas I got from Andy. And then from there I went into infant teaching, and then I went back here . . . and I've also taught various other stages from primary one to seven. So I've taught all ages in the primary school. And at the end of that year I had overactive thyroid, so I had to stop. I was only off work for about six to eight months. And the doctor said, 'It's clearing up fine. If you want to take a job again, you do that.'

So I heard about the autistic unit by this time, because it was in the same school that my daughter was going to. So I enquired of the Special Education Service about getting a job in a unit like that, and he said, 'Well that's the only unit, but if you like, you can do a spell of training there.' I was working with other teachers in what they call special reading units, and these are for children who have missed schooling, or fallen behind in school because of home circumstances, or illness. It's not because they're not bright, it's because things have been against them. They have so many units, so many places, and we push these children in, and we give them very high-powered teaching to bring them up to standard and give them confidence, and then they're put back into normal classes again. And all the time they're attending the unit, they're also attending school some of the time as well, so they don't really lose contact with their class. It's a really great set-up. So I worked with these people, and I worked at the unit.

When I went back first of all the lady downstairs looked after my youngest child, and when I went back to do my training for this job the girl on the ground floor looked after her, so she's always been with somebody. Then she went into nursery school, and that was when I went full time at the unit. It's worked out quite well. Now she's in the school, and I'm upstairs in the top part of the school, you know. So we all go round together, we all finish together, come home together, and it's really ideal. You have the sort of everyday problems about – is your kid going to be bright enough to make a go of things? I don't want particularly for her to be a crashing success or anything, I want her to be happy and able to cope, you know, that's the best I want for them. And what they do after that's entirely up to them, you know. But I think, given the sort of background we try to give them, they probably will want to go on, not necessarily to university, but do something . . .

They are both girls. I've got them and they're nice and that, and I enjoyed being pregnant, but I wouldn't want to go back through all the different stages again with a young baby, because we've got to the stage now where as a family we can go out and enjoy quite a variety of things together, and if you had another baby, it would set you back. I feel that I would be taken away from the children just when we're starting to enjoy each other's company so much.

They are different. The oldest is sort of proper and wants things done right and is quite conservative, and she wants to know why we don't have plastic fruit in a bowl like some people do, or, why don't we have a proper house with a garden, and this sort of thing. She's got very much – I don't know what kind of standards – very ordinary standards. She wants everything to be conformed and neat. And yet she's not an unimaginative child. I mean, she's – in her own way, she's quite imaginative, but she just likes things to be orderly and not upset. And the youngest is an extrovert – she doesn't give a bugger about anything, really, or anybody. The oldest is the sort of person who takes off her clothes and she'll lay them on a chair or a bed, and the youngest just chucks them about. And that's the difference in them. That one cares a bit about that sort of orderliness and the other doesn't.

You know, I don't want to be making them anything. Or at least I don't try to – well I suppose I do to a certain extent . . . but I always try to make them feel that they're not to be copies of anything. I want them just to be what they feel they want to be. It's difficult to explain . . . If one of them says, 'Girls can't do things like that,' I immediately say, 'Well, yes, girls can if they want to.' Or if she says, 'You shouldn't have such long hair, Daddy,' I say, 'Well they can if they want, why not?' You know, this sort of thing. We try not to – you're just trying to open up all the avenues for them. So they don't feel – because so often when I was young, I felt, there was things said – you don't do that because of what people would say. And I'd say, 'Well what would people say?' 'They'll talk.' 'Well what will they talk about?' 'They'll talk about you.' 'What's wrong with that?' 'I don't want it in my house,' – you know! And you never find a satisfactory reason for why you couldn't do it. And I don't want them to feel life's like that. I want them to feel that it's there and you just take what you want from it and enjoy it, and as long as you don't hurt people or damage yourself in a way, by making yourself too – I don't know – cheap . . . You know, have some sort of standards, but don't accept the standards that other people thrust on you – make up your own, stick to them if you think they're right.

14.   Linda Peffer

Linda Peffer is in her thirties and was born and brought up in a working-class district of North London. She had an unusual childhood owing to her mother's long illness, which necessitated the family being periodically separated – one of her sisters was sent to a local-authority boarding school.

Linda Peffer is married to a lorry driver and they have two young children at school. She now works in a canteen in a further-education college, where she has become active in the Union, despite her many criticisms of officials' attitudes to women workers.

Childhood

'We were really regarded as a weird family.'

I was born in Clapton, in June . . . I'm told there was a smell of roses coming from the garden. That was about all that was rosy about it, unfortunately.

My mum did work, before she was married, but she got TB when I was very young, and so, of course, she couldn't work. And my dad was a furrier. A very skilled sort of job, you know. The money wasn't really much. And he had his own factory at one time. Very small sort of business, but like most skilled jobs, you know, sort of highly paid, although the money wasn't *really* much. The drawback was it was dyeing, you see, you dyed the furs, which was quite a skilled job. It's also very dangerous because the dye gets on your chest. And he developed bronchitis, and it really got bad, so his job was gone. And then he got trouble with his legs – dye got through the socks – got ulcerated legs, this sort of thing, so he couldn't stand, and

when all that happened . . . and then you know, it really began to get ·
hard. Because, my mum was in and out of hospital all the time up
until I think I was about fifteen. Well even now she's still bad, though it's
not quite so bad now. Then when he lost the firm, my mum being so
ill, she couldn't work and she couldn't help out, so then things really
began to get bad.

There's me, and I've got a sister who's two years older than me,
and I've got a sister of eighteen, so there's three of us. I mean, really,
this was another thing – I mean, Mum was never in any fit condition,
from what I hear, and she was too embarrassed to go and get contraceptives or anything like that, which was, you know, very sad.
Because when she got pregnant she was about forty-five, so of course
she felt she couldn't be pregnant anyway – I mean, a woman of forty-
five just shouldn't get pregnant, which was, you know, how people
saw things then. An abortion . . . well, you see well I was never really
told the full story, my mum would never talk about it. But I don't
think that my mum would have had one, or whether it was left so
late that she just didn't have the chance to have one or not, I don't
know.

She had Christine, and it was quite a struggle. Of course we had a
house; at the time it was rented, so we had to pay the rent. But, we
got behind with the payments for the rent, and, er, my mum being
in hospital, my dad was ill, and we lost the house. But we were very
lucky really, because there'd been so much upset in the family, that
the council decided they couldn't break us up and put us in a children's
home . . . whatever they do with people. And they found us a place
in Stoke Newington High Street. We were really lucky. You hear
very sad stories of families being broken up, don't you? Christine,
she was about two when we moved there; I was fifteen.

My older sister, actually, she went to boarding school most of her
life, and so she just used to come home for holidays. It was a lovely
school she went to. My mum fought against her going, a lot, and it
made her feel very guilty. But in a way she was much more better off
than I was, because I was home for six months, shuttled back and
forward, and it was much more upsetting than if I actually stayed in
one place all the time.

We moved when I was fifteen or sixteen, I'd just started work –
terrible sort of upheaval that was. Cos they all wondered what was
going to happen to us. I think one of the things was always having
your own house, you know, I mean . . . big house – you know, it
wasn't a really decorated place or anything . . . of course we had
freedom. There was three self-contained flats, thirteen rooms in all of
them, and of course we could go, always, from one flight to the next
flight, this sort of thing. We had a big garden, lots of freedom. I
mean, most of my friends lived in council flats, and I didn't understand what it meant to be in a flat until we moved. And then we were
quite lucky because there again it was an old derelict place, in Stoke
Newington High Street. But there again there was still a certain
amount of freedom in it. You know, sort of big rooms, nobody was
cramped. It was all in a shambles, but we had a room with a record
player in where we could go, and there was different rooms.

And we missed the garden of course. If it was a nice sunny day, you
used to get your swimming costume on, out in the garden, you know,
things like this, you know, picnics in the garden – and you know, of
course, none of that – it ended, because there was no garden or anything. These aren't things that you think of immediately when you
move from one situation into another. I mean it just sort of dawned
on us, you know, when the summer come, that there was nowhere to
go. And we suddenly realized what it must be like for people who
didn't have gardens. You know, we were brought up a certain . . . I
mean, I never really thought much about people who lived in flats,
and who didn't have the sort of things that we had, because I'd
always had it, and for it suddenly to be taken away you start thinking,
oh, it must be like this for a lot of people. But there again, as I said,
we were still quite lucky, because, you know, although it was an old
place, it wasn't like these flats are now, it wasn't so restricted. You
could make as much noise as you liked. There was nobody underneath to keep the noise down – that sort of thing.

We had this thing – I mean I don't know if I got over it, probably
it's stayed with me all my life – me and my sister used to like to play
cowboys and Indians. At one time there used to be a series on the
wireless, I don't know what it was called, but there was a Geoff

Arnold who was the cowboy, and there was someone else, I forget who he was, but there was two sort of cowboys, you know, used to be on the wireless. And me and my sister used to like to dress up to be cowboys and we got an awful lot thrown at us for that. And because my mum was very sort of – now I realize it, she was very liberated – I mean she just wouldn't conform and buy us dolls. And we liked playing with guns and that, so we played with guns, you know. And I remember people actually – now, I realize what they were saying, I didn't at the time – but really they were saying, well, watch out, she might turn out to be a bit of a lesbian, you know, she's got those tendencies to play boys' games. And I remember all up the street, you know, we were really regarded as a weird family because of the way we lived. I mean, guns, and the way we all carried on, and mum was a very eccentric person. She was always sort of running about in trousers, you know, and doing really weird things which other people don't do.

She was really ill up to three years at a time. You know, in the summertime. I mean, it wasn't just a passing thing, this went on, she'd be one or two years away. Nothing for her to be away a year, so we got used to these big long gaps. He was on his own all the time trying to manage with us. At one time – which really shows that the system is just ridiculous – I wasn't going to school, and my dad, at this time he had ulcerated legs and he was on crutches, literally, he couldn't walk. They brought out a court action against us, and my dad couldn't appear in court, because he couldn't walk, and he had to appear, so they got him a wheelchair. Mind you, I must admit, when the judge saw what a state we were all in he just dismissed the case. But just the fact that it could have gone that far, to take us to court for not going to school. There again I never had any recollection of any help from the welfare people, never. They seemed to have no reality to us at all. I remember one woman coming down and saying to me, did I read poetry to my grandfather? – and all this sort of thing, you know. Well, I mean. . . They seemed to come from a different world.

School

'They wanted to pretend things weren't like they were.'

When I went to school I was thinking about reading and writing, and I used to read all these – er, Oscar Wilde, people like that who I liked – still do – and they really felt that was weird, and they really went into a whole motion of getting me out of it, you know. I think the thing was that I wasn't behaving the way that they wanted me to behave. The whole emphasis of school when I went there was put on to school uniforms, the most important thing, and behaving like a lady. The headmistress, I remember she sort of told us, how you had to behave like a lady. And you know, that was the whole emphasis was put on to it, how we spoke – you mustn't speak with a Cockney accent, you must try and speak properly. Well, really, I find that a bit stupid, because if you are Cockney, you're Cockney, and that's it. I mean I can't see why you shouldn't be. But she obviously did. She was trying to make the school give herself a name, you know, having all these neatly dressed girls. I remember, we even had a thing about how you sat down – you know, you must make sure that nobody can see up your kilt when you sit down. And she went through these long things: when you sit down, you only need to use one hand to brush your skirt down. This is to working-class kids. And most of them I'm sure ended up like me. I mean, I didn't work in Woolworth's, but lots of my friends ended up in – I worked in a shoe factory for a while, and they ended up working in shoe factories and Woolworth's and that, and they – it was of no relevance to them how they sat down.

But I mean it was this whole sort of stupid thing, I mean nobody really – I dunno if I can express it – there was no way you were going to get out of the situation you were in. But they wanted to pretend that things weren't like they were. You had to just pretend to put blinkers on. You know, if you put blinkers on you can pretend that this is how you're going to go on. There was a lot of emphasis on the girls . . . she wanted them to go into the office work. Everybody had to be a shorthand typist. And I really didn't want to be a shorthand typist. I couldn't stomach shorthand typing. And then it was a nursery nurse kind of thing. You know, you had to go into the nursery and look after children, and I found that was – I just couldn't do that.

And I just, I mean I just didn't fit in. I was far too masculine. And I know on one occasion, there was this flat, and we had a whole lesson on how to clean it perfectly. All the girls, naturally – well, there was no boys there then, but I mean even when there was boys the boys didn't do it, only the girls. And we done this cleaning the flat, and I was so fed up with it. I had my Oscar Wilde books, you know, poetry, and I sat there reading it – because I mean I didn't know why he was so good then, but I just enjoyed what he said. And she come in and caught me. And she said it was the most obscene book she'd ever seen. And she was absolutely disgusted and she wrote home to my dad and said that there was something wrong with me. I mean I was at home with my dad, I never had a mother, things were really going wrong, I didn't have a feminine . . . I suppose, somebody to show me how to be a lady. And she was really quite concerned about it. And she had my dad up there, and he absolutely cleaned the floor with her. He said she had the most filthy mind he ever met, you know. It was really lovely. And then afterwards, when we come out, the funny thing about it, I said to him, 'Well why is it obscene? I mean this is poems.' So he said, 'Well, the one you were reading, he'd actually written it to another man.' And I never knew that he was a queer. And then it fell into place and, you know, I remember saying, 'Well you know that makes it even better,' because I could understand it more.

But then again, I read Shakespeare, and they all thought I was pretty mad for reading it. You see, I was interested in things, really, that I shouldn't have been interested in. I mean, to them, reading people like Oscar Wilde or reading Shakespeare is really stupid, it wasn't for me. It really seems to me now, thinking back, what they said was, well look, we've told you what you can be, you've got this marvellous opportunity. You can be a shorthand typist, or you can be a nursery nurse. And here you are with all this sort of stupidness – it really isn't for you. And when you get out of it perhaps we can do something with you. And I suppose I never did, and then I was just written off as a failure. They'd absolutely written me off and they left me completely on my own. If I lost any time off from school, they used to bring me in the office and asked me if I was off because I was ill or because my mum was ill. But it was usually because I was ill, or just didn't want to go. I always said, well it was because I was ill.

I realized afterwards, when speaking to my mum, they were trying to find out if there was any way they could get me taken from home, on the grounds that I wasn't looked being after. And the whole basis of this was because of the family, because my dad was what you would call a very soft man, you know, he wasn't at all a hard working-class bloke. Mind you, I mean there again, that's fallacy, lots of blokes are like that anyway. But I mean he did . . . he sort of read poetry, and talked a lot, and he wasn't violent. He never settled arguments by punching people on the nose. And my mum *was* violent, you know, if people upset her. I mean, my mum would go out and say, er – I mean she never swore, I never ever heard my mum swear, but she wouldn't think twice of punching anyone on the nose.

We rented upstairs to this couple; they had to come through our kitchen to get to the garden, it was really funny. And most of the time my mum just let them through – I mean mum was free for all, you know, you could do anything with my mum. Then one day she was washing and the woman wanted to come through and she said to her, 'No you're not.' And there was a big argument, and she said, 'Well look, seeing as you're getting so stroppy with me, it's my house, and I'll let you come through two days a week to get your washing. So hang your washing out.' So she said, 'Oh, we won't do that, we'll have a pulley-line.' So my mum said, 'You can't do that,' – because the only place you could arrange a pulley would be directly over my mum's washing. And she did put a pulley-line up, this woman, and she hung a big heavy red chenille cloth out, a tablecloth – I don't know if you have ever seen them, but years ago we used to have these sort of heavy things – and all the dye ran. They had fringes round, and the colour dripped like mad, and she hung it out over my mum's washing. And my dad wouldn't do anything about it. He said, 'Oh, don't let's make a fuss.' So as my mum always had trousers on, my mum just climbed up the tree and tugged the washing-line down. You know, and this was the sort of thing . . . she didn't argue with her, you know – just that it was coming down, you know, and she would take anybody on.

So there was such a contrast, and obvious . . . I mean, they got on very well together. There again I was so mixed up with what was supposed to be a woman's role and a man's role, because I never really learnt it at home, because my mum did all the decorating – most of the decorating – and my dad was the one who done – he didn't do the sewing, but he used to bath Christine and tell us stories. But in fact my mum was much more the masculine one. My dad had much more of the feminine instincts. And of course you can imagine, I mean, the way people look at us all. It was really sort of weird, because we couldn't really be what we wanted to be. My dad was much more gentle than my mum. My mum and dad had had a very rough life. She'd had to really stand up for herself.

I think quite often I felt quite cross with her, because when you're a child you don't understand, you know, why people go off and leave you. But now I sort of see it differently. I mean, she was a very good woman, you know, very strong . . . but when you're a child you like your family to be like everybody else's, don't you? You know, Sunday dinner and the women being mum, and when you're young . . . and especially, I suppose, we were what would be classed as a typical working-class family. If it ever exists! You find there never is. But perhaps the difference is that a lot of people lead a sort of – cover-up, charade. They carry on and live a certain way and cover up, whereas our family wasn't so good at covering up, and we were more openly different than what other people were. I think my mum didn't cover up, because she wanted to be herself, and then I think because of all the pressures of society she must have got very guilty about it and so there must have been this terrible sort of mixture going on, partly wanting to be what she thinks is right and sod the others, and then the other half of her, you know, thinking, oh well, you know, it's not really right to be like it. And I think because of that, she sort of come out of it a bit confused.

My dad met my mum when they worked in the same place. My mum was in the fur trade, I mean she was a female flesher, which was very unusual, and he done the more feminine job, you know, the more delicate work. And she was this female sort of flesher – it's horrible really, they take the flesh off the fur – and there are very few women who can do that job.

Well I mean that was it, I suppose I come out as very confused. And for a long time I felt – you know, I just couldn't understand what I was. Because everybody was telling me, you know, look, well you're a woman, this is how you should be. And yet, on the other hand, I couldn't be like it.

I went to two council schools, one private school. Because when mum was ill I went to France, and the people in the place in France sort of said they'd pay for me to go to school, cos mum was in hospital, so there was no one to have me, and they wanted my dad to go over there and he said he couldn't go over there because he had me. So they said, well, you know, we'll pay her fees, which was really ridiculous, because of course I didn't fit in there, so I spent a very unhappy year or so there, when I was about thirteen. And then I come back, and I more or less left there, and it done me no good – nothing, you know.

The school was in Hastings. The only thing I can remember was standing up in the class and speaking and everybody looking around, because, you know, they'd never heard a Cockney accent. Or they had, and they thought, oh, how awful. And they taught me how to speak the Queen's English, and I come home and . . . I spoke with this sort of posh accent. You mustn't be too Oxford – that was as bad as being Cockney, you know, if you're too Oxford, that's wrong. Actually, I spent a year more or less just learning how to talk. It took me ages to learn how to talk that way and then when I come home I was talking like this, you know. And when I come home for holidays, in the break, it used to be really funny, because my dad said half of the sentence would be really . . . and the other half would lapse into Cockney, and I couldn't sort meself out. And then when I come home for good, I'd open my mouth, you know, and – people come to laugh at me, they knew I'd been back from school . . . talking, they said 'ooooooh', you know. It was really awful, and I was teased till – you know, I used to come home in tears, and I think it took me about three months to lose it. And there again it was this process of half of the words I was speaking exactly as they thought they should be spoken, and the other half was Cockney, and it was really confusing, because now I've been able to think about it, I mean they were really taking away every bit of identity that I had. I don't know if that would happen now. I mean it was a long time ago.

What I wanted to do, they just didn't do at school, so you see, everything I done, I done on my own. What I mean is that, if I read a poem, I had to come to my own conclusions about what the chap was saying, which was probably totally false, you know, and I never had anybody to discuss it with, only my dad, and he's sort of only . . . Anything I done sort of in the way of reading, or writing, would only be what I felt. I never had anybody to talk about it with. I mean I was really an odd bod. Actually my husband met a girl who knew me from school, and she summed me up by saying, 'Well that was the one who thought she was posh.' Well, mostly it was because I spoke differently when I come from the other school. It was so stupid, you know. It was such a mixture, because I really didn't fit in any-where. I certainly didn't fit in the school I was at, and I didn't when I come back – fit in with home. I did fit in with them, I mean, but because I spoke different that was a real big thing to them. I mean that they really teased me on it. Because it really wasn't me. And I can understand that, you know what I mean.

And there again, like most of my friends were really interested in boys, and you know we had to talk about boys all the time. I couldn't talk to them about books, cos they didn't want to talk about books. There again they found me very odd, cos to them boys used to be . . . who went out with who and how far they went. I mean a whole relationship to them with a boy was them saying no and wanting to and boys trying to, you know? I mean this was what it was. And whereas I couldn't think of boys like that really, I used to think of them as just people, like me. And that was really odd, because, when I went in the classroom, all the girls sat one side, and all the boys sat the other side. They would never mix, and first of all you know – I mean a whole rumour went round that I was a prostitute because I actually spoke to the boys. But I mean I just saw them as people.

They were very frightened of me I think, now I think about it, because I spoke to them. I mean if a boy had been off ill, and they came back, I used to say, you know, 'How are you?' and 'I am pleased to see you.' And they immediately took that as, 'Ooh, you're all right here,' you know, and all the other boys would tease him, and whereas I wasn't meaning it, I mean I just meant, you know. . . . So it was all very hard, because they couldn't understand me, and they wanted to put me in the role of . . . you know, I mean, when you're very young it used to be – blokes used to chase the girls round the playground and touch them up, really crude. And I wasn't having any of that, I didn't want to do that. I mean I wanted to talk to them and be friendly with them, but they didn't really want to be friendly with me. Some of them I think they did, really. It was funny, if there was no one else about they'd stand talking to me, but as soon as any of their mates come up, you know . . . I can't be caught talking to that odd bod, you know.

I mean there was such a division between them, the boys and the girls that I knew, it was always this . . . you know, they were out to get what they wanted, and the girls had to be, sort of, not wanting that, but sometimes they sort of . . . you know. There can't be any real genuine feeling between them. They can't, sort of, talk to women. I suppose they just can't see women as people, and that's it. I mean, you get, even now, they go in these discotheque places and they look the girls up and down, you know, sort of thing – who's got the biggest tits, boobs, and who looks the nicest, and if they fancy them.

Work after Leaving School

'Pretty hopeless again.'

School was a waste of time for me, quite honestly. When I left I went to the nursery first, and they just ripped me off, because I just wasn't – no good. I begin to realize that I was quite good, but there was this thing that you are better than them, the kids, you see. And then there's a matron. She was above all. It was a very sort of hierarchical ... you know. And I couldn't see myself as being any better than the kids. And they were very racialist. I mean I couldn't see that a black kid was any different to a white kid, and I just didn't fit in – as simple as that. I just saw the kids as my friends, in a way. Friends who needed, sort of, a little bit of help. You know what I mean. I couldn't see myself as above, telling them what to do. I liked them to call me Linda, you know. And they said, 'Ooh no,' you know, 'Nurse Smith.' Well I mean I wasn't a nurse. I was much too friendly with the kids, to what they wanted. I think really I just didn't fit in. I don't know if the same thing would happen now. I was interested in the kids, but I don't think I could have spent my whole life doing that. I was much more into reading, you know, I used to like to read a lot.

That was another thing we had fights over. The kids – they weren't allowed to develop. It seems to me what they done there was they said kids had to be made to think and act in a certain manner. They were just pushed into acting and behaving in a certain manner, you know. I wish I knew the words – I can't explain it. I mean it wasn't just that boys were always encouraged to play with boys' toys – you know, the lorries and that – and girls were always encouraged to play with girls' toys. It wasn't just that. I mean one little kid, he used to read these monster things, read monster books and that – you know, magazines – and he always loved the monster. Well, I mean, I was quite sorry for the monsters too. And I used to say, 'Oh, it's a shame they're going to shoot that man,' – or, you know, I used to feel the same for him. But to them you shouldn't say that. The monster's a bad man. I mean they wouldn't let him be what he wanted to be.

When they played, they had to be led along a certain pattern of play. You know, draw mummy, daddy and a house. And when a kid drew a room – and obviously they all lived in one room – they really didn't like that, they said, 'Oh no, go away and,' you know, 'draw us a house.' They said, 'Don't be silly, you can't have the bed in the front room.' He was only about three, so you can imagine what it looked like, but he was drawing life as he saw it. They didn't use those words, but what they were saying was, well, you can't draw what you see, you've got to draw something else. Probably, you know, it offended them.

This boy, the one who loved the monsters, I really loved him. He was a very violent kid as well, very violent – I remember I turned my back on him once and he smashed me on the back of the head with a blimmin' cowboy gun. But I remember we were drawing together and I drew him black – his parents were black – and you know, they really told me off for that! They said, 'Why have you done that? You shouldn't do that!' – you know, and I really felt – and I come home feeling that I'd done something wrong. I felt really bad, and they said, 'Oh well, what d'you think you've done to that kid?' And I felt, oh yes, it is wrong. And the next time I drew it I made sure I done 'em white. But I mean really, on thinking back, what I'd done to that kid was nothing really wrong. I mean all they were saying was, look, you should be ashamed of being black, weren't they?

Then a friend of mine went to work in the shoe factory and that was it. I went to see somebody about careers: 'What do you want to do, working in Woolworth's or what?' So I said, 'Well you know, I'd work in a shoe factory.' Which I did do. I was fifteen when I went to the shoe factory. I was absolutely hopeless at that. And I got really fed up. Well, you know, I mean, just packing shoes and doing all different odd jobs that they wanted done. Then I left there and I went to another shoe place, pretty hopeless again. I got on all right, but I wasn't interested in staying there, I just earned money. Then I decided I'd learn the fur trade, because my mum was in the fur trade. There was an advert, they wanted people to learn furriering, and that's what I went and done. I learnt that, right through. Well, I mean, I could have, but I got married, had the kids, and I didn't go on to do like Helen. Oh, she's skilled – I think they average fifty or sixty quid a week.

Sex, Courtship and Marriage

I tried to find out about sex – I mean, I didn't even know what a period was. I remember the girls at school had just started coming on with periods and asked me if I had – it was really funny – and I said yes, because on top of everything else, I mean let's face it, I didn't wanna be the odd one out there as well. And I didn't realize that a period meant losing blood, you know – I mean, I thought it meant having pain. And I used to get sanitary towels in the chemist with my sister, when I was with my mum. She always told me that it was something that she had because she had a lot of pain. So the girls at school said, 'Have you got any pads?' And I said, 'Oh no, I'm not bothered with a towel,' – because I had no cause. They said to me, 'Oh, you filthy thing!' And I didn't understand it. I really thought that a sanitary towel was something to stop you having pain, and I said, 'Oh well, I've not got any pain.' I mean I was that ignorant, which was really so stupid. When I did come on the periods, I didn't understand anything about it, and I knew nothing about sex at all. I was doing gym at the time and I came on; I didn't know what to do with the towel, someone had to actually show me how you used the towel. But it was then it was kept very quiet. Well you don't sort of talk about it. And then again, because I didn't understand it, I was very innocent about it, and I would sort of say things quite openly about periods. I mean I still do it now sometimes – forget that people get embarrassed. I just can't clue into it now, why it's not a natural thing.

I knew nothing about sex and that, so if I had a crush on a bloke I couldn't fantasize about him sexually, because I wouldn't know what I was fantasizing about. I used to read these books and go and see these romantic films that stopped at the vital point. I really thought that it was something that was going to happen that was going to be so marvellous and that, but I knew nothing about it. I was totally ignorant. I couldn't talk to my mum. I found I could with my dad much more. But there again, he was a bit het up about it. I think the difficulty was that my dad was basically a very open person, but if you live in a situation where everybody says it's wrong, you've got to comply, haven't you? And I think that was it. He wanted probably to talk to us – sort of in a very open way, I mean.

He wanted to be himself, like not being a masculine man. He liked sort of doing what is called feminine things, like reading poetry and that. He was much more the feminine out of my mum and dad. Mind you, she was very physically attractive – a fantastic figure – and she never used to make much effort, and she was always like electric. When she was in a room, everyone seemed to sort of listen to what she was saying. She was very physically a woman, the way she looked and that, but you know, in attitudes, she wasn't really a woman. My dad was really so quiet, and sort of knowing, through all this reading and talking. If there was a quarrel, he'd be the one to go out and reason and that. Whereas my mum would go out and punch them on the nose. Partly because she'd had to survive, she was always the one who stood up for herself. I mean, my dad would, but he used a different way to do it. Whereas my mum, if anybody upset her, she'd just march in there and say, 'Look . . .' – you know. But as I said, I think he was very confused about what he was. And I suppose we all are, really, because if you don't comply, a lot of pressure's put on you to, isn't it? This is it.

By the time I left school they'd written me off as a total waste of time, but before – you got the choice about two years before you left school, and they . . . it wasn't a choice, there was no thought at all. I mean they just weren't interested – it's as simple as that. Perhaps that's not right – perhaps they were interested, I don't know, but they just do not have the facilities or whatever it was, to give you anything. The headmistress sort of wanted everybody to pretend they were middle-class – that's really it. But we weren't. And if you wouldn't comply with what she wanted you to . . . I remember her giving us a whole lecture that you don't want to be like people who sweep the streets. And of course that was pretty hurtful, because, when you think of it, most of the girls at that school must have had parents who did jobs like that.

I mean, when I got married, I really think I done it and had children because that was what I had to do. There was no other opening to me – if I didn't get married I'd have been really odd. Now I really stop and think, well, should I have got married? I don't know. I mean, should I have had children? So much pressure was on me to do it, I never really had a chance to sit down and think out what

I wanted to do, it was just that – what if I don't get married, I'll be an old maid, you know. And I mean, most women I knew who weren't married, quite honestly, they were really odd, and I felt if I don't get married I'm gonna end up like them.

Mind you, my friend Helen never complied and got married. I don't know why she didn't. I think mostly because she'd never met the right bloke. You know, she was a working-class girl, and she needed sex. And if you're working-class you're not supposed to have sexual feelings, not if you're a woman. She never got married, but she wanted sex, and she had this terror – I mean the first time she slept with a bloke she actually knocked me up at five o'clock in the morning and told me that she'd done it. I envied her, really, because it was something that I wished to hell I could do, but I just couldn't bring myself to, I just couldn't. I think her biggest problem was that she was a woman who sort of – needed sex. She had very strong feelings, if she fancied a bloke she didn't know how to control herself. It was awful. She used to tell me, actually, never to leave her alone with him. It was that bad – 'If he asks to take me home, don't let me go, don't let me go!' This used to be before we went out. And of course it was so funny really, because I really envied her, for the fact that she could ever feel anything. She couldn't understand that. Well, I never told her – quite honestly I couldn't admit that I didn't feel anything.

I went out with a chap for a year, and we went away for a weekend and it was very funny because he actually assumed that I was going to sleep with him. He sat on the bed and started taking his shoes off, and it suddenly dawned on me that he thought he was going to get into bed! And I was so sure, I just wouldn't have any of it! On Canvey Island there's nowhere to go. It was very dramatic when I think about it – stupid old B films – I stormed out with all the suit-cases and everything. He followed me out to the car and he said, 'Where you gonna go?' And I said, 'Well take me to my friend's,' – cos I wasn't going back with him anyway. And afterwards, he turned round and said, 'Still, I respect you all the more for this!' It was so totally confusing. I just looked at him and thought, he just told me that he loved me. He really thought it was the right thing for us to do.

It was so exhausting going through it all, I just sort of couldn't work it out at all. A funny relationship to have with a person, isn't it, really?

I find that, with our friends who are single, they're very much the same. They go out to discos and places like this. They're all, sort of, old teenagers, if you know what I mean, and they like pulling the girls and that. They criticize them for it. It's not as obvious perhaps as it was, when we were young. I don't find it's quite as bad, but it's still there.

My husband, Fred, was the first chap I really got close to without sex coming into it. I mean we just went about for about two years with each other. We didn't even hold hands, we were just friends. I did meet boys I worked with, I had quite a few friends that I worked with. One friend in particular, I was very fond of him, and I used to go over to his flat and cook his dinner. I used to be able to talk to him and that. But nobody in work could understand it. They all thought that we were sort of – having it off together, to put it crudely. They couldn't understand that I wasn't interested in him from that point of view. I really wasn't. I think mostly it was because I didn't have any brothers, and I suppose in a way, I mean, he took the place. And I like men anyway. You know, it's very interesting . . . I always find it is nice to talk to a man about Women's Lib and women's problems, because I like to hear it from the other side of the fence, you know. And I know, I mean I could never sort of just see men as sort of sex. But don't get me wrong, I mean, there were men and boys that I really fancied like mad, you know. I used to sort of fantasize about them in all different situations – not sexually, because I mean I was so repressed.

Even when I met Fred I'm afraid that carried on for years and years because I was so repressed. Because I wasn't allowed to have any sexual feelings, you know. And it was so repressed, I mean none of my family talked about sex, and all the friends I had talked about it – well, they didn't know much about it themselves. It was very sort of crude. It was always the boys going out to get it. It always reminds me now when I think about it, about dogs – you know what I mean? I know it sounds awful. The men always sort of chase the women,

and I mean it was always a very sort of – almost a rapish thing. You
know, I mean it was never spoke about in. . . Probably it was because
it was the only way they could get hold of them; perhaps if a bloke
really forced them to it, then they could do it without feeling guilty,
I don't know. But it was always talked about like that.

I was at a friend's house, going home, and er, there was a dirty old
man down the road, exposing himself. So I got up there, saw this
dirty old man and come back again, and I was talking, and Fred was
in some flats and he'd come out on the landing and he heard this
going on, and he come down and said, 'Look, I couldn't help over-
hearing your conversation, if you want me to, I'll take you home on
my bike. You'll be all right, you know.' So I said yes, and that was
how it began. It was just purely a friendship. He said, 'Oh well, you
know, I love the bike and I love going fast on it.' And I said to him,
'I enjoyed the ride and that,' and he just said, 'Oh well, I'll pick you
up one night and we'll go for a drink somewhere, go out for a ride,
go in a pub, you know.' And this went on for quite a long time, you
know. Whenever we weren't doing anything, we used to see each
other; he'd give me a lift back – to a pub, we used to have a drink,
and this sort of thing. We used to sort of chat about all different
things, you know. I used to enjoy being in his company. Didn't
always talk . . . go out and find a nice pub, sit there having a drink, or
if it was nice we used to sit outside on the bike. I loved going out like
that. We used to do that regularly. And then we didn't see each other
for a year. Well, you know, it was just a friendship, and it sort of
petered off, and I was going with this chap at the time. Fred and me
were just like mates.

We broke for a year and then we saw each other again. Then I
started thinking of him a lot different. More of a man, more sort of
in that way. It just sort of clicked into place for me. I'm sure if we
hadn't have broke out from each other, we'd have never sort of
ended up having a sexual sort of thing. It was only probably because
we broke away for a year. When you're growing up, you know, a
year is a long time. We both sort of altered enough, and we'd been
out enough, and he just bumped into me, and he said, 'Would you
like to come out?' It was completely different then, begun to be

different. It was nice, because I mean, I also knew him as a friend as well, you know.

But I just wouldn't allow myself to have feelings – sexual feelings. It was really cold and calculated; I thought, well, you know, it's got to happen and I'll let it happen. When I got married I was pregnant. And it wasn't because I was swept away in a tide of passion. I mean it was a thing that I really had to come to terms with – it's all right to do it. The first time Fred and I had sex it was more or less one way – it was more or less like rape in a sense, that I gave him consent to. I don't mean he was rough, but I mean I didn't participate. And then when I slowly begun to get the feeling that it was really all right, and I got carried away and started to do things to him, and enjoy it, I used to apologize afterwards. And he said to me – you know, it took ages and ages to say to me, 'Look, don't be stupid. I mean women don't just lie there.' And I mean it took a long time before he really got me round to thinking, well, whatever I want to do it's all right ... openly enjoy it, and there's no right and wrong, you know.

Babies

'Motherhood is the best-kept secret in the world.'

I've had the kids . . . and when I had them it was like a nightmare, really. I suddenly realized what it was like to be married and have two kids, you know. Somebody said: 'Motherhood is the best-kept secret in the world.' They're right, because no one really owns up to what it's like. All this rubbish that's written about it.

I was pregnant when I got married. We found somewhere to live after a struggle. It was all lovely, it wasn't a bit sordid. I mean, we were going to get married anyway, and my mum sat down and said, 'Do you want to marry him or . . . you know, think it out.' There's no pressure on us at all to get married. It wasn't done like that. And everybody was so lovely, you know, and where I work, the chap said to me, 'Well if you don't want to get married, I know somebody where a flat's going, and your job's here if you come back.' I mean it really must have been a funny situation. And my mum said to me,

'Well if you don't get married I'll look after the baby when she's born, and you can go to work, and you can have your own . . . you know.' But I really wanted to get married, and I mean me and Fred sat down and spoke about it together. I said to him, 'Don't ever think you've got to marry me.' So he said, 'Oh no,' he said, 'it's really rubbish, you know; it's what I want to do, you know.' And he said, 'We will get married.' Well, we were engaged. He said, 'We wouldn't have gone this far . . .' – you know.

Then we found somewhere to live, and when I had the kids, well, it was just like – it was like a bomb. I can't describe it. When my first child was born I couldn't breast-feed her. They'd left the milk in, and I was a thirty-four bust and they went really big. When I got in and out of the bath it was like bricks, you know – doing, doing – so hard, and so painful, you know, and I was literally bleeding – I mean they left it too long. And I was full of these guilt feelings because people said to me, 'You should breast-feed, you should breast-feed,' and I couldn't. I mean, Karen was a sleepy baby and she wouldn't suck, and I couldn't keep waking her up to feed her, and plus the fact that, you know, I made lots of milk but it wouldn't come out. Actually I found out now, that there's something happens where your breast can get so overfilled with milk that you need an injection or something to loosen it. I don't know exactly, I mean I read it somewhere, so perhaps that's what happened to me. But of course nobody bothered; I mean, they don't bother about things like that!

And I come home and it was like – I couldn't describe. You see the thing was that I didn't feel any feeling for Karen whatsoever. And that really worried me. Because everything I read, everybody told me that I'd be filled with this love, and it just didn't come – it was nothing. I mean I remember looking at her and thinking, ooh, you know, there she is, you know, and a certain amount of feeling, because that was . . . I mean, she was inside me for nine months and here she is, this is what she looks like. But, you know, I sort of looked at her, and I had no feeling. I mean I thought I was going to be overwhelmed with love, you know, really I did. And I wasn't. And when I come home . . . and then it really started, because I mean, Fred was shocked a bit that I didn't have these feelings for her. It was like having a cat really – I know it sounds awful! I just didn't have all these feelings that everyone told me about. Plus the fact that I was ever so tired, and in the hospital you get no sleep at all. They kept trying to make me breast-feed, and they put curtains round me, and I was for an hour at a time breast-feeding, and you breast-feed three hours, every three hours, so for five or six hours a day I was just sitting with a curtain round me, nobody else could see me, so you could imagine what that does. There's a whole load of changes that go on inside you anyway when you have children, you know, so you've got this – thing.

When I come out I just couldn't cope with the housework, and I just felt that all I done with Karen was just fed and bathed her and kept her, and I just sort of used to burst into tears. And of course I couldn't tell anybody, because if I tried to tell anyone, you know, they'd think how terrible, you know, she's got this lovely baby, and what a horrible woman she is. So I just went into this absolute deep depression. Really – I mean, I was almost suicidal. Because I felt trapped. There was this little thing lying there, and I had to do everything for her, and nobody told me. You see, you're not really all keyed up with all these instincts. You don't automatically know what to do when the baby cries. It's all got to be found out, and I thought, oh Christ, what's wrong with me? I really don't know. Then of course I went back and thought, well I must really be a lesbian. You know, if I wasn't a lesbian, if I was an ordinary woman, I'd have all these feelings I should have.

The housework was hopeless. I suddenly realized – it really dawned on me then – that I really hate housework. Instead of normally sorting it out and thinking, well, there's nothing wrong with me, but there's something wrong with the situation I'm in, I turned it round the other way, which was the only way I could do. I mean all the women I met at the clinics and that were all saying, ooh, how lovely and how fulfilled they felt, and I just pretended. I'm much braver, I'm sure, since, because I've met people, you know, who are different. I started voicing opinions. It's surprising after you've said it a couple of times how many women say, ooh yes, you know, really – and they start opening up, and you find that a hell of a lot of women have felt exactly the same as you, only they've just been so scared to say it, you know.

I thought we were just going to split up. He used to go out every night, which is awful, and I couldn't go out, and I wanted to go out. I had a friend, a very close friend, and she used to keep telling me how to be a perfect wife. I mean, this was her way of things. She's really funny – she's very clever, she could add up in a flash, but if her husband's there she lets him do it. To make him superior she had to be inferior. Not that adding up makes a person inferior or . . . but you know what I mean? She used to tell me all about how I had to be a good mum, and I really used to try to do all this. I mean I just wasn't cut out for doing all the housework, looking after the baby on me own all the time. And of course I couldn't get out, because I had no baby-sitter, and you know, you go to the toilet, and the baby's screaming. I couldn't describe it to anyone, you're just drained. You can't think, because when the baby's asleep you're doing all this monotonous housework, that's supposed to be so important – half the time I was just too exhausted to do it anyway.

And what's the annoying part is, now I can admit to meself, it is monotonous and horrible, but then I couldn't, because every time I felt that way I thought, I mustn't think like that. It's so drummed into you, every time you used to watch a television programme, and there'd be a couple, and the woman always looked nice, for a start, which I didn't at the time, only when I went out, you know, I dressed up to suit – you know, the people I was with, so to speak. But you never see a television programme where the woman's house is all in a mess, do you? They're always all nice and clean and tidy and everything's going on all nice, and they've got a baby, and everything's wonderful, and you never see a whole load of messy nappies on the floor where she couldn't boil 'em up, or sitting there really depressed and fed up. I thought, oh Christ, you know. I must really be wrong.

I might make myself sound stupid trying to identify with the television, but in a lot of ways I was so cut off from everyone. You couldn't go out, and if you went out, most of the women I went round to see, well, they were the same. I found that out, it was really funny, a lot of them used to clean all up before I got there, and I done the same before they got there. If we'd have had the courage, I think we could have helped each other out a lot, if only we could have admitted it. It come out when I got a bit stronger, and actually confessed what a mess it was in, and gradually I found out that loads of women were like it, and we all pretended to be all right when we met each other, because we just couldn't confess that we were really in a right state at home.

So really, I suppose, I thought, well, what is it all about? I mean I was supposed to clean and do all the housework and I just couldn't do it – I didn't want to do it. And then I had John, because I knew, it was like falling off a bike, if I'd only got on again I'd have never had any more children, I knew that, and Fred wanted two. I felt, there again, it was the right thing to do, to have two. I'm glad I did apart from all this. And then I was back in the same situation – well, the only day nursery thing we had was with Karen. It was at George Downing Estate, which meant me getting on a bus and all that. And then it turned out that none of the women wanted to help, they were so depressed and fed up, and having the kids all day, and we were supposed to take a turn each. Of course, I ended up looking after all the kids, cos I felt so sorry for the woman in charge, you know – it become so hard, I just gave up. Really, I was stupid – I should have just said no, I'm not going to do it every week. But no, I felt sorry for her and that, and I felt I should do it as a woman, to prove I was a mother and that, and perhaps all these instincts would come flashing in if I do all this all the time, you know.

I mean, by then, Karen was about two and John was a year, so – or just nearly a year – so I did have feelings for her then. I mean she was a person then, I mean, I'd got sort of a relationship with her then, because, you know, she was a person, she wasn't just a bundle that was crying. Mind you, often I felt so angry with her, I used to just . . . I never hit her, I mean I was never a child-beater, my thing was that I just didn't do anything, and I used to let her play me up a lot. I was just blank, you know, because probably, you know, what I mean, all this tensed-up aggression must come out on the kids, and the thing I done is I never used to hit her or anything, I just used to let her get on with it, you know what I mean? Perhaps if I'd have hit her a bit actually it might have been better for both of us, but I just didn't, you know – I mean I used to switch off. I think if I had summed up my life when the kids were little, I think I could sum it up like that – being switched off, most of the time. I had to, otherwise I'd have gone insane. That's why I could have never thought of doing anything. I mean, I was talking to somebody and they were saying to me, 'Oh well, when you had the kids, and Fred had money' – I mean we weren't financially hard up – 'you could have gone and done a course or something.' But that was ridiculous, because I just couldn't have. I was put in such a hopeless situation, you know.

Karen goes to the Child Guidance. I think I was in such a state no wonder she was nervous. When I take Karen there they say how sensitive she is, and how she worries over things, but she is a very sensitive child. And they said she interprets everything in the class-room as violent, but it has to be when a teacher's trying to keep forty kids in a class in control.

Well, I used to sit there listening to the women. With the women I met at Child Guidance, a lot of it was brought on, I think, by financial things. One woman with kids, she asked them to take the kids away but they wouldn't. They were very patronizing with her, very patronizing, I really don't like that. Then, it's hard for them not to be, because most of them are middle-class women, who haven't really ever had the problem. I mean I'm not condemning them. One woman was married to a Greek chap, and you know the Greeks have this sort of attitude towards their women – you know, 'their little wife at home' thing. She had no money, they were skint, and she was really fed up and depressed. Well I think anyone would be, if you lived in an awful house, you'd got no money... What they were saying to her is, if you had the right attitude, you'd be all right. But I couldn't help looking at her and thinking, wouldn't anyone be like that, without any money and everything?

And you know, most of it come out was the guilt thing these women had about sex. Now this woman, she liked sex and that, she was attractive to men. And she was really frustrated over it, and really upset that she had these sexual feelings and that. It made it hard because he was Greek and she'd slept with him before they got married. This is so funny, he'd wanted to sleep with her, obviously, but then he kept bringing it up – that she was no good because she had slept with him. She had a pretty bad time as well, with her husband, he knocked her about a lot. I felt so sorry for her.

She was telling us about how she had been in a home, and they were frightened of the girls getting pregnant, so when they come on they had to go and ask for sanitary towels, so they knew when they'd come on. It seems so undignified. When she had her first period they said to her, 'You mustn't go out with boys, you mustn't let them touch you.' No wonder she grew up like she has. I just felt that all the tricks of the psychologist where she was concerned was just sort of . . . you know, this person who was trying to sort her out was employed by the council, but the council were the ones who had done it to her – they'd made her like she was.

Married Life

'People say children keep you together, and I think that's a great lie, because often it splits people up.'

We've been living together for ten years now and things have got great. I mean, things have really developed into a scale that I could have never dreamt that they would have done. Partly because, as the kids grew older, and the pressures were taken off. . . People say children keep you together, and I think that's a great lie, because often i⁺ splits people up. You've got to look at it from his point of view as well. He was brought up in a family where a man's a man and a woman's a woman, and he must have been really confused, because I suppose from his way he was thinking, well, if she's not a woman, well what am I? He used to come in and find me in tears nine times out of ten, and he really didn't know how to cope with it. He just didn't know what to do. Well I mean he'd never met a woman like it. He believed all the . . . well his mum was one of the sort of – a woman who was very much a woman, in that respect.

Anyway I didn't sleep . . . and Fred was very good but he was driving at the time, and can you imagine trying to sort of stay up half the night with kids and then you've got to get on the road and drive? He didn't do long-distance – he did do some long-distance, but not much. I mean he never left me overnight cos I couldn't have coped with it, and I just – he was the only thing that kept me alive, and of course when he come in from driving, all I wanted to do was pour out to him everything that was going on. It was hard for him to take it, you know, and he wondered what had hit him, I suppose really – I mean it was very awkward.

But we went on like this, and he used to be really good of a night, and he used to take a turn, because John just didn't sleep. And the older one wanted to get up in the morning – when John was born, Karen was fifteen months, and she was now going to bed and getting up in the morning at the right time. But I mean she didn't know that I'd been up all night. When she woke up she screamed, you know, she wanted to get out and do things. I mean, at fifteen months she was very lively and doing things, and I mean she didn't want to stay, it wasn't as if I could leave her in her cot to play. She was too old for that. And of course I had to get up with her. So what used to happen is I used to let him sleep. We done it in shifts. I stayed up till five o'clock with John, and I used to go up with his breakfast and wake him up, then I'd get into bed till half past seven when Karen woke up, and this is how . . . And we had baby-sitters, and I mean my mother-in-law was really excellent.

Every so often, she used to have the kids when we went out. But nine times out of ten that used to be very sort of energetic. To get out, I had to get them all ready to go round to my mother-in-law's, or if she come to me I was in such a state, and I felt so guilty, I had to clean all up before she could actually come and see me. You know, I wouldn't let her see what a mess we lived in. I'm sure if she'd have seen it she'd have been shocked, because . . . I make her sound like an awful person, but she's not. She really is a very good, very nice person. I mean she'd never interfere with what we done, she never had, there was no bitching with her. But also you know, I still felt I had to comply – complying to what people thought we had to be all the time. So when we went out it was a bit of an exhaustion, getting there and then having to get back again. Then of course I was up all night with the kids after that. And when they got a bit older and they got to school, and that was it – I thought, right, girl.

First they used to come home for dinner and that was a bit . . . I had a couple of hours and I used to wander round the shops and that without the kids, and it was like heaven – it really was. I know this sounds awful, but just being able to think, to actually think, to be able to sit down and read something, or do something. But that wore off, and I got so depressed again because I was only in the same situation, doing housework. It worked funny really, because before, I was so exhausted that any rest off from the kids was welcome. Then, of course, they were going to bed at six o'clock – well, seven o'clock – getting up, so I was getting my night's sleep, and there wasn't a lot to do during the day. So then I got bored. You know? Because I'd switched from one thing, where I was completely exhausted, and couldn't think, to another thing where if you've got a flat like this, it's quite easy to keep clean. We moved here when Karen was five, and John was just about going out to morning nursery.

One thing about our first flat was that there was always people in the house, you know. Well, they used to help out with the baby-sitting of the kids. Also, I'd gone through the really bad period and then things were going to shape up. A young couple moved upstairs. A black girl and a white chap, and it was really a nice atmosphere. They were young and there was always people in the house and we all seemed to get on so . . . it was very free and easy. And she didn't care about her housework, I mean it was lovely for me to actually meet someone who was like me. She didn't clear up for me – I mean that was me, you know, that was her – and I'd go up there . . . and she don't know what she done to me, you know. If you knew what it means to walk into someone's flat seeing a mess – it's such a relief. She was a very nice person. And he was as well. So that was really lovely because when Fred was out, and he was away, used to – her husband used to spend most of the time – he was a stockbroker or something – at home, so he used to come down to me. So there was always someone to have coffee with, and we used to have a chat – I mean it was a very friendly atmosphere. And when people come in, you know, they'd knock on the kitchen door, and I didn't feel alone. So that helped.

They said they'd baby-sit if we wanted them to, and of course it was lovely, because the kids were sleeping all night then, and I could just go out, and you've no idea what that was like. I nearly went mad, you know, I used to get ready and go out, every night. It was all I wanted to do, and it was like – well – coming alive. But see, to me I did come alive, but a lot of the women I know just never did. You know, I mean, because of their situation, they never ever do. That's ended to them. You know, they're like zombies. Really, they are – it's awful, but they are. I mean I was lucky.

Fred was marvellous, you know. Well, I mean, he used to go out drinking because he likes going out. But his whole attitude to me was – well, he was one in a million – I'll never get another one like him. I mean he really saw the situation. He really thinks I should have my own opinion and to do what I want and all that. And yet if you told him he was for Women's Lib he'd say, 'Oh no I'm not.' But he really does believe that. I mean, how many men would get up like that of a night, when they've got to go to work, and get up and look after the kids as he used to, and he did? I mean he'd come home and things were in a mess and he'd start clearing up and helping out. But I mean he didn't know how to help me emotionally. I mean he'd just try and do the best he could. It was just something he was never brought up to it. He'd never come across it. He didn't know what had hit him. I mean he thought everything was going to be, you know, nice, because before we were married I always looked nice and I'd been told to go into the beauty contest because I had a nice figure and all this sort of thing. I still used to get meself dressed up sometimes. But gradually I started to get depressed and sort of – I mean I wasn't quite the lively girl I was before, I suppose.

Actually it would have been even worse if we hadn't lived in that flat. If we'd have been in a flat like this I'd have been buried, I'm sure. But because we lived with people it did take it off an awful lot. Always someone there to talk to, and helping out. And then when you lived in closeness with people, you learn that everyone has their little quarrels and arguments. I mean, one of the nicest things, I was arguing with Fred because I hadn't washed his shirts, and he said, 'Oh I dunno what you are,' he said. 'I've never met a woman like you. You're not like a real wife, you never get out a clean shirt.' He opened the kitchen door to walk out and all of a sudden we heard Brian saying, 'Why haven't I got a fucking shirt?' [Laughs.] And you know, we just burst out laughing. Because it was that sort of situation – we couldn't argue any more.

People couldn't pretend, the way people have to pretend, because when you're living like that, near them, you see you can't pretend all the time, and it's a sort of lovely relief, whereas in these flats people do pretend, all the time. And it's so easy, because nobody knows how the other person lives. I mean it's so easy to pretend that you're a certain person, and you know, this is what goes – and they do. And out of interest, I mean, five of the women in this block of twenty are on tranquillizers. And they're the ones who pretend the hardest, you know, which I think is very frightening.

We wouldn't have lived in a tower block anyway. I was determined on that. But I mean when we moved here, the place we lived in, there was three rooms, and you know, it wasn't a bad place – I mean we had hot water. People take that for granted, but a lot of my friends didn't. We had a fairly reasonable sitting-room and a very big bedroom. And the kids were young so it didn't matter that they were in our room, but we foresaw it, we were trying to get a house. At the moment it was lovely, because we had baby-sitters there. But Fred said, 'You never know . . . Carol and Brian and the people we like won't stay here, they'll all be moving out soon, and new people that get in there, we might not get on with them like we do with them, and also we do need more room.' So, you know, it was a toss-up, he was sort of thinking of me really – and said, 'What's it going to do to you?' And I said, 'Oh no' – you know, I thought, ooh no, it would be nice you know. We must get away from this, you know. I mean, we were overrun by mice, plus the fact . . . also all those memories of what I went through, you know. So I thought, well let's get out, you know – I mean we've been offered a flat.

And then we took this. And when we come into this, well, I mean, already the worst was over, because I mean John was at nursery. And then we had no baby-sitter, and that was it, so I'm stuck in. Staying in – Christ, you know, I couldn't get over it. It was like a godsend – the girl next door said she wanted to baby-sit because she needed cash. It wasn't so nice as it had been because it did restrict us. We had to organize it in front, and we had to be back at a certain time. Then she went to work, and I was very upset, she didn't want the money any more, and it's only natural, once she'd got money – you know, buying clothes, going out with boyfriends. She didn't want to sit in baby-sitting. And quite right too.

Then Sally, across the road, said to me she wanted to baby-sit. I got talking to her mum about the problem and she said, 'Oh, Sally will baby-sit,' and we've had her ever since. And she's really lovely – you know, lovely relationship. Well the thing is, I mean, she wants the money, but also, the kids like her, and she's a very sweet girl, and also another thing that's lovely is that if ever we go out and we think we're going to be late, you know, her mum says she can sleep here. And I always give her a little bit extra because she slept here. And she sleeps in the kids' bed. So, I mean, we don't have to worry about getting back. So I'm really lucky, to what happens to most women. I mean most of them . . . they won't leave their kids – a lot of them have got this guilt thing about leaving them. My kids quite like us to go out, actually, because it means that they can play around with Sally, and they can play their Donny Osmond records.

Getting a Job

'To me – working-class girl, and no education – where am I going to start?'

Getting a job was absolutely – you see, for one thing, kids get colds. And another thing is getting a job that you can do the hours you want to do. I've got no qualifications at all. I wouldn't mind working in a shop or anything. If I do work in a shop, what do I do in the school holiday? I mean, there's play centres, but often they're not very well run, and the kids hate them. They've been in school all the term, and they want to think that they've got a break from school.

Not only that, they don't always have them, and they're all over the place and sometimes they're very difficult to get to. You've got to run in to work, and leave the kids there – it's so awkward during the holiday, there's no facilities. I mean, if there was a play centre at every school where the kids were it would be good. But there isn't. Sometimes we're lucky. At one time there was a play centre and it was up Stamford Hill somewhere. But when you're trying to get to work . . . I mean, most women, they time it from the time they leave school to when it gets to work, so they can do the job. People aren't at all sympathetic. Governors just don't want to know.

So I mean I was really trapped with getting a job. There was nothing that I could do, because I had no qualifications. If I'd have really been prepared to put the kids through it – say it had been a necessity – I would have had to have done something. If I'd have gone in the shoe trade, the hours start at eight o'clock in the morning, so what could I do? I don't take the kids to school till nine. Well, I did start back in the fur trade. I tried, but there again, remember, I'd been out of it for nine years, and I'd completely lost track. Perhaps they would have been prepared to train me, but I mean this what I'm saying, that to me – working-class girl, and no education – where am I going to start?

But I couldn't go back into a factory again, it was so restricting, you know, sort of sitting at a machine all day. And I thought, oh God, I can't do it. I just couldn't. I don't think I could ever go back to working in a factory. You had to get there at certain times . . . all the pettiness that went on, petty squabbling between the women. Mostly because they felt so insecure – that someone would pinch their job or something. You can understand it, why they were like it. But I thought I could never go through all that again. I really couldn't. I had had a bit of freedom, at home. I hadn't had anybody telling me what to do, so to speak. If I could have gone into a factory when the kids were little – yes; I mean, compared to being at home, the factory was a fun palace, really, the factory was utopia. But remember, I'd been all through that, and I'd got out of it. And then I'd had a year when I was just fed up and depressed and wanted something to do.

When I went into the fur trade there was the health thing, you got smothered in fur. I started having problems, the kids had bad colds, and I couldn't go in. And they weren't prepared to re-train me. You could see that they would have done, if I hadn't have had children. Plus I had to do part time. I done ten till half past three, and I was really lucky to get those hours, I was told afterwards. The boss had me over a barrel in a way. Mind you, I had him over a barrel, as well, because he couldn't get fur machinists, that's why he'd taken me. He would have never taken me if there was plenty of fur machinists. And yet then I just didn't want to do it any more, it was as simple as that. And so I gave it up and I thought, whatever can I do? And I had a friend that I was talking to and she said, 'Oh, do what I do. Go on school meals.' Which seemed to be the answer to all my problems. She said you get the school holidays, they let you do the hours you want to, and she said they're ever so sympathetic if the kids are ill. And that's what I done.

But I mean even now . . . I work at a college, not in the school – it's the same thing as a school meals, except it's a canteen, but the holidays aren't exactly the same. I get the summer breaks, I get the Easter breaks, but I don't get the half terms. And during that time my mother-in-law comes and looks after the kids. Most of the holidays coincide, and the odd differences my mother-in-law has the kids, so I mean I can do the job.

When you saw the adverts showing all these nice ladylike jobs, it's really heavy. Mind you, ten times better than being at home, but it is hard and heavy and dirty, and it's very manual, as well, you've got to empty big bins. It's not as bad as the school meals actually. But it really is a dirty, messy job. There's nothing ladylike about it. Anyone who's got any of this illusion, that it's catering and that, it's all frilly and light, is wrong. It really is a hard dirty job. And the attitude of a lot of the women there is they were so grateful to be there. So grateful to have a job, most of them.

One old lady there, she left, she was really – a really lovely old woman – and what she'd been through! The thing I liked – when she spoke about her life, there was no bitterness or anything, and yet she'd been through so much, and here she was, an old-age pensioner;

her husband was very ill, and she didn't have enough money to stay home, and in the end he died while she was at work. She just gave up the job, she was so upset about it all. But I thought, my God, both of them worked hard all their life, and they can't sort of have anything. She had to go and do that job, and she always worked harder than anyone there. She didn't want anyone to say she wasn't capable of doing a job.

Organizing Women in the Union

'So I thought, well I've got to show them at work how I'm as tough as what she is.'

Actually when I first tried to join the Union at work, the Supervisor, then, told me she didn't know how I could join it. So I was lost. So I thought, well how do you join, if she doesn't know? And then I bumped into a friend who said to me, well she'd get me the form, so she did, and I joined it. None of the other women would join it because the Supervisor was anti-union. I had no reason to get at her, but I wanted to be in it simply because of the job we do, heavy things and . . . cabbage, a whole load of cabbage – it's easy to get burnt, fall over. I thought, well if I'm in the union, if there's any trouble, it helps in the case. The first thing the Supervisor said to the girls was, 'Oh, if there's any trouble the head of the kitchen always wins.' So straight away she was on her guard and she fought. I mean since then, I admit, I will use the Union to get at the Supervisor, but I never thought of it like that until she said that to me. And then I was getting the girls to join it as well. And then she left.

And when she left I thought, right, you know, strike while the iron's hot, and I tried to get them all in then, and they wouldn't. And we had another cashier left and a new one come, so I said to her, 'Would you like to join?' And she said yes. She was a very good cashier, very good worker. We got this black Nigerian supervisor then. She'd got on a bit, and she had a chip on her shoulder, and she was very aggressive, and . . . 'I'm in charge' attitude. She obviously felt that people weren't going to listen to her because she was black, and she wouldn't give anybody a chance, so, you know, people were immediately against her. The girls at work, they were all scared stiff. They couldn't be too friendly with me. One who really would fight was on probation herself, and she knew she could lose her job. The other women were black anyway, and they're not on our side, but even if they were, they were scared to be too friendly with me, so I was really on me own.

So I thought, well I've got to show them at work how I'm as tough as what she is. Because I thought, if I fail now I've lost so much. I could show them that she can't get rid of me. So we went round – it was really funny. . . Every day I done something wrong. This went on from half past ten till half past three every day, and every day she done something wrong. And we followed each other round the kitchen like. Her telling me that I wasn't doing the job right and me saying, 'Oh well, I can't do that – against union principles.'

In the end she just broke down and ran out and sat in her office sobbing her eyes out. After that she got forcibly transferred against her wishes. Because you know, a lot of things had gone on – I mean, she'd upset a lot of people. And I just broke down. After she done it, I did. Well – I didn't break down in the kitchen, I carried right on, and then when I come home I was so ill I had to have the week off work. Just the exhaustion . . . when you're working it all the time, the whole atmosphere of it – and there was nobody to sort of supervise. It wasn't as if we were in it together, a crowd of people. I mean they weren't – I must be honest, they didn't stay on her side, but they didn't stay on mine. They were just watching, to see who had the power.

When she left I said to them, 'You've seen what she can do,' you know, and I said, 'That was on me own. You imagine if we all stood together what we could get done.' And they joined and now they're all in the Union. I've done it now. But I mean they really distrusted me, because I was white. And I talk to them and they say – their philosophy . . . they think that we all hate them, that we are just nice to their faces, but really we don't like them at all. This really hurts me sometimes, because they can be very hurtful towards me. I think they've been sold up the river so much by the white people that they're not going to let it happen again. They could be friendly with me, at a degree. But when it comes to coming to each other's home or getting too close – no. Friendly up to a point, but that's as far as they'll go.

The hatred of white people is really coming out now. I think it's like a lot of women – I mean, when you think of how oppressed women have been, when they come out they really come out, don't they? Perhaps it's the same with black people. They've been so oppressed, now it's coming out. I mean, if they come out and join in with the trade unions at work, and fight with the white people. . . Like us – I mean there's three whites, three blacks. If they won't stand with me, I'm lost – I mean, just the survival. If they sort of come out and they get aggressive and they join a union and say, right, we're not gonna take this – you know, I mean – that's going to be great. But what's happening in our place is, because they hate me they see that they can't join with me. Their emotions – I mean they can't sort of stand back and say, you know, she's white and we don't like her, but what she says is right, so we can stay together – you know what I mean? They just think, oh no, there's a catch in it somewhere. You don't tell me that white's going to help me, sort of thing – you know?

For blimming years they've been pushed down. Perhaps it gives them a kick to think that white people . . . I mean they always sit round in a clique when we're doing the work, talking and laughing. I suppose that must be a real contrast, to what they've been used to. And you can really understand them enjoying that situation, can't you? I had it out with them just the other day, when I done the floor; I said, 'Guess who it is, the old white honky again!' – because they say 'nig-nogs', you see, and we were laughing. Mind you, they all laugh, but you know I let them know that I play them at their own game, actually.

But I think one thing they learnt is that you can stand up to people. It was a good lesson. But the Union just didn't want to know. I got so annoyed I said I'd throw a brick through the window if they didn't come down. I was totally on my own in there. I was quite pleased, really, with the way I stood up to the Supervisor, but I didn't have enough support behind me. But now I have. And when

things go wrong they are inclined to come to me a little bit more now
and say, 'Oh, Linda,' you know – this has happened, or that's happened, you know. I don't know if I'd get them to union meetings,
but at least they're beginning to see that there was something in it.

Politics

Well, you see, I was always interested, because I think that I always
felt that society was wrong. But in what way it was wrong, I mean, I
couldn't really help on. But I think mostly I felt society was wrong
because pressure was put on people not to be themselves. You know, I
mean, it's bad to be a lesbian, and if they're a lesbian, you know, they
have a bad time. Of if you're a homosexual man, you know, you
have a bad time. And women have got to be such a way and men
have got to be such a way. And because of my upbringing I thought,
well surely this must be wrong? And why is it? You know, why
aren't people more tolerant of each other? And then when I looked
round and saw the sort of telly, I thought, well that's one of the worst
things, you know, they pump you with all these ideas in films and
the advertising and everything. And I thought, well you know, I
mean – why does it go on?

And when I joined the Parents' and Teachers' Group, when I went
there, to the Parents and Teachers, I listened to . . . got involved in
that, and then I saw that a few group of people can start to change
things. You know, I began to see my own power, so to speak.
Whereas before, politics to me was either voting for Harold Wilson
or voting for Ted Heath, which I didn't think it mattered a sod. All
right, so it might be marginally better if Harold Wilson is in. But
quite honest, I mean, I saw them all as the same. And really, to me,
what could I do about it? There just didn't seem any point in being
involved in politics. I thought it's all so corrupt, it's all such a mess,
what is the point in trying to sort it out from that level? So I could
never get involved in that.

When I met Celia, who was a member of the International
Socialists in the Parent–Teacher Group, I didn't know she was a

teacher. I thought she was one of the cleaners. I just met her on a person-to-person basis and I liked her. I mean she impressed me. Really, first of all because of her women's thing – she really made me see that I'm not a lesbian, because I thought she was very much like me. I mean, in many ways I think I know how she feels a lot, because I think she is like me. I mean of course she's come from a different background and all that, but I mean her feelings and that probably are very similar to our own, or perhaps a liberated woman or who wants to be liberated might feel. You know what I mean? But when they spoke about things it just sort of clicked into place. That perhaps this is why the world was like it was, because – not because people were so bad, but there was a group of people who manipulated us, you know what I mean? So then, we started talking about it all.

I liked people that I met who are involved in IS . . . I mean they seemed to have a lot to say, and what they said seemed to click in – you know, you have a sort of, 'Ooh yeah, that's how I thought.' But I never really put it in words before. In a way, you know, it's like sort of opening a door, you know what I mean – you see a little bit of light coming in, you know. You think to yourself, there's something out there. You know what I mean? And I thought, well perhaps this is what I am, all the time, and I haven't really been that odd, I'd just been a socialist, but not in a political sense. Because I could never . . . like, not from work, because I wasn't involved in unions, because I got married very young. Fred always supported me so I haven't had to worry about money, so I haven't had to be that involved. I mean I must go to union meetings but I haven't been going. Because I find it a bit hard to fit the union in, and the IS meetings and everything – and the house, and everything. And I feel at the moment that I must learn about IS. You know, I'm still trying to understand it, and come to terms with what goes on, I mean. I'm still battling with that. And to get out. It's a mental thing, really – trying to sort it all out when you've got two kids and everything else all round you, and the job that you do is so soul-destroying.

See, when I first joined IS I didn't think it mattered about knowing all this, and what I knew and what I didn't – well surely, being a socialist, I'm a working-class woman, what I've got to say must be of value, because surely this is what it's all about? But now I've been in it, I don't think so. I feel that I don't know enough to compete with what goes on. When I first joined, I felt, surely my life experience is enough? I mean they're talking about under-privilege and I am it, if you know what I mean, especially as a woman. I mean, when you talk about Women's Lib, a lot of middle-class people can talk about it, but I've been through it. And I felt that I was valuable just through that. But now after being in there for six months and listening to them, and going to the meetings, I'm beginning to think that my value isn't in that.

When I tried to get Fred involved he said, 'If they want to get people into it, they must get them into it on a level that they understand.' He said, 'I wouldn't do what you done. I'm certainly not going to give up all my time and sit there trying to read and understand it, and go to meetings every week.' Whereas if there was a way that he could have been introduced to it in a light way, on a sort of very basic level, then he'd have got interested in that perhaps. And then he'd have gone on a little bit. But you know, it's . . . to sort of throw someone in at the deep end. . . It's not that it's patronizing, it's just so stupid, because really, the thing I feel is that whether they're working-class or what they are – I mean they're just people, aren't they? When you try to treat someone as special or different, it just comes off as false.

I don't see any revolution taking place with middle-class people telling working-class people how to live their lives. I mean it's got to come from the working-class and middle-class. I mean a middle-class woman has faced . . . she's a woman like me.